WARRIORS
OF JAPAN
AS PORTRAYED IN
THE WAR TALES

Provinces of Premodern Japan
(Kantō Outlined in Dark Ink)

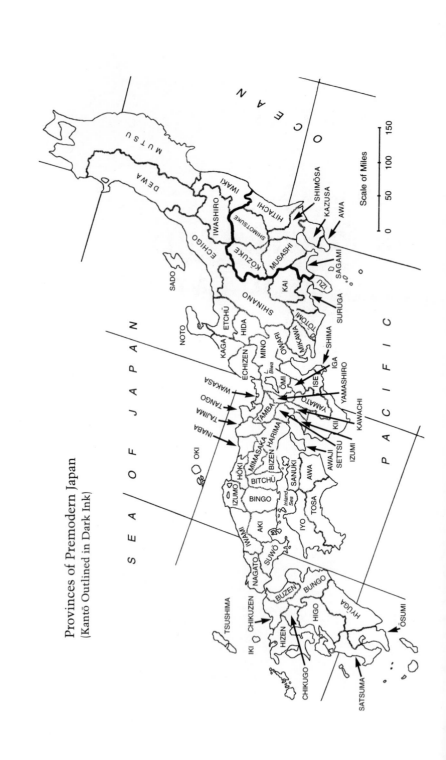

WARRIORS OF JAPAN

AS PORTRAYED IN THE WAR TALES

Paul Varley

UNIVERSITY OF HAWAII PRESS
HONOLULU

© 1994 University of Hawaii Press
All rights reserved
Printed in the United States of America

99 98 97 96 95 94   5 4 3 2 1

Library of Congress Cataloging–in–Publication Data
Varley, H. Paul.
    Warriors of Japan as portrayed in the war tales / Paul Varley.
        p.   cm.
    Includes bibliographical references and index.
    ISBN 0-8248-1575-0 (cloth). — ISBN 0-8248-1601-3 (pbk.)
    1. Japanese fiction—Heian period, 794–1185—History and
criticism. 2. Japanese fiction—1185–1600—History and criticism.
3. Tales—Japan—History and criticism. 4. War stories, Japanese—
History and criticism. 5. Generals in literature. 6. Japan—
Social life and customs—To 1600. I. Title.
PL747.25.W3V37   1994
895.6'3009358—dc20   93-43651
                                                          CIP

Frontispiece: From Paul Varley, *The Ōnin War* (New York: Columbia
University Press, 1966).

Publication of this book has been assisted by a grant from the Japan
Foundation.

Book design by Ken Miyamoto

To Betty Jane,
With Love

CONTENTS

Color plates follow page 72

Figures are on pages 116–125

vii

ACKNOWLEDGMENTS

I WISH to thank Columbia University and the University of Hawaii for making possible trips to Japan in 1991 and 1992 to gather materials for this book. I am also indebted to the Kajiyama Publication Fund for a grant to help pay for the book's illustrations.

A number of colleagues read parts or all of the book in its various draft versions: William T. deBary, Karl Friday, G. Cameron Hurst III, Imai Masaharu, James Lewis, Julia Meech, Barbara Ruch, Haruo Shirane, and Philip Yampolsky. I greatly appreciate the criticisms and advice they gave me. I am indebted to Barbara Ford, Miyeko Murase, and Barbara Ruch for assistance in gathering illustrations.

Finally, I wish to express my gratitude to Patricia Crosby of the University of Hawaii Press, who has aided and advised me in the publication of several of my books by the Press.

PREFACE

THE WAR TALES *(gunki-mono, senki-mono)* are a genre of literature recounting the stories of warriors and their battles from the tenth century, when a warrior class first emerged in the provinces of Japan, until the early seventeenth century. Almost all the war tales are based on real events, but even those that seem closest to history—primarily the early tales of the tenth and eleventh centuries—are composed in ways that suggest their authors were more interested in telling good or instructive stories than in recording events as accurately as possible. A number of the major war tales of the medieval age (1185–1573), moreover, were developed as texts for recitation by tale singers *(biwa hōshi)* who freely altered and embellished them to entertain their audiences.

The war tales can perhaps best be described as literary histories, mixtures of truth and fancy, although until recently they were regarded as generally reliable records of the past. They are, in any case, the most important sources of information we have about the customs and ethos of the warriors of ancient and medieval Japan, and the historian who wishes to study these warriors must rely heavily on the tales, even though he is constantly faced with the difficult (often impossible) task of trying to distinguish between fact and fiction.

This is a study in cultural history; no attempt is made to assess the war tales as works of literature. And since the focus is on the topic of how warriors are portrayed, discussions of the tales are limited primarily to those portions that deal with warriors, even though some of the tales relate much more than simply stories about these martial men and their battles. The great *Heike Monogatari* (Tale of the Heike), for example, is a romanticized recreation of life among both the courtier and warrior elites of the late twelfth century. But in this study, analysis of the *Heike* is limited primarily to its second half, which narrates the story of the epochal Gempei (Minamoto-Taira) War of 1180–1185 that ushered in the medieval age.

The Introduction presents a brief history of Japan before the war tales; attention is given mainly to the early stages in the evolution of a martial tradition and a warrior class. In the chapters that follow, each war tale, beginning with the first, *Shōmonki* (Chronicle of Masakado), is introduced by a section entitled "Historical Background" that presents the historical setting within which the tale's story occurs. Discussion of each tale is also preceded by a commentary on the tale's possible authorship, its date and means of composition (so far as they are known), and its general contents. This information is given to assist the reader in understanding and appreciating the tale as a work of literary history. Each tale is analyzed topically and selectively. The focus is always on how the warriors, its leading characters, are portrayed—how they fight, what they think, what their weapons, armor, and other battle accoutrements are, what customs and personal relationships govern their lives, who their heroes are.

One chapter of the book, Chapter 4, differs in format from the others. It deals with Minamoto no Yoshitsune, one of the most famous heroes of the war tales, who appears in the later chapters of *Heike Monogatari* as the field commander primarily responsible for defeating the Taira in the Gempei War.

The study ends with the fourteenth-century *Taiheiki* (Chronicle of Great Peace). Although war tales continued to be written for more than two centuries after *Taiheiki*, the great age of the genre was over. I decided to stop at *Taiheiki* mainly for a practical reason: Five centuries of war tales are enough to cover in one book. But I also believe that discussion of the later war tales would add little to the portrayal of warriors through *Taiheiki* that I wish to present.

It would be difficult—and tedious—to discuss all the war tales, including obscure lesser ones, that have come down to us from the period spanning *Shōmonki* and *Taiheiki*. Hence I have been selective. The tales I discuss in this study are: *Shōmonki*, the warrior stories in *Konjaku Monogatari Shū* (Collection of Tales of Long Ago), *Mutsu Waki* (A Tale of Mutsu), *Ōshū Gosannen Ki* (Chronicle of the Later Three Years War in Mutsu Province), *Hōgen Monogatari* (Tale of Hōgen), *Heiji Monogatari* (Tale of Heiji), *Heike Monogatari*, and *Taiheiki*.

Although most of the war tales examined in this study have been translated into English, I have made my own translations of all the passages I quote from them. I have done this both to deepen my familiarity with the original Japanese texts of the tales and to maintain consistency in usage of the specialized language of the tales.

The names of Japanese are given in the Japanese order, surnames followed by personal names. Thus Taira no Masakado is Masakado of the Taira family. Dates are based on the lunar calendar, which was used in premodern Japan, and are transcribed in the following manner: 1185:3:24 (the twenty-fourth day of the third month of 1185).

The bibliography is selective: it contains only the titles of books and articles used in this study.

WARRIORS
OF JAPAN
AS PORTRAYED IN
THE WAR TALES

Introduction
JAPAN BEFORE THE WAR TALES

JAPAN ENTERED its age of written history in the late sixth century, heralded by commencement of a period of three centuries of cultural borrowing from China. With China as a model, Japan created a centralized bureaucratic state headed by a *tennō* (emperor or empress), who presided over a court situated, from 710, in the capital city of Nara. During the late sixth through ninth centuries, some emperors and empresses were active, forceful rulers; but the trend even then was for the leaders of other families, the courtier families that served the *tennō*, to arrogate power to themselves, often by marrying into the imperial family. Beginning in the Nara period (710–784), a branch of the Fujiwara family gradually consolidated its control over the court,[1] and from the mid-ninth century the Fujiwara, as maternal relatives of successive emperors, became the real rulers of the country, holding the office of imperial regent *(sesshō, kampaku).*[2]

The economic basis of the Chinese-style imperial-bureaucratic state was tax revenue derived from the peasantry. In the Taika Reform of 645, all the rice-producing land of the country was nationalized with the aim of redistributing it in equal-sized holdings to peasants to work for their lifetimes. Each landholder was to be assessed three kinds of tax: a harvest tax; a special products tax (for example, a tax to be paid in cloth); and a corvée labor tax, which included the conscription of males for military service. Surviving records do not reveal how extensively this ambitious system of land allotment—called the equal-field system from its Chinese prototype—was implemented and maintained. The system was certainly successful enough to support the imperial-bureaucratic state for at least two centuries, but by the late ninth century, when the Fujiwara regents rose to power, it had greatly declined.

1

Meanwhile, the country's rice lands were steadily drawn into private estates *(shōen)*. The greatest beneficiaries of the estate system were the courtier families, headed by the Fujiwara, and Buddhist and Shinto religious institutions, which accumulated vast estate holdings. Thus the rise of the Fujiwara regents was accompanied by a process whereby the country's most important source of economic wealth, revenue from rice-producing lands, was diverted from the public treasury of the imperial-bureaucratic state into private hands. As we will see, the evolution of the estate system of landholding and related changes in the functioning of the imperial-bureaucratic state, comprising central government and provincial governments, set the stage for the emergence of a provincial warrior class beginning in the late ninth or early tenth centuries.

The Taika Reform provided for the establishment in the provinces of military units *(gundan)* under the command of the provincial governors *(kokushi)*. These units comprised both foot soldiers, who were peasants conscripted through the labor tax of the equal-field system, and mounted warriors drawn from the elite families of the districts *(gun)* into which each province was divided. In addition to service in the various *gundan*, foot soldiers and their mounted officers were also posted as border guards *(sakimori)* in Kyushu and as imperial guards in the capital (which was Nara from 710).

As provided in the Taihō Code of 702, which encouraged pursuit of the military arts *(bugei)*,[3] the *gundan* were organized along the lines of Chinese armies. Utilizing drums, gongs, and banners, they fought as coordinated forces, the peasant foot soldiers armed with crossbows *(ōyumi)* and their mounted officers bearing the longbow as their principal weapon.[4] Fighting on horseback with bow and arrow dates back to the late fifth or early sixth centuries in Japan, and the skills required for this method of warfare were cultivated especially by the local elite families who, from 645, held hereditary positions as district magistrates *(gunji)*. It was primarily from these elite district families that the warrior class later evolved.

For the peasantry, conscription into military service was the most burdensome aspect of the court's taxation. *Gundan* soldiers were often kept beyond their allotted terms of service, detained by the provincial governors, who used them for their own private purposes, including working in the fields. A saying of the time, for example, claimed that a man who left as a youth to serve in the imperial guards at the capital would return to his village with white hair.[5] Another saying asserted that the conscription of one man could lead to the destruction of his entire family.[6]

Resistance by the peasantry to conscription and other levies of the equal-field system became widespread during the Nara period. At first, able-bodied men sought to withhold their names from the tax registers or to substitute the names of women or old men, who would not be subject to conscription.[7] Later, increasing numbers of peasants abandoned their fields and absconded to other regions. The authorities called peasants who absconded *rōnin*, or "wave people," because they were no longer officially accountable and thus "adrift" in society. In many cases, *rōnin* were taken into the private estates that were beginning to form at this time.

The court moved from Nara to Heian, or Kyoto, at the end of the eighth century. One apparent reason for the decision to leave Nara was the wish to escape the direct influence of its Buddhist temples, some of whose priests had become deeply involved in politics. Other probable reasons were the need for greater space and better water facilities (both for drinking and for river travel to the Inland Sea) and the desire for direct access to the eastern and northern provinces, where the court was seeking to extend its authority.[8]

In 792, two years before the move to Heian, the court issued an edict ending most conscription and dissolving the *gundan*, except for those in outlying regions: Mutsu and Dewa provinces in northern Honshu, Sado Island in the Sea of Japan, and northern Kyushu. Conscription had proved difficult to administer and was socially disruptive. Moreover, most peasant conscripts were poor fighters. On those occasions when *gundan* forces were mobilized for battle in the late sixth and seventh centuries, the horse-riding bowmen of the elite district families provided the decisive fighting power.[9]

As Karl Friday and others have recently observed, the abandonment of most of the *gundan* system of military organization in the late eighth century did not, as often contended, mark the end of the court's efforts to maintain a national military.[10] Rather, it signaled a shift in policy based on recognition that peasant conscripts did not make good soldiers. From this time, the court focused mainly on developing new ways to employ the mounted warriors of the elite district families both as fighters in the provinces and as imperial guards in the capital.

Yet even as the court began this shift in military policy, it undertook to pacify the northern, Mutsu-Dewa region of Honshu, the homeland of a people called the Emishi, with Chinese-style *gundan* armies of conscripted peasant foot soldiers and cavalry officers. The Emishi appear to have been ethnically the same as the Japanese, but they were regarded by the latter as barbarians and were not treated as full members of the Japanese state.[11] The court attempted from at least the late seventh century to bring Mutsu-Dewa and the Emishi fully under its control, primarily by peaceful colonization and acculturation. Beginning in 780, the court turned to war.

The *gundan* armies the court sent against the Emishi were recruited from the areas bordering on Mutsu-Dewa, especially the Kantō (eastern provinces). From earliest times the Kantō had been noted for its stout fighting men and, along with Mutsu-Dewa, for breeding the best horses in Japan. As we will see, the war tales repeatedly praise the martial skills of the Kantō—or Bandō—horsemen.[12] These intrepid fighters are the warriors *par excellence* of the tales.

Despite the martial quality of the Kantō horsemen, one expedition after another sent by the court to Mutsu-Dewa failed. The Emishi themselves were fierce fighters, climatic conditions were harsh, and the expeditions had difficulty maintaining their supply lines. Perhaps most important, the expeditions suffered from poor leadership. Victory over the Emishi was not achieved until the selection of the redoubtable Sakanoue no Tamuramaro as commander of an expedition in 801. For his achievement in pacifying Mutsu-Dewa during this expedition and another sent the following year, Tamuramaro earned a reputation as Japan's greatest general before the rise of the warrior class. *Mutsu Waki*, a war tale describing the Former Nine Years War in Mutsu in the mid-eleventh century, has this to say about Tamuramaro:

> Our court in ancient times often sent forth great armies. Although these armies destroyed many barbarians within the provinces [of Mutsu and Dewa], they never completely defeated them. Then Sakanoue no Tamuramaro was called upon to go down to Mutsu-Dewa, and he bequeathed his fame to a myriad generations by conquering the barbarians throughout the six districts. He was like an incarnation of the god of the northern heavens, a general of distinction rarely to be seen.[13]

The memory of Tamuramaro lives in northern Honshu today at Buddhist temples and Shinto shrines throughout the region that was Mutsu-Dewa.[14] Tamuramaro is also remembered in Kyoto. It is said that generals who pray at his grave, not far from the old imperial capital, will surely be victorious; and in times of great peril for Japan, we are told, the grave will shake and rumble like thunder.[15]

The wars against the Emishi in Mutsu-Dewa in the late eighth and early ninth centuries accelerated the trend, already apparent, toward greater and greater reliance on mounted fighters in warfare in Japan. The Chinese-style armies employing units of foot soldiers or infantry as well as cavalry proved cumbrous against the fast-moving, elusive Emishi riders. One important technological change evidently motivated by the experience against the Emishi during these years was the switch from iron breastplates and chain-mail armor to armor made primarily of leather. Not only was leather more durable than iron, which easily rusted, but it was lighter and more flexible and hence better suited for mounted warriors.[16]

As the use of infantry in warfare steadily declined during the ninth century, the foot soldier's chief weapon—the crossbow—was gradually abandoned. The crossbow is a powerful instrument of war, and it was employed with great effectiveness by the Chinese. But while it is relatively easy to learn to use, it is difficult and expensive to produce.[17] On the other hand, the longbow, the preferred weapon of Japan's equestrian fighters, is easy to produce but difficult to master, especially from horseback. *Bugei*, the military arts, centered on horsemanship and mounted archery in ancient and medieval Japan—a fact we are repeatedly reminded of in the war tales and other writings by the characterization of the way of the warrior as the "way of the bow and horse" *(kyūba no michi)*. Horsemanship and archery, both arts in which the warriors of the Kantō excelled, constituted a formidable barrier between mounted warriors and all other fighters in Japan at least until the introduction of guns from Europe in the mid-sixteenth century.

The Heian court found it increasingly difficult to administer the provinces during the ninth century. Its main problem lay in dealing with the provincial governors. Governors were appointed from among the court aristocracy and held their offices for specified terms: at first six, later four years. They exercised broad powers over their provinces, performing administrative as well as police and judicial functions. Yet even during the Nara period the governors had tended to concern themselves more with self-enrichment, through such means as withholding taxes and unlawfully acquiring land, than with performing their proper duties.

The court tried to check the governors by requiring them, upon completion of their terms, to obtain documents of release *(geyu)* from their successors attesting that everything was in order in their provinces. But often disputes arose over preparation of the documents, and sometimes the outgoing and incoming governors colluded to conceal wrongdoing. From about 797, the court assigned release commissioners *(kageyushi)* to travel the provinces in order to audit the transfer of authority from one governor to another and ensure that the documents of release were properly and speedily issued.

The court itself contributed to the corruption and decline of the office of governor by allowing absentee appointments *(yōnin)*. Some courtiers, when appointed to governorships, sent surrogates *(mokudai)* to represent them; others simply allowed the vice-governors *(suke)*, usually men of the local aristocracy, to handle provincial administration for them.

Governorships were also misused by the practices of extending terms *(chōnin)* and purchasing offices *(jōgō)*. A governorship was purchased either directly by payment to someone at court or indirectly by obtaining it as reward for the achievement of merit (by repairing the imperial palace, for example, or by building or repairing a Buddhist temple or Shinto shrine).

The principal attraction of a governorship was the revenue it could provide. In addition to affording the opportunity for such illegal activities as the misappropriation of taxes and the imposition of private levies on the peasantry and local gentry, a governorship yielded substantial legitimate income. Approximately one-quarter of the rice land of each province was attached, in a holding called *kokugaryō*, to the office of governor.

While high-ranking courtiers appointed to governorships were apt to become absentee governors, middle and low-ranking courtiers usually regarded governorships—or even lower positions in the provincial governments—as important career opportunities. Many courtiers paid handsomely for the chance to serve in the provinces.

Among the courtiers who went into the provinces during the Heian period were former members of the imperial family. Because emperors were polygamous and maintained harems, they often had large progenies. Emperor Saga (r. 809–823), for example, sired fifty children by twenty-three women.[18] Periodically the imperial family engaged in "dynastic shedding," whereby princes and princesses were deprived of royal status, given surnames (the imperial family has no surname), and made subjects. One reason for dynastic shedding was the wish to lessen the economic burden of supporting a large number of royal offspring. A second reason was to allow princes to establish themselves independently as courtiers or accept positions in the provinces. And a third reason was pressure from the Fujiwara: Dynastic shedding was one means by which the Fujiwara regents manipulated the imperial family and gathered court power to themselves.

The surnames given to princes and princesses shed from the imperial family were Tachibana, Ariwara, Minamoto (or Genji), and Taira (or Heike). Minamoto, especially popular as a surname for former royals, was bestowed by many emperors during the Heian period. The various Minamoto branches are usually distinguished by reference to the sovereigns from whom they were descended—for example, the Saga Minamoto and the Murakami Minamoto. Most former royals remained in the capital to found courtier families, but some went into the provinces, including the forebears of the Seiwa Minamoto and the Kammu Taira, which became the most famous of the warrior clans in later times.

Former royals and courtiers, including Fujiwara, who took up positions in the provincial governments often continued to reside in the provinces—or at least to maintain residences in the provinces—after their terms of office.[19] Enriched as a group by profits derived from the abuses of office described above, they readily became leaders of provincial society, their status enhanced by their royal or courtier backgrounds.

The class of upper-level provincial officials, both those in office and those retired, was called the *zuryō* class. As a group, the *zuryō* are described in contemporary records as rapacious exploiters of the countryside. A saying from a slightly later time, referring to the *zuryō*'s insatiable appetite for land, claimed that "when a *zuryō* falls down, he comes up holding dirt."[20] Complaints about the *zuryō* from the court above and the people below were frequent. The court charged, for example, that the *zuryō* were often tardy in forwarding tax revenues and sometimes did not send them at all.[21] People in the provinces complained that the *zuryō* forced them to take unwanted loans *(suiko)* at usurious rates, perhaps fifty percent or higher.[22]

At a stratum of provincial society directly below the *zuryō* were the elite local families that hereditarily supplied leadership for the district governments—families that, as we have seen, also produced the mounted warriors who were the central force in warfare from earliest historical times. To counter the *zuryō*, these district families often commended their lands for protection to estates held by Kyoto courtiers or religious institutions. Such commendation stimulated a rapid increase in estate holding from the late ninth century, resulting in the gathering of nearly all the rice lands of the country into private estates by the late eleventh and twelfth centuries.

But the process of estate growth was not necessarily orderly; indeed it occurred against a background of mounting discord and disorder in the provinces. Groups of peasants, led by district magistrates, made frequent protests to the court about *zuryō* abuses, and on occasion these groups took up arms against the *zuryō*. In 857, for example, some three hundred peasants on Tsushima Island, led by officials of the island's two districts, attacked and burned the provincial governor's office, killing the governor (the *zuryō*), ten of his followers, and six frontier guards. And in 884 the magistrates of two districts in Iwami province led more than two hundred peasants in an attack on the governor.[23]

The provinces of the Kantō were especially afflicted with disorder in the mid-Heian period, the tenth and early eleventh centuries. This richly fertile, frontier region—the heartland of the mounted warrior— had been weakened and in places impoverished by demands made on it for men and supplies during the expeditions against the Emishi in Mutsu-Dewa in the late eighth and early ninth centuries. Yet even after settlement of the Emishi issue, the court continued to draw upon the Kantō disproportionately to the rest of the country for men to serve as guards in northern Kyushu and elsewhere.

Provincial disorder gave rise, at times, to robber gangs (tō), often led by locally powerful men and sometimes by zuryō. In the Kantō, especially the provinces of Kōzuke, Musashi, and Sagami, gangs of pack-horse handlers (shūba no tō) were particularly notorious. Often organized into networks whose marauding spanned broad areas, these gangs specialized in the seizure of tax goods being transported to Kyoto.[24]

The Kantō was further disrupted by periodic uprisings of relocated Emishi (fushū). In 875, for example, fushū rose up in Shimōsa province, and in 883 one thousand soldiers had difficulty quelling fushū who rebelled in Kazusa province. In an attempt to deal with the fushū, the court appointed men from the Bureau of Metropolitan Police (kebiishichō) to various districts in the Kantō provinces.[25]

We turn now to the story of warriors in the war tales, a story that begins with Shōmonki (Chronicle of Masakado), the tale of the revolt of Taira no Masakado in the Kantō in the 930s. Shōmonki provides us with basic information about the ancient warriors: They are, as observed, fighting men on horseback, relying primarily on the bow and arrow as their weapon of warfare; they are intensely concerned about honor and fame; and they are acutely fearful that their actions or the actions of others may cause them shame. But there is also much that Shōmonki does not tell us about these early warriors. We learn little, for example, about how they conducted themselves in battle or how a battle was fought by contending armies. Moreover, Shōmonki says almost nothing of the warrior leader's relations with his followers, whether they were bound by the lord/vassal relationship or whether that form of personal linkage between warriors had not yet evolved by the middle tenth century. Thus Shōmonki introduces us to the ancient warriors but gives only a rough sketch of them. This sketch is developed into a rich portrait in succeeding war tales.

1
THE ANCIENT WAR TALES

Historical Background to *Shōmonki*

The disorder in the Kantō described in the Introduction expanded into full-scale rebellion in the late 930s, centering on Taira no Masakado, a descendant in the fifth generation from Emperor Kammu (r. 781–806) and a scion of the military family of Kammu Taira. Kammu's great-grandson Prince Takamochi was given the Taira surname in 889 and was appointed vice-governor of Kazusa province. Takamochi remained in Kazusa after his term in office, and his many sons held a variety of positions in provincial offices throughout the Kantō.[1] By Masakado's time, the Taira descended from Prince Takamochi had proliferated into a number of branches, based primarily in the northern Kantō, where they formed an important part of the provincial *zuryō* aristocracy.

Not much is known about Masakado's early life.[2] He evidently traveled to Kyoto in his teens and served in the household of the imperial regent, Fujiwara no Tadahira. In 931 he returned to the Kantō and became embroiled in feuds with several of his relatives. *Shōmonki* refers to a dispute with an uncle over a woman, and there may also have been quarreling about land. In 935 a battle occurred between Masakado and some of his adversaries at a place called Nomoto. Masakado emerged the victor, while those killed on the opposing side included another of his uncles and three Minamoto brothers, whose family was intermarried with the Taira. This battle marked commencement of the fighting that led eventually to the Masakado Revolt. As just noted, *Shōmonki* is vague about what lay behind the fighting. But once begun, it took on a life of its own: The defeated in each battle were always determined to get revenge and the victors were zealous to win yet again.

From 935 until 939 there was a series of armed encounters in the northern Kantō that pitted Masakado against various relatives. Periodically, both Masakado and his enemies made appeals to the court. On at least one occasion, in 936, Masakado went to Kyoto to defend himself, although *Shōmonki* does not report what he said to the court. We see, in any case, how members of the provincial aristocracy tried to use the court for support of their activities during this age. Although the court had no standing army to send out to settle disputes, it could still exert its influence by appointing military enforcement officials to the provinces (who were often selected from the provincial aristocracy itself) and by arbitrating disputes.

Masakado's activities turned into rebellion in 939 when he attacked and captured the office of the governor of Hitachi. According to *Shōmonki*, he took this rash step in support of a man from Hitachi named Fujiwara no Haruaki, a "hooligan" and a "blight on the people" who illegally confiscated rice land and failed to pay taxes.[3] Within a month, Masakado also conquered Shimotsuke and Kōzuke provinces and declared himself the "new emperor" *(shinkō)* of the Kantō. He based his claim to this title on the grounds that he was descended from an emperor (Kammu). But Masakado's self-proclaimed reign over the Kantō was short-lived. In the second month of 940 he was killed in battle at Kitayama, a place not far from his residence in Shimōsa, by a joint force under Taira no Sadamori, his first cousin, and Fujiwara no Hidesato, the sheriff *(ōryōshi)* of Shimotsuke province.[4] As proof of their triumph, Sadamori and Hidesato sent Masakado's head to the capital.

Masakado's Revolt was unquestionably a severe blow to the Kyoto court, which as the central government was responsible for maintaining peace in the land. Yet the court was able to play a significant role in the revolt because provincial leaders—the *zuryō*—still coveted their ties to Kyoto and regularly solicited the court's support, requesting, for example, that the court issue orders branding their enemies outlaws or grant them commissions to subdue these enemies. In the end, the court was able to employ Kantō men, Sadamori and Hidesato, to settle a Kantō issue, thus pursuing the ancient Chinese strategy of "using the barbarian to control the barbarian."[5]

Shōmonki, stating that Masakado committed unspeakable crimes during his lifetime, claims that he suffered in hell after death.[6] But not everyone agreed with the assessment that Masakado had been a heinous villain. During his rebellion, for example, Masakado received considerable support from peasants oppressed by rapacious provincial officials *(zuryō)*; and in later centuries he became a folk hero in the Kantō, remembered for his willingness to stand up to overbearing authority. A number of mounded tombs in the Kantō are called "Masa-kado hills" (Masakado-*zuka*), and there are many Shinto shrines dedi-cated to his memory and to the deification of his soul. One of these shrines is in the Kanda section of Tokyo; another, called the Helmet *(kabuto)* Shrine, is at Nihonbashi, also in Tokyo.[7] In 1874 Masakado was condemned as an "enemy of the emperor" and, against the wishes of many local people, was removed as the deity of the Kanda Shrine. But a century later, in 1984, this action was reversed and, with much popular approval, Masakado was reinstated as the Kanda deity in a sol-emn ceremony.[8]

Shōmonki (Chronicle of Masakado)

A note at the end of *Shōmonki* states that it was written in the sixth month of 940, or about four months after Masakado was killed.[9] Although this date has been questioned, the weight of scholarly opin-ion appears to accept it as valid. Few dispute, in any case, that *Shō-monki* was produced soon after the events it chronicles and is therefore probably more reliable as history than most of the other war tales. But *Shōmonki* certainly cannot be accepted at face value as history. Its author (to use the singular for convenience) did not write with the intent simply to record events as accurately as possible. *Shōmonki* contains numerous embellishments (including many allusions to Chi-nese history and literature), moralistic injunctions, and hyperbolic descriptions of peoples' behavior, emotions, and the like that make it at least as much a literary as a historical work.

One of the most intensely pondered and argued questions about *Shōmonki* is its authorship. The quality of the writing and the knowl-edge displayed in it confirm the author as a man of learning, possibly a Buddhist priest, as many have suggested. But where did he live? Was his home in Kyoto, where he would have had access to government records concerning the Masakado Revolt, or was he a resident of the east, where the revolt occurred? Many scholars contend that the author was an eastern resident, citing three primary reasons. First, the author provides many details about places in the east, families living there, and personal relations among local people that someone residing in Kyoto or elsewhere would not likely have known or been interested in. Second, the author is brief if not terse when discussing Kyoto and court affairs, even though Masakado himself visits the court in *Shō-*

monki and the court is an active participant in the politics of the feuding that leads to the revolt and of the politics of the revolt itself. And third, the author expresses strong emotion as he tells his story, lamenting especially the suffering inflicted upon the common people of the Kantō by the incessant fighting of warriors. Such emotion suggests an author who actually witnessed the events in *Shōmonki* or learned of them firsthand soon after they occurred.[10]

The tone of *Shōmonki* changes in the transition from the first part, which deals with the early, interfamily feuding, to the second part, when Masakado becomes a rebel and seeks to assert his control over the Kantō. In the first part, the author treats Masakado sympathetically, relating his conflicts with relatives primarily from his standpoint and referring to his opponents in battle as "the enemy." But in the second part the tone is different. The author still has some sympathy for Masakado and can express regret about his descent and calamitous end. But Masakado is now a rebel (and is called a rebel, *zoku*), his actions cannot be condoned, and in the end he gets what he deserves.[11]

The language of *Shōmonki* is *hentai kambun*, which Judith Rabinovitch defines as " 'variant Chinese,' a now defunct, hybrid literary language combining Chinese and Japanese elements of grammar and sentence structure, vocabulary, and character usage."[12] *Hentai kambun* is, in short, Chinese with a strongly Japanese flavor.[13] In *Shōmonki* this flavor is probably most noticeable in the use of Japanese honorific expressions as well as words created by the Japanese using Chinese characters.

The Warrior

The most common term for warrior in *Shōmonki* is *tsuwamono*, written with a Chinese character whose original meaning was "weapon."[14] *Tsuwamono* probably refers to a mounted archer of the kind famous in the Kantō from earliest historical times. In addition to *tsuwamono*, the *Shōmonki* armies (called *ikusa*, a word that can also mean "battle") include peasant foot soldiers known as *banrui*. The combination of *tsuwamono* and foot soldiers in these mid-tenth-century armies reflects a perpetuation of the Chinese style of military organization first introduced to Japan during the Taika Reform and discussed in the Introduction.

Shōmonki armies are mustered for particular battles and campaigns and cannot be held together long. Sometimes armies are disbanded after battles so their men can return home to tend fields. Usually, however, the reasons for disbandment are not specified. The sizes of these armies fluctuate greatly, even from day to day. Thus we find a commander like Masakado supported on one occasion by fewer than ten men; at other times he leads eighty, a hundred, a thousand, or several thousand. Always ready to dissolve after battles, armies are difficult to assemble in preparation for them. Masakado's final defeat and death are attributed largely to the fact that his "usual army of eight thousand men had not yet assembled, and he found himself in command of scarcely more than four hundred."[15]

Fukuda Toyohiko speculates that when a commander like Masakado leads a small force of men in *Shōmonki* these men are, in most cases, primarily *tsuwamono* who have close personal ties with the commander. When, on the other hand, the commander is at the head of a large army, most of its members are apt to be foot soldiers. Temporarily recruited, foot soldiers are attracted by the anticipation of immediate rewards after battle and are likely to decamp if a battle goes badly.[16]

The archetype of the *tsuwamono* in *Shōmonki* is Masakado himself. In a letter written to the regent Fujiwara no Tadahira in which he seeks to justify his assumption of rule over the Kantō, Masakado observes that not only is he descended from an emperor, he is "endowed by heaven with martial prowess" and thus is like the "men of old who seized lands by force."[17] In the final pages of *Shōmonki*, its author, assessing Masakado's character and career (and revealing some of the sympathy for Masakado mentioned above), comments that although he could have attained great fame in history for "loyalty and devotion," Masakado instead "devoted his life to wildness and violence, engaging constantly in war." In the author's view, Masakado "took pleasure only in the military arts."[18]

The phrase "warrior way" (*tsuwamono no michi*) appears only once in *Shōmonki* and refers to a commander who purportedly was "not yet proficient" in it.[19] Although no precise explanation is given of this "way" of the warrior, very likely it connoted little more than skill in the military arts and might best be rendered in English as the "way of arms."

The Way of the Bow and Arrow

As the mounted warrior rose steadily to prominence in warfare in the Heian period, his chief weapon, the bow, dominated battles. In *Shōmonki*, there are hardly any references in battle accounts to weapons other than the bow. Use of this weapon set the premodern Japanese warrior apart from the mounted knight of medieval Europe, who disdained the bow and other missile-launching devices, assigning them to foot soldiers. The knight's weapons were the lance, sword, battle-ax, and mace.[20]

There are only two references in *Shōmonki* to the use of swords. One appears in the phrase "crossed swords with the enemy,"[21] and may be metaphorical: It may simply mean that one military force began fighting with another. The second reference is to Masakado's brandishing his sword as he rides into a battle toward the end of *Shōmonki*.[22] The Japanese of the tenth century probably still used a straight sword,[23] which was not suitable to the slashing technique generally practiced by mounted warriors. Not until the evolution of the curved sword later in the Heian period did the sword become a more potent tool in the battle equipment of the warrior on horseback.[24] Even then, the sword scarcely challenged the bow in value to the mounted warrior, at least so far as can be judged from the war tales.

Descriptions of battles in *Shōmonki* seldom exceed more than a few sentences. For example, a clash between Masakado and his uncle, Taira no Yoshimasa, in the tenth month of 935 is reported this way: "Yoshimasa and his men shouted their battle cries and attacked as planned, all fighting without regard for their lives. But fortune was with Masakado and he won. Deserted by fortune, Yoshimasa was in the end defeated."[25] And about an encounter between Masakado and another uncle, Yoshikane, in the eighth month of 937, we are told: "The gods were angry with Masakado that day and he was helpless. His followers were few, and they were ill-prepared. All they could do was shoulder their shields and retreat."[26]

Some battles are described in greater detail, but nowhere in *Shōmonki* is there information sufficient to give us more than a sketchy idea of how warriors and their armies actually fought in Masakado's day. A striking feature of *Shōmonki*'s battle descriptions, as remarked, is that they say almost nothing about the use of weapons other than the bow. Indeed, the only concrete reference to another weapon employed in battle is the second mention of a sword noted above, the sword that Masakado wields in an encounter near the end of *Shōmonki*. We read in one place of the stockpiling of *hoko*,[27] straight-bladed spears that were probably used by the *banrui* or foot soldiers and became common weapons of warrior attendants in later centuries. But *hoko* are not mentioned in *Shōmonki*'s actual battle accounts.

The Shield

Shōmonki's descriptions of battles contain many references to shields. We read, for example, of shields being repaired in preparation for battle, being carried in the proper manner when entering battle, or being discarded when fleeing in defeat from battle. Shields are prominent in this description of a clash between Masakado and Yoshikane ("the enemy"):

> Forming a wall of shields, the enemy advanced to smash Masakado. But before they could reach him, Masakado dispatched his foot soldiers to engage them in battle. More than eighty of the enemy's men and their horses were killed by arrows. . . . Dragging their shields behind them, the enemy all fled from the field of battle.[28]

This account, with its reference to foot soldiers and a "wall of shields," is one of the clearest proofs in *Shōmonki* that warriors, the *tsuwamono*, employed foot soldiers in Chinese-style mass maneuvers during battles.

At the beginning of *Shōmonki's* final battle, in which Masakado is killed, a fierce wind blows against the back of Masakado's army and into the faces of the enemy aligned against them. *Shōmonki* states that the wind is so fierce that it "blew down the shields of the new emperor's [Masakado's] army so they fell forward, and blew the shields of Taira no Sadamori's [the enemy's] army back into their faces."[29] Whereupon the armies abandon their shields and attack each other.

In battle accounts in later war tales, shields are often mentioned in the "exchange of arrows" *(ya-awase)* or opening stages of battle. Flat and rectangular in shape, about the height of a man, and equipped with folding legs so they could be stood upright, shields were commonly placed in a row to provide protection as an army exchanged arrows with the enemy. But the mounted warriors of an army usually left the shelter of the shields after the *ya-awase* stage of a battle and rode toward the enemy without the benefit of such protection.

So far as I am aware, warriors never used shields while fighting on horseback—for one thing, it would have been impossible to hold a shield while shooting arrows—and they do not use them in the war tales. As we will see in the discussion of armor and fighting methods in the next chapter, the warrior of the medieval war tales, in which we can discern techniques of warfare much more clearly, relies almost entirely on his body armor and helmet to deflect arrows.[30] And when paired off in close combat with swords, he has nothing but his armor and helmet to protect him.

The Horse

We have repeatedly noted that, from earliest times, the best fighters in Japan were men on horseback. So valuable were horses to warriors for the speed, mobility, and range they provided in combat, they were said to be esteemed more than the most precious jewels.[31] We have also noted that horses bred in the eastern (Kantō) and northern regions were especially treasured for their high quality, and the warriors of the Kantō gained fame as the country's finest in large part because they had ready access to excellent horses. In the frontier conditions of the Kantō in the ancient age, warriors figuratively spent their lives in the saddle.[32]

In *Hōgen Monogatari* (The Tale of Hōgen), the war tale dealing with a clash of arms in Kyoto in 1156, the first year of the Hōgen era (1156–1158), the chieftain Minamoto no Yoshitomo claims that even his younger brother Tametomo, a legendary warrior of enormous size and fabulous martial skills who grew up in western Japan, is no match on horseback for the warriors of the Kantō: "Since he [Tametomo] was raised in the west [Chinzei], he's no doubt good at fighting on foot. But when it comes to grappling on horseback, how can he hope to win out over the young warriors of the Kantō provinces of Musashi and Sagami?"[33] Since, as we will see, the early medieval war tales, beginning with the *Hōgen*, underwent extensive textual development over two or more centuries, we cannot be certain that a statement like this is not anachronistic: Perhaps it reflects what the thirteenth- or fourteenth-century shapers of these tales *believed* a twelfth-century warrior like Yoshitomo might say rather than what, as a man of the twelfth century, Yoshitomo was likely to have said. Nevertheless, the *Hōgen*'s comments about Tametomo and his young enemies from the Kantō are consistent with the admiration for the equestrian skills of Kantō warriors repeatedly expressed in the war tales from *Shōmonki* in the tenth century through at least *Taiheiki* in the fourteenth.

The war tales contain frequent, stereotyped references to horses that are "very big and powerful" (*kiwamete futō takumashii*). These references allude to the traditional warrior taste for large and high-spirited—even wild—horses.[34] In *Shōmonki*, Masakado is said to have led a force of "several thousand" warriors, each of whom rode a "dragonlike steed" (*ryū no gotoki uma*).[35] Dragonlike implies fierce and brave and was used to describe the same kind of animals as very big and powerful horses. The war tales also speak of *arauma* (literally, "untamed horses"),[36] horses known for testing the mettle of those warriors willing to mount them. Rough, wild horses were also valued in battle for the damage they could inflict with their hooves, especially upon foot soldiers.[37]

One of the most important technological advances in warfare in world history was the invention of the stirrup, which, in conjunction with the saddle, enabled a warrior to be seated firmly on his horse when handling a weapon. The stirrup was introduced to Japan from China, as observed in the Introduction, about the late fifth or early sixth century. Hence we can assume that the Japanese warrior of the tenth century had a long tradition of fighting on horseback with stirrups.

Knowledge of the stirrup, apparently transmitted to Europe, via Central Asia, in the eighth century, proved to be of inestimable value in providing lateral stability for the mounted knight in the kind of shock combat that was his specialty. Indeed, one line of scholars, beginning with Heinrich Brunner, believes that the stirrup revolutionized warfare and even gave rise to feudalism in Western Europe. As the mounted knight became dominant in warfare, society and the economy developed into the patterns we call feudal primarily to support him.[38]

More than anything, riding into battle on horseback became the true symbol of the ancient Japanese warrior. *Shōmonki* informs us that one of Masakado's enemies persuaded a servant (who was also a foot soldier, *banrui*) to spy on Masakado, his master, with the promise that he would be made "a mounted retainer" *(jōba no rōdō)*.[39] The lure of such a promise bespeaks the fact that, among other things, it was exceedingly expensive to obtain, outfit, and maintain a horse. Even presuming one was talented in the military arts, one could not hope to be a real warrior—a *tsuwamono*—without possessing a horse.

An important factor in battle between warriors on horseback armed with bows and arrows was the direction of the wind. In *Shōmonki*'s first battle, for example, Masakado prevails because he "was fortunate to have the wind in his favor, and his arrows flew through the air, each right on target."[40] And in the book's final battle—at the beginning of which, as we have seen, the shields of both armies are blown down by a strong wind—Masakado's enemies, Sadamori and Hidesato, achieve victory because, at a crucial point, the wind suddenly changes direction and gives them the advantage.[41]

The Warrior's Name

An attitude of the traditional warrior that is strongly articulated in *Shōmonki* is his concern for "name" *(na)*—a term that implies pride (including *menboku* or "face"), honor, fame, and material self-interest. At an early stage in the quarreling between Masakado and his relatives in the Kantō, one of Masakado's uncles criticizes a cousin (Taira no Sadamori) for being "friendly" with Masakado, who, he claims, has "murdered" some of their family relations and stolen a number of their valuables: "This does not become a warrior. A warrior must esteem his honor *(na)* above everything."[42] Shortly thereafter Masa-kado himself, having been temporarily driven into hiding, vows that he is determined to resume fighting in order to "bequeath his fame *(na)* as a warrior to future generations."[43] And at *Shōmonki*'s finish, its author observes that, despite his great promise as a warrior, in the end Masakado "lost his honor *(na)* and destroyed his life."[44]

In one of the battles described in *Shōmonki* we read: "Whipping his horse and shouting his name *(na o tonaete)*, Masakado pursued the enemy."[45] Here we have an early reference to "name-announcing" *(nanori)*, which became one of the most distinctive practices of warriors in later centuries. *Nanori* was much more than simply an announcement of one's personal name before or during a battle. Warriors might also give their ages, ranks, and positions, recite their family genealogies, recount the great achievements of their ancestors and themselves, and boldly challenge their enemies to combat. *Nanori* had several purposes: to identify oneself to the opposing army in the search for a suitable enemy (one of comparable rank and status) with whom to fight in one-against-one combat; to identify oneself to one's allies (a warrior was often difficult to recognize when encased in helmet and armor) for the purpose of establishing witnesses to support later claims to rewards; and to intimidate the enemy.

Still another purpose of the *nanori* was to promote the fame of oneself and one's family *(ie)*. Although the mounted warriors of ancient Japan fought in a highly individualistic manner, pairing off in one-against-one combat as their armies met in battle, they were as much concerned about representing their families as representing themselves. Very often warriors sacrificed their lives in battle not so much (or not at all) for their lords but in the anticipation that their families would be rewarded after their deaths.

Shame

The warrior's acute sense of *na*, as we find it in the war tales, led him to fear, perhaps above all, the *haji* or "shame" of defeat. *Shōmonki* records that when Masakado defeated his uncle Yoshimasa in battle, Yoshimasa's "shame as a warrior *(tsuwamono no haji)* spread to the other provinces, causing his enemy's [Masakado's] fame *(na)* to rise."[46] And another uncle, Yoshikane, is so chagrined at the bitterness of defeat by Masakado that he longs to "avenge his shame" *(kaikei no kokoro)*.[47] In her pioneering analysis of modern Japan as a shame society, Ruth Benedict observes: "A man is shamed either by being openly ridiculed and rejected or by fantasying [sic] to himself that he has been made ridiculous."[48] The warrior code of premodern Japan, as it is revealed in the war tales and other records, dictated that defeat or military failure inflicted public shame and this shame demanded reprisal or revenge. Thus Yoshikane desires to "avenge the shame" he experienced in defeat at the hands of Masakado. In its most dramatic form, the quest for revenge became the vendetta *(katakiuchi)*. Although the vendetta, discussed later in this chapter, usually involved more than shame—for example, the desire to avenge the killing of a parent or a lord—sensitivity to shame, with its overtones of pride and honor, no doubt in most cases also inspired a warrior to seek revenge.

Feudalism

The emergence of a provincial warrior class in Japan has long been thought to have heralded the beginning of feudalism, and many scholars have sought to compare Japanese feudalism with the feudalism of Western Europe in its medieval age.[49] There are three basic criteria of feudalism: a predominantly agrarian economy, a ruling warrior class, and the association of warriors as lords and vassals. Some scholars would add a fourth criterion: the fief, usually a holding of agricultural land, that supported the vassal economically and enabled him to serve his lord as a fighting man.

Recently, however, some scholars have questioned the appropriateness of describing as feudalism the institutions that evolved with warrior society in premodern Japan.[50] And even those who believe that Japan had feudalism are by no means in agreement about precisely when it began or how long it lasted. In Masakado's time in the mid-tenth century, only one of the three criteria for feudalism listed above —a predominantly agrarian economy—existed.

Although the *tsuwamono* of *Shōmonki* appear to be skilled fighters, they cannot be regarded as a ruling warrior class for at least three reasons: First, many, if not most, are only part-time warriors responding to calls for battle but otherwise devoting themselves to the management of their agricultural lands; second, the *tsuwamono*'s extensive use of peasant foot soldiers meant that warriors did not monopolize warfare as they would in later centuries; and third, the volatility of `Shōmonki` armies—hastily forming and quickly disbanding, their troop numbers fluctuating from less than a hundred to several thousand—implies that neither the armies nor warfare had become fully professionalized.

Shōmonki provides little information for us to judge whether the lord/vassal *(shujū)* relationship had evolved among warriors by Masa-

kado's time. References are made to the "followers" of warrior commanders—that is, the *jūrui*, identified by Fukuda Toyohiko as personal
tsuwamono supporters.[51] But we find almost none of the terminology
that was later to be used for lords and vassals, and there is scarcely any
hint of the attitudes of mutual obligation and personal loyalty that
joined fighting men in the late Heian and medieval centuries. Nearly
all the *jūrui* in *Shōmonki*, moreover, were related to their commanders
by either blood or marriage.[52] Although many vassals in later times
were also kin or in-laws of their lords, many were not.

Asakawa Kan'ichi, defining the lord/vassal relationship in feudalism, states that in a feudal society "the ruling class should exist of
fighting men, each group chained together by links of an exhaustive
personal bond of mutual service—a bond so personal that, in the last
analysis, it should obtain, in each link, between two armed men only,
lord and vassal: and so exhaustively personal that the one should swear
to the other fidelity even unto death."[53] As Asakawa suggests, the
lord/vassal relationship, at least in theory, is premised on exclusivity.
It is an association in which the vassal is devoted solely to serving his
lord; the lord in return bestows upon the vassal rewards,[54] protection,
various guarantees, and possibly a benefice, usually land. Such exclusivity, however, was in fact rare in Japanese feudalism. The term usually translated into English as lord/vassal is *shujū*. But this term literally means superior/inferior and is by no means limited to the lord/
vassal relationship of warriors in feudalism. For example, provincial
warrior leaders in the ancient age often established *shujū*, or what can
be called patron/client, relationships with prominent courtiers in
Kyoto. Thus Masakado in *Shōmonki* is a client of a courtier patron, the
regent Fujiwara no Tadahira.[55]

It was also common in Japanese feudalism, at least until 1600, for
warriors to have more than one lord. And in the age of the "country at
war," *sengoku* (1478–1573), it was expected that warriors, other than
those hereditarily bound in vassalage,[56] would seek new lords if the
lords they were serving failed to provide sufficient rewards or were
ineffective as commanders.[57] Lord/vassal relations were, in fact, so
unstable during the *sengoku* period that, as Katsumata Shizuo has
observed, rebellion against overlords was frequent and "hardly [war-
ranted] particular condemnation."[58] In *sengoku*, disloyalty, rather
than loyalty, seems indeed to have been the stronger guideline for a
warrior's behavior.

We will see much shifting of allegiances and disloyalty in the war
tales. At the same time, the tales are the main source in Japanese history for the *ideal* of the lord and vassal "chained together by links of an

exhaustive personal bond of mutual service . . . [swearing to each other] fidelity even unto death." Such intimate relationships may, in reality, have been rare; but in the war tales they are glorious manifestations of the warrior way. More will be said later in this chapter about lord/vassal ties in the war tales, including the ideals of absolute self-sacrifice by vassals for lords and of the bestowal by lords of a parental-like love upon their vassals.

The Suffering

Shōmonki devotes much attention to the suffering and losses inflicted upon noncombatants by war. Although its battle descriptions are brief, reports of the accompanying devastation to the countryside and the people are often detailed and graphic. For example, Shō-monki's opening battle, fought by Masakado and some relatives at Nomoto, is recounted in a few sentences; but the description of the agony suffered by the local people is effusive. Masakado's victorious army razes all the houses in four townships, shooting down people who try to escape the flames. Hundreds of houses are destroyed, as well as great quantities of supplies and many treasures. The screaming and weeping of the victims is heartrending; the roar of the flames sounds like thunder, and the smoke rises in huge black billows, covering the sky. Apparently horrified by the conduct of Masakado's army, the author even reflects upon the suffering of the victims' survivors—sons bereft of fathers, wives deprived of husbands.[59]

One of the reasons why Masakado's army pursues this scorched earth policy is to destroy the houses of his enemy's supporters.[60] Most houses are particularly easy to incinerate because they have grass (kusabuki) roofs.[61] The devastation is in any case frightful, and the description of it, along with similar descriptions in other Shōmonki battle accounts, suggests the true brutality of warfare in the Kantō in Masakado's time.

We will find frequent references to the burning of commoner houses in the later war tales. Often such burnings are intended to impress the enemy with an attacking army's aggressiveness and ruthlessness or to deceive the enemy into thinking that the attacking army is larger than it really is. In Heike Monogatari, as we will see in Chapter 4, Minamoto no Yoshitsune, probably the best-loved warrior of the war tales, burns houses to provide illumination during night attacks. Shōmonki is unusual for its vivid descriptions of the suffering of common folk during warfare. The later war tales, even while describing house burnings and the like, have little to say about such suffering.

Historical Background to the War Tales in
Konjaku Monogatari
Piracy in Central and Western Japan

At the same time that Masakado's Revolt was occurring in the Kantō, the court was troubled by disorder closer to home. Beginning in 939, the very year that Masakado launched his rebellion, a renegade member of court society, Fujiwara no Sumitomo, who had served as an official in the governor's office of Iyo province in Shikoku, began marauding the coast of the Inland Sea at the head of a band of pirates. The pursuit and seizure of Sumitomo took two years, and then were successful largely because his second-in-command betrayed him and revealed his secret hiding and storage places. The final victory over Sumitomo was at Hakata Bay in Kyushu in the fifth month of 941. Sumitomo himself escaped from the battle in a small boat, but he was later captured in Iyo and killed. His head, like Masakado's a year or so earlier, was sent to Kyoto for public display.

Sumitomo and his pirate band excelled in the naval warfare that was a specialty in the waterways of central and western Japan. In the twelfth century, the Ise branch of the Kammu Taira became a naval power in that region, and a number of battles in the Gempei (Minamoto-Taira) War of 1180–1185, which is the subject of the great war tale Heike Monogatari, were fought by warriors on water.

The Tadatsune Revolt

Some ninety years after Masakado, the Kantō was again plunged into war by the rebellion of Taira no Tadatsune. Although himself a former governor, Tadatsune seems to have been motivated by strong hostility toward members of the provincial officialdom of the Bōsō Peninsula, which comprised the three provinces of Shimōsa, Kazusa, and Awa. His rebellion did not begin, as Masakado's did, in private family quarreling. From the outset the Tadatsune Revolt was an open assault upon public authority.

After initial failure in its efforts to restore order to the Bōsō Peninsula, the court in 1030 commissioned Minamoto no Yorinobu as subjugator (tsuitōshi) to pursue and destroy Tadatsune. Yorinobu was the grandson of Tsunetomo, who received the Minamoto surname in 961 and founded what became the famous warrior clan of Seiwa Minamoto or Genji. The recipient of a number of appointments as governor or vice-governor, Tsunetomo firmly established his family in the emerging, warrior-oriented provincial aristocracy.

Tsunetomo's son, Mitsunaka, also had a long career of service in

Kawachi Minamoto

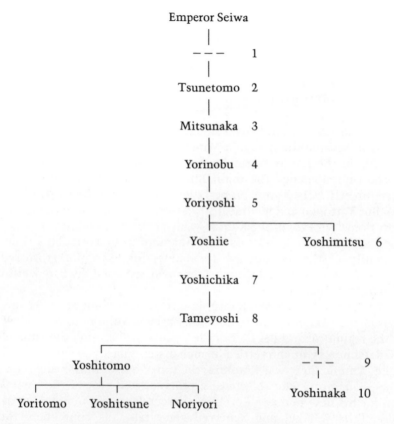

1, 2, 3 . . . indicate generations of descent from Emperor Seiwa

provincial offices and was one of the first of the Minamoto to act as warrior guard or "samurai" for the Fujiwara in the capital. The term samurai comes from the classical verb *saburau,* "to serve," and (as *saburai* or samurai) was used for "one who serves." In the eighth century, samurai were mere domestic servants assigned to care for old people.[62] But in the early Heian period the term was applied to private guards employed by the imperial and courtier families and organized into contingents called Samurai Units *(samurai-dokoro).* Members of these units normally held the fifth and sixth ranks at court. By the tenth century, leading warriors from the provinces regularly went to the capital to serve as samurai. Masakado, for example, became a samurai to the future imperial regent Tadahira, establishing the patron/client relationship discussed earlier.[63] The Seiwa Minamoto, from about Mitsunaka's time, became famous as the samurai "claws and teeth" *(sōga)* of the Fujiwara.

Minamoto no Yorinobu defeated Taira no Tadatsune and restored order to the Bōsō Peninsula without fighting. As Yorinobu was on his way to the Kantō, Tadatsune came to him and surrendered. In a report of the event, Yorinobu said: "Without beating of drums or waving of banners, without loosing an arrow, or even tightening our bow strings, we gained a great victory."[64]

The bloodless victory over Tadatsune brought renown to Yorinobu, who became the first in a Minamoto tradition of distinguished leadership in the Kantō. Yorinobu had his base in Kawachi province near the capital; hence the main line of the Seiwa Minamoto descended directly from him is properly identified as the Kawachi Minamoto. But Yorinobu and his lineal successors became famous above all as "overlords" *(tōryō)* of the Kantō. Many of the Taira branch families of the Kantō became vassals of the Minamoto from Yorinobu's time. The family of the vanquished Tadatsune, for example, prospered greatly in this new feudal arrangement and spawned such powerful houses as the Chiba and Kazusa.

Not all the Taira of the Kantō, however, were content to become vassals of the Minamoto or to accept a nascent Minamoto hegemony over the region. A number of Taira left the Kantō around the time of the Tadatsune Revolt and settled in such distant places as Shikoku and Kyushu. Among these was Korehira, the son of one of Masakado's conquerors, Sadamori, who selected Ise province just east of the capital region for his new home.[65] Korehira's descendants became known as the Ise Taira (Heike) and achieved great fame as contenders for national power with the Kawachi Minamoto in the late twelfth century.

Konjaku Monogatari (Tales of Long Ago)

Konjaku Monogatari belongs to a genre of literature called *setsuwa bungaku*, the "literature of stories." *Konjaku* contains more than a thousand stories, all beginning with the phrase *"ima wa mukashi,"* or "a long time ago." Although its author or compiler (assuming it was one person) is not known, *Konjaku* was probably produced in the early twelfth century. It is divided into four sections: stories of Buddhism in India, stories of Buddhism in China, stories of Buddhism in Japan, and secular stories of Japan. The sections are subdivided into thirty-one books, some of which are missing or incomplete. Because of the large number of stories about Buddhism, some scholars have speculated that *Konjaku* was compiled to provide Buddhist preachers with material for their sermons.[66] But this does not account for the fact that approximately one-third of the collection comprises secular stories.

Book 25 of the fourth section contains twelve stories about warriors and the titles of two others, which are either lost or were never written. Each story in Book 25 may be regarded as a short war tale. One is a summary of *Shōmonki* and another of *Mutsu Waki* (A Tale of Mutsu), which deals with the Former Nine Years War that was fought in northern Honshu in 1056–1062. Other stories relate the suppression of the early-tenth-century pirate Fujiwara no Sumitomo and the early-eleventh-century rebel Taira no Tadatsune. One of the missing or unwritten stories has a title indicating that its subject is the Later Three Years War (1083–1087), also fought in northern Honshu.

Konjaku is written in Japanese with some phrasing in Chinese, a style which prefigures that of the medieval war tales.[67]

Order of Battle

One of *Konjaku*'s stories in Book 25 tells of a battle fought in the early tenth century by Minamoto no Mitsuru and Taira no Yoshifumi, who was related to Masakado. In the course of "contending with each other for excellence in the way of the warrior (*tsuwamono no michi*),"[68] Mitsuru and Yoshifumi develop a fierce rivalry. Agreeing to settle their rivalry in combat, they select a place and day for battle and assemble armies (*ikusa*) of between five and six hundred men each. On the chosen day the armies take positions facing each other, separated by a distance of about 120 yards. After an exchange of envoys declaring intentions to do battle, the armies, at a signal, begin shooting arrows. But just as warriors from both sides start moving into closer firing range, Yoshifumi sends word to Mitsuru suggesting that, instead of allowing their armies to clash, he and Mitsuru fight alone. Mitsuru and Yoshifumi thereupon fight a series of encounters in which they gallop toward each other and shoot arrows. Both prove as skillful in defending themselves against arrows as in shooting them, and after a while they agree to stop, each satisfied that his military prowess has been well displayed and his honor upheld. Thereafter, the tale informs us, Mitsuru and Yoshifumi live as fellow warriors on good terms.[69]

Although probably fictitious, this tale describes the first stages of what some scholars believe was a prescribed "order of battle" fought between armies comprising mainly mounted bowmen in the ancient and early medieval ages.[70] According to this order, battles were arranged in advance—that is, armies agreed on when and where they would meet. Upon taking the field, each army sent an envoy to the other side to declare its intention to fight. "Humming" arrows (*kabura-ya*, arrows with turnip-shaped heads that made a humming sound when in flight) were then shot aloft by the armies to signal commencement of the battle. The first stage of actual fighting was a general exchange of arrows *(ya-awase)* by the warriors on both sides. In the Mitsuru-Yoshifumi conflict, the signal is made before the envoys have ridden back to their own sides, and the envoys display courage by continuing to ride at a steady pace without looking backward, even though arrows are by then flying around them. Before a certain battle in the late twelfth century, during the Gempei War, a Taira commander was so incensed by what he regarded as the rude language of the message brought by the Minamoto envoy that he beheaded the man. This grave breach of warrior etiquette so dispirited the men of his own army that it contributed to the army's defeat.[71]

Mitsuru and Yoshifumi make the unusual decision to stop the clash of their armies and engage, instead, in something like a Western joust. In this joust they fight exclusively with bows and arrows on horseback. Like those in *Shōmonki*, the warriors—*tsuwamono*—in *Konjaku* are primarily mounted archers. There are only a few scattered references to swords in *Konjaku*'s warrior section.[72]

There were six principal stages in what is thought to have been the classical order of battle between armies: (1) arrangement of the time and day for battle; (2) an exchange of envoys as the armies faced each other in the field; (3) the firing of humming arrows to announce the commencement of fighting; (4) a general exchange of arrows between the armies; (5) continuation of the shooting of arrows, with more accuracy, as the armies moved toward one another; and (6) the pairing off of warriors, as the armies came together, to fight one-against-one with swords.[73] Since it was difficult to deal a mortal blow with a sword from horseback, a warrior slashed at his opponent with the intent of knocking him from his horse.[74] Once the opponent was down, the warrior pounced on him and tried to kill him by stabbing with a knife.[75]

I will not attempt to estimate how many battles in ancient and early medieval times were actually conducted according to this six-stage order of battle; probably few, if any. Even in the war tales, adherence to such a ritualized order of battle is rare. The majority of battles in the war tales start with surprise attacks. Otherwise, battles (excepting sieges, which are especially common in the fourteenth-century *Taiheiki*) usually open with an exchange of arrows—the *ya-awase*—

and, if fought in an open field, reach their climax when the armies
come together and the mounted warriors pair off to fight one-against-
one. Such battles thus adhere roughly to stages 4 through 6 of the order
of battle given above.

The Taking of Heads

We have noted the practice of taking the heads of defeated rebel
leaders like Masakado and Sumitomo and sending them to Kyoto for
public display. By late Heian and early medieval times, it became the
custom to take the heads of all defeated enemies. Thus the typical warrior, once he succeeded in stabbing his enemy to death, took—or had
one of his attendants take—the enemy's head for display in an "inspection of heads" *(kubi-jikken)* after the battle. The purpose of this
inspection was to identify the various heads accumulated and to determine rewards, which were scaled according to the status of the warriors to whom the heads belonged. An embarrassing possibility was the
discovery of "friendly" or "allied" heads among those displayed. The
usual punishment for taking the head of an ally was the severance of a
finger from the right hand.[76]

In some cases in the war tales, however, warriors take the heads
of their slain or stricken allies and even their kin to prevent them from
falling into enemy hands. *Hōgen Monogatari*, for example, tells of a
warrior named Itō Go who leaps from his horse during a battle to take
the head of his brother, who has just been killed by an arrow that
pierced him and lodged in the armored sleeve of Itō Go riding at his
side.[77] And in *Heiji Monogatari*, a war tale that narrates the Heiji Conflict in Kyoto in 1159–1160, we read of a commander in battle who,
upon seeing that one of his warriors has been struck in the neck by an
arrow and is struggling to hold his seat on his horse, orders another of
his followers to take the warrior's head before the enemy gets it. Saitō
no Sanemori (whose story is told in Chapter 3), responding to the
order, rides up to the stricken warrior, explains what the commander
wants done, and, with the warrior's acquiescence and even assistance,
takes his head. Commenting on this incident, the *Heiji*'s anonymous author (to use the singular for convenience) observes: "There
is nothing so sad *(aware)* or admirable as the way of one who uses
the bow."[78]

The *Heiji* also contains the story of a commander in flight from
Kyoto after a major defeat who kills his son and takes his head because
the son has been severely injured and cannot continue traveling. The
commander, Minamoto no Yoshitomo, explains to his son that to be

captured by the enemy—and have his head taken and displayed—
would only "sully his name" (ukina).[79]

The Single Mounted Warrior

Although they do not use swords, Mitsuru and Yoshifumi fight in
the "single mounted warrior" style of battling (ikki-uchi) that had
evolved among horse-riding warriors over the centuries and pre-
dominated in warfare through the remainder of the ancient age and
well into medieval times. The persistence of this battle style is attrib-
utable in part to the continuing importance attached by warriors to
social status. Fighting a warrior beneath one's status brought no honor
and certainly no reward in the event one's army was victorious.
Defeating someone of higher status, on the other hand, was a boon to
the career of an aspiring warrior. Curiously, there is no reference in the
warrior section of Konjaku to the practice of name-announcing, one
purpose of which, as we have seen, was to identify oneself and one's
family status in the search for an adversary of equal or higher status.
But the Konjaku warrior stories as a whole are replete with references
to family pedigrees, indicating an acute consciousness of rank, status,
and achievement in warrior society.

Koremochi and Morotō

The contest between Mitsuru and Yoshifumi is the story of warrior chieftains punctilious about the etiquette of warfare. (Although
the setting of the contest is the early tenth century, the age of Masakado, it is described as though it were held in the late eleventh or early
twelfth century, when Konjaku was compiled.) Another Konjaku story
of two warriors, Taira no Koremochi and Fujiwara no Morotō, describes battling of a very different kind.

The Koremochi-Morotō story is one of violence and brutality,
deceitful strategies, and dog-eat-dog warfare. The leading figures are
descendants of the warriors who hunted down and killed Taira no
Masakado. Koremochi is the oldest son of a nephew of Taira no Sadamori, and Morotō is a grandson of Fujiwara no Hidesato. The fighting
in the Koremochi-Morotō story is reminiscent of Shōmonki: fighting
in which warriors give no quarter and ask none.

The animosity between Koremochi and Morotō arises from a dispute over land, a dispute that neither the principals themselves nor the
local officials can settle amicably. In frustration and anger, Koremochi
and Morotō challenge each other to a test of arms. Following the order
of battle described above, they exchange messages to settle on a time
and place to fight. But when Morotō learns that his army is outnum-

bered three thousand to one thousand, he declines the opportunity for combat and moves to another province.[80]

Persuaded by others that Morotō is no longer a threat, Koremochi allows his army to disband. But no sooner do they disband than he is attacked by Morotō. The attack comes suddenly in the early hours of the morning. Alerted only moments before by the noise of scattering birds, Koremochi attempts to erect shields and mount a defense with the small contingent of archers he has on hand. But the enemy force is too powerful. It advances rapidly on Koremochi's residence, sets it ablaze, and shoots down all those who try to escape. By daylight the residence is in ashes and the bodies of all inside are charred beyond recognition.[81]

Morotō assumes that Koremochi's body is among those in the ruins and departs with his army. In fact, Koremochi, disguised as a woman, escaped from the residence during the fire and clamor and hid in a nearby river, under overhanging trees. A group of Koremochi's vassals *(rōdō)* living in the vicinity gather at the ruins later in the morning and loudly lament what they assume is the death of their lord. They are overjoyed when Koremochi appears and informs them of his escape. The vassals recommend that they avoid any immediate encounter with Morotō's army of some four to five hundred men and instead devote themselves to rebuilding their own force to fight at a later time.[82]

Koremochi acknowledges their good sense but says that he cannot wait. He has no intention of bequeathing to his children and grandchildren the shame of one who has fled a scene of battle—indeed he cannot bear that shame for even one day before the eyes of his followers. Since he should have perished in the attack on his residence the night before, he now regards himself as no longer truly alive. He is prepared to pursue Morotō alone, if necessary, and die after firing at least one arrow at him. Aroused by their lord's words, the vassals assert their willingness to accompany him at once in pursuit of Morotō.[83]

Leading about one hundred men (some seventy mounted warriors and thirty soldiers on foot), Koremochi finds Morotō and his army resting by the side of a hill and completely offguard, both men and horses sated with food and drink. Koremochi's force falls on the army and routs it, killing many—including Morotō—and sending others into flight. Koremochi then rides with his force to Morotō's residence and sets it on fire. As the people within the residence attempt to flee, the men are killed and the women captured.[84]

In the Koremochi-Morotō story we find warriors engaged in merciless conflict of the kind that runs throughout *Shōmonki* but is described in that work with only a minimum of detail. Sneak attacks, especially at night, and arson are tactics that contrast sharply with those of the "order of battle" clashes between armies, such as the one in the story of Mitsuru and Yoshifumi. (Night attacks and arson are discussed more fully in the next chapter.)

Perhaps the most interesting passage in the Koremochi-Morotō story is that in which Koremochi speaks of his shame in having escaped death during Morotō's night attack. Shame, as noted, is closely bound with "name"—pride, honor, fame—and is one of the most powerful forces governing the behavior of warrior heroes in the war tales. We noted the shame of defeated warriors in Shōmonki. In the account of Koremochi we find shame so intensely felt that it cannot be borne even a moment beyond the time necessary to avenge it. The typical hero of the war tales is prepared to forfeit his life without a second thought when it comes to shame or name or, as we will see in the next section, when it is in the fulfillment of loyalty to his lord.

Konjaku states that, because of his triumph over Morotō, "Koremochi's fame (na) spread throughout the eight eastern [Kantō] provinces, and he was increasingly regarded as a warrior without peer (narabinaki tsuwamono)."[85] Koremochi was thus able to transform shame into fame and win the accolade of "warrior without peer," a stock form of tribute that is routinely bestowed upon warrior heroes in the war tales. A similar stock phrase found in the war tales from Shōmonki on is "a warrior the equal of a thousand" (ichinin tōsen no tsuwamono).[86]

Feudal Vassalage

Although the feudal institution of vassalage cannot be clearly identified in Shōmonki, Konjaku contains many references to warriors who are obviously bound as vassals to others (their lords). Among the terms in Konjaku that mean vassal are rōdō, kenzoku, and ruiban. Some of the Konjaku vassals are related by blood to their lords; others are non-kin adherents.[87] In certain cases the status of vassal is identified as hereditary, and there is frequent mention in Konjaku of the willingness of vassals to serve their lords in battle "without thought for their lives" (inochi o oshimazu) or with the expectation that they might "forfeit their lives" (inochi o sutete).[88] One of the most illuminating passages in Konjaku about the evolving lord/vassal relationship in warrior society appears in the story that is a summary of the war tale Mutsu Waki (A Tale of Mutsu), which recounts the fighting of Minamoto chieftains in the northern, Mutsu-Dewa region of Honshu in the mid-eleventh century.

Saeki no Tsunenori, a warrior from Sagami province in the Kantō, is informed during a battle that Minamoto no Yoriyoshi, his lord and the general of his army, is surrounded by enemies in another part of the battlefield and has little chance to survive. To his own followers *(zuihyō)*, Tsunenori says: "I have already served the general *(shōgun)* for thirty years. I have reached sixty and he is near seventy. Now that he is about to die, why should I not die with him? It is my wish to serve the general in the afterlife [literally, 'under the ground']."[89] After Tsunenori departs in search of Yoriyoshi, two or three of his followers declare: "Our lord has already gone to the general in order to join him loyally in death. How can we live on without our lord? Although we are rear vassals *(baishin)*, our loyalty is the match of his."[90] After fighting fiercely and shooting down many of the enemy, Tsunenori and all his followers are killed.

Tsunenori is portrayed in this story as a model warrior and vassal, loyal for a lifetime and even prepared to die for his lord; and Tsunenori's followers too are presented as models, ready to give their lives for him. In addition to illustrating loyalty the equal of Tsunenori's own, the followers provide us with a clear case of rear vassalage. For whereas Tsunenori is a vassal of Yoriyoshi and Tsunenori's followers are, of course, his vassals, the followers' relationship to Yoriyoshi is that of rear vassals.

The Warrior Army/Band

The word for army in *Konjaku* is *ikusa.* But *ikusa* can also mean "warrior band" (still another meaning, as noted earlier, is "battle"), and the difference between an army and a warrior band is important to note.[91] In its usual meaning (or at least its modern meaning), an army comprises soldiers who are governed by strict regulations—so strict, in fact, that their violation may result in punishment by death. The soldiers of an army are organized in a rigidly hierarchical structure, and the relationship between superiors and inferiors (between officers and men, for example) is basically impersonal. The warrior band that evolved in ancient Japan, however, was an association of mounted fighting men bound by personal (particularistic) lord/vassal ties.[92] Rear vassalage, moreover, involved a method of command within a warrior band that was significantly different from that of the usual army. The lord or leader of a warrior band gave commands only to his own vassals; he had no direct authority over the vassals of his vassals— that is, over those who were his rear vassals. The rear vassal received his commands exclusively from his immediate overlord, who was second in the hierarchical ranking of lord (of the warrior band), vassal, and rear vassal.

The warrior band and its evolution is one of the key subjects in the study of the institutional history of the warrior class in premodern Japan. The references I have cited from *Konjaku* concerning vassals and rear vassals tell us very little, beyond the rudimentary, about the warrior band as it took form in middle and late Heian times. Suffice it to note that, in *Konjaku*, *ikusa* sometimes means army and sometimes warrior band. Most battles were fought by armies that included foot soldiers. The warrior bands were essentially assemblages of mounted fighters or cavalries.

Idealization of Vassal Loyalty

We have observed that the lord/vassal relationship among warriors, although probably often tenuous in reality, is idealized in the war tales as a personal bonding in which the vassal is prepared to devote himself utterly in loyal service to his lord. In *Konjaku* and *Mutsu Waki*, Tsunenori and his followers relinquish their lives in battle voluntarily for their respective lords; and in *Mutsu Waki* we find a warrior saying: "I am ready to give my life for the general. I attach no more importance to it than to a goose feather."[93]

Watsuji Tetsurō has described this idealized ethic of warriors committed without reservation to the service of their lords—whether in the war tales or in reality—as *kenshin*, absolute self-sacrifice. He speaks of *kenshin* particularly in terms of an ancient "Bandō *musha no narai*" (way of the warriors of the Bandō), thus emphasizing the importance of Japan's "eastern frontier" not only in producing the best fighting men over the centuries but also in molding the warrior way.[94] In the ancient and medieval war tales it is almost always eastern warriors who are shown as exemplars of such idealized qualities as self-sacrificing loyalty, extreme aggressiveness, and legendary equestrian skills.

In historical reality, pure *kenshin* loyalty was impossible—except perhaps in isolated cases—because the lord/vassal relationship in warrior society was not unilateral but bilateral: A vassal served his lord as a fighting man in return for various rewards, including benefices (usually land). Warrior society would not have held together very long if warriors had simply given their existences for their lords without thought of reciprocity for themselves or their families. But even without referring to the bilaterality of the lord/vassal relationship, we can surmise from the nonexclusiveness of the relationship and the frequency of disloyalty and betrayal among warriors over the centuries (see the section on "Feudalism" earlier in this chapter) that self-sacrificing loyalty was at the very least an oft-violated ethic. Nevertheless, such loyalty remained a powerful ideal—a defining myth—of warrior life throughout the centuries. Even in periods when it was most abused, self-sacrificing loyalty was never displaced as a central concept of the warrior way—that is, of the way warriors *ought* to behave.

The perpetuation of self-sacrificing loyalty as an ideal was due in large part to the popularity of the war tales themselves, many of whose heroes are shining examples of the ideal. As described in the war tales, self-sacrificing loyalty is never sullied by reference to material gain by vassals or their families as reward for diligent, sometimes life-relinquishing, service. This does not mean that the war tales do not deal with the matter of warriors serving and fighting for rewards. *Heike Monogatari* in particular contains a number of passages that tell of lesser warriors driven by the desire to excel in battle solely for economic enrichment, and these passages give us important glimpses of medieval warfare as a hard means of livelihood. But when vassals are set forth as models of loyal behavior in the war tales, their loyalty is described in the purest, most unselfish terms of utter sacrifice for their lords.

The Vendetta

In one of *Konjaku's* stories we read of a man (it is not certain whether he is a warrior or merely a servant) who avenges the death of his father by murdering the father's killer, a real warrior, while he sleeps at night. Even though he does not clarify the status of the avenger, the author of the tale observes at its end that "it is the way of the splendid warrior to punish the enemy [that is, killer] of his parent" and that such punishment is "approved by heaven's way *(tendō)*."[95] Here is an early assertion of the belief that avenging the murder of a parent (or a lord) was not only the duty of the warrior but was approved by heaven itself. More commonly, justification for the pursuit of a vendetta—*katakiuchi* (sometimes translated as "blood revenge")—in premodern Japan was traced to an injunction received from China that appears in the *Book of Rites (Li-chi)*:

> Tzu-hsia asked Confucius, saying, "How should [a son] conduct himself with reference to the man who has killed his father or mother?" The Master said, "He should sleep on straw, with his shield for a pillow; he should not take office; he must be determined not to live with the slayer under the same heaven. If he meet with him in the market-place or court, he should not have to go back for his weapon, but [instantly] fight with him."[96]

Some premodern societies have sought to control the vendetta through law. In medieval Germany, for example, there was the law of

Wergeld, according to which a person who maimed or killed another was obliged to pay a sum of money to the victim or the victim's family. Schedules of payment were drawn up, specifying, for example, the amount owed for killing a nobleman or a freeman or for causing the loss of an arm, an eye, or some other part of the body.[97] The intent was to preclude a vendetta by the victim or his family.

In premodern Japanese warrior society, *katakiuchi* was regarded as virtually the duty of a warrior—a duty that was even thought, as observed above, to be approved by such venerable authorities as heaven and Confucius. The most celebrated case of *katakiuchi* in the medieval age was the vendetta of the Soga brothers, Jūrō and Gorō, who, in the late twelfth century, spent seventeen years in tracking down and murdering their father's killer. This vendetta is recounted and celebrated in *Soga Monogatari* (Tale of the Soga Brothers),[98] which is sometimes regarded as a war tale, and in later *nō* plays, ballad-dramas *(kōwaka)*, *kabuki*, and puppet plays. But *katakiuchi*, despite its appearance in *Konjaku*, is not a significant theme in the war tales as a whole.[99]

A Lesson in the Way of the Warrior

Minamoto no Yorinobu, the subduer of Taira no Tadatsune, appears in four of the *Konjaku* stories in Book 25, one of which recounts the Tadatsune Revolt itself. Another of the Yorinobu stories tells how he saved one of his vassal's children, a young boy of five or six who was taken hostage by a robber.

Yorinobu learns of the hostage crisis when his vassal, a "superb warrior" *(kiwametaru tsuwamono)*, rushes into his lord's residence and tearfully informs Yorinobu about the child being held in his own nearby home. Yorinobu's first words to the vassal, delivered with a laugh, appear to be shockingly callous; but they contain an important lesson in the way of the warrior as it is idealized in the war tales:

> "It is understandable that you are upset. But should you be crying this way when faced with an emergency? It's rather foolish for one who is supposed to be prepared to grapple with devils or gods to weep like a child. The boy's only an infant. Let him be killed. Only when you adopt such an attitude will you become a true warrior. If you are concerned about yourself or concerned about your wife and children, you will not be able to deal with things as a warrior should. To overcome timidity, you must forget entirely about yourself and your wife and children."[100]

Having said this, Yorinobu goes to the vassal's residence and talks the robber into releasing the child. But the principle enunciated by

Yorinobu of the warrior overcoming or transcending all personal considerations is in keeping with the *kenshin* ideal of absolute self-sacrifice in the service of one's lord—and is expressed even more dramatically in the medieval war tales, especially in regard to eastern or Bandō warriors. In *Heike Monogatari*, for example, we read: "Even though a parent or child is struck and killed, the Bandō warrior rides over the body and continues fighting."[101] And in the fourteenth-century war tale *Taiheiki* the description of a battle fought in 1333 contains this observation: "The attacking force were Bandō warriors, who gave no thought to living or dying. Even though their parents and children were cut down, they did not look back; and although lords and vassals were killed, they paid no heed to the number but rode over the bodies, pressing ever forward."[102]

Historical Background to *Mutsu Waki*
The Abe of Mutsu

We observed in the Introduction that Sakanoue no Tamuramaro achieved his great victory over the Emishi of Mutsu in 801–802. So decisive was this victory that Mutsu remained generally tranquil for two and a half centuries. On the other hand, Dewa, to which the first expeditions against the Emishi were sent in the late seventh century, was the scene of major uprisings in 878 and 939. Fortunately for the court, the Emishi of Dewa were not well organized, and provincial officials were able to bring about settlements of these uprisings mainly by correcting the administrative abuses that provoked them.

In both Dewa and Mutsu the court had continued to follow a policy, dating from the seventh century, of attempting to control the Emishi by appointing local Emishi leaders who accepted Japanese rule to serve as district magistrates. This policy worked particularly well in Mutsu through the ninth and tenth centuries. But by the eleventh century the very success of the policy produced a serious threat in enabling one family, the Abe, to establish control as district magistrates over six districts north of the Koromo River.[103] About midcentury, the Abe incited the ire of other provincial officials not only by seeking to expand their influence south of the Koromo but also by refusing to pay taxes or provide men for corvée labor service. The governor of Dewa attacked the Abe with a force of several thousand men, but was soundly defeated.[104]

The court selected Minamoto no Yoriyoshi, the son of Yorinobu, to deal with the Abe, appointing him governor of Mutsu and general for pacification (*chinjufu shōgun*). Yoriyoshi had accompanied his father in the campaign against Taira no Tadatsune in 1031 that resulted in

Tadatsune's submission without a fight. In 1051, when Yoriyoshi assumed his duties in Mutsu, the court issued an amnesty that included the pardoning of the Abe leader. Most of the next five years passed without incident; but just as Yoriyoshi's term as governor was nearing its end, Mutsu was suddenly plunged into the protracted fighting of the Former Nine Years War (which actually lasted only six years, 1056–1062).[105] *Mutsu Waki* blames the Abe for starting the war, but some historians believe Yoriyoshi goaded the Abe into fighting in order to expand his family's power in the north.

The Former Nine Years War

The war taxed Yoriyoshi's strength and determination to the utmost. Climatic conditions were harsh in the north, and Yoriyoshi, fighting far from his Kantō base, was often short of supplies and men. In the end, he prevailed over the Abe because, after much effort, he persuaded the Kiyowara family of Dewa to join him. When the Kiyowara leader, Takenori, crossed into Mutsu in the seventh month of 1062, he led an army, according to *Mutsu Waki*, of some ten thousand men.[106] Yoriyoshi's own force at the time numbered only three thousand. Together, the armies of the Minamoto and Kiyowara fought a series of battles in the eighth and ninth months of 1062 that culminated in the destruction of the Abe at Kuriyagawa, the site of modern Morioka city.

Mutsu Waki (A Tale of Mutsu)

Mutsu Waki begins with a commentary on the Abe family of Mutsu and how they flouted the authority of the Kyoto court; it then presents a brief biography of Minamoto no Yoriyoshi. The remainder of *Mutsu Waki* relates the story of Yoriyoshi's long period of service in the north, from his appointment as governor of Mutsu and general for pacification through his years as commander of the imperial forces in the Former Nine Years War. As is true of nearly all the war tales, the authorship of *Mutsu Waki* is not known. We do, however, have these remarks from its anonymous author at the tale's end: "I have compiled this record using official documents and stories currently being told. But since I am a great distance away, surely I have made many mistakes. Those who know the facts will have to correct these mistakes."[107]

It is generally believed that *Mutsu Waki* was written shortly after the conclusion of the Former Nine Years War and that these final remarks are a true statement by its author. Since the author lived "a great distance away," he was probably a resident of Kyoto. This would help explain his knowledge of Chinese, the language in which *Mutsu*

Waki is written, and also his access to "official documents." The "stories currently being told" may have been, as Helen McCullough suggests, accounts of the Former Nine Years War by soldiers returning to the capital.[108] It is in any case interesting to see the assertion that *Mutsu Waki* was composed by combining information from official sources with popular stories about the war and its origins. Probably much of the basic record of events in *Mutsu Waki* is historically accurate.[109] But the work itself is very much a war tale insofar as a large part of it comprises what are clearly embellished anecdotes.

Obligation

Prior to his appointment to pacify the Abe, Minamoto no Yoriyoshi was appointed governor of Sagami province. He established his base at Kamakura, which thenceforth served as the seat of the Kawachi Genji in the Kantō. *Mutsu Waki* informs us that Yoriyoshi so impressed the warriors of Sagami that most of them became his vassals. It goes on to say: "Because Yoriyoshi cared for them and saw to their needs, more than half of the men of bow and horse *(kyūba no shi)* east of Osaka became his followers."[110] Elsewhere in *Mutsu Waki* it states that, after an exhausting battle in the Former Nine Years War, Yoriyoshi

> fed his soldiers and put their equipment in order. He personally went around the camp, tending to the wounded. The soldiers were deeply moved and all said: "We will repay our obligations *(on)* with our bodies. We consider our lives as nothing compared to loyalty [or honor, *gi*]. If it is for the general, we do not in the least regret dying now."[111]

We see here the assertion that Yoriyoshi's success as a commander, at least in terms of attracting vassals and inspiring them to a loyalty that makes them ready to die for him, stems from his kindness and generosity, from his loving, personal care of them. These too are qualities at the heart of the *kenshin*, self-sacrificing ideal in the war tales. What binds vassals in loyalty to a lord even to the death is their sense of *on* or obligation toward him. If warrior society as portrayed in the war tales is a shame society, it is also an obligation society. Vassals incur an almost unlimited obligation to a lord simply by being his vassals and receiving his overlordship—that is, his kindness, generosity, and personal care. The *kenshin* ideal demands that a vassal be ever prepared to repay his obligation, although the obligation is typically thought to be of such magnitude that even death itself is not payment enough.

The nexus of personal favor and obligation that bound lord and vassal was given a particularly intimate coloration by the custom of treating the lord/vassal relationship in familial terms: lords conceived as parents and vassals as children. In its glorified form in the war tales, vassal loyalty is an ethic that guides the vassal's behavior in service to his lord in a way that is indeed as intensely personal as the behavior of a child toward his parent.

Minamoto no Yoshiie

The great battlefield hero of *Mutsu Waki* is Yoriyoshi's son, Yoshiie. Here is a description of Yoshiie in one of the battles of the Former Nine Years War:

> [Yoriyoshi's] oldest son, Yoshiie, was a warrior of peerless valor. He rode and shot arrows like a god. Defying naked blades, he broke through the rebels' encirclements, appearing first on their left and then on their right. With his large-headed arrows, he shot the rebel chieftains in rapid succession. He never wasted an arrow, but mortally wounded all those he attacked. Known throughout the land for his godly martial ways, Yoshiie rode like thunder and flew like the wind. The barbarians scattered and fled before Yoshiie, not one willing to confront him. The barbarians . . . called him Hachiman Tarō, the firstborn son of the war god Hachiman.[112]

The reference to naked blades is interesting, although we do not know whether these blades are wielded by men on foot or horseback. Yoshiie is clearly pictured as a fighter with bow and arrow from horseback, a warrior of the kind that had dominated warfare for centuries. After the final victory over the Abe, one of Yoshiie's fellow chieftains, the Kiyowara leader Takenori, asks him if he can test his strength with a bow. When Takenori hangs three suits of armor on a branch, Yoshiie pierces them with a single arrow. In wonder, Takenori exclaims: "This is a god in the form of a man. How could a mere mortal oppose him?"[113] As we will see, there are frequent references in the later war tales to this feat with the bow by Yoshiie as a classic demonstration of a warrior's strength.

Yoshiie became, in history, one of the greatest heroes of the Kawachi Minamoto. Later generations of the family looked upon him as their spiritual forebear, even though the founders of the family's martial fame were his grandfather and father, Yorinobu and Yoriyoshi. Yoshiie as hero was a product of two wars: the Former Nine Years War and a second conflict fought in the north two decades later called the Later Three Years War (which in fact lasted four years, 1083–1087). Since our knowledge of these wars is limited primarily to the information about them in two war tales, *Mutsu Waki* and *Ōshū Gosannen Ki*

(Chronicle of the Later Three Years War in Mutsu Province), Yoshiie is as much a hero of legend as of life.

In the passage quoted above, *Mutsu Waki* says that Yoshiie received his famous cognomen Hachiman Tarō (first son) from the enemy he fought in the Former Nine Years War, who wondered at his godlike prowess on the battlefield. In fact, the designation was attached to him because he was Yoriyoshi's oldest son and because the ceremony initiating him into manhood (the *gempuku* ceremony) was held at the Iwashimizu Hachiman Shrine in Kyoto. Yoshitsuna, Yoriyoshi's second son, had his initiation ceremony at the Kamo Shrine and was called Kamo Jirō (second son); and Yoriyoshi's third son, Yoshimitsu, was initiated at the Shiragi Shrine and was known as Shiragi Saburō (third son).[114] In addition to being a god of war, Hachiman also became the tutelary deity of the Minamoto. His association with the Minamoto was established during the time of Yoshiie's grandfather, Yorinobu.[115]

Chiyo Dōshi and Noritō's Wife

Mutsu Waki contains a touching story about the final battle of the Former Nine Years War:

Abe no Sadatō had a thirteen-year-old son, a handsome boy named Chiyo Dōshi. Clad in his armor, he sallied forth from the stockade and fought well and bravely. . . . Yoriyoshi was moved, and wished to pardon him. But Takenori came forward and said: "Don't think only about his conduct here and ignore the great harm he may cause later." Yoriyoshi agreed and had Chiyo Dōshi beheaded.[116]

Takenori is presumably concerned that the youthful Chiyo Dōshi will later seek to avenge the deaths of his kinsmen—that is, undertake *katakiuchi*. Such concern often leads chieftains in the war tales (and in reality) to round up and kill as many members of a defeated enemy as possible.

The story of Chiyo Dōshi is immediately followed in *Mutsu Waki* by that of the wife of Abe no Noritō. Defeat of the Abe comes when the joint Minamoto-Kiyowara force succeeds in setting fire to the stockade at Kuriyagawa in which the Abe have taken their stand, and a gale-force wind fans the fire into a conflagration. Most of the Abe warriors come rushing out of the stockade and are slaughtered. But inside, according to *Mutsu Waki*,

there were scores of beautiful women . . . choking on the smoke and weeping pitifully. As they emerged from the stockade, the women were given to the soldiers; and when the stockade fell, only Noritō's wife remained, clutching her three-year-old son. To her husband she said: "Since you are about to die, how can I live on alone? I wish to go first, before your eyes." So saying, she threw herself into a ravine, still holding the child. People called her a true heroine.[117]

In the later war tales there are numerous cases, such as this, of warriors' women committing suicide after (or in anticipation of) the warriors' deaths. Such suicides, the most poignant of which appear in *Heike Monogatari*, call our attention to the fact that women in the war tales often choose to share the fates of their men.

Historical Background to *Ōshū Gosannen Ki*

Twenty years after the Former Nine Years War, Minamoto no Yoshiie became embroiled in the Later Three Years War. This conflict developed from squabbling within the Kiyowara family, which after the Former Nine Years War had moved its base from Dewa to Mutsu and occupied the six districts previously held by the Abe. Two Kiyowara half-brothers, Kiyohira and Iehira, disputed overlordship of the Mutsu districts. Yoshiie, appointed governor of Mutsu and general for pacification, tried to mediate the dispute by dividing the districts between the brothers.

In 1086 Iehira attempted to murder Kiyohira. Yoshiie took Kiyohira's side and, with an army of several thousand, attacked Iehira at Numa Stockade in Dewa. What began as an attack became a grim siege that lasted four months. Great snows came with winter, and Yoshiie lost many of his men to cold and starvation. Meanwhile Iehira, joined by his uncle, abandoned Numa and took up a stronger position at Kanazawa Stockade, also in Dewa.

Yoshiie attacked Kanazawa Stockade in the fall of 1087, but he had no better success there than at Numa. Once again he faced the prospect of a severe winter and dwindling supplies. He was saved from another stalemate, however, when his brother Yoshimitsu joined him with reinforcements. Confronted with the combined armies of Yoshiie and Yoshimitsu and with their own food supplies exhausted, the defenders of Kanazawa Stockade surrendered in the eleventh month of 1087, thus bringing to an end the Later Three Years War.

The paucity of reliable sources makes it difficult to reconstruct the events of the Later Three Years War beyond the major battles and their outcomes. One thing is clear: As in the Former Nine Years War, the Minamoto underestimated the strength of their enemy. Committed to battle with a stubborn foe, Yoshiie was also frustrated by his repeated inability to secure the backing of the court. In the Former Nine Years War, the Abe were from the outset regarded as rebels. Accordingly, the court readily supported Yoriyoshi against them and provided him with men and supplies, although not always when promised.

In the Later Three Years War, the court claimed that the Kiyowara had done nothing publicly wrong and that Yoshiie's military action was an intrusion into the private affairs of a family.[118] Even after the war was won in 1087, the court, referring to the conflict as "Yoshiie's war" (Yoshiie *kassen*), refused to aid Yoshiie in rewarding his followers.[119] According to the war tale *Ōshū Gosannen Ki*, Yoshiie heard this on his way back to the capital. He had with him the heads of the defeated Kiyowara chieftains to present for display in Kyoto. In anger, he threw the heads away.[120]

The Later Three Years War thus proved very costly to Yoshiie, who was obliged to reward his warrior followers from his own resources. The real winner of the war was the man he had supported, Kiyowara no Kiyohira, who not only took possession of the disputed six districts in Mutsu but also asserted a hegemony over the entirety of Mutsu-Dewa. For a century Kiyohira and his descendants remained virtually unchallenged rulers of this vast northern territory. Known as the Ōshū Fujiwara (Kiyohira had been adopted from the Fujiwara), they left to history a priceless cultural legacy in Buddhist temples and art at Hiraizumi, their family seat.

From the standpoint of institutional history, the Later Three Years War was perhaps most significant for its role in furthering the development of the warrior band—or, more specifically, the warrior band of the Kawachi Minamoto. Although he needed help from his brother Yoshimitsu, Yoshiie achieved victory at the head of a personal force in a remote region under exceedingly adverse climatic and supply conditions. He could not have done this without good organization and firm control over the warriors he commanded.

Ōshū Gosannen Ki
(Chronicle of the Later Three Years War in Mutsu Province)

The preface to *Ōshū Gosannen Ki* states that it was written by the priest Gen'e in 1347, more than two and a half centuries after the Later Three Years War. *Ōshū*, however, is virtually identical to the text of *Gosannen Kassen Emaki* (Picture Scroll of the Later Three Years War), which was composed in 1171, less than a century after the Later

Three Years War.[121] Ōshū's principal value for this study lies in the anecdotes it contains that contributed to the legend of Yoshiie as one of Japan's greatest warrior heroes.

The Yoshiie Legend

Construction of the Yoshiie legend was begun in *Mutsu Waki*, where, as we observed, he is described as riding and shooting arrows like a god and as a godly fighter whom no mortal could hope to oppose. *Ōshū* does not focus so much on Yoshiie's divine fighting ability as on his qualities as a compassionate, wise, and inspirational leader. We read in *Ōshū*, for example, of Yoshiie warming soldiers with his own body during the bitter northern winters of the Later Three Years War, even reviving some who appear to have frozen to death.[122] This behavior is reminiscent of the kindness and care that *Mutsu Waki* says Yoriyoshi lavished on his followers. Such conduct is another example of the intimate, almost parental handling of vassals that, according to the *kenshin* ideal, imposed a sense of obligation on the vassals that inspired them to sacrifice themselves utterly in service to their lord.

Ōshū contains a number of stories that illustrate Yoshiie's wisdom and skill as a commander. To instill a fighting spirit in his men during the Later Three Years War, for example, he designates a "bravery seat" *(gōza)* and a "cowardice seat" *(okuza)* at camp to be occupied by those of his followers whom he judges to have fought best and worst in each battle.[123]

One of the most famous stories about Yoshiie in *Ōshū* concerns an incident that supposedly occurred as he led his army toward Kanazawa Stockade in what became the final battle of the Later Three Years War. As the army appoaches the stockade, Yoshiie sees a flock of geese rise from a field of grass and scatter. Surmising that enemy soliders hiding in the grass have disturbed the geese, he sends men to investigate. More than thirty of the enemy are driven out of the grass and promptly put to death. Yoshiie later reflects that study of Ōe no Masafusa's book on military strategy informed him that "when soldiers conceal themselves in the grasses of plains, they disturb flocks of geese." Yoshiie's followers are impressed and grateful that their lord is so learned in the art of war.[124]

The Limits of Warrior Pride

Among the most interesting stories in *Ōshū* is the account of a warrior named Kamakura no Kagemasa as he contends at the forefront of Yoshiie's army in an attack on Kanazawa Stockade. Only sixteen years old, Kagemasa fights with total disregard for his life. When an arrow pierces his right eye and lodges in his helmet, he breaks it off and shoots back an "answering arrow" *(tō no ya)*, killing an enemy. Back at camp another warrior, Miura no Tametsugu, comes to Kagemasa's aid. Placing his sandaled foot against Kagemasa's face as he lies on the ground, Tametsugu tries to withdraw the shaft. To Tametsugu's amazement, Kagemasa leaps up and attacks him with his sword, crying: "It is the warrior's wish to die facing bows and arrows. But so long as he lives he will allow no one to place a foot on his face!" All who hear these words are struck with admiration for this display of manly pride. Tametsugu, kneeling respectfully, removes the arrow.[125]

In an account of a battle in 1156 found in *Hōgen Monogatari*, two brothers who trace their lineage back to Kagemasa of the Later Three Years War begin their name-announcing with these words:

"We are Ōba no Heida Kageyoshi and Ōba no Saburō Kagechika, residents of Sagami province and the sons of Ōba no Shōji Kagefusa. We are also descendants in the fourth generation of Kamakura no Gongorō Kagemasa. At the time of the storming of Kanazawa Stockade by Lord Hachiman [Yoshiie] in the Later Three Years War, Kagemasa, who is now revered as a god, was only a youth of sixteen. When shot in the right eye with an arrow, Kagemasa, without even removing the arrow, shot an 'answering arrow' and killed an enemy. Thus did he bequeath his name to posterity."[126]

There is a discrepancy between *Ōshū* and *Hōgen* concerning whether Kagemasa broke off the arrow that struck him in the eye or simply ignored it as he shot his "answering arrow." Otherwise, the *Hōgen* name-announcing of the Ōba brothers reveals the careful preservation of an account of a single exceptionally dramatic event that supposedly occurred in a battle three-quarters of a century earlier. We may imagine the brothers recited this account before entering battle themselves both to publicize the fame of their family and to intimidate the enemy by implying that they will fight with as frenzied abandon as their ancestor, Kagemasa.

Reference to Kagemasa's feat of bravery appears again in the *Heike Monogatari* account of the Battle of Ichinotani during the Gempei War. Kajiwara no Kagetoki, a warrior of the Minamoto who is remembered by readers and audiences of the *Heike* both for his exploits in warfare and for his confrontations with Yoshitsune that lead eventually to Yoshitsune's downfall, claims in his name-announcing at Ichinotani that he is a descendant of Kagemasa and recites how Kagemasa killed a foe at the Battle of Kanazawa Stockade even after being struck in the eye with an arrow.[127]

History of the Aftermath of the Later Three Years War

The Later Three Years War occurred at a time of major political change in court government. In 1086 Emperor Shirakawa abdicated and inaugurated a period of some three-quarters of a century (until 1156) that historians call the age of rule by senior retired emperors (in). The ascendance of ex-emperors in court politics at this time resulted largely from the decline in effectiveness of rule by the Fujiwara regents. Support for the ex-emperors came primarily from two sources: court families other than the Fujiwara and families of the provincial warrior elite (the zuryō class), including Minamoto and Taira.

Minamoto no Yoshiie chose to spend most of the remainder of his life after the Later Three Years War living in Kyoto, where he sought to become more fully accepted by court society. In this he was badly disappointed, and his final years became a sad anticlimax to his earlier greatness as a warrior commander. Yoshiie was regarded as "the most valorous warrior in the land" (tenka daiichi buyū no shi),[128] and at the time of his death in 1106 a courtier wrote: "His military authority filled the realm. Here was a man truly worthy of being a great general (tai-shōgun)."[129] Yet Yoshiie and other warrior leaders from the provinces were still regarded in this age as mere underlings by the courtiers, whom they continued to serve as guards or samurai. The courtiers also held an inbred antipathy to the warriors' use of physical force and were strongly critical, from a Buddhist standpoint, of their taking of life. Taking life apparently troubled the warriors themselves. Konjaku Monogatari, for example, contains the story of Minamoto no Mitsunaka who, at the end of his fighting career, takes Buddhist vows to expiate the sins of many years of killing.[130] The courtiers were content to have warriors settle disputes for them by fighting and killing in distant provinces. But they were repelled by the presence of these martial men in the capital.

Yoshiie's final years were clouded by a great personal tragedy. His son and heir, Yoshichika, attempted to establish a power base in western Japan from his position as governor of Tsushima Island and was accused of rampaging through northern Kyushu, murdering people and stealing tax goods. In 1107, a year after Yoshiie's death, Yoshichika was finally tracked down and killed by Taira no Masamori. Masamori was the leader of the Ise branch of the Taira and was selected to pursue Yoshichika by the ex-emperor Shirakawa. Even before he returned to Kyoto from his campaign, Masamori was given lavish rewards by Shirakawa, including appointment as governor of Tajima province. A courtier remarked at the time in his diary: "It is only natural that reward should be given. But the sudden appointment of a person of Masamori's low status to a first-rank province can only be attributed to the special favor of the *in*."[131]

Whether or not Masamori deserved his rewards, his return to the capital was triumphant, as we see in these comments by the same courtier: "People high and low came in their carriages and on their horses to see the spectacle. The men and women of the capital filled the streets, and people behaved as though in a frenzy of excitement."[132]

Despite Masamori's apparent triumph, the Yoshichika affair left nagging doubts. People had difficulty understanding how an obscure warrior, with no outstanding military record, could in weeks track down and kill a chieftain of the family stature and fame—or notoriety —of Yoshichika. Rumors circulated that Yoshichika had not been killed by Masamori and was still at large. And for years there were reports that Yoshichika had been seen in one place or another, and even that he had been captured or killed.

Whatever the truth about Yoshichika, Masamori achieved a meteoric rise to prominence. It is clear in retrospect that Shirakawa had chosen to use him and the Ise Taira as his new samurai, his "claws and teeth," in place of the Kawachi Minamoto of Yoshiie. Thus, with the turn into the twelfth century, the fortunes of the Kawachi Minamoto, weakened by internal dissension, sank as those of the Ise Taira rose. In the century's second half, these two families would contend for national leadership.

2
THE EARLY MEDIEVAL WAR TALES
HŌGEN AND *HEIJI*

Historical Background to *Hōgen Monogatari*
Origins of the Ise Taira

The origins of the Ise Taira can be traced from at least 1006, when Taira no Korehira, a son of Sadamori, was appointed governor of Ise. Korehira held this appointment a bare two months and afterwards was assigned to positions in provincial governments in the east. Nevertheless, his branch of the Taira became firmly entrenched in Ise during the early eleventh century and gradually extended its influence into Iga province as well. Development of the Taira base and warrior band in Ise and Iga was achieved by a steady encroachment upon lands held by the Ise Shrine (in Ise) and Tōdaiji Temple (in Iga).[1]

By the time of Masamori, Korehira's great-grandson, the Ise Taira had attained court rank and served in the capital in the Bureau of Imperial Police. But the Taira family background and social position were far inferior to that of the Kawachi Minamoto of Yoshiie, the great hero of the wars in the north in the middle and late eleventh century. The decision of the senior retired emperor *(in)* Shirakawa to supplant Yoshiie with Masamori, noted at the end of the last chapter, presented an extraordinary historical opportunity to the Ise Taira. In selecting the relatively unknown Masamori as his new samurai, Shirakawa established with the Ise Taira the kind of patron/client relationship that, as we have seen, was much like the lord/vassal tie of warriors. This relationship between *in* and Ise Taira endured for three-quarters of a century and spanned the periods of three *in:* Shirakawa and his successors Toba and Goshirakawa.

With *in* patronage, Masamori served successively as governor of a number of provinces, including Tajima, Tangō, Bizen, and Sanuki, all of which were located to the west of Kyoto. Although Masamori was always an absentee governor, he had ample opportunity to expand his family's influence into western Japan, where he accumulated lands and formed vassalage ties with local warriors. From Masamori's time the Ise Taira became a distinctly "western" power and gained skills in the seafaring and naval warfare of that part of the west bordering on the Inland Sea.

Masamori's date of death is not known, but he probably died about 1122–1123.[2] He was succeeded as Ise Taira chief by his son Tadamori who, in his middle or late twenties, was already a distinguished warrior. In Tadamori's time (he lived until 1153) the Ise Taira became a major military force in western Japan. The family also rose to prominence at court when Tadamori was made *denjōbito*, courtier with the right of attendance upon the emperor.

Shirakawa, the dominant figure in Kyoto politics for nearly half a century, died in 1129. He was succeeded as *in* by his grandson Toba who, perhaps because of personal grievances toward his grandfather,[3] reversed many of Shirakawa's policies and replaced most of the major officials who had served him. One official who managed to survive the transition from Shirakawa to Toba was Taira no Tadamori. Indeed, Tadamori achieved his greatest prominence both as a warrior and as a courtier under Toba.

In *Heike Monogatari*, when Tadamori first visits the court in 1131, a group of courtiers, outraged that an upstart warrior has been allowed in the palace, mocks Tadamori in a song using wordplay involving the Taira name and plots to assassinate him.[4] But Tadamori, warned of the plot in advance, outwits the courtiers by displaying a sword and frightening them into abandoning their scheme. When later questioned about the sword, Tadamori reveals that it is made of wood. Thus he has not violated the prohibition against bearing arms at court.

There is no other evidence to support this story from the *Heike*, and it certainly sounds fictitious. But the story presents an interesting contrast between courtier and warrior in the mid-twelfth century. Ever arrogant and disdainful of social inferiors, the courtiers in the *Heike* story seem oblivious to the nature and extent of the power that warriors had by then acquired, even in the capital. The courtiers think only of berating and disposing of Tadamori. But Tadamori, alert and resourceful, has already come far by his wits, ambition, and physical prowess, and he has little trouble in turning the tables on his elegant but effete adversaries.

Ise Taira

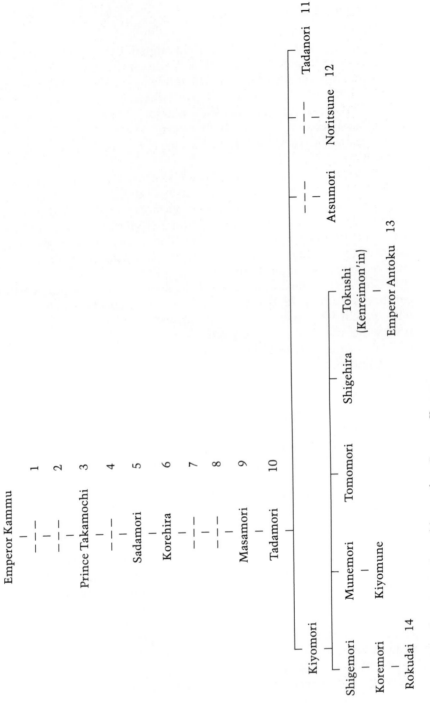

Emperor Kammu

— 1

— 2

Prince Takamochi — 3

— 4

Sadamori — 5

Korehira — 6

— 7

— 8

Masamori — 9

Tadamori — 10

Kiyomori

Shigemori — Munemori — Tomomori — Shigehira — Tokushi (Kenreimon'in) — Atsumori — Noritsune — 12 — Tadanori — 11

Koremori — Kiyomune — Emperor Antoku — 13

Rokudai — 14

1, 2, 3 . . . indicate generations of descent from Emperor Kammu

The Hōgen Conflict

Tadamori died in 1153 and was replaced as Ise Taira chief by his son Kiyomori. In 1156, the first year of Hōgen (1156–1158), Toba also died, bringing to an end twenty-seven years of dominance at court as *in*. Toba's death provoked a crisis that resulted in a brief clash of arms in Kyoto known as the Hōgen Conflict. This struggle has traditionally been regarded as marking the rise to national power of the warrior class. According to the priest Jien, writing in the early-thirteenth-century history *Gukanshō:*

> After senior retired emperor Toba died on the second day of the seventh month of 1156, fighting and strife began in Japan, and the country entered the age of warriors.[5]

Jien's words, however, should not be taken literally. Although warriors played an increasingly prominent role in national affairs from the time of the Hōgen Conflict, they by no means took immediate charge of the country or even the court. The evolution of warrior rule in Japan was a gradual process lasting well into the thirteenth century and beyond.

The cause of the Hōgen Conflict was factionalism, which afflicted all the major participants in court politics in the mid-twelfth century: the imperial family, the Fujiwara regent family, and the warrior houses of Ise Taira and Kawachi Minamoto. Each of these entities divided after Toba's death to form two contending camps with the former emperor Sutoku and his younger brother, the reigning monarch Goshirakawa, as titular heads. Sutoku, who greatly resented having been deposed by his father, Toba, in favor first of one brother (Konoe) and then another (Goshirakawa), was supported by Tadazane, patriarch of the Fujiwara regent family, and by his son Yorinaga, whom Tadazane made his successor as Fujiwara family head. Goshirakawa had the backing of Tadamichi, the regent and older brother of Yorinaga. Ordinarily, the regent and the Fujiwara family head were the same person. Division of the positions between the two brothers, Tadamichi and Yorinaga, reflected deep discord within the Fujiwara on the eve of the Hōgen Conflict.

Discord in the Ise Taira was minimal, since Kiyomori and most of the other family leaders joined Goshirakawa. But the Kawachi Minamoto became sharply split between the Goshirakawa and Sutoku camps. After the death of Yoshiie in 1106, the Kawachi Minamoto had lost almost all influence in court politics to the Ise Taira. While the Taira flourished under Masamori and Tadamori, the Kawachi Minamoto and their chief, Tameyoshi, languished in relative obscurity. Following in the path of his ancestors, Tameyoshi became a samurai to Yorinaga, head of the Fujiwara regent family.[6] (That is, Tameyoshi entered into the same kind of patron/client relationship with the Fujiwara regent family through Yorinaga that the Ise Taira had with the *in* from Masamori's time.) On the basis of this samurai relationship, Tameyoshi joined Yorinaga in the Sutoku camp.

Tameyoshi brought with him to the Sutoku camp other members of the Kawachi Minamoto (including his son Tametomo, who in *Hōgen Monogatari* is apotheosized as the great hero of the Hōgen Conflict). But Tameyoshi had long been on poor terms with his oldest son and heir, Yoshitomo, and Yoshitomo chose to defy his father and support the Goshirakawa side. Whereas Tameyoshi had spent most of his career in Kyoto and, according to his own admission as reported in the *Hōgen*, had "never fought a single battle,"[7] Yoshitomo was a man "reared in the Bandō who excelled in the way of the military *(buyū no michi)*."[8] When Yoshitomo rode into Goshirakawa's camp in 1156, he was accompanied by most of the leading vassals *(rōdō)* of the Kawachi Minamoto.[9]

The Hōgen Conflict was decided in a single battle: an attack before dawn on the seventh day of the seventh month by the Goshirakawa forces on the Sutoku encampment in northeastern Kyoto. Despite a stout defense, the Sutoku position was set ablaze and overrun. Fujiwara no Yorinaga attempted to escape but was killed by a stray arrow; the retired emperor Sutoku was captured and exiled to Sanuki province on Shikoku Island.

The Hōgen Conflict did not involve large numbers of warriors. The victorious Goshirakawa side had about six hundred men in its attacking army, and the Sutoku defenders had considerably fewer.[10] A principal reason why the Sutoku side kept to a defensive position on the night it was attacked was to await reinforcements from Nara.

The aftermath of the Hōgen Conflict witnessed the first executions in Kyoto since the early ninth century. To the horror of people then and later, Minamoto no Yoshitomo had his own father, Tameyoshi, killed, and Taira no Kiyomori enforced the execution of his uncle.

Hōgen Monogatari

Hōgen Monogatari, the first of the medieval war tales, is often linked with *Heiji Monogatari* and *Heike Monogatari* as one of a trio of related tales dealing with the three-decade conflict between the Ise Taira and the Minamoto that ushered in the medieval age. Unlike earlier war tales, such as *Shōmonki* and *Mutsu Waki*, which were written shortly after the events with which they deal, *Hōgen*, *Heiji*, and *Heike* evolved over long periods of time from both oral and written traditions and have been preserved in numerous versions.

Hōgen, *Heiji*, and *Heike* also differ from the earlier war tales in at least several other important respects. First, whereas the earlier tales are all set in places remote from the capital, such as the Kantō or the Mutsu-Dewa region, and involve warriors who, apart from a few leaders, have no direct contact with the court, these three tales are focused either entirely *(Hōgen)* or to a large extent *(Heiji* and *Heike)* on Kyoto and concern affairs and fighting in which both warriors and courtiers are embroiled. Second, these three works provide us with the first detailed descriptions of battle to be found in the war tales. They enable us to see the warrior as a fighting man engaged in warfare much more clearly than before. And third, *Hōgen*, *Heiji*, and *Heike* inform us, though in romanticized form, of the relations between courtiers and warriors in the first stage of transition to the medieval age. Even as warriors gradually displaced courtiers as rulers of the country, they were profoundly influenced by court life and culture. Some warriors, such as the Ise Taira, assumed courtly qualities to the point of becoming like courtier-warriors.

Hōgen, *Heiji*, and *Heike* also differ from the earlier war tales in having undergone substantial textual evolution, both as works intended to be read and as works to be memorized and recited by itinerant tale singers called *biwa hōshi*, blind Buddhist priests who accompanied themselves with lutes *(biwa)*. A collection of Buddhist writings for ritual use dated 1297 contains a reference to the recitation of all three of these early medieval war tales, the *Hōgen*, *Heiji*, and *Heike*, indicating that they were being used by tale singers at least by the late thirteenth century.[11]

Very likely the *Hōgen*, *Heiji*, and *Heike* were first written in the early thirteenth century, perhaps a half-century or so after the events they recount. The original *Hōgen* no longer exists, but there are more than thirty later versions extant. The oldest, dated 1318, is known as the Bumpō text (text of the Bumpō era, 1318–1339). The first and third books of the Bumpō text's three books are missing. But a text from the early modern age (1573–1867) containing all three books, called the Nakaraibon (Nakarai text), is believed to be a copy of the *Hōgen* representing the same stage in the tale's development as the Bumpō text.[12] Hence the Nakaraibon is the main text of the "old text" *(furubon)* category of *Hōgen* versions—that is, it is recognized as the oldest complete form of the work that has survived.

Another major category of *Hōgen* texts comprises the *rufubon* (literally, "circulating texts"), or versions of the *Hōgen* that have been most widely disseminated. The *rufubon* texts all date from the early modern age and, unlike the earlier *Hōgen* versions, which were hand-copied, are printed texts. The *rufubon* texts contain materials edited from a variety of *Hōgen* versions.[13]

The third major category of *Hōgen* texts are the Kotohirabon (Kotohira texts), which are regarded as the finest literary versions of the *Hōgen*. Nearly all the extant copies of the Kotohirabon are from the early modern age, but the text itself dates to a much earlier time, per-haps the late fourteenth century. The middle and late fourteenth cen-tury, called the age of war between the northern and southern courts (*nambokuchō jidai*, 1336–1392), witnessed the most important textual evolution of *Heike Monogatari* as a recitative work *(kataribon)*, culmi-nating in the great Kakuichi text of 1371. Quite possibly the *Hōgen* also underwent its most significant evolution—from the "old text" version to the Kotohirabon version—during the same time.[14]

The most significant change in the evolution of the *Hōgen* from the old text version to the Kotohirabon version was its transformation from a quasi-historical chronicle *(ki, kiroku)*, carefully arranged in chronological order with each passage precisely dated, to a tale *(mono-gatari)* in which the topical handling of stories often interrupts the his-torical chronology and much of the dating of passages has been dropped. The *Heiji* and *Heike* were similarly transformed from chroni-cles to tales. In all three cases—*Hōgen, Heiji,* and *Heike*—the transfor-mation was primarily the work of tale singers, who in effect changed these early medieval war tales into collections of stories held loosely together by historical chronology. For the tale singers, chronology and historical veracity were of far less importance than having good stories to tell.

Another important development in the transition from the old text version to the Kotohirabon version of the *Hōgen* was the creation of larger-than-life heroes, especially Minamoto no Tametomo. Other characters in the *Hōgen* are cast in a less favorable light in the Koto-hirabon than in earlier versions. We see this, for example, in the case of the Taira leader Kiyomori, who in the Kotohirabon is made to act cow-ardly. The Kotohirabon version of *Heiji Monogatari*, which represents a stage of development of the *Heiji* similar to that of the *Hōgen* Koto-hirabon, portrays Kiyomori not only as cowardly but also indecisive and buffoonish. And in *Heike Monogatari*, Kiyomori becomes the archvillain whose arrogance and cruel, arbitrary behavior sets the stage for the fall and destruction of the entire Ise Taira clan, the main theme of the *Heike*.

The *Hōgen* Kotohirabon also has biographical sketches, passages about historical events, stories of women, and commentaries, often sharply critical, about the personal conduct of characters that are not in the old text version. The Kotohirabon does not, however, contain the material about the fabulous adventures of Minamoto no Tametomo after the Hōgen Conflict that is found at the end of both the old text and *rufubon* versions of the *Hōgen*.

Hōgen and *Heiji* are about the same length and have similar structures. There are also, as we will see, striking similarities in the treatment of certain characters in the two works, especially the principal battlefield heroes, Minamoto no Tametomo in the *Hōgen* and Minamoto no Yoshihira in the *Heiji*. These facts suggest that the *Hōgen* and the *Heiji* may have been written by the same author or authors or, at the very least, were molded in similar ways by tale singers. The *Hōgen* and the *Heiji* are both divided into three books. In each, Book 1 recounts the circumstances and events leading to conflict, Book 2 describes the main fighting, and Book 3 deals with the conflict's outcome and repercussions.

This study of the *Hōgen* is based primarily on the Kotohirabon version. Where appropriate, comparisons are made with Nakaraibon *Hōgen Monogatari* and *rufubon Hōgen Monogatari*.

The Surprise Attack and Arson

When in *Hōgen Monogatari* the Sutoku side gathers to discuss plans before the Hōgen Conflict, Minamoto no Tametomo, observing that he has already fought in some twenty to thirty battles while living in Kyushu, proclaims that no strategy in warfare is superior to the night attack *(youchi)*. He urges that they attack the enemy's headquarters at Takamatsu Palace that night. His plan calls for setting fire to three sides of the palace and attacking from the fourth. As Tametomo envisions the assault, "those of the enemy who escape the fire will not escape our arrows, and those who escape our arrows will not escape the fire."[15] Intent upon all-out victory, Tametomo says that when Emperor Goshirakawa is forced to leave Takamatsu Palace and seek refuge elsewhere he, Tametomo, will shoot arrows at his palanquin. This will cause the bearers to drop the palanquin and thus enable the emperor's capture.

But Yorinaga, the Fujiwara leader, disdainfully rejects Tametomo's advice, attributing it to the excessive ardor of youth. According to Yorinaga: "The night attack is for a private fight among ten or twenty mounted warriors. It is hardly suitable to a struggle for the country between an emperor and a retired emperor."[16] Yorinaga insists that they wait until the following day, when he expects reinforcements from Nara. Tametomo replies that it is timing, not numbers, that matters, and if they do not attack that night, Yoshitomo will surely attack them. This is exactly what happens. Although the victory is not easily won, Yoshitomo and his allies finally succeed in setting fire to Shirakawa Palace, stronghold of the Sutoku side, and dispersing its occupants. In the panic that follows, many on the Sutoku side are killed, while others are captured. A few escape.

This confrontation between Yorinaga and Tametomo in the *Hōgen* suggests the probable arrogance—and ignorance—with which courtiers sought to deal with warriors even as the warriors, in the mid-twelfth century, were poised to begin their rise as the new ruling class of the land. Yorinaga contends that a major conflict, especially one that involves an emperor and a retired emperor, must be conducted according to proper rules of behavior. We have noted that some battles in the war tales are conducted according to rules of behavior by adherence to part or all of a six-stage order of battle. (See the section "Order of Battle" in Chapter 1.) But in many other battles there are no rules. Surprise attacks, including attacks at night, are frequent; and warriors do what they must to achieve victory. (Most of the famous battles in the Hōgen Conflict, the Heiji Conflict, and the Gempei War were, in fact, precipitated by unannounced attacks.)

Night attacks are described in most of the early war tales, including *Shōmonki* and the war tales in *Konjaku Monogatari* (for example, the attack of Fujiwara no Morotō on Taira no Koremochi). In *Mutsu Waki*, Minamoto no Yoriyoshi says: "The warrior does not necessarily choose his time for battle. He looks for the best chance. . . . When an opportunity presents itself in warfare, one should take advantage of it."[17]

Whereas Fujiwara no Yorinaga in the *Hōgen* insists that the Sutoku side act in a manner befitting an encounter between an emperor and a retired emperor, the most influential courtier in the Goshirakawa camp, Fujiwara no Shinzei, takes a far more realistic view of the impending conflict, endorsing Yoshitomo's proposal of a night attack by stating that military planning is the business of warriors.[18] Shinzei displays his pragmatism again when he authorizes Yoshitomo to set fire to Shirakawa Palace, even though he knows that the flames might also destroy Hōshōji, a nearby temple much admired for its beauty. The *Hōgen* claims that the Shirakawa defenders are actually winning the battle and the attackers' only chance for victory is to resort to arson. Faced with the alternative of victory or defeat,

Shinzei chooses arson and victory, observing rather casually that Emperor Goshirakawa can easily rebuild Hōshōji.[19]

We observed the use of arson as a weapon of combat by warriors in the war tales surveyed in the last chapter. In premodern Japan, nearly all structures, military and civilian, were made of wood. If an enemy was established in a defensive position in a wooden building or group of buildings, an attacking force often, if not usually, sought victory by setting the position on fire. In the final battle of *Mutsu Waki*—the attack on Kuriyagawa Stockade in which the Abe family is decisively defeated—Minamoto no Yoriyoshi, after directing his men to cut reeds and grass and pile them "like a mountain" around the stockade, bows toward the imperial capital and implores His Majesty: "Let a mighty wind repay the loyalty of an old minister. . . . Send the wind! Kindle the flames! Burn the stockade!"[20] Far from regarding arson as a violation of the proper rules of battle, Yoriyoshi seeks to employ it to complete what he regards as an imperially sanctified mission.

We also noted in the last chapter cases in the early war tales of the particularly vicious practice of burning down the residences and other structures of enemies and suspected enemies following battles. Thus after the first battle described in *Shōmonki*, the victorious Taira no Masakado "burned to the ground all the houses [in four villages], down to the small huts of his enemies' followers. . . . Supplies sufficient for a thousand years were reduced to ashes in a moment, and more than five hundred enemy houses . . . went up in flames."[21] After defeating the Sutoku side in the Hōgen Conflict by torching Shirakawa Palace, Minamoto no Yoshitomo, Taira no Kiyomori, and others of the Goshirakawa side remorselessly set fire also to the residences of Sutoku, Fujiwara no Yorinaga, and Yoshitomo's father, Tameyoshi.[22]

When faced with enemy attacks they wish to avoid, warriors in the war tales often burn their own residences—and frequently the residences of others as well—before fleeing. To cite an example from *Heike Monogatari*, the Taira in the Gempei War, when driven from Kyoto by the Minamoto in 1183, "burned to the ground in a single blaze more than twenty residences belonging to the high nobles and courtiers of the family, the dwellings of their many followers . . . and forty to fifty thousand homes of townspeople in the capital and Shirakawa."[23]

One of the most famous acts of arson in Japanese history was the burning of Sanjō Palace, which precipitated the Heiji Conflict of 1159–1160, an encounter that emerged in the aftermath of the Hōgen clash and pitted Ise Taira against Kawachi Minamoto. Much of the fame of the Sanjō Palace burning arises from the magnificent portrayal of it in the "Illustrated Scrolls of the Tale of Heiji" *(Heiji Monogatari Emaki)*.

Tametomo and the Loser as Hero

Hōgen Monogatari set a pattern for the medieval war tales insofar as it deals with or is told primarily from the standpoint of warrior losers. (Among the earlier war tales, *Shōmonki* is also about a loser, Taira no Masakado.) Two observations may be made here about this preference for losers in the medieval war tales. First, there is a distinct liking in Japanese literature, discernible in the earliest writings, for stories of the sufferings and tragic fates of those who lose out in particular events or affairs.[24] Second, in the medieval age, whose advent was accompanied by a despairing pessimism about entry into a period of darkness and disaster, the period of *mappō* or the "end of the Buddhist Law" (to be discussed in the next chapter), losers served as fitting symbols of the decline of the world in general. The sense of *mappō*, which is not particularly noticeable in *Hōgen Monogatari* and *Heiji Monogatari*, is presented with almost overpowering force in *Heike Monogatari*. The descent to extinction of the Ise Taira family in the *Heike* drew the sympathy of medieval readers in part because they believed that what happened to the Taira was in a larger sense happening to the world as a whole.

The great loser-hero in *Hōgen Monogatari* is Minamoto no Tametomo. Although Tametomo was a real person, the Tametomo in the *Hōgen* is almost entirely a creation of the authors of the *Hōgen* in its various versions. We deduce this from the fact that Tametomo appears as barely more than a name in most contemporary accounts of the Hōgen Conflict. The diary *Hyōhanki* by the courtier Taira no Nobunori, regarded by historians as the best source of factual information about the conflict, does not even mention him on the night of battle.[25] Tametomo was literally invented and "heroicized" in the process of the textual evolution of the *Hōgen*, especially by the tale singers who were primarily responsible for the development of the *Hōgen*'s Kotohirabon version. In this version, Tametomo becomes a veritable superman: "More than seven feet tall, Tametomo exceeded the ordinary man's height by two or three feet. Born to archery, he had a bow arm that was some six inches longer than the arm with which he held his horse's reins. . . . [He used] a bow that was more than eight and a half feet in length."[26] Elsewhere in the Kotohirabon version, Tametomo is called "frightful" *(osoroshii)*, "unlike a human being," and "a demon *(kijin)* or a monster *(bakemono).*"

Tametomo is an extreme example of a particular kind of personage found in the war tales called *aramusha* or "rough warrior," a warrior who may be likened to the *arauma*, rough or untamed horse (discussed in the last chapter), that was so esteemed by the ancient Japanese fighting man. Wild and unruly from childhood, Tametomo was sent by his father to live in Kyushu, which in ancient times was frequently chosen as a place of distant exile. In Kyushu, according to the legend, Tametomo became a feared fighter, terrorizing the populace and virtually asserting his military control over the island. In the *Hōgen* account of the Hōgen Conflict, the Sutoku side bases its hopes for victory almost entirely on the prowess of Tametomo, even though his strategy for battle is rejected by Fujiwara no Yorinaga.

When Yoshitomo, Kiyomori, and the other commanders of the Goshirakawa side attack Shirakawa Palace at night, Tametomo holds them off almost single-handedly. Much of the *Hōgen's* lengthy description of the attack on the palace is a recitation of how Tametomo's arrows fell one attacker after another and keep still others at bay. At one point, an arrow loosed by Tametomo against two attacking brothers goes through one brother, killing him, and lodges in the armor of the other. Witnesses to this remarkable display of archery recall the story, from *Mutsu Waki*, of how Tametomo's ancestor Minamoto no Yoshiie shot an arrow through three suits of armor as a demonstration of his skill with the bow after the Former Nine Years War.[27]

Taira no Kiyomori, who was more generously rewarded than any of the participants on the victorious Goshirakawa side after the Hōgen Conflict, is portrayed in particularly unflattering terms in his meeting in combat with Tametomo. Upon learning that the gate of Shirakawa Palace he has chosen to attack is guarded by such a "dreadful fellow" (*susamajiki mono*) as Tametomo, Kiyomori decides it is wiser to withdraw and attack elsewhere.[28] Here we see the first stage in the process, remarked upon earlier, of the denigration of Kiyomori's character in the textual evolution of the early medieval war tales (the *Hōgen*, *Heiji*, and *Heike*), mainly by the same tale singers who transformed Tametomo and others into great heroes.[29]

Although Tametomo becomes, by virtue of the defeat of the Sutoku side in the Hōgen Conflict, a loser-hero, he differs from most of the other major loser-heroes of the early medieval war tales in that he is not also a tragic hero. The tragic warrior hero is one who fails or comes to grief at least in part because of some weakness or flaw of his own—he is not done in entirely by others or by outside forces—and whose end is made especially moving because his reduced state evokes memories of an earlier time of fame and glory. The three most prominent tragic heroes of the war tales of the late-twelfth-century conflicts that ushered in the medieval age are Minamoto no Yoshitomo (in *Heiji Monogatari*), Minamoto no Yoshinaka (in *Heike Monogatari*), and Minamoto no Yoshitsune (in *Heike Monogatari* and *Gikeiki*). As we will see, all three of these heroes fail primarily because of shortcomings, not as military commanders, but as statesmen or politicians.

Unlike the tragic hero, Tametomo is brought low entirely by others. First his advice about making a night attack is rejected. Despite this rejection of a strategy that probably would have led to victory, Tametomo becomes the main defender of Shirakawa Palace and, according to the *Hōgen*, has the battle almost won when the attackers resort to arson. With the palace in flames, Tametomo, his father Tameyoshi, and his brothers flee. Tametomo alone remains undefeated in spirit, urging that they go to the eastern provinces and, like the tenth-century rebel Taira no Masakado, establish a capital there and continue their resistance to the imperial forces (the Goshirakawa side).[30] When Tametomo is finally captured, after a fierce struggle, he is sentenced to exile on the island of Ōshima off the Izu Peninsula. Before dispatching him to Ōshima, his captors dislocate his arms to prevent him from once again becoming a superhuman archer. But although Tametomo's arms are thus weakened, they are also lengthened and, we are told, he is soon able to shoot arrows even more powerfully than before.[31]

The Kotohirabon version of the *Hōgen* ends its account of Tametomo with the disquieting report that once in Ōshima, which was part of Izu province, he commences behaving without regard to the wishes of others and the Izu official appointed as his warden does not know how to control him.[32] We have seen that other versions of the *Hōgen*, which include the old text and *rufubon* versions, contain accounts, taken from the legends that grew up around Tametomo, of his exploits in exile. Briefly, these are stories of how he ruthlessly subjugates the seven islands of Izu, beginning with Ōshima, and then sails to a mythical Island of the Devils and conquers it as well. Eventually, when the court sends a force in some twenty warships to attack Tametomo, he abandons the thought of further resistance (after sinking one ship with a single arrow) and commits suicide.[33] Still another story in the Tametomo legend relates that he does not commit suicide but makes his way to the Ryukyu Islands, subjugates them, and founds a dynasty of kings.

The Ever-Faithful Follower

Among the most appealing characters in the medieval war tales are men—I will call them ever-faithful followers—who are leading vassals of the tragic heroes and serve these heroes with utter devotion and a sense of absolute self-sacrifice (in the manner of Watsuji Tetsurō's concept of *kenshin*). Tametomo, who is not a tragic hero, has no such vassal. But his older brother, Yoshitomo, whose story begins in *Hōgen Monogatari* and who becomes a tragic hero in *Heiji Monogatari*, has an ever-faithful follower in Kamada no Masakiyo. The end of the story of Yoshitomo and Masakiyo must await the discussion of the *Heiji*, but we can observe the general character of the relationship between these two men as it is revealed in the *Hōgen*.

When, in the attack on Shirakawa Palace, Yoshitomo prepares to confront his fearsome brother Tametomo, Masakiyo holds him back, asserting that the commander-in-chief *(tai-shōgun)* does not enter a battle personally until his forces have been greatly reduced and the fighting is desperate. Masakiyo states that he will test Tametomo in Yoshitomo's place and, advancing, announces his name.[34] Tametomo responds by saying that Masakiyo, as a hereditary vassal of the Kawachi Minamoto, has no business attacking him. It is clear also that Tametomo does not regard Masakiyo, a vassal, as a worthy opponent to fight. Shouting that Tametomo has defied an imperial decree and is now a rebel, Masakiyo shoots an arrow that strikes Tametomo in the cheek and lodges in his helmet. Tametomo sets out with twenty-eight riders in pursuit of Masakiyo and his band of thirty. With Tametomo's enraged voice sounding in his ears like "the clapping of thunder," Masakiyo barely manages to escape, although he still has the presence of mind not to draw Tametomo in the direction of his lord, Yoshitomo. Friend and foe alike admire Masakiyo's stratagem of maneuvering Tametomo away from his lord.[35]

The character of Masakiyo, as he appears in the *Hōgen* and *Heiji*, is not drawn as clearly as the two greatest of the ever-faithful followers in the war tales of this age: Imai no Kanehira (in the service of Minamoto no Yoshinaka) and Musashibō Benkei (in the service of Minamoto no Yoshitsune). Nevertheless, we see in him the basic qualities of the ever-faithful follower, including unqualified devotion and loyalty and a readiness to advise and even guide his lord. The tragic heroes —Yoshitomo, Yoshinaka, Yoshitsune—characteristically falter and grow weak as their fortunes decline. The ever-faithful followers encourage and bolster them as they approach their ends.

The Warrior House, Status, and Genealogies

Takeuchi Rizō has observed that, by the eleventh century, there had evolved in warrior society a strong sense of elite status based on birth into warrior houses *(tsuwamono no ie).*[36] This sense of status by birth, and the obligations attendant upon it, is expressed by several of the warriors in the Hōgen Conflict as narrated in the *Hōgen*. Thus Minamoto no Tameyoshi, after ignoring several calls from the Sutoku side, reluctantly joins them because it is his duty as one "born into a house devoted to the bow and arrow *(yumiya no ie)*."[37] And Tame-yoshi's son Yoshitomo, pressed into the military leadership of the Goshirakawa side, remarks: "It is my fortune, having been born into a military house *(bubi no ie)*, to deal with such matters."[38]

The sense of elite warrior status deriving from birth is revealed also in the prominence given to genealogies in the name-announcings found in the *Hōgen*. The earlier war tales, while referring to name-announcings, provide little information about their contents. From the *Hōgen* on, name-announcings are not only presented in detail in the war tales, they appear as prominent features of the descriptions of most battles. As Kenneth Butler, writing about *Heike Monogatari*, explains, name-announcing is a formulaic technique used by tale sing-ers in many countries to elaborate their stories.[39] We may presume that the extensive use of *nanori* from the *Hōgen* on in the war tales reflects the oral contribution to their evolution.

The highlighting of genealogies in name-announcings in the *Hōgen* can be illustrated by an exchange of "names" between a Taira warrior, Kiyomori's son Motomori, and a Minamoto warrior, Uno no Chikaharu (or Chikaharo), who encounter each other during a recon-naissance mission led by Motomori immediately before the Hōgen Conflict. Coming across Chikaharu and a group of some thirty follow-ers at the southeastern entry to the capital, Motomori, after informing the new arrivals that many warriors are gathering in the city and a dis-turbance is brewing, proclaims himself: "The police lieutenant of Aki, Motomori; descended in the twelfth generation from Emperor Kam-mu; a distant relative in the eighth generation of the Taira general *(shōgun)* Masakado; grandson of the minister of punishments, Tada-mori; and second son of the governor of Aki, Kiyomori." Not to be out-done, Chikaharu then recites his lineage: "I am the resident of Yamato province Uno no Shichirō Chikaharu; descended in the tenth genera-tion from Emperor Seiwa; a distant relative of the Sixth Grandson Prince; five generations removed from the governor of Yamato, Yori-chika, the younger brother of the governor of Settsu, Raikō; grandson of the vice-minister of central affairs, Yoriharu; and oldest son of the governor of Shimotsuke, Chikahiro."[40]

Apart from the recitation of genealogies, there were other pur-poses of name-announcings (as summarized in the last chapter): iden-tifying oneself to an enemy army in the quest for a suitable opponent with whom to do battle; identifying oneself to one's allies to establish witnesses for later claims to rewards; intimidating the enemy; and promoting the fame of oneself and one's family. Name-announcings were common, indeed virtually obligatory, when warriors encountered each other or were about to enter battle. Warriors in the medieval war tales frequently announce their names and demand that their opponents do the same. When, for example, Taira no Kiyomori in the *Hōgen* approaches the gate defended by Tametomo during the night attack on Shirakawa Palace, he shouts his name and demands to know his opponent. The brief response from the gate—"The defender here is Chinzei no Hachirō Tametomo"—is sufficient to dampen Kiyomori's fighting ardor and prompt him, as noted, to try another gate.[41]

Name-announcings were also delivered during battle in the form of *kachi-nanori* or "victory name-announcings." These were shouted claims to triumph over individual enemies or to other special achievements, such as leading an attack or being the first to breach an enemy's position. When warriors were killed performing meritorious acts in battle, the attendants or grooms who accompanied them on foot (*ge'nin* or *shojū*) often shouted the *kachi-nanori* for them.

One of most rousing *kachi-nanori* in the *Hōgen* is made by a nineteen-year-old warrior named Kaneko no Ietada of the Goshirakawa side, who claims that the attack on Shirakawa Palace is his initiation to battle. Challenging Tametomo and his crew of defenders, Ietada wrestles with two brothers, known for their strength and prowess, who venture from the palace to deal with him, and he stabs them to death. Taking their heads, Ietada remounts his horse and loudly announces: "I, Kaneko no Jūrō Ietada, a resident of Musashi province, have come forth, before the renowned Tametomo of Tsukushi [Kyushu], and with my own hands have taken the heads of two noted warriors (*samurai*). Observe this, both enemy and ally! A feat rarely achieved either in ancient times or the present! . . . I am the Ietada who wishes to bequeath his name (*na*) to generations to come. If there are warriors among Tametomo's band who feel they are my match, let them come and grapple with me!"[42]

Of all the heroes in the *Hōgen* among ordinary warriors, Ietada is singled out as an exemplar of the finest warrior qualities: "With his martial prowess, he has established his fame (*menboku*) in this life. His loyalty will live through the ages, his name imprinted on future generations and his achievements bequeathed to his descendants."[43] With a didacticism that marks both it and the *Heiji*, but not the *Heike*, the *Hōgen* warns the warrior who may eschew bravery in favor of cautious, if not cowardly, behavior: "You will not only lose the stipend from your lord. No, not only that. You will live with shame and, after your death, become the target of censure."[44]

Finding a "Worthy Foe"

One purpose of the name-announcing, as noted, was to find a suitable opponent to fight—an opponent of equal or higher status. When Kiyomori shies away from attacking the gate of Shirakawa Palace that Tametomo is defending, a vassal, Itō Kagetsuna, and Kagetsuna's two sons advance to challenge Tametomo, announcing their names. But when Tametomo hears that his challengers are mere "Taira retainers (rōdō)," he declares they are not worth wasting arrows on. He relents, however, when one of his followers informs him that, although only Taira vassals, the challengers are worth fighting because of their achievements in earlier battles.[45] Facing Kagetsuna and his sons, Tametomo, in a remarkable display of power archery, fires an arrow that, as described earlier, goes through one of the sons, killing him, and lodges in the armor of the other.[46]

Later in the battle of Shirakawa Palace, Tametomo rejects the challenge of Kamada no Masakiyo, the ever-faithful follower of his brother Yoshitomo, because—as we have observed—Masakiyo is a hereditary vassal of the Kawachi Minamoto. But Masakiyo attacks anyway, holding that status distinctions are not valid when contending with someone like Tametomo who has defied an imperial edict and become a rebel.[47]

The medieval war tales contain many encounters between warriors in battle in which one questions the other to determine whether he is a "worthy foe" (yoki kataki) or, conversely, an "unworthy foe" (awanu kataki). In one of the battles in Heike Monogatari, for example, a warrior, seeking to disguise his identity for a special reason, refuses to announce his name to an opposing warrior but assures him that "We are worthy foes for each other."[48] And in the famous encounter in the Heike between the young Taira chieftain Atsumori and the low-ranking warrior Kumagae no Naozane (discussed in detail in the next chapter), Atsumori, after hearing Naozane's name-announcing, says that Naozane is not of sufficiently high status to merit hearing Atsumori's nanori. But Atsumori assures Naozane, who already has him on the ground and is ready to kill him, that he, Atsumori, is a worthy foe.[49]

Kumagae no Naozane, as we will see in the next chapter, represents a breed of lesser warrior who, as portrayed in the Heike, must fight for a living and hence is constantly in search of suitable enemies or even prize enemies (like Atsumori) to fight. As Naozane puts it:

"Fame *(kōmyō)* depends on your enemy. You can't just accept anyone who comes along."[50] Naozane's determination to achieve fame and its accompanying rewards is graphically illustrated in the description of the Battle of Ichinotani in the Gempei War in *Gempei Seisui Ki* (or *Gempei Jōsui Ki;* "Chronicle of the Rise and Fall of the Minamoto and Taira"). Naozane and his son approach a fortress occupied by a Taira army, announce their names, and demand that warriors come forth to do battle with them. When nobody responds to this demand, Naozane shouts at the fortress, describing the fighting spirit that he and his son possess and declaring that they are worthy foes. Still there is no response. In desperation, Naozane taunts the occupants of the fortress, calling them warriors without shame and even reciting the names of members of the Taira army who should come out and fight. Naozane's reward for this taunting is a shower of arrows from the fortress tower that forces him and his son to take cover.[51]

Dressing the Hero

Another formulaic technique used by singers of military tales in Japan and elsewhere is "dressing the hero," a detailed description of the attire and outfitting of a warrior as he prepares for battle or enters the fray. Dressings can be found in earlier war tales, such as those in *Konjaku Monogatari*,[52] but they become common, along with name-announcings, from the *Hōgen* on. Like the name-announcing, the dressing reflects primarily the oral influence in the making of the medieval war tales. Dressings were especially popular with the tale singers' audiences, who relished them as preludes to the narration of battles.

The dressings give a powerful visual quality to the war tales in both their oral and written forms. And they provide warriors with a certain distinctiveness. Since very little is said in the tales about the physical appearances of even the most prominent warriors (Tametomo, who is vividly depicted in the *Hōgen*, is an exception), we tend to picture the warriors who populate these tales figuratively as suits of armor, visualizing them primarily in terms of their battle garb as described in the dressings.[53]

As an example of a dressing, here is how Taira no Kiyomori's oldest son, Shigemori, is described in the *Hōgen* as he approaches Shira-kawa Palace to do battle with Tametomo and the other palace defenders: "Over a red brocade robe, he wore armor with lacing in the form of reversed water plantains. The tassets of his armor had metal fittings in the shape of butterflies; and he had a silver-studded helmet and an arrow-deflecting hood that billowed in the wind. He rode a light bay horse, sitting in a lacquered saddle flecked with gold and silver dust and bordered with gold."[54]

Punishing the Losers

It became the custom in warrior society for victors in battles not only to execute their enemies (usually by decapitation) but to round up the enemies' families, including women and children, and exterminate them as well. This was done primarily to avoid later vendettas. It was not unusual, then, that many of the warriors defeated in the Hōgen Conflict were executed. What horrified nearly everyone was that the two leaders of the victorious Goshirakawa side, Taira no Kiyomori and Minamoto no Yoshitomo, executed their own kin. Kiyomori killed his uncle, Taira no Tadamasa, and four of his cousins (Tadamasa's sons) and Yoshitomo had his father, Tameyoshi, and no less than nine of his brothers put to death.

In the Hōgen, Kiyomori deliberately executes his uncle in order to force Yoshitomo to kill his father.[55] Although Yoshitomo repeatedly pleads for his father's life, the court (Emperor Goshirakawa) adamantly demands that he be executed. Carried out by a group led by Yoshitomo's ever-faithful follower, Kamada no Masakiyo, the execution described in the Hōgen is an agonizing confrontation between Tameyoshi and his killers. Expressing bewilderment at the fate that has led him to be captured by his son and put to death by hereditary vassals of the Minamoto, Tameyoshi speaks of his sense of mortification and resentment and tells Masakiyo and the other executioners that they will attain no glory for what they are about to do.[56]

Yoshitomo's brothers are killed in two groups: a group of five adult brothers who participated in the Hōgen Conflict and a group of four infant brothers ranging in age from seven to thirteen. The executions of the infant brothers are especially pathetic. The oldest, thirteen-year-old Otowaka, rallies the spirits of the others to die bravely; and before his own death he admonishes Yoshitomo for killing his father and brothers and predicts that he will meet his end in three to seven years.[57] This prediction is fulfilled in the Heiji Conflict, precisely three years later, when Yoshitomo is defeated in battle and, attempting to escape to the east, is killed.

Suicide by Disembowelment

In a foregoing passage about name-announcings, we met Uno no Chikaharu, the Minamoto warrior who encounters Taira no Motomori while Motomori is leading a reconnaissance party on the outskirts of Kyoto before the Hōgen Conflict. Upon learning that Chikaharu intends to join the Sutoku side, Motomori attempts to force him to go instead to the Goshirakawa camp. Portrayed in the *Hōgen* as a man of high principles, Chikaharu says that he has committed himself to the Sutoku side and that "the man of bow and arrow, once having given his word, cannot be expected to change it."[58] In the fighting that ensues between Chikaharu and Motomori, the latter emerges the victor when he is joined by a host of reinforcements. Confronted with the suddenly expanded Motomori party, Chikaharu and his men are captured so quickly that they do not have time "to draw their swords or cut their bellies."[59]

This is the first reference to suicide by "cutting the belly" *(hara o kiru)* to appear in the war tales we have surveyed so far. In the account of Minamoto no Tametomo's adventures after he is exiled that is appended to some versions of the *Hōgen*, Tametomo commits suicide in this manner when attacked by an armada of warships sent from the capital.[60]

Chiba Tokuji states that belly cutting or disembowelment *(seppuku)* had in fact become fairly common among warriors by the time of the Hōgen Conflict. He suggests, however, that it was confined to eastern warriors.[61] Noting that there is no record of Ise Taira committing *seppuku* at the time of the family's annihilation in the Gempei War, Chiba speculates that the practice had not yet spread to warriors in central and western Japan.[62]

Although we do not know the origins of *seppuku*, it surely derives from the primitive belief among the Japanese that the spirit or soul resides in the abdominal cavity. The persistence of this belief is reflected, for example, in a number of idioms in modern Japanese, such as:

hara o watte hanasu (to open one's stomach and speak)—
to speak sincerely

hara no suwatta hito (stomach-seated people)—
people who are resolute

haraguroi hito (black-stomached people)—evil people

Although *seppuku* was not limited to warriors,[63] it became a central feature of the warrior tradition. Chiba Tokuji observes that *seppuku* was a form of purification for the warrior, a means of preserving his honor in even the most desperate or adverse circumstances.[64] There were several reasons for committing *seppuku:* to avoid capture in battle, which was regarded as dishonorable; to atone for an error; to assume responsibility; and to admonish a superior. In the Tokugawa period (1600–1867), *seppuku* was also widely used in capital punishment for warriors.

Cases of *seppuku* become increasingly common in the later war tales. But warriors also often commit suicide by other means, such as falling on their swords, especially when they do not have time to perform *seppuku*.

Historical Background to *Heiji Monogatari*

Settlement of the Hōgen Conflict did not bring peace to Kyoto for long. The seeds for another clash of arms, the Heiji Conflict of 1159–1160, were sown in the days following the Hōgen fighting.

Although he was the warrior leader chiefly responsible for the victory of the Goshirakawa side, Minamoto no Yoshitomo was not well rewarded. Whereas Taira no Kiyomori was made governor of Harima province, Yoshitomo was given a relatively insignificant position at court and appointed to a rank well below Kiyomori's. The person behind this inequity of rewards was Fujiwara no Shinzei, a member of a lesser branch of the Fujiwara whose wife was a former wet nurse of Emperor Goshirakawa. Shinzei, who appears in the *Hōgen* as the realistic-minded courtier who authorized the night attack on Shirakawa Palace and, later, its burning, sought to advance in court politics by reducing the influence of both the regent branch of the Fujiwara and their samurai, the Minamoto.

Goshirakawa abdicated in 1158 and was succeeded by his son, who became Emperor Nijō. Before long a group opposed to Goshirakawa as the new *in*—or, more precisely, opposed to his adviser Shinzei —formed behind Nijō. The principal members of this group were Fujiwara no Nobuyori (an archrival of Shinzei) and the disgruntled Minamoto no Yoshitomo.

In the twelfth month of the first year of Heiji, 1159, the Nobuyori-Yoshitomo group suddenly moved to take control of the government. The group chose this time because of the departure a few days earlier of Kiyomori on a pilgrimage to the Kumano Shrines in Kii province. Attacking and setting fire to the *in*'s residence, Sanjō Palace, the group moved Goshirakawa to the imperial palace and incarcerated him there with Emperor Nijō. Fujiwara no Shinzei, whose residence was also burned, fled the capital for safety but was captured and killed. His head was later displayed like a common criminal's on the gate of a jail.

Kiyomori, who had only a small party of retainers and few weapons, learned of the coup on his way to Kumano. With the help of warriors from Kii province, he made his way back to the capital and to his

residence in the Rokuhara section of the city. There he made concilia-
tory gestures toward the insurgents while secretly recruiting supporters. On the night of the twenty-fifth, Kiyomori's supporters managed to smuggle the emperor, disguised as a lady-in-waiting, from the
palace to Rokuhara. Possession of the emperor greatly bolstered the
morale of the Taira and their backers and, conversely, stigmatized the
Nobuyori-Yoshitomo side as "rebels." The latter were further isolated
when Goshirakawa escaped from the palace and took sanctuary in Ninnaji Temple.

On the twenty-sixth the Taira attacked the Minamoto-held position at the imperial palace. Yoshitomo repulsed the attack and even
took the offensive. But when one of his allies, Yorimasa of the Tada
branch of the Minamoto, broke his pledge to provide support, Yoshitomo was routed. Fujiwara no Nobuyori went to Ninnaji to beg
Goshirakawa to save his life but was captured and beheaded. Yoshitomo managed to escape from Kyoto with a small band and got as far as
Owari province on his way to the Kantō. He was killed in Owari
through the treachery of a vassal.

As remarked earlier, both the Hōgen and Heiji conflicts were relatively small in scale, involving only several hundred warriors. Yoshitomo, whose base was in the eastern provinces and who was awaiting
reinforcements from the east that never came, seems to have been at a
distinct numerical disadvantage in the Heiji Conflict. It is possible
that Kiyomori, in going on the Kumano pilgrimage, hoped thereby to
encourage Yoshitomo and Nobuyori to act as they did. Kiyomori left
most of his family and retainers at Rokuhara and was able to return to
the capital with relative ease.[65]

Heiji Monogatari

The textual evolution of *Heiji Monogatari*, so far as it is known,
was very similar to that of *Hōgen Monogatari*. There are extant thirty-
three versions of the *Heiji*, which scholars divide into eleven categories.[66] As in the case of the *Hōgen*, the most important categories of
Heiji versions are the *furubon* (old text) versions, the *rufubon* (circulating text) versions, and the Kotohirabon versions. The principal old text
version is called the Yōmei-Gakushūin text, because it combines parts
or books from copies of old text versions of the *Heiji* held by the Yōmei
Bunko and the library of Gakushūin University.[67] Although both the
Yōmei Bunko and Gakushūin copies date from the late Muromachi
period (1336–1573) or after, they are believed to represent a form of the
Heiji from the Kamakura period.[68]

As pointed out in discussing the textual evolution of the *Hōgen*, the old text versions of all three of the major war tales dealing with the Gempei period of the late twelfth century—*Hōgen*, *Heiji*, and *Heike*— are quasi-historical chronicles that follow a fairly straightforward chronology of narration with frequent dating. In the case of the *Heiji*, scholars have in particular used the criterion of chronological structuring in attempting to judge which versions of the work are the oldest—that is, the more strictly chronological a version is, the older it is.[69]

The *Heiji* has a special old text version in the *Heiji Monogatari Ekotoba*, "Text of the Illustrated Scrolls of the Tale of Heiji," which, along with the scrolls themselves, dates from the middle or late Kamakura period. Although only three of what was presumably a larger set of scrolls dealing with the Heiji Conflict survive, they are magnificent works of art and invaluable pictorial documents for the study of the early medieval warrior. The text of the scrolls is of limited value, however, since it is highly abbreviated and in places either inadequate or erroneous in describing the events depicted in the scrolls.

The *Heiji* Kotohirabon, like its *Hōgen* counterpart, represents the highest development of the *Heiji* as a "tale," shaped mainly by tale singers in the late thirteenth and fourteenth centuries. Literarily the most refined of the *Heiji* versions, the Kotohirabon is less concerned with chronology and more with stories or topics within the general sequence of events before, during, and after the Heiji Conflict. Characters are more vividly drawn—as heroes, cowards, villains—than in the old text versions, and there are more stories about women, more critical commentaries, and more passages providing biographical and other background information.

The *rufubon* versions of the *Heiji*, again as in the case of the *Hōgen*, were printed in the early modern period and became the most widely circulated and read versions of the *Heiji*. The main text used in this study of the *Heiji* is the Kotohirabon. Where there are significant differences, the Yōmei-Gakushūin *Heiji Monogatari* and *rufubon Heiji Monogatari* are cited.

The Bun (Civil) and the Bu (Military)

The *Heiji* explains the Heiji Conflict in emphatically moralistic terms, attributing it to the machinations of a "bad minister," Fujiwara no Nobuyori. In singling out Nobuyori as the culprit responsible for the conflict, the author or authors of the *Heiji* observe: "In inquiring how sovereigns from early times to the present in both Japan and China have rewarded their ministers, we see that they have given primacy to the two ways of the civil and the military *(bunbu no nidō)*.

Sovereigns have selected ministers who by means of the civil *(bun)* have handled the manifold affairs of government and by means of the military *(bu)* have pacified the barbarians of the four directions."[70] In the *Heiji*, Nobuyori is utterly lacking in both civil and military skills. He seeks only to advance himself by currying favor, aspiring to office beyond his station in court society.

The distinction drawn between the "two ways of the *bun* and the *bu*," although advanced here in regard to a courtier, becomes an important concept also in warrior society from about this time. When applied to warriors, however, the terms *bun* and *bu* usually imply cultural and military rather than civil and military. We will see an example of the cultural/military distinction in the next chapter when we consider the *Heike Monogatari* portrayal of the Ise Taira as warriors who, in their long residence in Kyoto during the late twelfth century, acquired courtly cultural tastes and assumed the airs and manners of courtiers.

The overly ambitious Nobuyori precipitates the Heiji Conflict, according to the *Heiji*, because of his determination to destroy his principal rival at court, Fujiwara no Shinzei. But although Nobuyori and his supporters, including Minamoto no Yoshitomo, achieve early success by burning Sanjō Palace and Shinzei's residence, they start on the road to their downfall when Nobuyori, like Fujiwara no Yorinaga in the *Hōgen* version of the Hōgen Conflict, rejects the advice of a warrior leader. In the *Heiji*, the warrior leader is Yoshitomo's oldest son, Yoshihira (Akugenda). Nobuyori dismisses as a "rash scheme" Yoshihira's proposal that he be given a force to lead south of Kyoto to ambush Taira no Kiyomori on his return from the pilgrimage to Kumano. Nobuyori insists that, instead, they wait and seize Kiyomori and his party when they attempt to reenter the capital.[71] We find in this another example of a courtier portrayed in a war tale as arrogantly hardheaded and rigid at a time, during the transition to the medieval age, when he should earnestly solicit the advice and support of a warrior leader to deal with a pending military conflict. Yorinaga of the *Hōgen* and Nobuyori of the *Heiji* seem almost to be caricatures intended to symbolize why the courtiers were losing out as a ruling class at this time.

Yoshihira as Loser-Hero

Minamoto no Yoshihira is the main loser-hero in the *Heiji* just as his uncle Minamoto no Tametomo is in the *Hōgen*. Like Tametomo in the *Hōgen*, Yoshihira in the *Heiji* appears to be largely, if not entirely, a fictional character—for example, he is not even mentioned in the fairly lengthy account of the Heiji Conflict in Jien's *Gukanshō*. Unlike Tametomo, however, Yoshihira is not inflated into a superman. Although a redoubtable fighter, he does not dominate the Heiji Conflict as Tametomo did the Hōgen Conflict.[72]

Yoshihira's most conspicuous appearance in the *Heiji* is in the Battle of Taikenmon Gate.[73] The Taira, having secretly smuggled the emperor to their residence and camp at Rokuhara, attack the Minamoto position at the imperial palace. Their plan is to draw the Minamoto out of the palace, occupy it themselves, and force the Minamoto to fight in the streets of Kyoto. The Minamoto commander, Yoshitomo, orders his son Yoshihira to lead the battle against the Taira. The battle begins at the palace's Taikenmon Gate, and after fierce fighting within the palace grounds, moves into the streets, as the Taira had planned. Yoshihira, leading a band of only seventeen, calls upon his men to ignore all others and seek to capture or kill the enemy leader, Taira no Shigemori. This sets the stage for a personal confrontation between Yoshihira and Shigemori, the oldest sons of Yoshitomo and Kiyomori.

Although Shigemori has five hundred men under his command, Yoshihira is the aggressor, attacking time and again. This agressiveness, however, plays into the hands of Shigemori, who, in a series of calculated retreats, leads Yoshihira and the Minamoto force to the Taira residence at Rokuhara, where they are decisively defeated. The Minamoto defeat is ensured by the refusal at the last minute of a relative, Minamoto no Yorimasa, to provide promised support.

Yoshitomo and the other Minamoto flee first to Lake Biwa across the mountains to the northeast of the capital and then toward the Kantō. Yoshitomo instructs Yoshihira to leave the party and go to the Hokuriku region to raise troops and continue the fight against the Taira.[74] Later, when Yoshihira learns that his father has been killed by a traitorous vassal in Owari province, he returns secretly to Kyoto to spy on the Taira. He is soon captured and brought before the Taira leader Kiyomori.

Kiyomori inquires how Yoshihira, who during the Heiji Conflict had been able to break through an encirclement of three hundred enemy troops, could have been captured at this time by a mere fifty. Yoshihira replies that he was taken because "his luck had run out" *(un ga tsukinu)* and warns Kiyomori that when his own luck runs out he will suffer a similar fate.[75] Here, in a vague prediction, Yoshihira announces the great theme of *Heike Monogatari:* the decline and annihilation of Kiyomori and the Ise Taira, who are hounded as much by the dark forces of fate as by the Minamoto enemy in the Gempei War of 1180–1185.

Yoshitomo as Tragic Hero

In a quotation from the *Hōgen* given earlier in this chapter, Minamoto no Yoshitomo is described as a man "reared in the Bandō who
excelled in the way of the military."[76] More than once we have
observed that warriors from the frontier-like region of the Bandō or
Kantō enjoyed an especially high reputation as fighting men. Born on
horseback, they practiced the warrior skills throughout their lifetimes.
Heike Monogatari contains any number of references to the superiority
of eastern warriors over those, including the Ise Taira, from the central
and western provinces. The Taira possess certain skills in naval warfare; but, the *Heike* emphatically informs us, they are really no match
for the Minamoto and other fighting men from the east (and in fact the
Taira are finally destroyed by the Minamoto in a sea battle at Dannoura in 1185).

This disparity in fighting ability adds to the poignancy of the
Taira decline and destruction in the *Heike* account of the Gempei War.
But little is said of any disparity in the *Hōgen* or *Heiji*. Indeed, it is a
warrior from the west, Tametomo, who excels everyone in battle in
the *Hōgen* version of the Hōgen Conflict, although his older brother
Yoshitomo (as quoted in the last chapter) says: "Since Tametomo was
raised in the west, he's no doubt good at fighting on foot. But when it
comes to grappling on horseback, how can he hope to win out over the
young warriors of [the Kantō provinces of] Musashi and Sagami?"[77]

Yoshitomo was the archetypal Kantō warrior of his age. So far as
we can judge from the historical information we have about him
(which is admittedly scant) and from the portrayal of him in the *Hōgen*
and *Heiji*, he was a good if not outstanding military commander. He
was handicapped in the Heiji Conflict because reinforcements from
the Kantō, his power base, did not materialize.[78] But his great failing,
which transforms him into a tragic hero in the *Heiji*, is his political
ineptitude. In this he resembles his nephew Yoshinaka and his son
Yoshitsune, the other leading tragic heroes of the war tales of this age.
For example, Yoshinaka in the *Heike*, after driving the Ise Taira from
Kyoto in 1183, finds himself regarded as an uncouth barbarian and un-
welcome outsider by court society and, finally, is virtually destroyed
by court politics. But Yoshitomo also differed from the countrified
Yoshinaka, since by the time of the Hōgen Conflict he had lived in
Kyoto for nearly a decade and should have been reasonably sophisti-
cated in the ways of court politics.

Yoshitomo is completely outstripped by Kiyomori of the Ise Taira
in the politics of the Hōgen and Heiji conflicts. Even though, as
portrayed in the *Hōgen*, Yoshitomo is the commander primarily

responsible for the victory of the Goshirakawa side in the Hōgen Conflict, he is, as we have seen, far less generously rewarded than Kiyomori. Yoshitomo's discontent over this difference in rewards leads him to make what the *Heiji* depicts as the incredible blunder of allying himself with Fujiwara no Nobuyori, the archvillain of the *Heiji*, in a conspiracy against the Taira.

The *Heiji* account of Nobuyori's behavior at the climax of the Heiji Conflict, when the emperor is smuggled to Rokuhara and the Taira attack and defeat the Minamoto, ranges from the pathetic to the ludicrous. Although he has practiced riding and the military arts, his knees are knocking so badly, the *Heiji* tells us, that he cannot mount his horse to join in the defense against the Taira. When some men try to push him onto the horse—he is fat and has the additional weight of armor—he falls off the other side.[79] Later denounced by Yoshitomo as a coward and "the biggest loser in Japan,"[80] Nobuyori flees the scene of battle and seeks refuge with retired emperor Goshirakawa. But Goshirakawa rejects his plea, and he is seized and beheaded.

The story of Yoshitomo in flight from Kyoto after the defeat at Rokuhara is a paradigm of the tragic hero of the early medieval war tales: the defeated leader seeking sanctuary from his enemies and pursuers; his following reduced to a few; the leader himself increasingly uncertain and hesitant, more and more reliant on his chief vassal, the ever-faithful follower.

Yoshitomo's first plan is to escape by boat across Lake Biwa. But when he and his group reach the lake the winter wind is blowing fiercely, waves are crashing on the shore, and there is not a boat to be found. Heading instead toward Seta and the east, Yoshitomo dismisses twenty or so of his followers, instructing them to make their own way to the Kantō.[81] This leaves him with only seven companions—his sons Yoshihira, Tomonaga, and Yoritomo and four vassals, including Kamada no Masakiyo.

Encountering a raging snowstorm, Yoshitomo and his small band are forced to abandon their horses and discard their armor, including precious Minamoto heirlooms.[82] When they finally reach a resting place in the home of an ally in Mino province, Yoshitomo instructs his older sons, Yoshihira and Tomonaga, to proceed in other directions—Yoshihira to the Hokuriku region and Tomonaga to Shinano province—to raise forces for a later attack on the Taira in the capital. But Tomonaga is badly weakened from a wound suffered earlier and is unable to carry out his father's orders. To prevent Tomonaga's falling into enemy hands, Yoshitomo kills him before setting out again toward the east.[83]

Early fourteenth-century helmet and suit of armor, thought to have belonged to Ashikaga Takauji. The helmet has the horn-shaped *kuwagata* attachment, and the fabric covering the corselet is decorated with a painting of the Buddhist god Fudō. The Metropolitan Museum of Art. Gift of Bashford Dean, 1914. (14.100.121)

Heiji Conflict. Warriors raiding and burning Sanjō Palace.
Court ladies have been driven from the palace, and some
have jumped into a well seeking relief from the flames. The
well, stuffed with bodies, is at bottom center. "Illustrated
Scrolls of the Tale of Heiji" *(Heiji Monogatari Emaki).*
Fenollosa-Weld Collection. Courtesy of the Museum of
Fine Arts, Boston.

Hōgen Conflict. Battle of Shirakawa Palace. The cartouche to the left identifies the sprawling figure above it as Ōba no Heida Kageyoshi, who has
just been thrown from his horse after being struck by an arrow fired by
Minamoto no Tametomo. Below and to the left of the cartouche, Ōba no
Kagefusa has leaped from his horse to carry his brother from the battlefield. Late sixteenth-century screen painting by an unknown artist. The
Metropolitan Museum of Art, Rogers Fund, 1957. (57.156.5)

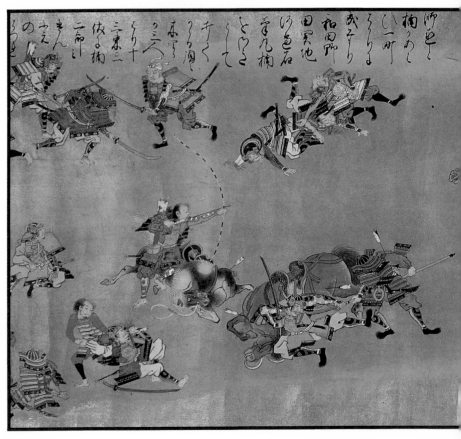

War between the northern and southern courts. Battle of Shijō-Nawate. In the upper right corner Ueyama Rokurōzaemon prepares to don the armor of his commander, Kō no Moronao. (When Rokurōzaemon is later killed by Kusunoki Masatsura, Masatsura believes he has achieved his single-minded aim of destroying the Kō leader.) "Illustrated Scrolls of *Taiheiki*" *(Taiheiki Emaki)*. Spencer Collection. The New York Public Library. Astor, Lenox and Tilden Foundations.

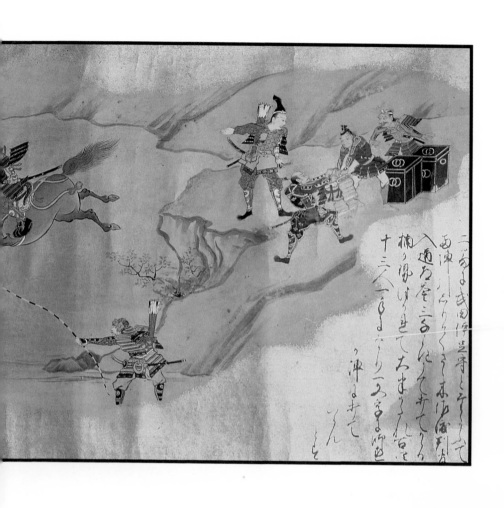

二郎よ武田伊豆守とてして
西陣へよりくさ本化国有
入通方を三ろんてまてくる
楠り渡りまてをまう九を
十三人しまなり一ス車前色

沖をまて

て東をうけ
とくるさと
包くろのゝか
わうのめ会
くやくくら
せさおつゝし
阿院とむか
ものかてう
やせとる卯
東とす゛
うりとえく
も打り卯る
ひらそ気前
しうを卯る
ゝよかうれ
も皇卯な
と皇卯な
うつらて
竹稙免の中
納るうすて
そゝけさ
ゆりくるいろ
ありなろ捐
わすろいと二
活を、渚ふ
ノ子まきしき包よ

War between the northern and southern courts. Toki Yoritō and his party encounter the procession of former emperor Kōgon in the streets of Kyoto. Yoritō's companion, Nikaidō Yukiharu, has dismounted and is kneeling in obeisance to the retired emperor (bottom, slightly left of center). But when Yoritō, the mounted figure to the left, is ordered to dismount, he shoots arrows at Kōgon's ox-drawn cart (right). "Illustrated Scrolls of *Taiheiki*." Spencer Collection. The New York Public Library. Astor, Lenox and Tilden Foundations.

Gempei War. Composite view of scenes from the Battle of Yashima. Part of one wing of the temporary palace that the Taira built for Emperor Antoku can be seen at upper left. The Taira, with red banners, are arrayed in boats on the right, while the Minamoto with white banners attack from the shore at left. At center, Nasu no Yoichi shoots at a target placed on a Taira boat. Slightly to the right of top center, Yoshitsune attempts to recover his "dropped bow" with a bear claw rake (the rake is not mentioned in *Heike Monogatari*). Detail from a seventeenth-century six-panel screen. The Metropolitan Museum of Art. Gift of General and Mrs. Hugh J. Casey, 1960. (60.40)

His band reduced to only the four vassals (the youthful Yoritomo has been lost along the way), Yoshitomo reaches Owari province and the residence of another vassal, Osada Tadamune, in the last days of the twelfth month of 1159. Yoshitomo has been repeatedly supported and encouraged on the journey by his ever-faithful follower, Masakiyo, and he welcomes refuge at the Osada residence in part because Tadamune, in addition to being his vassal, is Masakiyo's father-in-law. But Tadamune, thinking of possible reward from the Taira, has treachery in his heart. On the third day of the new year he and his son dupe Yoshitomo into taking a bath without a guard, and Yoshitomo is slaughtered by Osada henchmen. When Masakiyo, distracted by the offer of wine in another room, hears the commotion and realizes what has happened, he rushes to the bath but is cut down by Tadamune's son hiding behind a door. His last words, apropos of the ever-faithful follower, are: "Masakiyo joins you, My Lord!"[84]

The Warrior Attendant

The mounted warrior of the age of the Hōgen and Heiji conflicts was accompanied into battle by one or two attendants on foot called *ge'nin* or *shojū* in the war tales. These warrior attendants saw to the grooming and feeding of their masters' horses; they carried their masters' equipment; they gathered the heads of enemies taken by their masters in combat; and, as noted, they performed the name-announcings when their masters were killed in battle.

In paintings of the age, the warrior attendant appears wearing a light armor corselet known as *haramaki* or *dōmaru*, which was like the European cuirass with the addition of a protective skirt (*kusazuri*).[85] The attendant is usually barelegged and sometimes barefooted. Often he carries the *naginata*, a curve-bladed polearm.[86] The portion of the Heiji Scrolls that depicts the burning of Sanjō Palace, for example, shows several warrior attendants ferociously wielding *naginata* as they chase courtiers and servants in the palace. Other attendants in the Heiji Scrolls are armed with bows and arrows and even swords, although they may be carrying these weapons for their masters.

As Ishii Susumu points out, warfare in the period of transition to the medieval age continued to be centered on the individual mounted warrior, and attendants did not usually participate in battles. They were always on hand to be of service to their warrior masters, but during the actual fighting they were primarily bystanders.[87]

The *Heiji* tells the story of a warrior attendant who may have been an exception insofar as he regularly joined in battle with warriors. He is Jirō, an attendant of Kamada no Masakiyo, and is known as

"Eight Block" Jirō because he is so fleet of foot that he can overtake a warrior on horseback within a distance of eight blocks. Dressed in *haramaki* and wearing other protective gear, Jirō attempts to pull Taira no Yorimori from his horse with a rake-like instrument called a *kumade* (bear's claw) during the Battle of Taikenmon Gate. But when Jirō finally succeeds in catching hold of Yorimori's helmet with his *kumade*, Yorimori cuts the *kumade* in two at its handle with his sword, a Taira heirloom known as Nukemaru.[88]

Armor and Weapons

The early war tales provide only a general idea of the appearance of the ancient Japanese warrior, his attire, his weapons, and his equipment. Not until the "dressings" in the *Hōgen*, *Heiji*, and *Heike* are we able to envision with any clarity how the warrior looked when prepared for battle. Using, for example, the dressings in the *Heiji* along with the visual representation of these dressings in the Heiji Scrolls, we observe the early medieval warrior as a mounted fighting man attired in armor and helmet that, at their most resplendent, are the equal artistically of any protective gear ever devised for a warrior in any culture. And his armament includes a sword that in quality and excellence of craftsmanship has never been surpassed in the world.

Chieftains and other warriors of high status in this age wore the Great Armor (*ō-yoroi*). The Great Armor comprised a corselet with protective skirt similar in appearance to the corselet of the warrior attendant, but more solidly and elaborately constructed, and broad, flat shoulder protectors called "great sleeves" (*ō-sode*).[89] The Great Armor was mainly constructed of overlapping, horizontal layers of leather and metal plates (lames) coated with lacquer to give them greater strength and bound together with thick lacing called *odoshi*. Among helmets used with Great Armor, perhaps the most common was the "star helmet" (*hoshi kabuto*), so named because of the numerous rivets protruding—like stars—from its surface. Attached to the bowl of the helmet was a widely flaring neck guard (*shikoro*) that folded back as flaps at each cheek. The most extraordinary feature of the helmet, and indeed of the entire assemblage of Great Armor, was the *kuwagata*, a huge vee-shaped or horn-shaped decorative device attached to the front of some helmets, usually those worn by chieftains.

The description, given above, of Taira no Shigemori's Great Armor as he is "dressed" in the *Hōgen* in preparation for the Battle of Shirakawa Palace suggests the elegance, intricate craftsmanship, and beauty of a fine suit of armor at the dawn of the medieval age. We know from surviving suits of early medieval armor that armor makers of the time attained a level of artistry that was never exceeded.

Identification in battle was, as we have seen, important to the warrior for various reasons. Name-announcing was one means of identification; armor was another. The most readily distinguishable feature of a warrior's armor in the tumult of battle was the color of its lacing. Thus, for example, in the frequent postbattle disputes over who had killed which enemy, witnesses were often called upon to identify the responsible warriors by verifying the colors of their armor lacings.[90] Still another device used for identification in battle was a small flag called *kasa-jirushi* (hat marker) that was attached to the back of a warrior's helmet. Because of the placement of the *kasa-jirushi*, it was clearly intended to provide identification for allies rather than enemies.[91] But flags were also sometimes attached to warriors' sleeves.[92]

The war tales contain many references to suits of armor bearing names and identified as heirlooms. In the *Hōgen*, for example, Minamoto no Yoshitomo is described as wearing armor called Hachiryū (Eight Dragons) that had been "passed down in his house." The armor is decorated with a design of eight dragons that is associated with Yoshitomo's famous ancestor Yoshiie.[93] In the *Heiji* we find Yoshitomo's oldest son, Yoshihira, wearing this same Hachiryū armor as he enters the Battle of Taikenmon Gate.[94] And when Yoshitomo, Yoshihira, and others flee from Kyoto after their defeat in the Heiji Conflict, the Hachiryū armor is among the priceless family heirlooms they are forced to abandon as they struggle through a snowstorm in their attempt to escape to the eastern provinces.[95]

The Taira too have their prized suits of armor. One of these becomes an issue in the *Heiji* when Yoshihira encounters Taira no Shigemori during the early skirmishing in the Battle of Taikenmon Gate and, as we have seen, commands his soldiers to concentrate solely on pursuing him. As arrow after arrow shot by the Minamoto fails to penetrate Shigemori's armor, Yoshihira, in exasperation, shouts: "It's the armor known as Karakawa (Chinese Leather), which is famous among the Taira. Aim lower and shoot at his horse!"[96] The Karakawa armor is also mentioned in *Heike Monogatari*. Shigemori's son Koremori, starting out on an expedition from Kyoto in 1180 at the beginning of the Gempei War to fight the Minamoto in the Kantō, has it carried in a Chinese lacquered chest, perhaps as a talisman, while he wears other armor.[97]

Purportedly laced with tiger skin, the Karakawa armor is unusual —assuming that we can believe its description in the *Heiji*—in its resistance to arrows. This resistance is unusual because the armor of the age was deliberately made light to allow its wearer, an archer on horseback, as much freedom of movement as possible.[98] When charging into battle, the warrior usually bent over the pommel of his saddle, hoping to deflect enemy arrows mainly with the top of his helmet, his flaring neck guard, and his great sleeves, which protected not only his upper arms and shoulders but, in a bent-over position, also his back. But arrows frequently found their way between the lames (plates) of armor, and if the neck guard accidentally turned upward the neck and head could become tempting targets. In a *Heike Monogatari* account during the Gempei War, a warrior cautions his son: "Keep pushing your armor up. Don't let an arrow through. See that your neck guard is low. Don't get shot in the face!"[99]

The Heiji *Survivors*

The *Heiji* ends with a series of stories about how Yoshitomo's sons Yoritomo and Yoshitsune are spared after the Heiji Conflict, grow up, and eventually overthrow the Ise Taira in the Gempei War.

Yoshitsune, less than a year old at the time of the Heiji Conflict, was the youngest of three sons born to Yoshitomo and the court lady and renowned beauty Tokiwa. Learning after the defeat of the Minamoto that her sons are to be seized and executed, Tokiwa flees with them from Kyoto to seek sanctuary with relatives. But when she learns that her mother is to be tortured and executed if she does not reveal Tokiwa's whereabouts, Tokiwa returns to the capital and surrenders to Kiyomori. Smitten with Tokiwa's beauty, Kiyomori allows the sons to be spared in return for her becoming his concubine.

Yoritomo, who fell behind and became lost as his father, Yoshitomo, and his small band fled from Kyoto after the Heiji Conflict, is captured by the Taira and also condemned to execution. But he too is spared when Kiyomori's stepmother takes pity on him because he reminds her of a dead son and persuades Kiyomori to limit his punishment to exile in the Kantō.

On the eve of his departure for the Kantō, Yoritomo prays at a shrine to Hachiman, the tutelary deity of the Minamoto, asking that he one day be allowed to "return to the capital"; and a Minamoto vassal tells him of a dream he had that predicted Yoritomo in his manhood would be given "bow and arrow," that is, become a great military leader.[100]

We saw in the last chapter that victors in battles often rounded up and executed the families and followers of their defeated foes in order to prevent future vendettas. In these stories that form the final portion of the *Heiji*, Kiyomori is pictured as committing, at the behest of women, the cardinal error of allowing future enemy chieftains to survive. This error brings him great grief when, the year before his death in 1181, Yoritomo and other Minamoto rise against Kiyomori and the Ise Taira and precipitate the Gempei War. On his deathbed, Kiyomori requests that no tributes be made to him, only that Yoritomo's head be placed on his grave.[101]

3
THE TALE OF THE HEIKE

Historical Background
The Glory of the Taira

The period from the Heiji Conflict, 1159–1160, until the beginning of the Gempei (Minamoto-Taira) War in 1180 has traditionally been regarded as the age of the power and glory of the Ise Taira. *Heike Monogatari* asserts that so grand did the Taira become during this time that there were none in the world to match them.[1] In 1160 Kiyomori was given the senior third rank at court, becoming the first warrior to be made a senior noble *(kugyō)*.[2] The following year, 1161, he was appointed head of the Bureau of Imperial Police; in the same year his wife's younger sister gave birth to a child of the retired emperor Goshirakawa, who later became Emperor Takakura. In 1164 Kiyomori married one of his daughters into the Konoe branch of the Fujiwara, and in 1167 he advanced to the peak of the court system of ranks and offices when he was given the junior first rank and was made chancellor *(daijō daijin)*. Meanwhile, Kiyomori's sons and brothers also rose rapidly in both rank and office at court.

Yet recent scholarship indicates that the Taira under Kiyomori did not, as long thought, establish a new and dominant regime of their own in Japan following the Heiji Conflict.[3] Although they had no challengers after Heiji to their military preeminence in the capital, the Taira—at least until the late 1170s—continued essentially to serve the venerable court regime whose leader was their patron, the retired emperor Goshirakawa. The Taira ascent to ever-higher court ranks and offices reflected not so much the assertion of newly created power as acceptance of the traditional way of participating in court government.

Moreover, the Taira failed to develop a significant network of support among warriors in the provinces, giving their attention instead primarily to court politics in Kyoto.[4] Weakness in provincial warrior support contributed greatly to the undoing of the Ise Taira in the Gempei War.

With the passage of years, the alliance between the Ise Taira and Goshirakawa, which had served both so well in the Hōgen and Heiji conflicts, evolved into competition and, finally, outright opposition. This opposition burst into the open in the revelation in 1177 of the Shishigatani plot against the Taira by supporters of Goshirakawa. The plot, which is prominently featured in the first three books of *Heike Monogatari*, symptomized mounting distress among Goshirakawa and his circle of courtiers over what they perceived as the steady rise of the Taira as upstart participants in court society and government. When word of the plot leaked out, Kiyomori ruthlessly suppressed it by executing some of the plotters and sending others into exile. The most sensational aspect of the Shishigatani plot (the plotters met secretly at a residence in the Shishigatani section of northeastern Kyoto) was the disclosure that Goshirakawa himself was privy to it.

In 1178 Kiyomori's daughter Tokuko gave birth to a prince (by Emperor Takakura) who two years later would become Emperor Antoku. With the prospect of becoming grandfather to a sovereign, Kiyomori stood on the verge of attaining a position of undisputed power at court. He took the final step in his ascent to power in 1179 when, in the face of renewed opposition by Goshirakawa, he placed the retired emperor under house arrest and replaced all the leading ministers at court who opposed him with his own kinsmen. Kiyomori and his family were at last prepotent in Kyoto. But their enemies were legion, and they stood on the verge of a great countrywide war that was to lead in five years to their destruction.

The Gempei War

In the fourth month of 1180 an imperial prince named Mochihito, disgruntled because he had been passed over in the succession to the emperorship in favor of Antoku, the two-year-old grandson of Kiyomori, issued a decree to Minamoto chieftains in the provinces. As given in *Azuma Kagami* (Mirror of the East), a record of the Kamakura military government or Bakufu compiled in the late thirteenth century, the decree stated:

> To the Genji [Minamoto] and their warriors in the provinces of the three circuits of Tōkai, Tōsan, and Hokuriku: You are ordered to immediately pursue and destroy the lay priest Kiyomori, his followers, and other rebels.[5]

Mochihito himself joined an armed rising in the capital region and was killed the following month. But his decree was interpreted even after his death as a valid imperial order by members of the provincial Minamoto and others, who used it to legitimize the military activities they launched against the Ise Taira that became the five-year Gempei War (1180–1185).[6]

Traditionally the Gempei War has been conceived as a climactic struggle for national power between two great warrior clans, the Taira and the Minamoto, that was won by the Minamoto, who founded a military government (the Bakufu) at Kamakura in the Kantō. But the war was much more complex. For one thing, no single Minamoto family or group rose to oppose the Ise Taira. Rather, a number of Minamoto leaders took up arms in response to Mochihito's edict. They included Yoritomo, scion of the Kawachi Minamoto based in the Kantō, his cousin Yoshinaka of Shinano province, and the Minamoto of Kai province, who were particularly active in the early stages of the war. Moreover, Yoritomo, who gradually emerged as the supreme Minamoto leader and the eventual winner of the war, devoted his primary attention not to defeating the Ise Taira but to establishing his hegemony over the Kantō. Defeat of the Ise Taira was almost incidental to the process by which Yoritomo constructed the first military government in Japanese history during the Gempei War.

In the eighth month of 1180, Yoritomo attacked and seized the government offices of Izu province, where he had spent two decades in exile after the Heiji Conflict. Claiming that the Mochihito decree placed "within his jurisdiction" all the "public and private domains" of the east, Yoritomo, while faithfully acknowledging the final authority of the imperial court, gradually asserted his de facto control over the Kantō. In so doing, he drew to himself as vassals the leading warrior chieftains of the region. These included men from branch families of both the Taira and Minamoto: the Kazusa, Chiba, and Miura families (who were Taira of Kazusa, Shimōsa, and Sagami provinces), for example, and the Satake, Nitta, and Ashikaga families (who were Minamoto of Hitachi, Kōzuke, and Shimotsuke provinces).

We see how meaningless it is to think of the Gempei War simply in terms of Minamoto versus Taira. The Kantō was the most important theater of the war, insofar as that was where Yoritomo established his military regime. Yet the warrior chieftains of the Kantō scarcely had time or reason to reflect upon the fate of the Ise Taira in Kyoto or where they stood in regard to what we call the Gempei War. Each was faced with the pressing need to decide how to deal with the rapid rise of Yoritomo as a regional hegemon—whether to support or oppose him—

and each was far more likely to make his decision on grounds of direct family interests rather than any loose association with the Minamoto or Taira.

In his first regular battle against a force representing the Ise Taira, a battle that occurred at Ishibashi Mountain in Sagami province on 1180:8:23, Yoritomo was routed and barely escaped alive. Nevertheless, warriors of the Kantō continued to flock to his banner, and two months later he won a major encounter with a Taira army, sent by Kiyomori from the capital, at Fuji River in Suruga province, a clash that decisively influenced the course of the war.

The two armies took up positions on opposite banks of the Fuji in the evening of 10:20 in anticipation of battle the following morning. But, according to *Azuma Kagami*, when a commander from Yoritomo's side tried to move around behind the Taira position, he disturbed some water birds in a marsh and they rose in flight with a great flapping of wings. The alarmed Taira believed they were about to be surrounded by a vast enemy force and, without awaiting morning, withdrew from the Fuji River and began a long retreat back to the capital.[7]

The Battle (or Nonbattle) of Fuji River marked a turning point in the Gempei War, just a few months after the commencement of hostilities. Never again did the Taira send an army to the Kantō; and Yoritomo made the critical decision—on the advice, according to *Azuma Kagami*, of his leading followers—not to pursue the Taira to the west but to devote himself first and foremost to extending his control over the Kantō.[8] Yoritomo selected as his military seat Kamakura, which had been a headquarters of the Kawachi Minamoto since the time of Yoriyoshi in the eleventh century. And in 1180:11 he established at Kamakura his first major governmental office, the Board of Retainers (*samurai-dokoro*) with Wada no Yoshimori as its head.

The period 1181–1182 was a time of relative quiescence. Taira no Kiyomori died early in 1181, calling from his deathbed, the *Heike* tells us, for the head of Yoritomo.[9] And Minamoto no Yoshinaka, who took up arms only a month after Yoritomo, began a series of hard campaigns that led, in the seventh month of 1183, to Kyoto, from which he drove the Ise Taira. The latter fled westward with the child emperor Antoku, their days of glory at an end.

From the beginning there was strong competition between the cousins Yoritomo and Yoshinaka, a competition that intensified after Yoshinaka occupied Kyoto. Securing the title *sei-i tai-shōgun* from the court,[10] Yoshinaka sought to assert himself as the main leader of the Minamoto and the new dictator of the capital. But Yoritomo, taking advantage of the court's profound displeasure with the rough, countri-

fied Yoshinaka, obtained an imperial edict late in 1183 that gave him
police and judicial authority in the Tōkai and Tōsan regions. Historians have long debated the precise meaning of this edict and its significance in the evolution of the Kamakura Bakufu.[11] Essentially it
acknowledged powers that Yoritomo had already acquired. But it also
marked the first time the court took formal note of Yoritomo's emer-
gent warrior government, thereby legitimizing its existence.

Toward the end of 1183, Yoritomo finally undertook to deal with
the unruly Yoshinaka, dispatching an army from Kamakura under the
command of his half-brothers Noriyori and Yoshitsune to attack
Yoshinaka's position in Kyoto. *Heike Monogatari*'s romanticized account of the destruction of Yoshinaka is among the most moving sections of this great work, and it is enhanced by the irony (known to
audiences of the medieval war tales) that Yoshinaka's principal destroyer, Yoshitsune, would later join him as one of the most prominent
tragic heroes of the Gempei age as portrayed in the war tales.

In 1184 the Minamoto forces from the Kantō, having eliminated
Yoshinaka, began their major offensive against the Ise Taira. In a series
of brilliant victories, Yoshitsune led these forces to final triumph over
the Taira, which he achieved in the naval battle of Dannoura in the
Straits of Shimonoseki (separating Honshu and Kyushu) in the third
month of 1185. Among the casualties at Dannoura was the seven-year-
old Emperor Antoku, who drowned along with many of his Taira
kinsmen.

Heike Monogatari

Heike Monogatari is the finest of the war tales; indeed, it is
among the supreme masterpieces of Japanese prose literature. One
thing that sets the *Heike* apart from nearly all other war tales is its
sheer length. It is, for example, almost six times as long as *Hōgen
Monogatari* and seven times as long as *Heiji Monogatari*. Both the
Hōgen and *Heiji*, in addition to describing the armed conflicts on
which they are focused, provide information about court life and politics in the late twelfth century. But the *Heike* is a panoramic recreation of life among the courtier and warrior elites during that age, the
epochal age of transition to the medieval period.

The origins and authorship of the *Heike*, like those of the *Hōgen*
and *Heiji*, are not precisely known, although there is no shortage of
speculation about them. Scholars appear generally to believe that the
Heike, again like the *Hōgen* and *Heiji*, was first written in the early
thirteenth century and like the original *Hōgen* and *Heiji* was probably

arranged as a quasi-historical chronicle *(kiroku)*, its passages marked with frequent notation of dates. Almost certainly the original *Heike*, perhaps bearing the title *Jishō Monogatari* (Tale of the Jishō Era, 1177–1180), was much shorter than later versions of the work. Whereas most *Heike* versions we have today are in twelve books, the original *Heike* may have consisted of as few as three.[12] The original *Heike* very likely focused on the career of Taira no Kiyomori, and its author or authors probably used a variety of sources, including court diaries, Jien's *Gukanshō*, eyewitness accounts, and fictional stories about the great struggle between Taira and Minamoto in the late twelfth century that no doubt began circulating shortly after, or even during, the Gempei War.[13]

At least sixteen people have been suggested as possible authors of the original *Heike*.[14] The likeliest of these is a courtier identified as the *Heike*'s author in a passage in Yoshida Kenkō's *Tsurezuregusa*, written sometime in the 1330s:

> During the reign of Emperor Go-Toba [r. 1183–1198], a former official from Shinano named Yukinaga enjoyed a reputation for learning. Once, when he was chosen to participate in a discussion on the *Lo-fu*, he forgot two of the military virtues described in the poem *Dance of the Seven Virtues*. He accordingly acquired the nickname of Young Man of the Five Virtues. The nickname so distressed him that he abandoned scholarship and became a priest. The priest Jichin [or Jien], who made a practice of hiring men with artistic talent even as menials and treating them kindly, employed this lay priest of Shinano.
>
> Yukinaga wrote the *Heike Monogatari* and taught a blind man named Shōbutsu to recite it. That is why the temple on the mountain [the Enryakuji on Mount Hiei] is described with special dignity. He wrote about Yoshitsune with detailed knowledge, but omitted many facts about Noriyori, perhaps because he did not know much about him. Shōbutsu, a native of the Eastern Provinces, questioned the soldiers from his part of the country about military matters and feats of arms, then got Yukinaga to write them down. *Biwa* entertainers today imitate what was Shōbutsu's natural voice.[15]

The Yukinaga mentioned in this passage from *Tsurezuregusa* was Fujiwara no Yukinaga who, despite his unfortunate lapse in describing the *Dance of the Seven Virtues*, was a man well educated in Chinese language and literature and, as Kenkō observes, "enjoyed a reputation for learning." He had close ties with the Kujō branch of the Fujiwara and sometime in the late twelfth century served Kujō no Kanezane,[16] the imperial regent and author of the diary *Gyokuyō*, one of the probable sources for the original *Heike*. Jien, the author of *Gukanshō*, was Kanezane's brother and the abbot of Enryakuji Temple on Mount Hiei. It is entirely possible that Yukinaga, having suffered his humiliation in the poetry discussion and entered the Buddhist priesthood, was taken into the employ of Jien, presumably in the early thirteenth century. If Yukinaga was the author of the original *Heike*, his association with Jien would help explain the considerable attention given to the affairs of the Enryakuji in the *Heike*'s pages.

The collaboration between Yukinaga and the blind man Shōbutsu mentioned in *Tsurezuregusa* is intriguing to scholars of the textual evolution of the *Heike*. Shōbutsu seems clearly to have been an early tale singer and, if we are to believe *Tsurezuregusa*, served as a model for later singers, at least in recitation of the *Heike*. If Shōbutsu was a native of the east, he may well have been a primary source for stories, both real and fictional, about the eastern warriors and their ways of fighting that were incorporated into the original *Heike*.

The comments in *Tsurezuregusa* about Yukinaga writing with detailed knowledge about Minamoto no Yoshitsune but neglecting his half-brother Noriyori are also interesting. The historical records indicate clearly that Yoshitsune was by far the finer of these two as a field commander in the great campaigns beginning in 1184 that led to the final destruction of the Ise Taira at the Battle of Dannoura in the third month of 1185; and the *Heike*, in its accounts of Yoshitsune's exploits, firmly places him in the firmament of Japan's greatest warrior heroes of history and legend. But the reader of the *Heike* is nevertheless apt to question why, in its lengthy coverage of the Gempei War, this work says so little about one of the war's leading commanders, Noriyori. *Tsurezuregusa* seems to answer this question.

The *Heike*, from its probable origins in the early thirteenth century, developed in two streams: a stream of texts to be read *(yomibon)* and a stream of texts to be memorized and recited by tale singers *(kataribon)*. The first stream, the *yomibon*, reached its high point of development about the mid-thirteenth century in *Gempei Seisui Ki*. Although sometimes called a variant of the *Heike* because it tells essentially the same story, *Gempei Seisui Ki* differs quite substantially in its handling of the story from the *Heike*.

As a recitative text, the *Heike*, once again like the *Hōgen* and *Heiji* but to a much greater extent, was molded and expanded during the great age of tale singers in the late thirteenth and fourteenth centuries. The finest recitative version of the *Heike* is also its most widely disseminated text *(rufubon)*. It was completed in 1371 and is known as the Kakuichi text after its compiler, the tale singer Akashi no Kakuichi.

In its evolution during a period of a century and a half, from its original form to the greatly expanded Kakuichi recitative version, the *Heike* was transformed, as the *Hōgen* and *Heiji* were transformed, from a chronicle into a tale *(monogatari)*. Most of its chronicle-like dating disappeared, along with much of its factual material, which even in the original *Heike* was not always well integrated with the stories that were the *Heike*'s true basis. The language too was changed from the Chinese of the original *Heike* to the "mixed Japanese and Chinese" that first appears in the war tales in *Konjaku Monogatari*.

Anyone studying the *Heike* is confronted with the fact that there are extant more than one hundred versions of the work.[17] Thorough textual comparison of even a single chapter would entail considerable labor, and would probably be impossible because of the inaccessibility of many versions. This study is based on the Kakuichi recitative text of the *Heike*. Comparisions are made, where appropriate, with the *Enkei-bon Heike Monogatari*, a major variant from the early thirteenth century (the Enkei era, 1308–1310), and *Gempei Seisui Ki*.

The "End of the Buddhist Law"

The opening lines of the *Heike* are among the most famous in all Japanese literature:

> The sound of the bell of the Gion Temple tolls of the impermanence of all things, and the hue of the Sala tree's blossoms reveals the truth that those who flourish must fade. The proud ones do not last forever, but are like the dream of a spring night. Even the mighty will perish, just like dust before the wind.[18]

This passage beautifully expresses the Buddhist concept of impermanence, *mujō*. The first of Buddhism's Four Noble Truths is that life is suffering; the second is that people suffer because they try to possess things, even though nothing can be truly possessed because nothing is real—all is transitory, insubstantial, impermanent.[19] These truths are fundamental to Buddhism at all times, but in the medieval age *mujō* was felt with particular intensity because of the widespread strife and suffering of the age. It is no exaggeration to say that medieval thinking and writing were dominated by a powerful belief in *mujō*.

The sense of human helplessness that accompanied the medieval fixation on *mujō* was further heightened by the notion, drawn from Mahayana Buddhism, that the world had entered the age of *mappō*, the "end of the Buddhist Law." According to this notion, the world, from the time of the historic Buddha, Gautama, circa 500 BC, would pass through three ages: an age of the flourishing of the Law; an age of the decline of the Law; and, finally, an age of the end of the Law, when the world would descend into darkness, disorder, and destruction.[20] The Japanese calculated that the first age lasted a thousand years and came to an end in AD 552, when (according to *Nihon Shoki*) Buddhism was formally introduced to Japan from Korea. The second age would last only five hundred years and would yield to *mappō*, the third and final age, in 1052.

Mappō thinking in Japan formed the basis of a profoundly pessimistic view of history as a path of steady decline leading ultimately to the degenerate, lawless time of *mappō* itself. To Heian period Buddhists, *mappō* seemed sadly to explain the deterioration of their world in the final years of the Heian period and the rise of warriors as the country's new ruling elite. When, for example, the sacred sword of the imperial regalia sank beneath the waves with Emperor Antoku at the Battle of Dannoura in 1185, people took this as a sign that the imperial court had lost its vitality and would thenceforth need to be defended by warriors, whose ascent to prominence was itself an indication of the world's fallen state.[21]

With the coming of *mappō*, many Buddhists lost confidence in their ability to save themselves from worldly suffering through *jiriki*, "self-power." They believed that from this time on they would be obliged to seek the help of another: to rely on *tariki*, "other-power." This belief led to the establishment of new salvationist sects of Buddhism, the most prominent of which was the Pure Land (Jōdo) school, based on the vow of the Buddha Amida to save all beings who placed their faith in him by transporting them, upon death, to a Pure Land paradise in the western realm of the universe. People mired in the despair of living in what they regarded as a "world of filth" *(edo)* in *mappō*'s degenerate age were in this way promised release and a future life of bliss in the Pure Land of Amida.

The most important use of the *mappō* idea in the study of Japanese history is to be found in Jien's *Gukanshō*.[22] But the sense of gloom and impending disaster that accompanied *mappō* thinking is nowhere more powerfully expressed than in the *Heike*. Much of the *Heike*'s excellence as literature derives from its consistently maintained theme of the nearly helpless decline of the world. Frequently this decline is explicitly attributed to *mappō*.[23] But even more frequently the *Heike* refers to the workings of great and mysterious forces, such as fate *(unmei)*,[24] karma *(inga*, retribution), and the will of the gods. In some cases, characters in the *Heike* are blessed with good fate or fortune *(unmei hiraku*, the "beginning of good fortune")*; but far more often they are driven remorselessly to the "end of their fortune" *(unmei tsukiru)*.[25]

Hōgen Monogatari and *Heiji Monogatari* both contain references to the age of *mappō* and to a parallel theme that is continued in the *Heike:* the decline not only of the Buddhist Law but also the Imperial Law *(ōhō)*—that is, the waning of rule by the imperial family and the courtier class. The *Hōgen* and *Heiji* also speak of fate and of "fortune running out," and many of their characters—including such warrior chieftains as Tameyoshi and Yoshihira—pray to Amida for salvation in the Pure Land as they face death. But, compared to the *Heike,* the *Hōgen* and *Heiji* are essentially this-worldly works, devoted mainly to matters over which people are seen to have control based on their own actions. The *Hōgen* and *Heiji* view the world more in terms of Confucian morality than the deeply pessimistic Buddhism of the *Heike*.[26]

The *Heike* is also concerned with morality and karmic retribution, especially in regard to the behavior of Kiyomori and the Ise Taira. But the themes of morality and retribution are secondary, I believe, to the conviction that everything is ultimately governed by an unfathomable, relentless fate. In the *Heike*, the past is almost invariably seen as better than the present and the future portends only further deterioration and decline.[27] Yet the *Heike* is by no means an entirely negative work. Even while picturing protracted warfare as an inevitable result of the time of *mappō*, it glorifies warriors and the warrior spirit. In Yasuda Motohisa's analysis, this spirit became the basis for a new "world view" of the medieval age.[28]

Kiyomori as Villain

Taira no Kiyomori is a prominent personage in both the *Hōgen* and *Heiji*. In the *Heike*, he is the leading figure of the work's first half, or until his death in Book 6. As adumbrated in the last chapter, the tale singers who shaped the *Hōgen, Heiji,* and *Heike* as recitative texts in the thirteenth and fourteenth centuries systematically defamed some characters, including Kiyomori, even as they made great heroes of others. It will be recalled that in the *Hōgen* Kiyomori is shown as cowardly when he approaches a gate at Shirakawa Palace, discovers that its defender is the fearsome Tametomo, and decides to go to another gate. In the *Heiji*, as Minamoto no Yoshitomo approaches the Taira residence at Rokuhara in a continuation of the fighting that started in the Battle of Taikenmon Gate, a startled Kiyomori, attempting to don his armor, places his helmet on backwards. When his attendants call attention to this, Kiyomori says that he has placed the helmet this way in order not to appear to turn his back toward the emperor, who is at Rokuhara, as he leaves the residence. Kiyomori's oldest son, Shigemori, observes that, whatever his father says, his conduct seems cowardly.[29]

In the old text version of the *Heiji*, Kiyomori's behavior as the

Minamoto approach Rokuhara is entirely different. He dons his armor, mounts his horse, and grandly leads a force of Taira out to meet the attackers.[30] This description of Kiyomori's behavior is probably close to the historical truth, since it is almost identical to that found in Jien's *Gukanshō*.[31]

Having been made to appear cowardly and also foolish in the earlier tales, Kiyomori is transformed into an archvillain in the *Heike*. To illustrate that "the proud ones do not last forever" and "even the mighty will perish," the *Heike* presents in its opening chapter a list of villains in both Chinese and Japanese history who "did not obey the rule of their old lords or former sovereigns, led dissolute lives, ignored admonitions, were not aware of the world's disorders, and were blind to the suffering of the people."[32] At the end of this list is the name of Kiyomori, whose behavior in the present is described as "beyond the mind's imagining and the power of words."[33]

Thus Kiyomori is shown as an immoral, villainous ruler who is headed for a fall and will take the entire Ise Taira family down with him. But Kiyomori's villainy is only one reason for the impending fall. At the most basic level, the fall is caused by *mujō*, the law of constant change. The *Heike*, as revealed in its opening lines, is especially concerned with a particular kind of change: the change that will come to those (the Taira) who have scaled great heights, who have "flourished," become "proud," and are "mighty." This change will inevitably be downward, and it will occur with great speed, like the vanishing of the "dream of a spring night" or like "dust before the wind."[34] As we read on, however, we find that the speed and timing of the predicted decline and fall of Kiyomori and the Ise Taira cannot be precisely known. They are determined primarily by fate, and there appears to be no way of estimating when fate has run its course.

Hence, although Kiyomori's villainy certainly helps accelerate the process of Taira decline as narrated in the *Heike*, the main force behind the decline seems to be an unknowable fate. We see this perhaps most clearly in Book 2—in the events in 1177 following discovery of the Shishigatani plot by supporters of the retired emperor, Goshirakawa, to overthrow Kiyomori and the Taira. Kiyomori reacts to discovery of the plot with characteristic bluster and rashness, summarily executing some of the plotters and sending others into exile. But Kiyomori's actions elicit something that in the *Heike* invariably distresses and intimidates him: admonition from his oldest son, Shigemori. The *Heike*'s Shigemori is the conscience of the Taira. Shigemori seems also to represent, as many commentators have suggested, the voice of the courtier class, speaking out with anguish against the rise of warriors, led by Shigemori's own family, as the new rulers of the land.[35] In the *Hōgen* and *Heiji*, Shigemori is one of the principal fighters among the Taira, playing a particularly prominent role in the *Heiji*'s Battle of Taikenmon Gate. But in the *Heike*, Shigemori is always dressed in courtly robes, and he speaks and behaves like a courtier rather than a warrior.[36]

When Kiyomori dons his armor in order to lead a Taira force to arrest Goshirakawa, Shigemori admonishes him by invoking a variety of Shinto, Buddhist, and Confucian principles. He charges that, in putting on armor and helmet and taking up arms, Kiyomori, as a chancellor, violates the propriety of the land of Amaterasu the Shinto Sun Goddess. Kiyomori also sins against Buddhism, since he has taken Buddhist vows and is technically a monk. Finally, he contravenes Confucian laws of ethical behavior.[37] Having made these general charges, Shigemori gets to his main point, a point that can be taken to represent the political views and interests of the courtier-based Heian government. Of all the obligations one has in life, the obligation to sovereign *(kokuō no on)* comes first.[38] The Taira have been the recipients of extraordinary imperial favor, including appointment to the office of chancellor and to the governorships of half the provinces of the land. They have, moreover, been given free rein in acquiring agricultural estates. By going against the wishes of the retired emperor, they can only invoke the wrath of Amaterasu and Hachiman, who as gods of Japan, the divine land *(shinkoku)*, will not tolerate such impropriety.[39] But, Shigemori avers, something can still be done. The Shishigatani plot has been discovered "because the fortune of the Taira has not yet run out." It is still possible for Kiyomori, working as a loyal official of the court, to deal with the plotters properly and to the satisfaction of both gods and buddhas.[40]

Shigemori sternly criticizes his father for disobeying and offending the *in*, whom he identifies as a sovereign,[41] and predicts dire punishment if Kiyomori does not change his ways. But, Shigemori infers, the ultimate determination about the Taira depends on an inscrutable fortune or fate *(un)* that he believes has not yet run out but may, presumably, come to an end at any time. In reading the *Heike*, it is often difficult if not impossible to distinguish among the various forces of *mujō*, fate, *mappō*, bad karma (as retribution for evil acts), and the will of the gods and to judge which is most powerfully at work at any particular time in determining people's actions or the course of events. But I believe that, in the overall scheme of the *Heike*, retribution, although vividly and dramatically emphasized from the work's opening lines in regard to the personal villainy of Kiyomori and the hubris of the Taira in general, is of secondary importance to fate. The central theme of the *Heike* is how the Taira, having risen to dizzying heights of power, splendor, and affluence, are driven to annihilation less in punishmènt for their sins than because of fate, which appears to be especially intense and destructive in the age of *mappō*. This becomes clear, I believe, in the *Heike*'s second half, after the Gempei War has begun and Kiyomori is dead. We find many references to the Taira suffering setbacks and defeats during the war because of what is believed to be karmic retribution. But it is the fearful, dark force of fate that is the main determinant of what happens to them. They are propelled toward extinction chiefly because their fate/fortune is running out.[42]

We noted that, in its opening lines, the *Heike* refers to *mujō* in terms of particularly rapid change—change occurring like the "dream of a spring night" or like "dust before the wind." Although the role of fate makes it difficult to judge the exact speed and timing of the Taira fall, in fact it happens quite rapidly: The Taira are demolished in the Gempei War and the last member of the family (Rokudai, Kiyomori's great-grandson) is killed a few years later. Thus the Taira rise and fall occur within a matter of decades. To the extent that it is fate, it is a fast-working fate; insofar as it is bad karma, that karma seems to have been set in motion primarily by Kiyomori's evilness and to have been carried swiftly to retribution against his entire family.[43] Such speed of change is a recurrent motif in the *Heike*;[44] it is often expressed in phrases like "yesterday . . . today" or "last year . . . this year."[45] When the Taira, for example, are driven from Kyoto by Minamoto no Yoshinaka in 1183 and begin their wanderings in the western regions of Japan, the *Heike*'s author observes: "Yesterday they were ten thousand riders, their horses' bits aligned at the foot of the eastern barrier. Today they are a mere seven thousand, their mooring lines cast off and their boats adrift on the waves of the western sea."[46] And when Yoshinaka himself is expelled from Kyoto the following year by an army sent from the east by Yoritomo, we read: "The year before when Yoshinaka left Shinano province he was said to command fifty thousand riders. Today, as he passed through Shinomiya [in Kyoto], he and his followers numbered only seven."[47]

Shigemori, according to the *Heike*, commits suicide—or, rather, allows himself to fall sick and die—after receiving a sign from the god of the Kumano Shrines that the good fortune of the Taira will indeed run out in "a single generation"—that is, it will end soon and not extend to the sons and grandsons of Kiyomori.[48] Shigemori's death, which occurs in 1179, symbolizes the beginning of the end of the Taira. Within a year the Gempei War has begun, and the year after that

Kiyomori dies. Although he was evil, Kiyomori was at least a strong leader. From this time the Taira suffer from conspicuously weak leadership, beginning with Munemori, Kiyomori's second son, who becomes the family head upon his father's death.

The "Death of the Lay Priest" is one of the most dramatic, horrifying chapters in the *Heike*. Kiyomori contracts a fever that makes his body so hot that people cannot approach him. When water is thrown on him to provide relief, it boils and turns to steam. He dies writhing in agony. But he is unrepentant to the end. Unlike so many other characters in the *Heike* when they face death, he says nothing about fate or karma, or even a desire to be reborn in Amida's Pure Land. Instead, in one of his last conversations with his wife, Kiyomori asks that there be no tributes or memorials for him when he dies. His only wish is that the head of Yoritomo be taken and hung before his grave.[49]

Sanemori and the Bandō Warrior

The leader of the Taira army that marched to the Kantō in 1180, confronted Minamoto no Yoritomo at Fuji River, and retreated without fighting was Kiyomori's grandson Koremori. Among the Taira commanders in the *Heike*, none is more courtier-like and less martial than Koremori.[50] When in 1183, for example, the Taira are forced by Yoshinaka to flee from Kyoto, Koremori alone refuses to take his wife, a court lady, and his children with him. He cannot bear to subject them to the hardships he knows lie ahead. Later, he is so overcome with nostalgia for wife and children and for the capital that he deserts the Taira camp; finally, he commits suicide.[51] The selection of Koremori to lead a force to the east to fight the ferocious Kantō (Bandō) warriors portends how unequal the conflict between Minamoto and Taira will be, at least as that conflict is narrated in the *Heike*. The Taira are simply no match, in fighting skills or spirit, for the Minamoto and other provincial warriors who rise to oppose them.

The contrast between what the *Heike* categorizes as "eastern" warriors and "western" warriors is perhaps most graphically expressed in the following remarks made by an eastern warrior in Koremori's army on the eve of the Fuji River debacle. The warrior, Saitō no Sanemori, replies to a query about how many other warriors in the east are as powerful with bow and arrow *(yunzei, tsuyoyumi)* as he:

> "Do you regard me as a shooter of long arrows? My arrows are scarcely thirteen hand-breadths in length. Many warriors in the eight provinces [of the Kantō] can match me. Those known as 'long arrows' never draw a shaft of less than fifteen hand-breadths. A strong bow requires five or six stout men to string. When a fine east-

ern warrior shoots arrows, he can easily penetrate two or three suits of armor laid one on another. To be considered a chieftain *(daimyō)*, one must command at least five hundred riders. When the eastern warrior rides, he is never unseated; although he gallops over rough terrain *(akusho)*, he keeps his horse from falling. In battle, even though a parent or child is struck and killed, the eastern warrior rides over the body and keeps on fighting. In warfare in the west, on the other hand, if a parent is killed in battle Buddhist services are held and the fighting does not resume until after a period of mourning. If a child is killed, the western warrior is so overcome with grief that he stops fighting altogether. When concerned that his food supplies may run short, the western warrior takes time off to plant his fields in the spring and harvest them in the fall. He doesn't like to fight when it is hot in summer or cold in winter. Warriors of the eastern provinces are not at all like this."[52]

The western warriors of the Taira armies, as pictured in the *Heike,* are not only far less impressive as fighters than their eastern counterparts, they are also apt to flee as soon as the battle goes against them. The primary reason for this, it seems, is that many of the warriors recruited by the Taira are not regular or hereditary vassals but "temporarily assembled warriors" *(kari-musha)*, who are said to be "unconcerned about shame" and "interested only in seeing their wives and children again."[53] In a discussion of strategy between Koremori and a subcommander, Tadakiyo, before the confrontation with the Minamoto at Fuji River, Tadakiyo points out that although their expeditionary force has swelled from thirty thousand to seventy thousand as warriors from various provinces have joined them on their way to the Kantō, the newcomers are *kari-musha* and cannot be relied on to fight well.[54]

Kari-musha appear again in the Battle of Shinohara fought between Minamoto no Yoshinaka and the Taira expeditionary force sent to the Hokuriku region in 1183. A general from the Taira side advances at the head of five hundred horsemen and is met by a force of three hundred from the Minamoto side. Although the Taira contingent has a great numerical advantage, its troops are "temporarily assembled warriors from various provinces." After fighting briefly, they desert their commander en masse, each seeking to flee faster *(ware saki ni)* than the other.[55]

The flight of the *kari-musha* from the Battle of Shinohara is the beginning of a full-scale rout that leads to the retreat of the entire Taira expeditionary force from the Hokuriku region back to Kyoto and sets the stage for Yoshinaka's advance upon the capital. Despite the disgraceful behavior of the *kari-musha* troops, there are others of the

Taira force who, in the *Heike*, conduct themselves with great heroism during the Battle of Shinohara and the ensuing retreat. Chief among these is Saitō no Sanemori, the eastern warrior whose remarks about the differences between eastern and western warriors before the Battle of Fuji River are quoted above.

Sanemori fought with Minamoto no Yoshitomo in the Heiji Conflict but, like many others, entered the employ of the Taira after the decimation of the Minamoto in that conflict.[56] When the Gempei War began in 1180, Sanemori, although an eastern warrior with long-standing ties to the Minamoto, chose to remain loyal to the Taira. At the time of the Battle of Shinohara, he was more than seventy years old. In the *Heike* account of the battle, Sanemori has dyed his white hair black to disguise his age and has stated his determination to die in the fighting at Shinohara. He gives as his reason the shame he feels for failing to fire even a single arrow at the enemy at Fuji River three years earlier, when the Taira army was startled by birds and fled back to Kyoto without fighting.[57]

As the Taira army runs away from the Battle of Shinohara, Sanemori continues to fight alone to slow the enemy pursuit. An opposing warrior, Tezuka no Mitsumori, sees Sanemori, is impressed by his valor, and challenges him to combat. Sanemori accepts the challenge, tells Mitsumori that they are worthy foes for each other, but refuses to announce his name because he does not wish to reveal his age. In the ensuing combat Sanemori, who is exhausted and must contend with both Mitsumori and his retainer, is killed.[58]

When Mitsumori reports the killing to his commander, Yoshinaka, he expresses puzzlement over the fact that the warrior he killed, whose identity he still does not know, looked like a commander but did not have a following of retainers. The warrior seemed to be a commander because he wore a red brocade robe under his armor and had various decorations on his helmet, armor, and saddle usually reserved for commanders. The author of the *Heike*, referring specifically to the red brocade robe, informs us that Sanemori, before leaving Kyoto, had received special permission from the Taira leader, Munemori, to wear a commander's robe because he intended to die in the coming campaign and, in a tradition received from China, wished to return home for the last time "wearing brocade."[59] When Yoshinaka guesses that the dead warrior is Sanemori, he has Sanemori's hair washed and finds that, with the dye gone, it is pure white.

First in Battle

Aggressiveness is surely a quality desirable in all warriors. The premodern Japanese warrior, at least as we see him in the war tales, was an unusually aggressive fighter. No doubt his aggressiveness derived in large part from the single mounted warrior style of fighting that prevailed in ancient times and through much of the medieval age as well. Fighting mainly as an individual seeking reward for his battlefield successes, the warrior had to be aggressive or find himself without reward and possibly seen as a slacker or coward.

One manifestation of this aggressiveness was the name-announcing. Although used to serve other purposes as well, the name-announcing was always an important part of the psychological combat between warriors. For example, a stock ending to many name-announcings in the war tales is a challenge by the warrior to those enemies who "think they are my match" to come forward and try their luck at arms with him. This challenge was presumably intended both to intimidate potential opponents and to persuade them that the warrior was worthy to be met in combat, even though the chief criterion of a worthy opponent continued to be his social status.

Probably the most conspicuous way in which warriors display their aggressiveness in the war tales is in their constant competition to be "first in battle" (sakigake, senjin). References to such competition are found repeatedly in battle accounts, which describe warriors "striving to be first" (ware saki ni; literally, "Me first!"), "contending for the lead" (saki o arasou), or determined to be "second to none" (ware otoraji). Thus in Hōgen Monogatari, Tametomo feels obliged to caution his brothers—who are vying with one another to be the first to engage the enemy (ware saki o kaken to araso[u]) as they await the night attack on Shirakawa Palace—that he, Tametomo, will defend against the main assault.[60] And in the Battle of Taikenmon Gate in Heiji Monogatari a group of Minamoto warriors, at the urging of their commander, Yoshitomo, compete to lead the advance against the Taira (ware mo ware mo to susumikeri).[61]

But the Heike contains the best, most exciting examples of sakigake. Among these is the competition between two Minamoto warriors, Sasaki no Takatsuna and Kajiwara no Kagesue, to be first to cross the Uji River on horseback as members of the army sent by Yoritomo from Kamakura early in 1184 to destroy his cousin Yoshinaka, the occupier of Kyoto. Both Takatsuna and Kagesue are astride famous horses, Ikezuki (Natural Biter) and Surusumi (Inkstick),[62] that were given to them by Yoritomo himself and are prime examples of the "wild horses," the "very big and powerful" horses described in Chapter 2. The quality of these splendid steeds ensures that surely one of them will lead the crossing of the Uji River. In fact, it is Takatsuna riding Ikezuki, recognized as the finer of the two horses, who first reaches the river's opposite bank. Upon climbing the bank, Takatsuna stands in his stirrups and announces his name—including the proclamation, which will remain a permanent part of his *nanori* and that of his descendants, that he is the first to cross the Uji River.[63]

Gempei Seisui Ki, in discussing the planning at Kamakura for sending the army to ford the Uji and attack Yoshinaka, provides us with additional information about the importance of horses to warriors in the war tales. In requesting that Yoritomo lend him one of his famous horses for the campaign against Yoshinaka, Kajiwara no Kagesue observes: "Even though he may possess a fierce spirit like [Taira no] Masakado or [Fujiwara no] Sumitomo, a warrior riding a weak horse will surely die a dog's death."[64] And Yoritomo himself, anticipating that the army will be sorely challenged both by the swift current of the Uji River and by the spikes *(sakamogi)*, tautened ropes (to trip the horses), and other impediments placed in the river by the enemy, directs that the army be equipped with "fine mounts" *(yoki uma)*. *Gempei Seisui Ki* then lists a number of warriors and their mounts, all of which, like Ikezuki and Surusumi, are identified by their names (White Wave, Rough Shore, Ring of the Moon). Here is a case where, in assembling an army, greater attention appears to be given to the caliber of the horses than to their warrior riders.[65]

The *Heike* account of the crossing of the Uji River describes an amusing incident concerning the competition among warriors to be first. Hatakeyama no Shigetada, leading some five hundred riders, has to abandon his horse in midstream when an enemy arrow lodges in the beast's head. Using his bow as a staff, Shigetada manages to get to the other side of the river. As he is about to climb the bank, he feels someone catch hold of him from behind. It is a young warrior, his godson, named Okushi no Shigechika, who has also lost his mount and needs assistance getting ashore. But when Shigetada seizes him and throws him onto the bank, Shigechika leaps to his feet and loudly proclaims that he is the first warrior to cross the Uji River on foot. Hearing this name-announcing, allies and enemies together burst into laughter.[66]

One of the most informative accounts in the *Heike* of the competition to be first in battle occurs on the eve of the Battle of Ichinotani and during the battle's opening stages. Fought in the second month of 1184 on the shore of the Inland Sea, this battle resulted in the first major defeat of the Taira by the Minamoto after the Taira were forced to flee from Kyoto by Yoshinaka the year before. The *Heike* relates how two men, Kumagae no Naozane (whom we met in the last chapter) and Hirayama no Sueshige, both archetypes of the eastern, Bandō warriors, compete for the lead in the Minamoto assault on the western entrance to the Taira fortification at Ichinotani.[67] The lowly status of both these warriors is attested by their name-announcings, for they have nothing to say about their backgrounds except that they are "residents of Musashi province."[68] These men are in the business of warfare to earn a living. As another resident of Musashi participating in the same battle puts it: "Even if he does nothing himself, a chieftain (daimyō) gains fame through the exploits of his vassals (ke'nin). But we vassals have to earn our reputations ourselves [that is, do the real fighting]."[69]

The term for chieftain in the preceding quotation, daimyō, means "big name,"[70] and in later centuries it became the standard designation for warrior leaders who controlled substantial territories and had large vassal followings. In another quotation from the Heike, given earlier in this chapter, a daimyō is defined as a chieftain who commands at least five hundred riders.[71] The converse of a daimyō is a shōmyō or "little name."[72] Shōmyō are warriors like Kumagae no Naozane and Hirayama no Sueshige who have no vassals and essentially do the "real fighting" by themselves. At the Battle of Ichinotani, Naozane is accompanied by his son Naoie and a standard bearer (hatasashi) and Sueshige has only a standard bearer.

Both Naozane and Sueshige were, by the time of the Battle of Ichinotani, recognized as warriors willing to undertake the daredevil job of leading the attack in battles. For example, both were rewarded by Yoritomo for their exploits as advance fighters in the campaign in the eleventh month of 1180 in which Yoritomo, seeking to extend his hegemony over the Kantō, conquered the Satake family of Hitachi province. According to Azuma Kagami: "Among the soldiers [who fought against the Satake], Kumagae Jirō no Naozane and Hirayama no Musha-dokoro Sueshige especially distinguished themselves. Rushing ahead of the others in one encounter after another, with no regard for whether they lived or died, they collected many enemy heads. Accordingly, it was immediately ordered that they should be more generously rewarded than their fellow warriors."[73]

Another passage in Azuma Kagami contains Yoritomo's decree bestowing land and a stewardship upon Naozane for his conduct in the fighting against the Satake. The decree includes these words: "In that day's battle [against the Satake], Naozane led all the others in the attack and, advancing first to smash the enemy position, established a reputation for himself as a warrior 'the equal of a thousand.' "[74]

As various commentators have pointed out, those who, like Naozane and Sueshige, competed to be the first to attack often accomplished little.[75] Azuma Kagami says that Naozane and Sueshige took many heads in the Satake campaign. But in many, if not most, of the competitions to be first-in-battle described in the *Heike*, the contending warriors manage to do scarcely more than place themselves in unnecessary danger. Although their acts of derring-do may bolster the fighting spirit of their comrades, these acts are frequently carried out in contravention of their commanders' orders. In the *Heike* account of the Battle of Ichinotani, for example, one of the Minamoto commanders, Noriyori, warns that there will be no rewards for those who "forge ahead to attack, leaving the rest of the army behind."[76] But Kajiwara no Kagetaka ignores this order and, shouting loudly, dashes into the lead. Kagetaka's father, Kagetoki, fearful that his son will be killed, orders his force of five hundred riders to rush after him, and in the ensuing combat all but fifty of these riders are killed.[77] We are left to wonder whether Kagetaka's reckless behavior was not responsible for this decimation of the Kajiwara force.

On the night before the Battle of Ichinotani, Kumagae no Naozane decides to disobey the orders of his commander, Minamoto no Yoshitsune, and be the first to attack the Taira the following day. Anticipating that his old comrade and competitor Hirayama no Sueshige—who, like Naozane, "has no liking for mass attacks *(uchikomi no ikusa)*" in which the individual warrior is lost in a crowd—aspires also to be first at Ichinotani, he steals out of the Minamoto encampment during the night. Accompanied by his son Naoie and his standard bearer, Naozane makes his way along a little-used path to the shore at Ichinotani and to the shield barrier *(kaidate)* in front of the western gate of the Taira fortification. It is the dead of night and not a sound comes from the fortification. But Naozane announces his name in a loud voice: "Kumagae no Jirō Naozane and his son Kōjirō Naoie, residents of Musashi province, are the first *(senjin)* at Ichinotani!"[78]

There is no response from the Taira.[79] Meanwhile Sueshige, who has been delayed through the trickery of still another warrior who wishes to lead the way at Ichinotani, arrives accompanied by his standard bearer.[80] The group of five waits until dawn. Then Naozane proceeds once again to the shield barrier and announces his name loudly. He repeats his name-announcing of the previous night but adds the familiar, aggressive challenge: "If there are Heike samurai who think they can handle me, let them come and confront me! Let them come and confront me!"[81]

Finally, the Taira open the gate of their fortification, twenty warriors ride forth, and the fighting begins. Naozane and Sueshige match each other exploit for exploit. Naozane loses his horse and must secure another mount; Naoie is wounded by an arrow in his bow arm, and

another arrow fells Sueshige's standard bearer. In the end, both Naozane and Sueshige claim to have been the first at Ichinotani—Naozane
for reaching the Taira fortification first and Sueshige for leading the
way into the fortification when its gate was opened.[82]

More attention is devoted to the Battle of Ichinotani than to any
other fight described in the *Heike*. But neither the assault at the western gate nor the attack at Ikuta-no-mori to the east is decisive. Victory
is achieved by one of the most daring and celebrated military exploits
in Japanese history: the descent by Yoshitsune and a band of riders
down the precipitously steep Hiyodorigoe Cliff to attack the Taira from
the rear (the north). This descent, presented in the *Heike* as the high
drama it undoubtedly was, is discussed as part of the story of Yoshitsune in the next chapter.

A number of sections in the *Heike* are devoted to encounters
between individual warriors during the Battle of Ichinotani and after,
as the surviving Taira attempt to escape. These sections too will be discussed later, for they contain some of the best-known and most poignant battle scenes in the *Heike*, including the death of Atsumori at the
hands of Kumagae no Naozane.

Battle Descriptions

Komatsu Shigetō identifies three types of battle descriptions in
the war tales: one warrior fighting against another *(ikki-uchi)*; one
fighting against many; and many fighting against many (group combat).[83] Battles in *Shōmonki*, which are only sketchily described, are
presented almost exclusively as group combat—that is, one army contending against another. The *Konjaku Monogatari* war tales also contain primarily descriptions of group combat, although we can see the
contours of what became the classical order of battle in the ancient
age: commencement of a battle as group combat when two armies confront each other and engage in an exchange of arrows *(ya-awase)*; then
division into individual fights as the armies clash and warriors pair off
one against another.[84]

The principal battle in *Hōgen Monogatari*, the night attack on
Shirakawa Palace, is pictured at first as a group combat, but soon it
becomes a description of a series of individual encounters as Tametomo takes on one comer after another. In *Heiji Monogatari* the climactic Battle of Taikenmon Gate is treated throughout as a group
combat, although there are interlude descriptions of encounters between individual warriors within the overall pattern of two armies
clashing.

Heike Mongatari presents far more detailed and varied battle descriptions than any of the war tales that precede it. Examples of *Heike* battles that are described strictly as group combat are Yoshinaka's victory over the Taira at Kurikara in the Hokuriku region and Yoshitsune's spectacular descent of the Hiyodorigoe Cliff, which routed the Taira in the second phase of the Battle of Ichinotani. Most of the battles in the *Heike*, however, are described as a mixture of group combat and individual fights. Cohering essentially to the classical order of battle, a description in this category typically presents us, first, with a general overview of the conflict and then with scenes of fighting between small groups or individual warriors. This division of a battle description into overview and scenes was congenial to the art of the tale singer, for it enabled him to devote much of his attention to the subject that appealed most to his audiences: accounts of the exploits or fates of individual heroes in a battle. Of the ten chapters in the *Heike* that cover the Battle of Ichinotani, nine are concerned exlusively or mainly with individual or small group encounters, most of which occur as the surviving Taira try to escape from the rout at Ichinotani.

Komatsu's third type of battle description—one warrior or a small group fighting against many warriors—is used mainly for two special kinds of conflict highlighted in the war tales: the competition to be first in battle and the self-sacrificing act of one or more warriors fighting to delay the enemy while their defeated army retreats.[85] An example of the former is the attack of Kumagae no Naozane and Hirayama no Sueshige, accompanied by Naozane's son and two standard bearers, on the Taira fortress at Ichinotani; and an example of the latter is Saitō no Sanemori's gallant defense against Yoshinaka's hordes as the Taira retreat from the Battle of Shinohara.

One general aspect of battle accounts in the medieval war tales is the infrequency of reference to warriors' attendants. We know that each mounted warrior was accompanied into battle by one or two attendants (see the section in Chapter 2 on "The Warrior Attendant"), but they are seldom mentioned in the war tales except in certain passages where they are featured, such as the passage about "Eight Block" Jirō in *Heiji Monogatari* and several *Heike* passages to be discussed later in this chapter. The reader of the war tales is likely to envision battles as essentially groups of mounted men meeting in combat. Yet the attendants on hand at battles may have outnumbered the warriors by as many as two to one. We know, as discussed in Chapter 2, the general functions of these attendants. But the authors of the war tales apparently did not think they were sufficiently worthy or interesting as subjects for inclusion in most of the battle accounts.

Witnesses to Battlefield Exploits

We have noted the importance to the warrior of fighting an enemy of equal or higher status. As Kumagae no Naozane bluntly puts it during the Battle of Ichinotani: "Fame depends upon the enemy [that is, the kind of enemy you fight]."[86] Fame also depended on having one's exploits properly witnessed. Hence we find frequent references in the war tales to witnesses (shōnin) and the need for warriors to have them along when entering battle. In Hōgen Monogatari, for example, a Taira warrior, Yamada no Koreyuki, referring to the disgraceful behavior of Kiyomori in avoiding combat with Tametomo in the night attack on Shirakawa Palace, calls for witnesses as he rashly decides to advance toward the superhuman Tametomo.[87] Koreyuki's announcement that he is a "resident of Iga province" informs us that, like Kumagae no Naozane and Hirayama no Sueshige, he is a warrior of little account. Indeed, he enters combat with Tametomo "without even a single soldier on foot (kachihashiri)" but only a groom (toneri) to hold his horse.[88] (Here is a rare case of a groom or attendant being featured in a scene in a medieval war tale.) Since all the others in the Taira party, including Kiyomori, have by this time withdrawn from the scene of battle in fear of Tametomo, Koreyuki is obliged to take the unusual step of recruiting his own groom as a witness. In his instructions to the groom, Koreyuki observes: "It seems certain that I will be struck and killed by one of Hachirō-dono's [Tametomo's] arrows. But for a man of bow and arrow this is a golden opportunity to acquire land [as a reward]. Whether I live or die, it is assured that I will achieve great merit."[89] But the groom, as described in the Hōgen, is as foolhardy as his master. When Koreyuki is mortally pierced by one of Tametomo's arrows, the groom rushes into the enemy's ranks, wildly wielding a naginata, and is also killed.[90]

In the competition between Kumagae no Naozane and Hirayama no Sueshige to be first in the Battle of Ichinotani, Sueshige says he was late in arriving at Ichinotani because a companion he regarded as a friend duped him by saying he should not get ahead of his witnesses. By witnesses, the friend meant the other members of their army. According to Sueshige, the friend said: "What's to be achieved by a single horseman dashing into the enemy horde and getting himself killed?" But when Sueshige paused to await others from the army, the duplicitous friend galloped past him, heading toward Ichinotani. The ruse, however, did the friend little good, because Sueshige, riding a stronger horse, was soon able to catch up and outdistance him.[91]

In the attack on Ichinotani two brothers named Kawara, who are also "residents of Musashi," literally forfeit their lives to gain merit in battle.[92] (The older of the brothers is the warrior who, as quoted in the section on "First in Battle," observes that whereas chieftains gain fame through the exploits of their vassals, the vassals—the common warriors—must achieve their own fame by hard fighting.) After the Kawara brothers are killed, their attendants immediately perform a substitute name-announcing for their masters, shouting out that the masters have just perished leading the attack on the Ichinotani fortress.[93] Their purpose is to recruit witnesses to the brothers' deeds and thus gain posthumous rewards for the brothers' families.[94]

The Warrior's End: Yoshinaka

Much attention is given in the war tales to descriptions of the deaths of warrior heroes. Seven chapters in the *Heike*, for example, are entitled the "death" (or end, *saigo*) of such-and-such a warrior, and the fourteenth-century *Taiheiki* is replete with chapters bearing titles that indicate they are records of the deaths, by suicide or other means, of warriors. No doubt one reason for this heavy focus on death was the inherent dramatic appeal, to readers and audiences, of accounts of how fighting heroes of the war tales met their ends.

In later centuries from about the *sengoku* (provincial wars) period (1478–1573)—after the war tales had lost their vigor as a genre of literature—the "way of the warrior" increasingly stressed the importance of the warrior being ever prepared to die bravely and even "beautifully." There was almost incessant fighting in the *sengoku* period, and chieftains apparently felt ever more keenly the need to instruct their vassals in how to deal with the grim likelihood of meeting death in battle. For example, Katō Kiyomasa, who served the late-sixteenth-century unifier Toyotomi Hideyoshi and later fought for the Tokugawa at the Battle of Sekigahara in 1600, stated in his house precepts: "Those who are born into warrior *(bushi)* houses must devote themselves to the way of handling swords and meeting death. If one does not constantly study the warrior way *(bushidō)*, one will find it difficult to achieve a brave *(isagiyoki)* death. . . ."[95] And in *Hagakure*, compiled in the early eighteenth century, we are told that "the way of the warrior is death."[96]

The war tales contain no precise code of behavior in regard to death, although they present many examples of brave and perhaps even beautiful deaths to serve as models for warriors in later centuries. As in so many other ways, the *Heike* surpasses all the war tales in its handling of the death scenes of warrior heroes. Of these scenes, none is

more finely drawn, more dramatically affecting, or more informative
of a warrior's behavior as idealized in the war tales than the death of
Minamoto (Kiso) no Yoshinaka.[97]

Although Yoshinaka raised the banner of revolt against the Taira
just one month after Yoritomo in 1180, we find only scattered references to him in the first half of the *Heike*. As we begin the *Heike*'s second half (from Book 7), however, Yoshinaka is suddenly catapulted
into prominence and becomes the central character of the work's middle section. After the disastrous failure of the Taira army at the Battle
of Fuji River in the tenth month of 1180, the Gempei War had settled
into a state of virtual inactivity, although Yoritomo made valuable use
of this time to consolidate his control over the Kantō and neighboring
areas. In mid-1183 the Taira decided to march against Yoshinaka, sending a vast army into the Tōsan and Hokuriku regions. Yoshinaka
defeated this army in one battle after another, including the Battle of
Shinohara described earlier in the section on "Sanemori and the Bandō
Warrior." In the seventh month of 1183 Yoshinaka swept into Kyoto,
forcing the Taira to abandon the city and flee to the west.

In the *Heike* account, Yoshinaka is welcomed by the Kyoto courtiers as a conquering hero and is even given the designation "Morning-
Sun General" *(asahi shōgun)* by an elated former emperor Goshirakawa.[98] But the honeymoon between Yoshinaka and Kyoto is short-
lived. We know from history that the central provinces of Japan,
including Kyoto, were at the time barely recovering from a severe famine,[99] and Yoshinaka's arrival in the capital with an army of thousands
placed an intolerable strain on food supplies. But the *Heike* attributes
Kyoto's rapid disenchantment with Yoshinaka primarily to his uncouth behavior and crude manner of speaking.

Yoshinaka in Kyoto is transformed in the *Heike* from a brilliant
military commander into an incredible buffoon and bully. He mocks a
courtier, calling him a cat because the word "cat" appears in the name
of the place where the courtier lives; he wolfs down his food; he falls
unceremoniously from a carriage on his way to court.[100] In a surge of
arrogance, he even toys with the idea of making himself emperor or
retired emperor.[101] Perhaps this gross satirization of Yoshinaka is
meant to mock all rustic warriors who go to the capital and ape courtly
ways. Or perhaps the rude and vulgar Yoshinaka is intended as a foil to
highlight the role of the Taira in the second half of the *Heike* as courtier-like fugitives, hounded and hunted by rough warriors from the
provinces.

Yoshinaka's supremacy in Kyoto lasts less than a half year.
Opposed by the retired emperor Goshirakawa, unsuccessful in armed

forays against the Taira outside the capital, and the target of plotting and hostile maneuverings by Yoritomo, his competitor for Minamoto overlordship, Yoshinaka is increasingly isolated and endangered. Finally, in the first month of 1184, he is destroyed by the army under Noriyori and Yoshitsune sent from the Kantō.

First portrayed as a victorious commander and then as a loutish occupier of Kyoto and brash intruder into court society, Yoshinaka in his final hours assumes a third persona: the tragic hero. He becomes hesitant and uncertain, is increasingly dependent on his ever-faithful follower, Imai no Kanehira, and finally falls, alone except for Kanehira, before a vastly superior foe. As much as Kiyomori or any of the Ise Taira, Yoshinaka fulfills the prophecy of the *Heike*'s opening lines that those who flourish must fade and the mighty will perish in the end.[102]

Even as the great eastern army thunders toward Kyoto, Yoshinaka fails to react decisively, revealing the vacillation that, except for a few gestures of bravado, will characterize his behavior in the final hours. Instead of mustering his forces for defense, he wastes precious time in a farewell visit to a mistress. One of his vassals, alarmed that the enemy has entered Kyoto and still the commander is with his mistress, commits disembowelment to bring Yoshinaka to his senses.[103] Yoshinaka rushes from the mistress' residence, alert at last to the crisis. But by this time tens of thousands of enemy horsemen are in the capital, and Yoshinaka's efforts to disperse them are futile. Before long his force is reduced to a mere remnant. In the words of the *Heike*: "The year before when Yoshinaka left Shinano province he was said to command fifty thousand riders. Today, as he passed through Shinomiya [in Kyoto], he and his followers numbered only seven."[104]

As a number of commentators have pointed out, there is a subtle but striking change in the *Heike*'s tone as Yoshinaka is driven from Kyoto to his desperate final battle outside the capital in the chapter entitled "The Death of Kiso." Whereas the language used to describe him in Kyoto is abrupt, at times derisive, in this chapter it becomes respectful, and his words and actions are couched in grammatical forms more likely to be used for courtiers than warriors.[105] This change in tone reflects, at least in part, the tendency for the authors of the war tales to display sympathy—and respect—for loser-heroes in their times of extremity, often disregarding the flaws, mistakes, and evil acts that may have done them in.

Among Yoshinaka's tiny band is a redoubtable woman warrior named Tomoe, who is described as having white skin, long hair, and a beautiful face. Such a description, although brief, is unusual since, as discussed earlier, the war tales seldom say anything about the personal appearances of warriors, other than their armor and weapons. Tomoe is a powerful fighter, the "equal of a thousand," capable of dealing even with "demons or gods." She is, in particular, a rider of untamed horses (arauma-nori) who is prepared to take them over rough terrain (akusho-otoshi).[106] This capacity to take horses over rough terrain is much admired in the war tales as an indication of outstanding horsemanship. The great example in the Heike of negotiating such terrain is, of course, Yoshitsune's descent of Hiyodorigoe Cliff at the Battle of Ichinotani.

Tomoe is an intriguing but puzzling character. She is one of only two women warriors I have come across in my reading of the war tales. (The other, who appears in the Gempei Seisui Ki version of "The Death of Kiso" and is also a follower of Yoshinaka, is said to have been killed "the year before," 1182.)[107] Although scholars have valiantly sought to identify Tomoe as a historical figure, they have thus far been unable to adduce evidence sufficient to prove that she is other than a creation of the Heike's authors.[108] Yet even the Heike is unclear about Tomoe's relationship to Yoshinaka. The Kakuichi text, for example, introduces her as an "attendant" or "servant" (binjo) whom Yoshinaka has brought with him from Shinano, but the text then asserts that in battles she is assigned as Yoshinaka's "leading commander" (ippō no taishō).[109]

Despite Tomoe's obviously sterling qualities as a warrior, Yoshinaka, determined to fight to the death against the eastern horde, orders her to leave the battlefield, saying: "It would be a disgrace to have it said that Lord Kiso was accompanied by a woman in his final battle."[110] Forced to obey Yoshinaka despite her reluctance to leave him, Tomoe looks for a "worthy foe" to slay before she departs. Her selection is Onda no Moroshige, known in his native province of Musashi as a warrior of great strength. Riding forward and engaging Moroshige in one-against-one combat, Tomoe pins him against the pommel of her saddle, "twists his head off" (a euphemism for decapitation that appears frequently in the war tales), and throws it away. She then sheds her armor and heads toward the eastern provinces.[111]

Some scholars have suggested that Tomoe, although probably a fictional character, represents those warriors and others attached to armies who survived battles and went on to tell about them, taking special care to recount how great chieftains met their ends. One can, in any case, imagine that Tomoe or someone like her, who participated in this clash with the Kantō army, became such a teller of battle tales (katarite) and provided the material that eventually became the nucleus for the Heike's version of "The Death of Kiso."[112]

Having fled Kyoto with a following reduced to a handful, Yoshi-naka thinks only of his ever-faithful follower, Imai no Kanehira, whom he earlier dispatched to defend the Seta Bridge approach to Kyoto. The two are far more than lord and vassal. They grew up together in Shinano province and are "brothers of the bosom," having shared the same wet nurse. They have vowed that, when the time comes, they will "die together in the same place."[113]

As Yoshinaka heads toward Seta in search of Kanehira, the latter starts back toward Kyoto looking for Yoshinaka. The two meet in a highly charged reunion near Ōtsu and, gathering three hundred riders from among those of their followers who had scattered in the earlier fighting, they attack a nearby force of the enemy. The commander of this force is Ichijō no Jirō, whom Yoshinaka pronounces to be a worthy foe.[114] In the combat that ensues, Yoshinaka's greatly outnumbered group is reduced from three hundred to fifty, then to five (it is at this point that Tomoe is ordered to leave), and finally to two, Yoshinaka and Kanehira.

Yoshinaka complains that his armor feels heavier than usual. Recognizing this as a sign of discouragement,[115] Kanehira attempts to bolster Yoshinaka's spirits by saying that he, Kanehira, who is the "equal of a thousand," will hold off the enemy while Yoshinaka does what he must do, commit suicide. When Yoshinaka continues to talk about dying together in the same place, Kanehira leaps from his horse and imploringly addresses his master:

> "No matter how much fame the handler of bow and arrow may achieve, if he behaves poorly at the end it will become a lasting stain on his honor. You are tired, and there is no great army following you. If we become separated by the enemy and you encounter somebody's insignificant vassal who kills you, people will say: 'Lord Kiso, famous throughout Japan, has been killed by so-and-so's vassal.' How regrettable that would be. Please, go into those pine woods [and kill yourself]."[116]

We see here the importance attached by warriors to dying a proper death. What matters most, as Kanehira emphatically points out, is to avoid being killed by somebody "insignificant." Sensitivity to rank and status was a hallmark of warrior society in the ancient and early medieval ages, at least as described in the war tales. At a later time—as in the *sengoku* period—when there was much opportunity for upward mobility among warriors based on individual ability, rank and status came to mean far less.

Here is the *Heike*'s description of how Yoshinaka meets his end:

A lone rider, Yoshinaka headed toward the Pine Woods of Awazu. It was dusk on the twenty-first day of the first month, and the ground was covered with thin ice. When Yoshinaka, not realizing that he was riding into a mud-filled rice field, drove his horse quickly forward, the animal sank into the mud until even its head could not be seen. No matter how much Yoshinaka dug with his spurs and beat with his whip, the horse did not move. Though caught in this quandary, Yoshinaka was anxious to know Kanehira's whereabouts, and turned to look behind him. Just then Ishida no Jirō Tamehisa, following behind, drew an arrow to its fullest and sent it smashing into Yoshinaka's helmet. Mortally wounded, Yoshinaka slumped forward, the front of his helmet striking the horse's neck. Two of Ishida's vassals came up and took his head.[117]

This description of Yoshinaka's end, one of the favorite passages in the *Heike*, has been highly aestheticized to appeal to the tastes of medieval audiences: the lone rider entering the woods; the shadows of dusk gathering and a thin layer of ice on the ground (enhancing the desolation of the setting); a backward glance toward the ever-faithful follower; and the sudden, sickening impact of the arrow, shattering the existence of a mighty chieftain at the height of his manhood.

To give Yoshinaka the chance to enter the woods of Awazu, Kanehira holds off fifty of the enemy single-handedly in an example of the one-against-many type of battle found in the war tales. Against such odds, Kanehira fights like a "berserk warrior," firing arrows furiously and, after exhausting his arrows, slashing with his sword like a man possessed. When he hears Ishida no Tamehisa shout that he has killed Yoshinaka, Kanehira replies with his own shout *(nanori)*: "Observe, you eastern warriors, this model of how the bravest man in Japan kills himself!" Placing the tip of his sword in his mouth, Kanehira leaps over backward from his horse and dies, run through by the sword.[118]

Many of the warriors and other characters in the war tales are stereotypes. Kanehira in the "Death of Kiso" chapter is essentially a stereotype: the ever-faithful follower imbued with the *kenshin* spirit of self-sacrifice for his lord; the berserk warrior capable of inhuman feats of derring-do and prepared to meet a grisly death without a moment's hesitation. Yoshinaka, on the other hand, is revealed in this chapter as a person of distinctly human frailties. He briefly displays what may be faintheartedness when he complains that his armor is too heavy; in his fervent wish to die with Kanehira he shows, in a most human way, the kind of emotional attachment that could govern the feelings of both vassal and lord in a feudal relationship. Yoshinaka's death is surely one of the saddest moments in the *Heike*, because we see in him a person of real, complex sentiments, unlike so many of the characters in the *Heike* and other war tales.[119]

The Taira as Courtier-Warriors: Tadanori

We have noted that one of the *Heike*'s major themes is the transformation of the Ise Taira into courtier-warriors during their years of residence in Kyoto between the Heiji Conflict and the Gempei War. Socializing with courtiers, receiving ever-higher court ranks and titles, acquiring courtly tastes, and learning courtly manners, the Taira came to exemplify the "two ways of the *bun* and the *bu*," the ways of the civil or courtly and of the military. Kiyomori's grandson Koremori, as observed, is probably the most courtier-like—the most *bun*-like—of the Taira in the *Heike*. Appointed to command armies, he has no taste for warfare and is a dismal failure as a general. Faced with the rigors of camp life and the mounting threat of annihilation by the pursing Minamoto after the Taira are driven from Kyoto in 1183 by Yoshinaka, Koremori is overcome with yearning for the capital and for his wife and children who are still there. Finally, he absconds from the Taira camp and commits suicide by drowning.[120]

The best example in the *Heike* of a Taira leader who truly exemplifies both the *bun* and the *bu* is Kiyomori's youngest brother, Tadanori. A stout warrior and reliable leader, Tadanori is called upon time and again to command forces against the Minamoto. He is, in fact, the commander of the Taira force in the western part of the fortress at Ichinotani, where Kumagae no Naozane and Hirayama no Sueshige contend to be first in battle, and is killed attempting to escape after the Taira defeat.

Tadanori was, in reality, a distinguished poet who studied with Fujiwara no Shunzei, one of the leading masters of the age. He earned lasting fame as a poet by the inclusion of sixteen of his poems in *Kin'yōshū* and other imperially authorized anthologies.[121] When the Taira, in the *Heike* account, leave Kyoto in 1183 in sad procession as the army of Yoshinaka bears down on the capital, Tadanori turns back to call for a last time at Shunzei's home. At first, Shunzei's servants will not let him in, but he is admitted when the master himself comes to the door. Tadanori gives Shunzei a scroll with more than a hundred of his poems, imploring the master to consider them for inclusion in the anthology that, Tadanori believes, Shunzei will be commissioned by the court to compile when the country is once again at peace. Reflecting the extraordinary honor attached to the acceptance of poems for an imperially authorized anthology, Tadanori tells Shunzei that he will "feel joy in his grave and from a distance become Shunzei's guardian spirit" if even one of the poems on the scroll is selected for the anthology.[122]

Shunzei was indeed commissioned after the Gempei War to compile an anthology, the *Senzaishū*, which he completed in 1187, and he included in it one of Tadanori's poems. But because Tadanori was then regarded, along with all the Ise Taira, as an "enemy of the court," Shunzei wrote beneath the poem "author unknown."

In the *Heike* version of his death, Tadanori is seen riding away from Ichinotani after the Taira defeat astride a "very big and powerful" horse and proceeding unhurriedly in the company of some one hundred warriors.[123] A Minamoto partisan, Okabe no Tadazumi, spies Tadanori and gallops toward him, demanding that he announce his name. Tadanori tries to deceive Tadazumi by replying that he is an ally, but Tadazumi observes that Tadanori's teeth are blackened in the courtier manner and knows he is a high-ranking Taira. As Tadazumi closes in to grapple with Tadanori, Tadanori's hundred companions, who are temporarily assembled warriors, scatter hastily *(ware saki ni)* in flight.

Tadanori, we are told, possesses enormous strength. After smashing Tadazumi several times with his sword, but not cleanly penetrating armor or helmet, Tadanori seizes his opponent and is about to decapitate him when one of Tadazumi's attendants rushes up and, with a deft slash of his sword, severs Tadanori's right arm. Realizing that his end has come, Tadanori quickly recites prayers to Amida Buddha, beseeching him for rebirth in the Pure Land. As he finishes, Tadazumi, from behind, lops off his head.[124]

Defeat of the hero in battle because of the intervention of one of his opponent's attendants or vassals is a recurrent theme in the *Heike* and other war tales. The old and gallant Saitō no Sanemori, for example, is killed fighting against Tezuka no Mitsumori when Mitsumori's retainer confronts Sanemori to protect his master. Holding the retainer against the pommel of his saddle, Sanemori beheads him; but this gives Mitsumori time to move to Sanemori's weak side (his left side), raise the skirt of his armor *(kusazuri)*, and stab him.[125]

Tadazumi realizes that he has killed a "worthy general" *(yoi tai-shōgun)*, and in examining the body and its armor learns from the signature on a poem attached to the quiver that the general is Taira no Tadanori. Affixing Tadanori's head to the tip of his sword, Tadazumi raises the sword and shouts his victory name-announcing. There are none among friend or foe, we are told, who do not shed tears upon hearing this report about how Tadanori was killed: "How sad! He was a person who excelled in both the military arts and the way of poetry. He is a general who will be sorely missed."[126]

The Taira as Courtier-Warriors: Atsumori

One of the best-loved and most moving stories in the *Heike* is the account of the death—also following the Battle of Ichinotani—of the young Taira general Atsumori at the hands of the Bandō "rough" warrior Kumagae no Naozane. Motivated by the insatiable desire of his breed of warrior to achieve reward for killing worthy enemies, Naozane, after the rout of the Taira from their Ichinotani fortress, heads for the nearby beach, hoping to find a "worthy general" among the Taira attempting to escape on boats moored offshore. The situation at the boats is grim. A number have already sunk, as hordes of heavily armored men attempt to board them, and the decision has been made to allow only "worthy warriors" (*yoki musha*; i.e., warriors of status) on the boats. The lesser warriors are to be driven away with swords and *naginata*, and indeed some, attempting desperately to cling to the boats, have already had their arms chopped off.[127]

From the shore, Naozane sees a warrior astride his horse in the offing whom he readily identifies, by his resplendent armor, as a general. He calls to the warrior, admonishing him for turning his back on an enemy and demanding that he come back to shore. Without hesitation, the warrior (his name is not revealed until later) returns to engage Naozane in combat, but he is quickly unseated and pinned to the ground. When Naozane removes the warrior's helmet to behead him, however, he gazes upon the beautiful face of a youth of sixteen or seventeen, lightly made up and with teeth blackened in the courtier manner.[128] Naozane's reaction to this face is twofold: He is virtually overwhelmed with pity because the warrior's youth and beauty remind him of his own son, Naoie, who is about the same age, and he is struck with awe at the face's elegance and refinement, qualities like those of a courtier.

This is the second usage in the *Heike* of a theme that can be described as that of "the older warrior who encounters a younger warrior and is struck with pity because he is reminded of his son."[129] The theme first appears in Book 7 in the description of the Battle of Shinohara, where the Taira expeditionary force sent against Yoshinaka in 1183 is soundly defeated and begins its flight back to Kyoto. Takahashi no Nagatsuna of the Taira side is pursued by the Minamoto warrior Nyūzen no Yukishige, who appraises Nagatsuna as a worthy foe. But as Yukishige rides alongside Nagatsuna, the latter seizes him and demands that he announce his name. When Yukishige gives his name and says he is eighteen years old, Nagatsuna says: "How pitiful! My son who died last year would this year have been eighteen. I should twist your head off and throw it away, but I will spare you."[130] Nagatsuna says that he would throw the head away because it is of no value to him: He is a commander and Yukishige, as he reveals in his name-announcing, is merely a "resident of Etchū province." Nagatsuna's pity is ill-placed. When he and Yukishige dismount to rest, Yukishige waits until Nagatsuna is offguard and treacherously stabs him. Just then, three of Yukishige's retainers gallop up to help him kill the hapless Nagatsuna.[131]

In the older warrior versus younger warrior confrontation of Kumagae no Naozane and Atsumori we find much more than simply the older warrior taking pity on the younger and wishing to spare him. When he is forced to kill Atsumori because he sees some fifty of his Minamoto allies riding toward them and knows they will show Atsumori no mercy, Naozane, the prototypal Bandō warrior, is literally filled with revulsion for warfare and the profession of killing: "Alas, there is nothing more grievous in life than to be a man of the bow and arrow. If I had not been born into a warrior (bugei) house, surely I would never have had this wretched experience. The agony of having killed him so coldly!"[132] This is the strongest statement in the Heike against the butchery of the martial profession, a statement all the more remarkable because it is delivered by a lesser warrior like Naozane, for whom battle and killing are a way of life. Although not so stated in the Heike, it has traditionally been believed that Naozane, who in the Heike only tells Atsumori that he will conduct memorial services for him, became a Buddhist priest to devote his life to praying for the salvation of Atsumori's soul.[133] Thus, for example, Naozane appears in the Muromachi-period nō play Atsumori as the priest Rensei, who visits the Ichinotani battle site to pray for Atsumori.[134]

Naozane's behavior in the presence of Atsumori, whom he regards as the same as a courtier, impresses us as an affirmation of how courtier-like the Taira, as described in the Heike, have become. It also provides a striking example of the almost reverential way in which an ordinary warrior of this age might speak to a courtier, a person who from his social standpoint is figuratively "above the clouds." In addressing Atsumori, Naozane uses the most respectful language of which classical Japanese is capable—and classical Japanese is a language unusually rich in this capability. Atsumori, on the other hand, speaks to Naozane as a master might speak to a servant. When (as noted in the last chapter in the section "Finding a 'Worthy Foe' ") Atsumori hears Naozane's name-announcing, for example, he curtly replies: "Well, then, there is no need for me to announce my name to someone like you. Let's just say that I'm a worthy foe (a 'good catch') for you."[135]

After Naozane—so distraught and blinded by tears that "he does not know where to strike with his sword"—finally beheads Atsumori, he discovers, attached to Atsumori's waist, a brocade pouch containing a flute. With a great sense of pity ("*Ana itoshi!*"), Naozane realizes that it must have been Atsumori whom he heard playing the flute in the Taira fortress at dawn that morning. He observes that not one among the "ten thousand riders" of the army of eastern warriors to which he belongs was likely to bring a flute to camp before a battle. In admiration he exclaims: "These lofty people [the Taira] are truly men of refinement!"[136] Here, in the words of Kumagae no Naozane, is perhaps the most telling characterization in the *Heike* of the Taira as courtier-warriors.

Although he appears only in this single chapter of the *Heike* and speaks barely a few sentences, Atsumori is one of the work's more memorable characters. With his beauty, his elegance, and his refined accomplishment as a flutist, he is a fitting symbol of the Ise Taira as surrogates for the courtiers who are losing out as a ruling elite to provincial warriors in the tumultuous transition to the medieval age. We sense that Atsumori, even allowing for his youth, is probably not physically powerful: He certainly is no match for the rugged Naozane.[137] Yet, in turning back after hearing Naozane's shouted challenge from the shore, Atsumori displays an uncommon gallantry. The *Heike* is full of brave—sometimes insanely brave—acts by warriors in battle. But few elicit our admiration as does Atsumori's, largely because it is truly a *beau geste*, a noble but meaningless gesture, as though a courtier had symbolically sacrificed himself to a fierce warrior as the warrior was about to overrun his world.

The Warrior as Prisoner: Shigehira

There is no clearly identifiable code in the war tales for the treatment of prisoners. In most cases, prisoners are simply executed and their heads added to those taken in battle for display in the traditional inspection of heads. Prominent prisoners, however, are often detained and subjected to public disgrace before execution. Among the prisoners taken in the *Heike*, Shigehira, the only Taira commander captured at the Battle of Ichinotani, endures the most prolonged captivity before his execution.

A son of Kiyomori, Shigehira was in historical fact one of the ablest of the Taira commanders, although we get little sense of this in reading the *Heike*. One reason, as Uwayokote Masataka points out, is that the *Heike* says little about Taira victories during the Gempei War, instead focusing on the battlefield superiority of the Minamoto and making the ultimate Minamoto triumph appear more one-sided than it was.[138] Some of Shigehira's victories are not even mentioned in the *Heike;* some are credited to other Taira commanders.

Shigehira becomes the most hated of the Taira leaders, save Kiyomori, when early in the Gempei War (1180:12) he is accused of destroying two of Japan's most venerable Buddhist temples, Tōdaiji and Kōfukuji of Nara. To people living in the age of *mappō* and the Gempei War, the burning of these temples—one patronized by the imperial family, the other by the Fujiwara—appeared to symbolize the destruction of Japanese civilization itself. The *Heike* account of the temple burnings, for example, cites a document supposedly written by Emperor Shōmu, builder of Tōdaiji during the Nara period: "If my temple prospers, the realm will also prosper; if my temple declines, the realm will decline." The *Heike*'s author gloomily observes: "Thus it seemed that the realm was assuredly doomed to decline."[139]

Hostility between the Nara temples and the Taira arises in the *Heike* when the temples support Prince Mochihito and Minamoto no Yorimasa in the uprising against the Taira in the fourth and fifth months of 1180 that leads to the Gempei War. Although the Taira readily suppress the rising, Kiyomori resolves to assert control over the Tōdaiji and Kōfukuji monks. According to the *Heike,* Kiyomori wishes to do this while avoiding an armed conflict. But when he sends a force of five hundred riders without armor or bows and arrows to Nara, the ferocious monks—fighting monks of the kind called *akusō* (rowdy monks), who were employed by the leading temples of the central provinces during the Heian period—capture and decapitate sixty of the riders. Outraged, Kiyomori dispatches Shigehira with a real army to bring the monks to heel.[140]

Helmeted and armed, the monks join battle with Shigehira's army. The *Heike* description of this battle, like so many of its other combat accounts, is high in excitement and drama—a monk with spear in one hand and oversized sword in the other keeps scores of Taira horsemen at bay, for example—but not very clear about the tactics of the battle or the precise progress of the fighting. Shigehira, we are told, has an army of forty thousand horsemen and the monks number only seven thousand, all on foot. Although the monks have the advantage of defense works they have constructed, the battle soon becomes a melee and the monks are "chased in all directions." This would appear to signal the end of the fighting; but in fact the battle, which began at eight in the morning, continues to rage until nightfall.[141]

In the darkness of night, Shigehira calls for a fire to illuminate the battlefield. One of his followers torches a peasant's house and the flames, fanned by a fierce wind, rapidly spread to the buildings of Tōdaiji and Kōfukuji, burning both temples to the ground. More than thirty-five hundred people, having sought refuge in the temples, are killed in the blaze.[142]

There are other examples in the *Heike* of the deliberate and wanton burning of peasants' homes, often to provide illumination at night. That this was a common practice, in the Gempei age at least, is suggested by a remark of Minamoto no Yoshitsune during a night attack on a Taira force just before the Battle of Ichinotani. When asked by his men what to do about the dark conditions as they prepare to attack, Yoshitsune suggests: "How about lighting big torches in the usual way?" His men thereupon set fire not only to some peasants' homes, but also to grass and trees in the fields and hills nearby, making the night "bright as day."[143]

A number of scholars have observed that the *Heike*, at least half of which is devoted to battling in the Gempei War, conveys little sense of the real horror and brutality of warfare.[144] The work, of course, contains many descriptions of the slaughter of warriors and others during and after battles. But the descriptions are not graphic. A warrior is stabbed to death, another is captured and decapitated—there are few references to the personal agonies or bloodiness that must inevitably have accompanied these killings. The account of the burning of Tōdaiji and Kōfukuji during the battle between Shigehira's army and the monks of Nara is unusual for its vivid recreation of the terror and tragedy of the event: not only the loss of ancient and priceless temple buildings and treasures, but also the incineration of "aged monks unable to walk, eminent scholar-monks, pages, women, and children" who seek shelter in the temples and whose "shrieks . . . could not have been surpassed by the sinners in the flames . . . of hell."[145]

There is no indication in the *Heike* that Shigehira intended to burn the Nara temples. But having given the order to start a fire, he bore responsibility for its spread to the temple buildings.[146] Public opinion indelibly branded him an enemy of Buddhism and of the state, an enemy whose heinous crime could never be fully expiated.

Shigehira's capture after Ichinotani results from the treachery of a cowardly vassal. Few of the warriors identified by name in the *Heike* are cowards. We do find frequent conventionally phrased descriptions of the troops of routed armies vying one with another—"Me first! Me first" (*ware saki ni, ware saki ni*)—to flee the field of battle, having abandoned all sense of dignity and pride. But the great majority of the warriors who appear as individual fighting men in the *Heike* bear themselves well—sometimes with notable or even extraordinary brav-

ery—in the Gempei battles. Shigehira has the misfortune to be paired
with a truly craven warrior, identified as his foster brother Morinaga,
when he attempts to escape from Ichinotani. As the two men ride away
from the Ichinotani fortress, Shigehira's horse is wounded by an arrow
—a lucky shot fired from a considerable distance. Morinaga, pretend-
ing not to hear Shigehira's shouts for assistance and apparently fearful
that his horse will be commandeered, discards the identifying insignia
on his armor and rides away as rapidly as possible. People later speak of
him as a truly shameless fellow.[147]

In captivity, Shigehira is transformed into a courtier, revealing
the other side of the warrior-courtier duality of character that he shares
with many other Taira in the *Heike*. After being paraded through the
streets of Kyoto in an open carriage past gaping crowds, Shigehira is
placed under guard in the chapel of a courtier. His guards treat him
decorously, even deferentially; he is allowed to send messages, including one to his wife and another to a court lady who is his mistress. His
words to the mistress and hers in return are elegant and graceful, inter-
spersed with lyrical expressions of undying love. The two are even
allowed a brief meeting, from which they reluctantly part with tearful
verses comparing their lives to dewdrops. When the mistress later
learns of Shigehira's death, she cuts her hair and becomes a nun to pray
for his enlightenment.[148] She is one of a host of women in the *Heike*—
some of them prominent characters; others, like her, merely fleeting
figures—who, for love of their warrior men, either commit suicide
(usually by drowning) or embrace religion to pray for the warriors'
souls after their deaths.

Shigehira is persuaded by the retired emperor Goshirakawa to
appeal to his brother Munemori and the Taira at Yashima to exchange
the imperial regalia (mirror, sword, and jewel)—which the Taira took
as symbols of Emperor Antoku's sovereignty when they fled Kyoto in
1183—for Shigehira's life.[149] Despite the anguished pleas of Shigehira's
mother (Kiyomori's widow) that he be saved at all costs, Munemori
rejects Goshirakawa's scheme, suspecting, on the one hand, that Shigehira might still be executed even if the sacred objects are relin-
quished and acutely aware, on the other hand, that without the regalia
Antoku would cease to be emperor and the Taira cause would be
lost.[150] Throughout the Gempei War as it is reported in the *Heike*,
Goshirakawa, at best an indistinct figure in the book's plot, makes
repeated attempts to regain the regalia, thus highlighting the immense
symbolic importance attached to these objects in the Imperial Law
thinking that, as observed earlier in this chapter, is one of the philo-
sophical foundations of the *Heike*.

Informed of the failure of his appeal to Yashima, Shigehira turns his thoughts to religious salvation. As so many Taira (but no Minamoto) do in the *Heike* when faced with death,[151] he seeks assurance of rebirth in Amida Buddha's Pure Land paradise. Refused permission to become a monk, he receives instruction in the commandments from Hōnen, the founder of Pure Land Buddhism.

Shigehira is sent to Kamakura, where he has an audience with Yoritomo. The reason for this trip is unclear, although it may simply have been intended to satisfy the curiosity of Yoritomo, who questions Shigehira about his "heinous crime" in burning the Nara temples.[152] The *Heike*'s authors use the trip, during which Shigehira is treated with extreme courtesy and consideration, to further emphasize his courtliness. We find Shigehira, for example, responding with sensitive awareness and appropriate verses to the trip's famous sites; and in Kamakura he charms everyone with his lute playing and chanting, eliciting from Yoritomo himself the observation that "he is the most cultivated of men."[153] Shigehira has a brief affair with a girl, Senju-no-mae, assigned to serve him and she becomes another of the *Heike*'s victims of love for warriors: Upon learning later of Shigehira's execution, Senju-no-mae, like the court lady mentioned earlier, takes holy vows and devotes the remainder of her life to praying for him.[154]

Shigehira is finally executed in 1185, after the destruction of the Ise Taira at the Battle of Dannoura. He is given to the Tōdaiji and Kōfukuji monks, but some of the monks suggest such barbaric methods of execution—sawing off his head, for example, or burying him alive—that their superiors decide it is wiser to return him to the Minamoto. Shigehira is decapitated by his warrior captors at a riverbank in Nara as he intones prayers to Amida, and his head is nailed to the Shinto gateway *(torii)* near where he purportedly stood when Tōdaiji and Kōfukuji burned. His wife, who was sorely neglected while Shigehira dallied with various mistresses, later manages to retrieve both his head and corpse and to have them properly cremated. This admirable woman, like the two mistresses discussed, then becomes a Buddhist nun to pray for Shigehira's soul.[155]

Heiji Conflict. Warriors raiding and burning Sanjō Palace. Slightly to the left of bottom center, warriors are beheading a courtier. At bottom right, a warrior attendant, wearing cheek protectors and the corselet and skirt of a suit of armor, brandishes a *naginata* as he pursues a courtier during the raid upon and burning of Sanjō Palace. "Illustrated Scrolls of the Tale of Heiji." Fenollosa-Weld Collection. Courtesy of the Museum of Fine Arts, Boston.

Later Three Years War. Warriors attacking soldiers hiding in a field of grass who have revealed their presence by disturbing a flock of geese. Damage to this mid-fourteenth-century scroll makes some of the figures indistinct. The head and upper torso of one of the hiding soldiers can be seen below the front portion of the horse at center. "Picture Scroll of the Later Three Years War" *(Gosannen Kassen Ekotoba)*. Collection of the Tokyo National Museum.

同寅刻〻信西ゟ婦小路西洞院乃常而退補
志く火を放川これ三四耳八参伎禁制なと
あっそ天下静謐あり〇〻、をれ天〻る乱む
弟く禁中〻宣中兵軍兵〻こ〻くたを〻こ
ちつ〻〻なつまね〻〻ふりと貴賤〻ふ〻三あつり

Heiji Conflict. Lead rider and attendant of the procession escorting former emperor Goshirakawa from the burning Sanjō Palace. "Illustrated Scrolls of the Tale of Heiji." Fenollosa-Weld Collection. Courtesy of the Museum of Fine Arts, Boston.

Heiji Conflict. Procession escorting former emperor Goshirakawa away from Sanjō Palace after the burning of the palace. "Illustrated Scrolls of the Tale of Heiji." Fenollosa-Weld Collection. Courtesy of the Museum of Fine Arts, Boston.

Gempei War. Warriors fighting during the Battle of Ichinot. From a seventeenth-century six-panel screen. The Metrop tan Museum of Art. Gift of General and Mrs. Hugh J. Ca 1960.

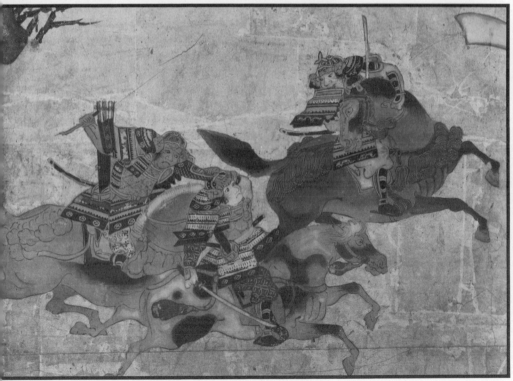

Gempei War. Yoshitsune and his band (top center) prepare to descend Hiyodorigoe Cliff during the Battle of Ichinotani. Below them is the Taira fortress with a watchtower manned by archers. The deer sent by Yoshitsune
to test the feasibility of descending the cliff can be seen to the left of the
watchtower. From a seventeenth-century six-panel screen. The Metropolitan Museum of Art. Gift of General and Mrs. Hugh J. Casey, 1960.

Gempei War. Kumagae no Naozane beckons to Atsumori with a fan to
return and fight as Atsumori attempts to escape after the Battle of Ichinotani. (*Heike Monogatari* does not mention the fan.) At bottom, a boat has
overturned after heavily armored Taira warriors have tried to board it.
From a seventeenth-century six-panel screen. The Metropolitan Museum
of Art. Gift of General and Mrs. Hugh J. Casey, 1960.

Three men string a bow (center) as another tests an already strung bow
(upper right). Shields, propped on their folding legs, can be seen at lower
right. "Picture Scrolls of Obusama Saburō" *(Obusama Saburō Ekotoba).*
Collection of the Tokyo National Museum.

Warfare leading to the Kemmu Restoration. The army of
Ashikaga Takauji, having marched from Kamakura to quell
the loyalist uprising in 1333, moves through a mountain
pass in the central provinces in preparation for joining the
loyalists and attacking the Rokuhara magistrates in Kyoto.
"Illustrated Scrolls of *Taiheiki.*" New York Public Library,
Spencer Collection.

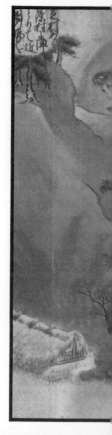

Warfare leading to the Kemmu Restoration. Battling of the Ashikaga and other loyalists against the forces of the Rokuhara magistrates in Kyoto in 1333. At upper left a courtier or court lady is being transported to safety in a palanquin as agitated townspeople rush about. At right is the grisly scene of a warrior who, having pulled a young enemy from his horse and severed his legs, is about to cast the remainder of his body aside. "Illustrated Scrolls of *Taiheiki*." New York Public Library, Spencer Collection.

4
YOSHITSUNE

Yoshitsune in History: To the End of the Gempei War

No hero in the war tales has been more dearly loved by readers and audiences over the centuries than Minamoto no Yoshitsune, who has also been regarded both in history and in the popular imagination as one of Japan's most brilliant field commanders. Yet this lofty reputation as a commander is based on a surprisingly brief career: a series of one-day battles fought over a period of about fifteen months during the Gempei War from the first month of 1184 until the third month of 1185. Chief among these battles were the destruction of Minamoto no Yoshinaka in 1184:1, the Battle of Ichinotani against the Ise Taira a few weeks later in 1184:2, and the battles of Yashima and Dannoura in the second and third months of 1185, which brought the annihilation of the Taira and the end of the war. Although Yoshitsune's battles spanned fifteen months, they were actually concentrated in two much shorter periods: two weeks in early 1184 (from the twenty-seventh of the first month through the seventh of the second month) and five weeks in 1185 (from the nineteenth of the second month through the twenty-fourth of the third month).

Meeting with Yoritomo

Our knowledge of Yoshitsune before the Gempei War is limited almost entirely to an entry in *Azuma Kagami* describing how he appeared, unexpected and unheralded, in the camp of his half-brother Minamoto no Yoritomo at Kisegawa in Suruga province on 1180:10:21, two months after the Gempei War began and only a day after the Battle of Fuji River, when the Taira expeditionary force invading the Kantō fled from Yoritomo's army without fighting:

126

Today a young man stood in front of the residence of the Lord of Kamakura [Yoritomo], requesting to see His Lordship. Doi no Sanehira, Tsuchiya no Munetō, Okazaki no Yoshizane, and others were suspicious and refused to inform Yoritomo. But as time passed, Yoritomo learned of the visitor's presence. Judging from the visitor's age, Yoritomo guessed that he might be Kurō [Yoshitsune] of Ōshū [Mutsu province] and ordered that he be brought to him immediately. Accordingly, Sanehira spoke to the visitor and found that indeed it was Yoshitsune. Yoshitsune was thereupon promptly brought before Yoritomo, and together the two reminisced about the past, shedding tears over thoughts of the old days. Yoritomo spoke with feeling about the time in 1083:9, during the reign of Emperor Shirakawa, when their great grandfather, the governor of Mutsu Minamoto no Yoshiie, fought the generals Kiyowara no Saburō Takehira, Kiyowara no Shirō Iehira, and others in Ōshū. At the time, Yoshiie's brother Saemon-no-jō Yoshimitsu was in Kyoto. Learning about the fighting in the north, Yoshimitsu resigned his position as guard at court and, submitting his bag of bowstrings to the court [as a sign of resignation], secretly went down to Ōshū. When Yoshimitsu added his army to his brother's, together they promptly destroyed the enemy. Yoritomo observed with sincere thanks that the present arrival of his brother was in keeping with this splendid precedent of a century earlier. This lord Yoshitsune was born in 1160:1, and while still in swaddling lost his father Yoshitomo. Later, with the aid of his stepfather, Ichijō Ōkura-no-kyō no Naganari, he entered the Buddhist priesthood at Kurama Temple. Upon reaching adulthood, he thought constantly of avenging his father's death. Conducting his own coming-of-age ceremony and putting his trust in the mighty power of Fujiwara no Hidehira, he went down to Ōshū. Years passed, and upon learning of the opportunity to fulfill his long-standing wish as a warrior, he expressed the desire to Hidehira to set out to join Yoritomo. When Hidehira sought forcibly to prevent his departure, Yoshitsune secretly left Hidehira's residence and started on the road. Hidehira thereupon relented and, following after Yoshitsune, directed the stout warriors Satō no Tsuginobu and his brother Tadanobu to accompany and serve him.[1]

We are told in this *Azuma Kagami* account that Yoshitsune was barely a month old in 1160 when his father, Minamoto no Yoshitomo, was killed in the aftermath of the Heiji Conflict. Yoshitsune's mother, the court beauty Tokiwa, remarried, this time to Ichijō no Naganari. When Yoshitsune was about eleven, Naganari arranged to have him enter Kurama Temple to study for the Buddhist priesthood. About five years later, Yoshitsune left the temple and made his way to Mutsu province, where he was taken in by Fujiwara no Hidehira, scion of the family whose leaders had presided as virtually independent territorial barons in northern Honshu for a century following the Later Three Years War.

Historians have questioned the historicity of this *Azuma Kagami* account, but most appear willing to accept as true its principal points about Yoshitsune's early life: that he spent some five years at Kurama Temple and then went to Hiraizumi, where he lived with Fujiwara no Hidehira until departing to join Yoritomo in 1181.[2] According to the legends that later developed around Yoshitsune's life, the young Minamoto lord made his way to Hiraizumi in the company of a gold merchant. Watanabe Tamotsu, noting that there was a flourishing trade between Kyoto and Hiraizumi in the late twelfth century, suggests that Yoshitsune may very well have been guided to the north by a traveling merchant.[3] But why, if Yoshitsune did go to Hiraizumi, was Hidehira willing to take him in? Hidehira and his predecessors, as leaders of the northern Fujiwara, had consistently followed an isolationist policy, zealously protecting their Mutsu satrapy and avoiding involvement in the politics of the rest of Japan.[4] By extending patronage to Yoshitsune, Hidehira ran the risk of being drawn into the still unresolved competition for warrior supremacy between the Ise Taira and the Kawachi Minamoto.

The description of the meeting between Yoshitsune and Yoritomo at Kisegawa raises another puzzling question. When Yoshitsune arrived at Yoritomo's camp he was presumably accompanied by the Satō brothers from Hiraizumi. But there is no reference to any other warrior followers in his company. If Yoshitsune, in fact, had no other followers—no warrior band of his own—why would Yoritomo have likened his coming to the arrival of Yoshimitsu in Mutsu during the Later Three Years War? Yoshimitsu and his army, after all, provided the additional force that enabled Yoshiie to win the war.

We have no way of knowing what Yoritomo really thought about Yoshitsune when he appeared in 1180. It seems likely that he did not regard him as a major contribution to the war effort against the Taira since, so far as we know, he did not give Yoshitsune a battle assignment for more than a year. (One can also argue that Yoritomo failed to use Yoshitsune against the Taira during this time because he was not conducting a "war effort" against them—that is, he was devoting all his attention to asserting his hegemony over the Kantō.)

In the eleventh month of 1181 Yoshitsune was ordered, along with four other commanders (Ashikaga no Yoshikane, Doi no Sanehira, Tsuchiya no Munetō, and Wada no Yoshimori), to lead a Minamoto army westward to engage a Taira expedition under Koremori headed for the Kantō. As it happened, the Taira expedition showed no intention of proceeding beyond Ōmi province; hence Yoritomo canceled the order for departure of the Minamoto army.[5]

The Destruction of Yoshinaka

Yoshitsune did not enter the Gempei War until the attack on Yoshinaka in Kyoto in the first month of 1184, more than three years after he joined Yoritomo. Late in 1183, Yoshitsune and Nakahara no Chikayoshi led a contingent of several hundred riders to the central provinces to conduct reconnaissance in preparation for the attack. In 1184:1 Yoshitsune's half-brother Noriyori brought a Minamoto army from Kamakura, and with Yoshitsune as co-commander, this army routed and destroyed Yoshinaka. Although Yoshitsune and Noriyori shared the command against Yoshinaka, the operation was widely regarded as Yoshitsune's victory.[6] It was, in fact, a victory that marked the first step in Yoshitsune's rise to fame as a military leader.

As an indication of how little known Yoshitsune was at the time of the attack upon Yoshinaka, the courtier Kujō no Kanezane, writing in his diary, *Gyokuyō*, about the advance of the Minamoto army on Kyoto, refers to one of the army's commanders as "Yoritomo's younger brother Kurō (I don't know his proper name [*jitsumyō*])."[7] Yoshitsune burst onto the scene of the Gempei War like a meteor, his proper name soon to be on everyone's lips.

The Battle of Ichinotani

Having destroyed Yoshinaka, Yoshitsune and Noriyori immediately turned their attention to the Taira. The recent conflict between competing branches of the Minamoto, headed by Yoritomo and Yoshinaka, had provided the Taira with the opportunity to renew their strength and plan a campaign to reoccupy Kyoto. In preparation for this campaign, the Taira had established themselves at Fukuhara, a port on the Inland Sea near present-day Kobe that had long been a Taira base and had even been the imperial capital briefly in 1180.[8] The extensive Taira fortification at Fukuhara became the site of what is known in history as the Battle of Ichinotani, although Ichinotani was only one of several nearby locales where the fighting took place.

Yoshitsune and Noriyori departed Kyoto for Ichinotani within a week after their victory over Yoshinaka. There is no evidence that the decision to attack Ichinotani so quickly was made by Yoshitsune, although such a decision certainly accorded with his liking as a commander for rapid movement and sudden strikes. In any case, the Minamoto won at Ichinotani when, as mentioned in the last chapter,

Yoshitsune led a daring attack down Hiyodorigoe Cliff to fall upon the Taira from the rear (the mountainous north) while the Taira were defending against the main Minamoto assaults from the east (at Ikuta-no-mori) and the west (Ichinotani). Routed, the remnants of the Taira force escaped mainly on ships moored in readiness offshore from Ichi-notani.

Completely overshadowing Noriyori, Yoshitsune returned to Kyoto a conquering hero. There he remained for nearly a year before receiving another assignment from Yoritomo to reenter the war against the Taira. Historians have long wondered why Yoritomo did not direct a Minamoto force—whether commanded by Yoshitsune or someone else—to pursue the Taira immediately after Ichinotani, when they were in disarray and on the run. Not until 1184:8:8, half a year after the Ichinotani fighting, did Yoritomo again move against the Taira, this time bestowing upon Noriyori a commission as subjugator (tsuitōshi) with directions to proceed from Kamakura to Kyushu and destroy the Taira support on that western island.[9] But Noriyori, complaining about a shortage of ships, horses, and other supplies, became bogged down attempting to cross from Honshu to Kyushu.[10] Noriyori's failure in this Kyushu campaign has contributed to the belief that he was a mediocre if not inferior commander.

Why did Yoritomo not use Yoshitsune, by then a proven leader and winner in battle, instead of Noriyori? It is possible that Yoritomo deliberately held Yoshitsune in reserve with the thought of sending him against the main Taira force, which had by this time established itself at Yashima Island off the coast of Shikoku, after Noriyori eliminated Kyushu as a principal source for Taira support throughout the Inland Sea. But it also appears that the long delay in giving Yoshitsune another battle assignment stemmed at least in part from personal estrangement between Yoritomo and Yoshitsune that first surfaced after Ichinotani but may have had its origins earlier.

There is not enough information in the sources to determine precisely when Yoritomo began to look unfavorably upon Yoshitsune— much less perceive him, as he came to perceive him, as a threat to himself and his rule that had to be physically eliminated. According to the sources, Yoritomo's distress with Yoshitsune either stemmed from or was first brought to light in the matter of rewards given to the victors after Ichinotani. On 1184:6:20 Yoritomo issued a rewards list bestowing the title of governor of Mikawa on Noriyori but omitting mention of Yoshitsune.[11] This was startling because Yoshitsune was widely regarded as the leader most responsible for the destruction of Yoshinaka and the victory at Ichinotani. Yoshitsune himself, according to *Azuma Kagami*, was greatly displeased at not being given a court appointment.[12] As though to rectify Yoritomo's oversight, the retired emperor Goshirakawa in the eighth month gave Yoshitsune two court positions: one in the Imperial Guards (the position of *saemon-no-shōjō*) and the other in the Bureau of Metropolitan Police *(kebiishi-chō)*, which provided Yoshitsune with the title *hōgan* (lieutenant).[13] This title later became famous in Yoshitsune lore because of the concept, first enunciated in the Tokugawa period,[14] of *hōgan biiki*, "sympathy for the underdog" (literally, "sympathy for the lieutenant [who is an underdog]").

Why Goshirakawa bestowed these court positions on Yoshitsune remains unknown. Notorious as a political schemer, Goshirakawa may have hoped to foment trouble between Yoshitsune and Yoritomo, who had an iron rule against vassals accepting appointments from the court without his approval; or he may simply have wished personally to reward Yoshitsune, whom he apparently greatly favored. Yoshitsune claimed that he found it impossible to refuse appointments from such an exalted personage as the retired emperor, but this did not appease Yoritomo, whose anger was great. *Azuma Kagami,* reporting on the matter, says: "This is not the first time Yoshitsune has opposed His Lordship's will."[15]

Yashima and Dannoura

Yoshitsune was not given a new command assignment by Yori-tomo until the first month of 1185, when he was ordered to lead a Minamoto force to attack the Taira at their main base on Yashima Island. Moving with his customary speed and braving powerful winds, Yoshitsune, with five ships and a band of selected warriors, crossed from Honshu to Shikoku in about a day on a trip that normally took three days. Marching rapidly to Yashima, Yoshitsune destroyed the camp of the Taira who, duped into believing that Yoshitsune was approaching with a much larger force than theirs, took to their boats and headed for the sea. Four hundred boats carrying the remainder of the force Yoshitsune led from Kyoto did not reach Yashima until after the Taira were driven from their encampment and after Yoshitsune, leading eighty warriors two days later, defeated a contingent of Taira, apparently intent upon reoccupying Yashima, in a battle at nearby Shido Bay.

A month after Yashima, Yoshitsune decisively defeated the Ise Taira at the naval battle of Dannoura in the waters between Honshu and Kyushu, thus ending the Gempei War. All the Taira leaders not killed in earlier battles either lost their lives at Dannoura or were captured.

Although Dannoura is one of the most famous battles in Japanese history, we actually know little about it. How, for example, were the Minamoto under Yoshitsune able to achieve such a great triumph over the Taira in a region where the Taira had long had one of their principal bases of support and in a style of battle—on the sea—in which the Taira supposedly excelled? Beyond a few hints, the records provide no answer to this question.[16] Apparently, during the month between Yashima and Dannoura, Yoshitsune was able to recruit a substantial fleet of boats and the personnel to man them from warrior families in the region of the Inland Sea. Very likely many of the families that supported Yoshitsune at this time were Taira adherents who decided to defect to the Minamoto after Yashima. Unlike Noriyori, who in late 1184 and early 1185 tried unsuccessfully to invade Kyushu with an army comprising predominantly eastern, land-based warriors, Yoshitsune evidently chose to confront the Taira at Dannoura with their own kind and at their own game. His success in doing so was another measure of his genius as a commander.

One of the saddest results of the Taira defeat at Dannoura was the drowning of the child emperor, Antoku. According to *Azuma Kagami*, a Taira woman took Antoku in her arms and leaped into the sea. Kiyomori's widow, Taira no Tokiko, also threw herself into the sea.[17] She clutched the sacred sword, one of the three imperial regalia, which was never recovered.

Yoshitsune in *Heike Monogatari:*
To the End of the Gempei War
The Battle of Ichinotani

Although Yoshitsune was co-commander with Noriyori in the Minamoto attack on Kyoto that led to the defeat and death of Yoshinaka and the destruction of his army in 1184:1, we learn little from the *Heike* account of this attack about Yoshitsune's qualities as a warrior leader. The one glimpse we get of the daring, dashing Yoshitsune of battles to come is in his decision, upon the advice of a follower, to promptly forge the Uji River, whose bridge has been destroyed by the Taira, rather than waiting for the river's swift current to subside or circling around and attempting to approach Kyoto from the west.[18] This decision provides the occasion for the celebrated competition between Sasaki no Takatsuna and Kajiwara no Kagesue, described in the last chapter, to be first to cross the Uji.

Although widely praised for his victory over Yoshinaka, Yoshitsune, as portrayed in the *Heike*, does not display his true brilliance as a commander until he makes his surprise attack down Hiyodorigoe

Cliff to rout the Taira at the Battle of Ichinotani. The plan at Ichinotani, as noted in the last chapter, was for Noriyori to lead the Minamoto frontal assault force *(ōte)* of fifty thousand riders in an attack on
Ikuta-no-mori, the eastern approach to the Taira fortification at Ichinotani. Simultaneously, Yoshitsune was to lead the rear assault force
(karamete) of ten thousand riders against the western (Ichinotani)
entrance to the fortification.

One distinctive attribute of Yoshitsune as commander in the
Heike is his practice of seeking the advice of followers—sometimes a
selected follower or followers, at other times his followers as a whole—
about strategy and battle tactics. In each case, Yoshitsune accepts
advice that is daring and direct. We have just observed, for example,
his decision, upon a follower's recommendation, to forge the Uji River
to make a rapid entry into Kyoto against Yoshinaka rather than waiting
cautiously for the turbulent Uji to subside or circling around to
approach the capital from the west.

When he encounters a Taira contingent at Mikusa as he leads the
rear assault force toward Ichinotani, Yoshitsune again turns to his followers for advice, asking whether they should attack the enemy at
night, while they are bivouacking and off guard, or wait until morning.
The advice, accepted by Yoshitsune, is to attack immediately.[19] This is
the occasion, discussed in the section "The Warrior as Prisoner: Shigehira" in Chapter 3, when Yoshitsune suggests "lighting the big torches
in the usual way" (that is, setting fire to peasants' houses) in order to
provide nighttime illumination.

After defeating the Taira at Mikusa by this unexpected night
attack, Yoshitsune divides the rear assault force into two groups,
assigning the bulk of the riders to Doi no Sanehira and taking the
remainder himself for the descent upon the Ichinotani fortress from
Hiyodorigoe Cliff. The *Heike* says that Yoshitsune gave seven thousand riders to Sanehira and kept three thousand. But most of the troop
figures in the *Heike*—as in other war tales—are notoriously inflated.
The historically more reliable *Azuma Kagami* states that Yoshitsune
had about seventy riders under his command when he descended Hiyodorigoe Cliff. In view of the nature of the terrain at Hiyodorigoe—
Azuma Kagami observes that it was thought to be traversable only by
boars, deer, rabbits, and foxes—seventy sounds like a much more plausible figure.[20]

Proceeding toward Hiyodorigoe Cliff at Ichinotani, Yoshitsune
once again seeks advice from his followers, this time inquiring about
how to find the way to the cliff. Beppu no Kiyoshige of Musashi province, quoting an old adage of his father's, suggests that the best way to

cross unfamiliar, mountainous terrain is to throw the reins over the neck of an old horse and follow him. Yoshitsune agrees with this advice, and he and his band continue on, following an old horse.[21] But later another follower, Musashibō Benkei, brings a man of the region to Yoshitsune to act as a guide. When the man, a hunter, protests that he is too old to undertake a rigorous march, Yoshitsune recruits his son, Washinoo no Yoshihisa, as guide. The *Heike*, informing us that Yoshihisa will become one of Yoshitsune's most devoted followers, observes that "when Yoshitsune died in Ōshū . . . Yoshihisa perished at his side."[22]

These passages about Yoshitsune's progress toward Ichinotani provide us with important new information about the kind of commander he is and who his followers are. Whereas virtually all other chieftains in the *Heike* operate as rear-echelon commanders, Yoshitsune is always found with his men, personally leading them into battle.[23] We picture him most vividly—as at Ichinotani and, later, Yashima—at the head of a small band of fighters, chosen for their personal loyalty to him, moving with great speed and decisiveness and taking full advantage of surprise.

In the march to Ichinotani we encounter for the first time the names of warriors, including Musashibō Benkei and Washinoo no Yoshihisa, who are (or become) members of Yoshitsune's personal band. Others of the band are the Satō brothers, Tsuginobu and Tadanobu, who the *Azuma Kagami* says were assigned to Yoshitsune by Fujiwara no Hidehira of Hiraizumi, and Ise no Saburō Yoshimori.

No other commander in the *Heike* has such an odd and socially inferior assortment of followers. For example, Musashibō Benkei—who, in the legends that grew about Yoshitsune after his death (as found primarily in *Gikeiki*, "The Chronicle of Yoshitsune"), becomes Yoshitsune's foremost follower and a hero almost the equal of his master—is a mere monk. Washinoo no Yoshihisa is the son of a hunter, and Ise no Yoshimori may even have been an outlaw.

Benkei plays only a slight role in the *Heike*. Apart from the reference, just noticed, to his introducing the hunter to Yoshitsune, he appears in only a few other places in the *Heike*, and then simply in listings of Yoshitsune's followers.[24] Ise no Yoshimori, on the other hand, emerges as Yoshitsune's principal adviser and confidante, especially at the Battle of Yashima, discussed in the next section of this chapter. Allusions to Yoshimori's apparently disreputable background—and also to Yoshitsune's background—appear in the *Heike* when, just before commencement of the Yashima fight, Yoshimori exchanges insults in a war of words with one of the enemy on the Taira side,

Etchū no Moritsugi. Moritsugi disparagingly refers to Yoshitsune as "the lad who served as a page at Kurama Temple and later became the lackey of a gold merchant, managing to get to Ōshū carrying provisions for the merchant on his back." Moritsugi claims he has heard that Yoshimori "supports his family and manages to get by as a mountain bandit *(yamadachi, sanzoku)* in the Suzuka Mountains in Ise."[25]

There is no doubt that Yoshimori was a real person, for his name appears in such historically reliable sources as *Gyokuyō* and *Gukan-shō*. Yet these sources do not explain how Yoshitsune became associated with Yoshimori or with most of the other men of low social standing who became his close followers. One possible answer to this question can be found in a letter Yoshitsune wrote—the Koshigoe Letter—when, after final defeat of the Ise Taira in 1185, he became dangerously estranged from Yoritomo. The letter, which appears in almost identical form in both *Azuma Kagami* and the *Heike* and will be examined more fully later in this chapter, was written as a plea for reconciliation with Yoritomo. Yoshitsune refers to his life after leaving Kurama Temple as a time of "wandering through the provinces, hiding myself here and there, making distant places and provinces my home, and following the orders of local people and peasants."[26] This statement seems at variance with the passages already noted in *Azuma Kagami* and the *Heike* about Yoshitsune traveling with a gold merchant to Ōshū after leaving Kurama Temple. Yet both versions of the post-Kurama experiences—traveling with the gold merchant or wandering (presumably alone) through the provinces—suggest extensive contact with commoners of a kind that few warriors of Yoshitsune's eminent lineage were likely to have had. We may speculate that Yoshitsune formed ties with most of his peculiar band of followers during this time in the provinces.[27]

Some commentators, studying the battle tactics of the Yoshitsune band in the *Heike*, have described its members as guerrilla fighters.[28] This is a suggestive characterization, especially in regard to the Battle of Ichinotani, where Yoshitsune and his men strike with the suddenness, surprise, and fierceness of guerrillas in their attack down Hiyodorigoe Cliff.

The chapter entitled "Descending the Cliff" begins with one of the most vivid battle descriptions in the *Heike*, a description of the clash between the Taira and Noriyori's main Minamoto force at Ikuta-no-mori, the eastern approach to the Ichinotani fortress:

The Chichibu, Ashikaga, Miura, and Kamakura clans and the bands of Inomata, Kodama, Noiyo, Yokoyama, Nishitō, Tsuzukitō, and

Shinotō all rushed into the melee of Minamoto and Taira. As they mingled foe against foe, announcing their names, their voices reverberated through the mountains and the hoofbeats of their horses, charging here and there, sounded like thunder. The arrows they shot back and forth fell like rain. Some, with wounded men on their backs, withdrew to the rear. Those only slightly wounded continued to fight, while those gravely hurt died. Some grappled with enemies, fell, were stabbed, and died. Some seized their opponents, held them down, and cut off their heads; others had their heads cut off. Neither ally nor foe could find an advantage. Thus it appeared that the main force of the Minamoto could not, by itself, prevail.[29]

In the midst of this stalemate at Ikuta-no-mori, Yoshitsune and his men descend Hiyodorigoe Cliff and fall upon the Taira from behind. Yoshitsune tests the descent by first driving several deer and some saddled but unmounted horses down the cliff's precipitous trail. The deer and three of the horses make it safely to the bottom; the other horses fall and break their legs. Despite the mixed results of this experiment, Yoshitsune is convinced the descent can be made by men on horses and, calling upon his followers to "take him as a model," starts down Hiyodorigoe Cliff.[30]

With "the stirrups of those behind touching the helmets and armor of those in front," the force makes its way along the Hiyodorigoe trail. Halfway down, it reaches a ledge and is confronted with what appears to be a sheer drop of more than one hundred feet. Sawara no Yoshitsura says that in his home district of Miura in Sagami province they ride after birds day and night on terrain like this. Proclaiming the setting a "Miura racetrack," Yoshitsura takes the lead in urging the force once again down the steep trail.[31]

Nearing the trail's bottom, members of the force shout their battle cries *(toki)* and plunge into the Taira,[32] setting fire to their quarters and driving them in disarray out of the Ichinotani fortification. Most of those not killed fleeing seek to escape in boats moored offshore.[33]

Yoshitsune's descent of Hiyodorigoe Cliff at the Battle of Ichinotani is one of the most celebrated military achievements in Japanese history. As described in the *Heike*, it is also probably the finest display of horsemanship in the war tales. As Kajiwara Masaaki observes, the two principal criteria of horsemanship in the war tales are "riding spirited horses" *(arauma-nori)* and "descending difficult terrain" *(akusho-otoshi)*.[34] No other warriors in the voluminous pages of the war tales match the breathtaking descent of such "difficult terrain" as the terrain Yoshitsune and his band descended at Ichinotani.

The Battle of Yashima

The *Heike* says nothing about the discord that arose between Yoshitsune and Yoritomo over Yoshitsune's acceptance of court positions after the Battle of Ichinotani. We are simply told that Noriyori and Yoshitsune both received court appointments in 1184:8.[35] In fact, as we have seen, Noriyori's appointment as governor of Mikawa was made two months earlier. The *Heike* also gives no indication that this appointment was approved by Yoritomo while Yoshitsune's appointments were not.

Book 11 of the *Heike* begins with Yoshitsune, after a year's hiatus, once again commissioned to pursue the Taira. He leaves Kyoto with a Minamoto force and heads toward Watanabe on the shore of the Inland Sea in Settsu province, where he assembles boats for the sea journey to Shikoku and the Taira encampment at Yashima.[36] As they gather and prepare boats, the Minamoto discuss naval warfare, an art at which the Ise Taira, based in the central and western provinces, excel, but about which the land-fighting Minamoto of the east know little. Kajiwara no Kagetoki, assigned by Yoritomo to serve as Yoshitsune's adviser, makes the sensible suggestion that they equip their boats with "reverse oars" to enable them to sail in any direction, according to the dictates of battle. Yoshitsune scornfully rejects this suggestion, remarking that even to consider the possibility of moving in reverse or retreating is defeatist thinking and unworthy of a true warrior. When Kagetoki retorts that the commander who knows only how to rush forward is a "wild boar warrior" and not a real leader, he and Yoshitsune nearly come to blows.[37]

What caused this sudden clash between two leading warriors of the Minamoto at the commencement of a major campaign against the Taira? Was there animosity between Yoshitsune and Kagetoki before the clash? If so, the *Heike* says nothing about it. Did Yoshitsune believe it was sufficiently important for the morale of the Minamoto to contradict and embarrass a prominent chieftain in front of others? Perhaps, but one may also conjecture that the reverse oars controversy is precipitated by the hotheaded, impetuous streak we find in Yoshitsune in the *Heike:* Kagetoki's suggestion angers him and he summarily rejects it.

Whatever the reason for the controversy, it ultimately leads to the gravest of consequences, for Kagetoki, in later submitting a negative report to Kamakura about Yoshitsune's conduct, is primarily responsible for Yoritomo's decision after the Gempei War to track down and kill Yoshitsune. In the legends contrived about Yoshitsune in the medieval age, Kagetoki is pictured as the most evil of men, the real destroyer of Yoshitsune; but in the *Heike* he is by no means such a one-dimensional villain. In the Battle of Ichinotani, for example, Kagetoki displays admirable human emotion when he risks his life to save one of his sons;[38] appointed to escort Taira no Shigehira, taken prisoner at Ichinotani, to Kamakura, he is a respectful and considerate warden; and in the Battle of Dannoura Kagetoki becomes a hero when he and his band attack a Taira boat and are the first to have their names recorded for merit.[39] Even in his clashes with Yoshitsune—before Yashima and then, as we will see, before Dannoura—Kagetoki does not appear to be unreasonable and certainly not evil. On the contrary, it is Yoshitsune who impresses us as arrogant and inflexible and quite prepared to goad Kagetoki. There is little in the *Heike* as a whole to suggest that Kagetoki is anything other than a good warrior doing his job.[40]

When the time for departure of the Minamoto flotilla for Shikoku approaches, gale-force winds arise and the boats' sailors recommend waiting for the weather to clear. But Yoshitsune threatens to shoot those who refuse to sail immediately, and soon he and some seventy or eighty men depart in five of the flotilla's two hundred boats. There is no explanation why, after Yoshitsune's dire threat, all but five of the boats are allowed to remain behind.[41] In any case, Yoshitsune and his small band cross the Inland Sea in record speed, land on Shikoku at a place with the auspicious name of Victory Bay (Katsuura), and promptly set out for Yashima. Approaching the Taira encampment, which includes a temporary palace for Emperor Antoku, they set fire to commoners' houses and deceive the Taira into believing they are a great horde. Only after retreating to their boats offshore do the Taira realize how few Minamoto actually oppose them from the shore.[42]

The Battle of Yashima is a conflict between land (the Minamoto) and sea (the Taira). Providing only a rough overview of the battle, the *Heike* focuses instead primarily on several memorable scenes. The battle commences with the war of words, mentioned earlier, in which a Taira partisan mocks the backgrounds of Yoshitsune and Ise no Yoshimori. When the firing of arrows begins, Satō no Tsuginobu is killed as he and others of Yoshitsune's most intimate followers seek to shield their lord with their bodies: "[A band of] warriors, each the equal of a thousand, vied with one another to align their horses's heads and protect the commander from arrows."[43] Tsuginobu's death is a memorable moment in the *Heike*, both because of its inherent drama and because of the insight it gives us into the relationship between Yoshitsune and his special group of personal followers.

Carried to the rear, Tsuginobu dies holding Yoshitsune's hand. His last words are:

> "I regret that I must die without seeing my lord rise to fame in the world. Apart from that, he who wields bow and arrow must expect to meet his end before an enemy's shaft. It is an honor for this existence and a memory for the next that the war tales of future generations will record that 'In the war between the Minamoto and the Taira, Satō no Saburōbyōe Tsuginobu gave his life for his lord on the beach at Yashima in Sanuki province.' "[44]

Yoshitsune summons a priest to copy sutras on Tsuginobu's behalf and, as a reward, gives the priest the very horse that he, Yoshitsune, rode on the descent of Hiyodorigoe Cliff at the Battle of Ichinotani. Yoshitsune's remaining followers are so moved by this gesture that they say: "We would regard giving our lives for this lord as no more important than a dewdrop or a speck of dust."[45]

This scene—Tsuginobu mortally wounded while protecting his lord, Yoshitsune holding Tsuginobu's hand as he dies, Yoshitsune's other followers expressing their willingness, even eagerness, to die for him—reminds us of the relationships of the eleventh-century Minamoto chieftains Yoriyoshi and Yoshiie to their men. *Mutsu Waki*, it will be recalled, says that Yoriyoshi personally tended to his men after a hard battle in the Former Nine Years War, eliciting from them vows that they would repay their obligations *(on)* to him "with their bodies"; and Yoshiie in *Ōshū Gosannen Ki* bonds himself to his followers by warming them with his own body during the bitterly cold winters of the Later Three Years War in Mutsu.[46]

The *Heike* contains many examples of warriors bound to each other even unto death—for example, Minamoto no Yoshinaka and his ever-faithful follower, Imai no Kanehira, who vow to "die in the same place."[47] But Yoshitsune and his band are the only case of a lord and his group of followers who are so intimately associated that the followers do not think twice about sacrificing themselves for the lord. This pure, *kenshin*-type loyalty of vassals to lord becomes the central theme of the post-Gempei part of the Yoshitsune legends as we find them in *Gikeiki*. In these legends, our sympathies are, in fact, drawn more to the vassals—models of self-sacrificing feudal service—than to the lord, Yoshitsune, himself.

Following Tsuginobu's death, there occurs an incident that pro-

vides one of the great tableaux of the *Heike*, a scene that remains fixed
in the minds of the works' readers and audiences and has been a favorite of artists through the ages. Evening has come, and both sides in the
Battle of Yashima prepare to retire for the night. Suddenly, a splendidly
decorated Taira boat rows closer to shore and an elegant, beautiful
young lady of eighteen or nineteen emerges from the cabin. Erecting
a pole with a fan attached to the top, the young lady beckons toward
the shore. One of Yoshitsune's men remarks that the fan, which has
a gold rising sun design against a background of red, has apparently
been set up as a target for an archer; but he suspects that the real intent of the young lady's appearance and the hanging of the fan is
to lure Yoshitsune himself into firing range to enable someone to
shoot him.[48]

It is decided that, nevertheless, someone among the Minamoto
must accept the challenge and fire at the target, and Nasu no Yoichi of
Shimotsuke province is selected. A rather small man noted more for
accuracy than strength with a bow, Yoichi expresses doubts about his
ability to hit the fan. Concerned that a failed shot will bring lasting disgrace to the Minamoto, he requests that someone else be designated
the shooter. But Yoshitsune, displaying the temper that is one of his
characteristic traits in the *Heike*, rails that no one who has come from
Kamakura with the Minamoto army has a right to disobey his orders.[49]
Gempei Seisui Ki, in its version of this story, adds drama by informing
us that the Taira have brought the fan from the Itsukushima Shrine, a
place of special importance to them. If Yoichi hits the fan, the Minamoto will win; if he misses, they will lose.[50]

Praying to the god Hachiman and vowing to kill himself if he
fails, Yoichi, after riding some thirty-five feet into the sea to get closer
to the boat, launches a shaft that travels unerringly to its mark. As the
fan, cut from its pole and spun high into the sky, is caught by the wind
and falls into the sea, both friend and foe—Minamoto and Taira—
applaud and express their appreciation for Yoichi's achievement by
beating on the sides of their boats or slapping their quivers.[51]

Yoichi's feat of shooting the Taira fan as it flutters in the wind on
a boat off Yashima Island is perhaps the best known of a number of cel-
ebrations of the art of archery in the war tales. We have noted, for
example, how Minamoto no Yoshiie displays his physical power with a
bow in *Mutsu Waki* by shooting a shaft through three suits of armor. In
Hōgen Monogatari, Yoshiie's grandson Tametomo duplicates this feat.
Whereas Nasu no Yoichi uses accuracy and Yoshiie and Tametomo display their sheer power, still another warrior achieves supremacy in

shooting an arrow for distance in a competition between the Taira and Minamoto during the Battle of Dannoura as described in the *Heike.*

As the sea battle of Dannoura begins, Wada no Yoshimori of the Minamoto, firing arrows from the shore, beckons to the Taira to shoot back one of his shafts that has traveled an especially great distance. The Taira select Nii no Chikakiyo to return the shaft, which Yoshimori has inscribed with his name, and Chikakiyo sends it more than a thousand feet, some thirty-five feet beyond the distance achieved by Yoshimori.[52]

When a second arrow fired by Chikakiyo thuds into the side of Yoshitsune's boat, Yoshitsune inquires who among the Minamoto is capable of firing it back. The selection this time is Asari no Yoichi, a hunter who is said never to have missed a running deer even at seven hundred feet. Using a nine-foot bow, Asari no Yoichi dispatches an arrow of fifteen hand-breadths that travels more than fourteen hundred feet and strikes Nii no Chikakiyo himself.[53]

At the Battle of Yashima, Nasu no Yoichi's triumph is followed by another scene centering on the bow. This is not a celebration of the bow or of archery, but a revelation about a particular warrior's bow. Amid the applause from both Minamoto and Taira following Yoichi's shot, a Taira warrior emerges from the boat's cabin and performs a dance where the fan had hung. Upon orders from Yoshitsune, Yoichi fires a second arrow that strikes the warrior's neck and fells him.[54] The brief period of empathy between friend and foe inspired by admiration for Yoichi's first shot is immediately ended by his second, which many observers regard as a wantonly cruel act (although the Minamoto shout and slap their quivers again).

Aroused by this shooting, some Taira warriors attack the beach, where they are met by a group of Minamoto. As other warriors join in on both sides, Yoshitsune leads some eighty warriors in a charge that drives the Taira back into the sea. While fighting in the sea, Yoshitsune loses his bow and manages to retrieve it only after repeated attempts. Later, Yoshitsune's followers criticize him for risking his life for a mere bow. He says to them:

"I was not concerned about losing the bow. But my bow can be strung by two men. If it were a 'three-man stringer' *(sannin-bari)* or were like my uncle Tametomo's [five-man] bow, I would probably have dropped it deliberately and let them recover it. But I could not bear to think how the enemy would laugh if they got their hands on my weak little weapon: 'This is the bow of the Genji general Kurō Yoshitsune?' That is why I risked my life to get the bow back."[55]

Yoshitsune's followers, we are told, were deeply impressed by these words.

Apart from its inherent interest as a story, the "dropped bow" incident offers a clue to Yoshitsune's physical appearance: As the user of a weak bow, he is probably slight in stature. (As noted in Chapter 2, the war tales contain little information to enable us to distinguish most warriors physically one from another.) This guess about Yoshitsune's size is confirmed as correct in the *Heike*'s later description of the Battle of Dannoura, where Yoshitsune is identified as "short" *(sei chiisaki)*. The Dannoura account also says that Yoshitsune is "white" or fair-complexioned and has protruding teeth. Because these physical characteristics make him readily identifiable even in battle, Yoshitsune attempts to confuse the enemy by frequently changing his armor and under-robe.[56]

After the fighting that produced the dropped bow incident, the Taira withdraw to their boats and once again both sides ostensibly settle down for the night. The Taira, however, begin preparations for a night attack, but fail to launch it when two of their commanders argue over who should be allowed to lead the attack *(senjin)*. The *Heike* sees the aborting of this night attack as still another sign that the fortune *(un)* of the Taira has run out.[57]

The following day the Taira retreat to nearby Shido Bay. Pursued and defeated in battle once again by Yoshitsune, they depart from Shikoku and make their way to the western end of Kyushu, setting the stage for the climactic Battle of Dannoura a month later.

In the *Heike* account of the Battle of Yashima, Ise no Yoshimori emerges as Yoshitsune's right-hand man. The portrayal of Yoshimori in this account is of particular interest because nowhere else in the *Heike* are we provided with information sufficient to observe one of Yoshitsune's followers as an individual and not merely a stereotype. (Satō no Tsuginobu, for example, is presented as a stereotype of the self-sacrificing—*kenshin*—vassal in the scene of his death during the opening exchange of arrows at Yashima.) The Yoshimori we see in the Yashima campaign is noteworthy both for his temper, which he displays in the unseemly exchange of insults with Etchū no Moritsugi of the Taira side before commencement of the battle, and for his craftiness, which, in the world of the *Heike*, is a quality not typical of warriors. As it happens, Yoshimori's temper and craftiness are both shared by his master, Yoshitsune.

We see Yoshimori's—and Yoshitsune's—craftiness when, after the remnants of the Taira have been chased from Shido Bay, Yoshitsune directs Yoshimori to seek out a local warrior and Taira partisan named

Noriyoshi and, by "making up a story," bring him back to camp. Setting out with a small band of only sixteen riders, unarmed and without armor, Yoshimori finds Noriyoshi and tells him a story of how the Minamoto have defeated the Taira, a story that contains the following untruths: The Taira commander Munemori and his son have been captured; Noritsune, the best Taira general, has committed suicide; all the other Taira leaders have either been killed in battle or have drowned themselves; Noriyoshi's own father has been taken prisoner; and the few remaining Taira found at Shido Bay have been destroyed. Faced with these daunting "facts," Noriyoshi surrenders and, with his three thousand followers, returns with Yoshimori to Yoshitsune's camp.[58]

Praising Yoshimori for his "splendid deception," Yoshitsune asks his opinion about what should be done with the prisoners. Yoshimori recommends that they be incorporated into Yoshitsune's army: "These provincial warriors don't care whom they serve. They'll follow anyone who can quell the disturbances and restore order to the land."[59] These words, although no doubt fictional, suggest what may well have been a prevailing attitude among the warriors who participated in the Gempei War. Far from joining armies and engaging in battles out of devotion to the Taira or Minamoto causes or to individual commanders, many warriors may simply have done what they believed best to restore order to the land—specifically, to the locales where their own holdings and families were situated.

In this regard, the Minamoto appear to have had serious difficulty during the Gempei War in motivating eastern warriors to join armies to march to battles in the distant central and western provinces. To be sure, there was the lure of rewards in the distribution of lands that might be seized in those regions after victories over the Taira. But, in the view of Watanabe Tamotsu at least, this lure was not great.[60] Indeed, Yoritomo himself was probably not enthusiastic about sending armies westward, which may help to explain why he chose personally to remain in Kamakura throughout the war.

The casualties in the Battle of Yashima appear not to have been great. Yoshitsune's principal accomplishment was to dislodge the Taira from a chosen base. But as Nagano Jōichi remarks, the Minamoto failed to inflict greater damage on the Taira at both Ichinotani and Yashima because they lacked a navy with which to pursue when the enemy fled in boats.[61] In this sense, Yoshitsune's greatest achievement as a commander was to assemble a navy in a very short span of time— little more than a month after the Battle of Yashima—in order to deliver a decisive blow to the Taira at the Battle of Dannoura in the third month of 1185.[62]

The Battle of Dannoura

The records say little about how Yoshitsune assembled his navy to engage the Taira at Dannoura. The *Heike*, however, suggests that this navy was manned at least in part—probably in large part—by men of the Inland Sea who joined the Minamoto after Yashima, including those who had theretofore supported the Taira. Immediately before commencement of the battle, for example, a former Taira partisan named Tanzō crosses over to the Minamoto with two thousand men in two hundred boats, and Kawano no Michinobu of Iyo province in Shikoku joins the Minamoto with one hundred and fifty boats. According to the *Heike*, this gives the Minamoto a three thousand to one thousand advantage in boats.[63] *Azuma Kagami*, however, says that the Minamoto had eight hundred and forty boats and the Taira five hundred.[64] These *Azuma Kagami* figures, which give the Minamoto less than a two to one advantage, are more plausible than the *Heike* figures if only because of the almost physical impossibility, as Nagano Jōichi observes, of cramming four thousand boats into the narrow straits at Dannoura.[65]

The *Heike*'s description of the amassing of boats and the preparation for battle at Dannoura is replete with signs and portents that are unfavorable to the Taira and even suggest they will suffer a disastrous defeat. In rendezvousing for the battle, for example, the Taira gather at "Retreat Island" (Hikushima), while the Minamoto select as their gathering place "Pursuit Bay" (Oitsu). And Tanzō decides to defect to the Minamoto after he first is advised by the deity of a Shinto shrine to join the white banner (of the Minamoto) and, second, observes seven white cocks defeat seven red cocks (the Taira banner is red) in a cockfight.[66]

Despite their apparently great advantage in numbers, the Minamoto nearly jeopardize their chances when another argument erupts between the commander, Yoshitsune, and Kajiwara no Kagetoki. The issue this time is who will lead the attack—be "first in battle"—against the Taira. When Kagetoki requests that he be allowed to lead the attack, Yoshitsune replies that this would be fine if he, Yoshitsune, were not there to do the leading. In response to Kagetoki's remark that it is improper for a commander *(tai-shōgun)* to lead an attack, Yoshitsune advances the hairsplitting argument that he is not the commander—the only "commander" is the lord of Kamakura, Yoritomo. This prompts Kagetoki to observe that Yoshitsune does not possess the qualities to be a commander. Yoshitsune in turn labels Kagetoki "the biggest fool in Japan." Only the physical intervention of others prevents Yoshitsune, Kagetoki, and their entourages from drawing swords. The description in the *Heike* of this second Yoshitsune versus Kagetoki confrontation concludes with the author's ominous remark that "from this time Kagetoki despised the lieutenant *(hōgan)* and finally, through slander, destroyed him."[67]

Curiously, the opening scene of combat in the *Heike*'s account of the Battle of Dannoura is the scene, mentioned earlier, of Kagetoki and a band of fourteen or fifteen warriors boarding a Taira boat, killing many enemies, seizing booty, and having their names recorded as the first to distinguish themselves in the battle. We are left to wonder whether Kagetoki was not, in fact, the "first in battle" at Dannoura, despite Yoshitsune's refusal of his request to be granted that honor.

Kazusa no Kagekiyo of the Taira observes that the Minamoto have no experience in fighting on water and predicts they will be as easy to seize as "fish climbing trees"; and Etchū no Moritsugi calls upon the Taira to seek out the "white-skinned, short, and buck-toothed" Yoshitsune.[68] Despite the numerical advantage of the Minamoto, the Taira appear at first to get the better of the fight, largely because the flow of the tide favors them. But omens appear which indicate that the tide of battle too will soon turn. A white banner, at first thought to be a cloud, floats down to a Minamoto boat and is seen by Yoshitsune as a sign of victory from the great god Hachiman; and the movement of a school of dolphins is similarly interpreted as an indication that the Minamoto will win. But the Minamoto victory is, in fact, made possible by the defection of a Taira partisan, Awa no Shigeyoshi, who informs the Minamoto which boats carry fighting men and which do not.[69] Tomomori, the Taira battle commander at Dannoura, had suspected that Shigeyoshi (whose son Noriyoshi was duped by Ise no Yoshimori into joining the Minamoto after the Battle of Shido Bay) might turn traitor, but his advice to "cut off his head" had been ignored by the commander-in-chief, Munemori,[70] who is repeatedly portrayed in the *Heike* as a hesitant, ineffectual leader.

The *Heike*'s account of the death agonies of the Taira at Dannoura is one of the most poignant and tragic scenes in Japanese literature. Kiyomori's widow, embracing her grandson, the child emperor Antoku, and carrying also the jewels and sword of the sacred regalia, leaps into the sea (the jewels are retrieved, but the sword is lost);[71] Lady Kenreimon'in, Antoku's mother, also plunges into the sea, but is fished out by the Minamoto. Many Taira warriors, including Tomomori, commit suicide by drowning. Donning additional armor and holding or shouldering anchors to ensure that they sink to the bottom, they leap into the sea one after another. In several cases, they go to their deaths holding hands. Thus Tomomori and his foster brother Ienaga, having earlier vowed to die together, plunge hand-in-hand into the waves.[72]

The most spectacular suicide at Dannoura is that of Taira no Noritsune. Firing off a barrage of arrows and then wielding a sword in one hand and a *naginata* in the other, Noritsune fights with great ferocity—as if berserk—in the last moments of the battle, wounding and killing many.[73] Tomomori, even as he himself prepares to commit suicide, sends a messenger to Noritsune to admonish him for committing the sin of slaughtering those who are not worthy foes. Noritsune, however, interprets Tomomori's admonishment to mean that he should stop wasting his time with lesser warriors and seek out and kill the Minamoto commander, Yoshitsune.[74]

As Noritsune fights his way from one Minamoto boat to another, Yoshitsune does his best to evade him, finally making a spectacular, desperation leap to another boat when he is almost in Noritsune's grasp.[75] This is the only instance in the *Heike* when Yoshitsune "runs away" from a foe. Since he is the Minamoto commander, he is no doubt wise to avoid the frenzied Noritsune, whose wild attack can have no influence on the outcome of the battle, which the Taira have already lost. But perhaps most surprising, Yoshitsune has been left exposed. We noted that in the *Heike* Yoshitsune is nearly always accompanied by his special band of personal followers, each ready to die for him. At the Battle of Yashima these followers form a human shield to protect him from the arrows of the same Taira no Noritsune, and Satō no Tsuginobu is killed. But at Dannoura, for whatever reason, the followers are conspicuously absent when Yoshitsune needs them most.

Having seen Yoshitsune escape, the frustrated Noritsune throws his sword and *naginata* into the sea, tears off his helmet and most of his armor, and, standing unarmed in only his cuirass (*dō*), challenges all who "think they are my match" to combat. At first there are no takers. Then three of the enemy—two brothers from Tosa province, noted for their strength, and one of their retainers—board Noritsune's boat with the thought that together they can surely subdue him. But Noritsune, after kicking the retainer overboard, seizes the brothers and, with one clamped under each arm, leaps into the sea, shouting that he and the brothers will visit the world of the dead together.[76] The death of Noritsune at Dannoura symbolizes the final defeat of the Taira, inasmuch as he was the victor in most of the few battle successes attributed to the Taira in the *Heike* version of the Gempei War.

To the shame of the Taira in particular but to the warrior class as a whole, Munemori allows himself to be captured along with his son

Kiyomune. Despite the example of other Taira, who are leaping to their deaths, Munemori and Kiyomune stand uncertainly at the side of their boat until some Taira retainers, under the pretext of accidentally bumping him, knock Munemori into the sea. But Munemori and Kiyomune, who jumps in after his father, are excellent swimmers, and they easily remain afloat until dragged from the water by Ise no Yoshimori using a bear-claw rake. Munemori's humiliation is increased when his foster brother, Hida no Kagetsune, seeks to aid him and is slain before his eyes. Boarding Munemori's boat, Kagetsune attacks Ise no Yoshimori. But Yoshimori, like many others in the *Heike*, is saved by a self-sacrificing follower—a page *(warawa)* who interposes himself between his master and Kagetsune and is felled by sword blows intended for Yoshimori. As Kagetsune thus disposes of the page, he is struck by an arrow and then stabbed to death by enemy warriors.[77]

Munemori in captivity is pathetic. After being paraded through the streets of Kyoto with the other Taira prisoners captured at Dannoura, he and Kiyomune are taken to Kamakura by Yoshitsune. As they set out, Munemori begs Yoshitsune to intercede with Yoritomo for his life, and in Kamakura he is obsequious toward Yoritomo.[78] He is finally executed by Yoshitsune on the way back to Kyoto. Throughout his ordeal as a prisoner, Munemori is frightened of impending death and concerned about his son Kiyomune, who is executed immediately after him. But at the very end he achieves tranquillity of mind through the instructions of a priest and faith in Amida Buddha.[79]

Yoshitsune in History: After the Gempei War

News of the Minamoto victory at Dannoura reached Kyoto on 1185:4:4, ten days after the battle was fought. Yoshitsune, ordered by Kamakura to take the Taira prisoners captured at Dannoura to Kyoto, did not arrive in the capital until 4:26, more than a month after the battle. His arrival should have been a moment of great personal triumph. But even before he entered Kyoto a letter from Kajiwara no Kagetoki, severely criticizing him, was delivered to Yoritomo in Kamakura. Kagetoki accused Yoshitsune of arrogance and overweening pride in his handling of the campaign that accomplished the destruction of the Taira. Rather than encourage cooperation and seek advice, Yoshitsune, according to Kagetoki, conducted the campaign entirely as he alone saw fit. The author of *Azuma Kagami*, supporting this last charge, observes that whereas Noriyori consulted regularly with the adviser assigned to him, Wada no Yoshimori, Yoshitsune ignored his adviser, Kagetoki.[80]

On 4:29, three days after Yoshitsune entered Kyoto, a letter arrived from Yoritomo ordering those warriors who wished to give their loyalty to Kamakura to desist from serving Yoshitsune. Yoritomo accused Yoshitsune of having caused resentment among the warriors assigned to him for the campaign against the Taira by willfully demanding rigid subordination to him. In messages sent about the same time to Kagetoki and Noriyori, Yoritomo referred to Yoshitsune as a "criminal" *(zainin)* who had sought to alienate eastern warriors from their responsibilities and loyalty to Kamakura.[81]

From the evidence we have, Yoshitsune was thunderstruck by these charges. He immediately dispatched a letter to Yoritomo, through the latter's adviser Ōe no Hiromoto, vowing his unswerving loyalty. *Azuma Kagami* claims that this declaration of loyalty, made after the receipt of censure, only heightened Yoritomo's anger toward Yoshitsune.[82]

On 5:7 Yoshitsune left Kyoto for Kamakura, taking with him the Taira prisoners Munemori and his son Kiyomune. But when he reached Kamakura eight days later, he was prevented from entering the city by order of Yoritomo. Obliged to surrender the prisoners to Yorito-mo's envoy, Hōjō no Tokimasa, Yoshitsune began what became nearly a three-week wait at Koshigoe outside Kamakura. During this time, he was almost entirely ignored by Yoritomo. On 5:24 Yoshitsune wrote the famous Koshigoe Letter to his brother. (The *Heike Monogatari* version of this letter, which is very similar in content to the version contained in *Azuma Kagami*, is reproduced in its entirety in the next section.)

In the Koshigoe Letter—sent, like earlier correspondence, through Ōe no Hiromoto—Yoshitsune recounts his great military achievements in vanquishing the Taira and avenging the death, in the Heiji Conflict, of his and Yoritomo's father, Minamoto no Yoshitomo. He speaks of the hardships of his early life after his father's death and the sacrifices he has made for the Minamoto cause, and he seeks to justify his receipt of court appointments as a great honor for the Minamoto. In an effusion of self-pity, he bewails the slanderous falsehoods that have turned Yoritomo against him. Although deserving great reward, he is not even allowed to enter Kamakura to refute this calumny. Invoking various Shinto and Buddhist deities, Yoshitsune once again vows his unqualified and eternal loyalty to Yoritomo.[83]

There is no evidence that Yoritomo even acknowledged receipt of the Koshigoe Letter. On 6:9 he returned Taira no Munemori and Kiyo-mune to Yoshitsune and ordered him to escort them back to Kyoto. A few days later, even as Yoshitsune made his way to Kyoto, Yoritomo issued a decree dispossessing him of the twenty-four holdings of former Taira lands that had been bestowed upon him as a reward for victory in the Gempei War.[84] At Shinohara in Ōmi province, Yoshitsune, acting under Yoritomo's orders, executed Munemori and Kiyomune.[85]

By the time he reached Kyoto at the end of the sixth month, Yoshitsune's anguish at being punished by Yoritomo had turned to anger. He continued to enjoy considerable support among people at court, especially the advisers of the senior retired emperor Goshirakawa.[86] Moreover, he was increasingly drawn into association with his uncle, Minamoto no Yukiie, who as a general during the Gempei War had achieved little military success but who, like Yoshitsune, had been branded an enemy of Kamakura and hence shared Yoshitsune's antipathy for the Yoritomo regime. Together, Yoshitsune and Yukiie represented an unmeasurable but still potentially dangerous threat to Yoritomo.

In the middle of the tenth month, an assassin sent by Yoritomo, Tosabō no Shōshun, was repulsed in an attack on Yoshitsune's residence in Kyoto. Galvanized into action by this attempt on his life, Yoshitsune—with Yukiie—requested and received from Goshirakawa an edict to chastise Yoritomo. We cannot know precisely why Goshirakawa agreed to issue this edict. He and others at court certainly sympathized with Yoshitsune in the aftermath of Tosabō's attack. But more likely Goshirakawa granted the edict as part of his overall policy of "using the barbarian to control the barbarian." Realizing that it would be difficult in any case to deny the request for an edict, since Yoshitsune and Yukiie were in Kyoto with the potential to force its issuance,[87] Goshirakawa may have reasoned that any repercussions from Kamakura would simply have to be dealt with later.

Yoshitsune and Yukiie left Kyoto on 11:3. Many people in the capital thought they would take Goshirakawa with them and establish a court in Kyushu. Yoritomo, on the other hand, believed they would march eastward to attack Kamakura, and even assembled an army under his personal command to meet and repel them. In fact, Yoshitsune and Yukiie headed westward, although not with Goshirakawa. Their call to warriors in the central provinces to join them had met with little response, and they decided to go to Kyushu to raise forces there. As they departed Kyoto, they had under their command only two hundred riders. Their hope lay in a new edict from Goshirakawa appointing them to positions of command over Shikoku and Kyushu islands and granting them the right to collect commissariat rice from estates and public lands in those regions.[88]

Three days out of Kyoto, Yoshitsune, Yukiie, and their followers encountered disaster. After repelling opposition from pro-Bakufu,

Minamoto forces in Settsu province, they tried to set sail for Kyushu
from Daimotsu harbor in Settsu. But a storm arose, destroying some of
their boats and scattering the others. Before long, Yoshitsune and
Yukiie were separated,[89] Yoshitsune's mistress Shizuka no Gozen was
captured in the Yoshino Mountains of Yamato province, and Yoshitsune and a small band of followers went into hiding, disguising themselves as mountain priests *(yamabushi)*.[90]

Given the paucity of reliable information, little can be said with
assurance about the movements of Yoshitsune from this time, at the
end of 1185, until about the spring of 1187, when he appeared at
Hiraizumi in Mutsu,[91] where he had spent much of his youth under
the protection of Fujiwara no Hidehira. Yoritomo, armed with decrees
from the court to track Yoshitsune down, made repeated efforts to find
him, sending agents throughout the country. Apparently Yoshitsune
spent much of his nearly two years in hiding in the central provinces,
even Kyoto itself. He continued to receive support from the court, possibly even from Goshirakawa, and he was abetted by many prominent
temples, including Enryakuji, Kōfukuji, Kuramadera, and Ninnaji.[92]
Clearly, Yoritomo had more to be concerned about than just the continued independence of a rival chieftain. He faced the possibility that
Yoshitsune might be able to mobilize significant opposition to his
regime in the central provinces.

Upon his arrival in Hiraizumi in 1187, Yoshitsune was warmly
greeted by his old patron, Hidehira, who pledged to protect him against
Yoritomo. For his part, Yoritomo may have been pleased to learn that
his brother was in the north. This meant that he was no longer a threat
to assume leadership of an anti-Bakufu rebellion in the central provinces. Yoritomo could now devote his attention entirely to the Mutsu
Fujiwara, an autonomous power that he had long perceived as a challenge to his rule at Kamakura. From at least 1185 Yoritomo had
regarded the Bakufu as a national government. He could not tolerate
indefinitely the existence of a separate Fujiwara regime outside his
control at Hiraizumi.

In 1187:10 Fujiwara no Hidehira died. Among his final instructions were admonitions to his heir, Yasuhira, and his other sons to
stand by and defend Yoshitsune against Yoritomo—indeed to use
Yoshitsune as their commander in such a defense. But Yasuhira and
the other sons not only lacked their father's commitment to Yoshitsune, they did not agree among themselves about how best to continue the management of family affairs. Shrewdly sensing opportunity,
Yoritomo adopted a carrot-and-stick policy, alternately threatening
Yasuhira with edicts he obtained from the court and enticing him to

surrender Yoshitsune in return for reward.[93] Finally, in the intercalary
fourth month of 1189, Yasuhira attacked Yoshitsune's residence on the
Koromo River with several hundred riders. Yoshitsune's small band of
supporters was quickly overcome, and Yoshitsune, after killing his
wife and child, killed himself. Yasuhira sent his head, preserved in
sweet sake in a black lacquer box, to Kamakura.

One reason why Yasuhira finally decided to kill Yoshitsune was
the knowledge that Yoritomo was assembling an army to invade
Mutsu. Yet if he hoped thereby to forestall the invasion, he was sadly
disappointed. In 1189:7, three months after the death of Yoshitsune,
Yoritomo set forth from Kamakura at the head of the army. By 1189:9
Yasuhira was dead and the domain of the Mutsu Fujiwara, established
a century earlier, was only a memory.

Yoshitsune in *Heike Monogatari:* After the Gempei War

The *Heike* is primarily a collection of stories, many if not most of
which have been dramatically embellished by innumerable tale singers
to arouse the interest and excite the imaginations of their audiences.
The stories are told essentially as an eyewitness or bystander might
tell them. Little attention is given to the plotting and planning—the
political maneuvering—that inevitably lie behind decisions and actions, such as those of the courtiers and warriors who are the main
actors in the events leading up to and during the Gempei War. We are
told, for example, almost nothing about the intense political struggle
between Yoshinaka and Yoritomo, as both sought to influence Goshirakawa and the court in their competition to assume leadership of the
Minamoto during the half year, from mid-1183 until early 1184, when
Yoshinaka was in Kyoto. And Goshirakawa, described in all histories
as a wily, duplicitous politician who was forever stirring up trouble,
appears in the *Heike* as a rather benevolent patriarch who is just trying
to maintain some semblance of order at court as Kyoto is threatened
and buffeted by one contending warrior chieftain after another.

We know from *Azuma Kagami* and other sources that there was
friction between Yoshitsune and Yoritomo during the Gempei War,
especially over Yoshitsune's acceptance of court appointments from
Goshirakawa in 1184:8 without Yoritomo's approval. But the *Heike*
misreports how and when these appointments were made and gives no
indication that there was anything unusual about Yoshitsune's receiving them. Apart from the ominous warning—after the second confrontation between Yoshitsune and Kajiwara no Kagetoki at the Battle of
Dannoura—that Kagetoki will eventually slander Yoshitsune and

cause his destruction, the reader of the *Heike* is given no hint until the
end of the Gempei War of trouble between Yoshitsune and Yoritomo.

Trouble is finally indicated in two brief passages after the victory
at Dannoura. In the first passage, we are told that Yoritomo is angered
when he learns that Yoshitsune, in Kyoto, is assuming personal credit
for vanquishing the Taira and has taken as his wife a daughter of one of
the captured Taira leaders, Tokitada.[94] In the second passage, Kajiwara
no Kagetoki reports to Yoritomo about Yoshitsune, presenting the lord
of Kamakura with the "slander" predicted earlier. Yet the slander, as
recorded in the *Heike*, is rather mild: Kagetoki simply informs Yoritomo that Yoshitsune has claimed personal responsibility for the victory at Ichinotani and has insisted that all the Taira prisoners taken at
Ichinotani be placed in his, rather than Noriyori's, custody.[95] Nevertheless, upon receiving this report from Kagetoki, Yoritomo promptly
orders that Yoshitsune, who is on his way to the east with Munemori
and other prisoners taken at Dannoura, be denied entry to Kamakura.

So far as we know in reading the *Heike*, Yoshitsune has until this
point no idea whatever that Yoritomo might be upset with him. He is
literally confronted for the first time at the gates of Kamakura with
Yoritomo's unalterable wrath, the full implications of which he cannot
know but which will eventually lead to his destruction.

Who is Yoritomo? Who is this lord of Kamakura who so abruptly
indicts and banishes his brother? The Yoritomo of the *Heike* is a
remote, shadowy figure. He stays in Kamakura, distant from the setting of almost all of the *Heike*'s action. Directives come from him;
reports are made to him. But he is not directly involved in what is happening and has almost no personal contact with most of the book's
main characters. Yoshitsune, for example, never sees Yoritomo in the
Heike.[96]

While the motivations and sentiments of Yoritomo remain
largely obscure—he offers no explanations and does not even deign to
communicate with Yoshitsune after forbidding him to enter Kamakura
—Yoshitsune's feelings are tellingly revealed in the Koshigoe Letter,
which he sends to his brother, through Ōe no Hiromoto, from his camp
outside Kamakura:

> Having been appointed a deputy [of His Lordship, Yoritomo] and hav-
> ing received an imperial edict, I, Minamoto no Yoshitsune, defeated
> the enemies of the court and avenged the shame of my dead father.
> Although deserving of reward, instead I vainly shed crimson tears
> because of a wicked person's slander. The slanderer's charges have
> not been examined for their truth or falsity; yet still I am barred from
> entering Kamakura. Unable to express my true feelings, I languish in

idleness here at Koshigoe. How long it has been since I gazed upon my brother's beloved countenance! Yet our fraternal tie is already rent. Is it because the fate that bound us is exhausted? Or is it the result of a bad karma from a previous existence? How very sad. Unless my dead father's revered spirit is born again, who else is there to tell of my anguish? Who is there to take pity on me? To discuss such matters again may sound like grumbling, but no sooner did I receive life from my parents than my father died and I became an orphan. Clutched by my mother to her breast, I was taken to the Uda district of Yamato province. From that time on I have not known peace of mind for a single day, even for a moment. My worthless life was prolonged, but since it was too dangerous to go about Kyoto, I hid myself here and there, in this place and that. I made remote regions and distant provinces my home and was employed as a servant by country folk and peasants. But fortune suddenly came my way, and I was given the opportunity to go up to the capital to track down the Taira. After first killing Kiso no Yoshinaka, I set out to destroy the Taira. At times I whipped my fine steed over rugged peaks, with no thought that my life might be crushed by the enemy; at other times I braved fierce gales on the boundless ocean, heedless that I might sink to the ocean's floor and my body become the feed of whales. Moreover, using my armor and helmet as a pillow and pursuing the way of the bow and arrow, I aimed only to assuage the anger of the spirit of my dead father and fulfill the long-cherished wish of the Minamoto. My appointment to lieutenant with fifth rank is an assignment of significance for our house of Minamoto. What higher honor could there be [than to serve the court]? Nevertheless, my grief now is profound, my sorrow great. Without the divine assistance of the buddhas and Shinto gods, how will my supplications be heard? I have sent a number of pledges, using the backs of Ox King amulets,[97] proclaiming to all the gods and buddhas of Japan that I harbor no ambitions. But still I have received no pardon from Yoritomo."[98]

Yoshitsune here assumes no personal blame for the estrangement from his brother, but attributes it entirely to what he regards as groundless slander. Although he does not identify the slanderer by name, it is clearly Kajiwara no Kagetoki. Above all, Yoshitsune is alarmed by the prospect that he may be given no chance to rebut the slander or tell his side of the story. The implications of his remark that the receipt of a court appointment should be regarded as an honor for the Minamoto cannot be appreciated by the reader of the *Heike*, who has not been informed that Yoshitsune was made "lieutenant with fifth rank" in contravention of Yoritomo's strict rule against such appointments without his approval.

But what is perhaps most striking about the Koshigoe Letter is its pervasive tone of self-pity and its depiction of Yoshitsune as a humble supplicant, pleading, almost groveling, for forgiveness from the intransigent Yoritomo. Since self-pity, pleading, and groveling are qualities distinctly at variance with the character of Yoshitsune as we find it elsewhere in the *Heike*, the Koshigoe Letter strikes a discordant note in the work's overall portrayal of this most colorful of commanders in the Gempei War.

The *Heike*'s Yoshitsune is, above all, a shrewd and skilled military commander. Decisive and imaginative, he represents a new breed of warrior leader who is unconcerned about the traditional rules and etiquette of warfare (to the extent that there were such rules and etiquette) and who is determined to achieve victory by any means, even deception. Hotheaded, he shows particularly bad judgment in venting his temper on Kajiwara no Kagetoki, assigned by Yoritomo to be his adviser.

Unlike most commanders in the *Heike*, Yoshitsune personally leads his men in battle. He is beloved by his intimate band of followers to an extent, as noted in the death scene of Satō no Tsuginobu at Yashima, that their feelings for him are a model of the *kenshin*—self-sacrificing—loyalty that is the central ideal of warrior society in the ancient and medieval ages, at least as it is presented in the war tales. No other warrior chief in the *Heike* commands such adulation from his followers as Yoshitsune.

The *Heike*'s Yoshitsune is not a man of elegance. Although far superior to the rude Yoshinaka, he is said to be less than "the dregs" of the courtier-like Taira.[99] Yoshitsune is also no match for his half-brother Yoritomo in lineage, breeding, or appearance. Whereas Yoritomo's mother was the daughter of an important shrine official, Yoshitsune's—Tokiwa—was a menial in a courtier household.[100] Throughout the *Heike*, Yoshitsune is pictured as essentially rough and ready, while Yoritomo appears as a man always attentive to the proper forms and rituals of his position. (This comparison is perhaps unfair, since Yoshitsune was fighting a war and Yoritomo was merely directing it from afar.) Although both brothers are described as small of stature, Yoshitsune is additionally portrayed as pallid and buck-toothed. Yoritomo, on the other hand, is "elegant" or even "comely" *(yubi)*.[101]

Though he lacks certain personal graces, Yoshitsune becomes extremely popular among the courtiers of Kyoto and is especially favored by the senior retired emperor Goshirakawa. This does not mean that the courtiers or Goshirakawa in any sense regard him as worthy of true acceptance into courtly society: It merely indicates that they like him as a warrior chief, particularly compared to the barbarian

Yoshinaka and the threatening, often inscrutable, Yoritomo. Yoshitsune spends much time with women, even irking Yoritomo, as observed, by taking as wife a daughter of the prisoner Taira no Tokitada, who was captured at Dannoura. To other warriors, Yoshitsune can be courteous and thoughtful—as when he treats the captured Taira leader, the pusillanimous Munemori, with unusual sensitivity—or cruel, as when he orders Nasu no Yoichi to shoot the warrior who dances on the Taira ship at Yashima after Yoichi has hit the fan presented to the Minamoto as a target.

We noted earlier that the theme of sympathy for the underdog, which later becomes so strong in the Yoshitsune legend, is not especially to be found in the *Heike.* If the Koshigoe Letter were removed, it would be almost totally absent. Hence the Yoshitsune so beloved in the literature and theater of later centuries, the victim of persecution by Yoritomo and others, is not the Yoshitsune of the *Heike.*

We have noted too that Yoshitsune is, along with his father Yoshitomo and his cousin Yoshinaka, one of the three great tragic loser-heroes of the war tales dealing with the conflict between Taira and Minamoto in the late twelfth century—*Hōgen Monogatari, Heiji Monogatari,* and *Heike Monogatari.* The loser-hero, it will be recalled, becomes a tragic hero when his failure results from a personal flaw. Yoshitomo, Yoshinaka, and Yoshitsune—ranging from good to great military leaders—all ultimately fail because of political ineptitude. In Yoshitsune's case, this ineptitude is revealed in the *Heike* primarily in his rash handling of Kajiwara no Kagetoki.

The tragic loser-hero possesses other characteristics: He is aided by an ever-faithful follower, and, as he approaches his end, he becomes indecisive, even passive, and is increasingly reliant on the ever-faithful follower. Yoshitsune in the Kakuichi text of the *Heike* reaches only the first stage in his transformation into a tragic loser-hero. His principal ever-faithful follower, Musashibō Benkei, is a nonentity in the *Heike,* and Yoshitsune himself, even as we see him for the last time toward the book's end, leaving Kyoto in 1185:11, is still very much a vigorous commander.

The last two chapters of the *Heike* in which Yoshitsune appears are those dealing with the unsuccessful attack by Tosabō no Shōshun, sent by Yoritomo to Kyoto to assassinate Yoshitsune, and with Yoshitsune's departure from Kyoto shortly thereafter with an edict from Goshirakawa to chastise Yoritomo. In historical fact, as observed, Yoshitsune had by this time become allied with his uncle Yukiie, who both aided him in repulsing Shōshun and accompanied him when he left Kyoto. But Yukiie is absent from the *Heike* version of the Shōshun story and is mentioned only in passing in the account of Yoshitsune's departure from Kyoto.

In the *Heike*, Yoshitsune overcomes Shōshun with only a close group of followers, including Eda no Genzō, Kumai no Tarō, and Musashibō Benkei. He is impressed with Shōshun's gallantry as a warrior and offers to spare his life. But Shōshun says he has already given his life to Yoritomo—in accepting the mission to assassinate Yoshitsune—and requests only that he be executed forthwith. There are none who fail to praise him.[102]

The *Heike* states that Yoshitsune is accompanied by five hundred riders when he leaves Kyoto.[103] (*Azumi Kagami* says he has about two hundred riders.)[104] But his party is soon scattered when it encounters a storm on the Inland Sea as it attempts to travel by boat to the west. The storm was caused, people say, by the vengeful spirits of the Taira. Yoshitsune returns briefly to Kyoto after this calamity and then sets out for the northern provinces. There is no mention of companions. This is the last we hear of Yoshitsune in the Kakuichi version of the *Heike*, although other versions provide information about his subsequent adventures, up to his death in Hiraizumi in 1189.[105]

A Note on *Gikeiki* (Chronicle of Yoshitsune)

More legends have grown up about Yoshitsune than any other character in the war tales.[106] At least several reasons can be adduced for this. First, Yoshitsune is one of the most dynamic, exciting, and successful warriors in the war tales. Second, he suffered the fate of a martyr at the hands of Yoritomo, arousing a powerful sense of sympathy for him (sympathy for the underdog) among those who read or heard stories about him. Third, little is known about his life before he appeared in the Gempei War in 1180:10 or after he left Kyoto in 1185:11 under threat from Yoritomo. This scarcity of facts about all but a few years of Yoshitsune's life—the glory years—encouraged the invention of stories about, first, how he grew up and, second, how he fared in the fugitive period from 1185:11 until his death in Hiraizumi in 1189.

The most important collection of legends about Yoshitsune is *Gikeiki*, which was probably compiled sometime in the second half of the fourteenth century or the first half of the fifteenth century. Although sometimes called a war tale, *Gikeiki* differs significantly from the regular war tales. The regular war tales, including those examined in this study, deal with warriors and their battles and are based on history. If we regard warriors, battles, and historical bases as the principal criteria of war tales, *Gikeiki* is a war tale only insofar as it concerns warriors.

Gikeiki lacks the "battles" criterion of war tales because virtually all of its fighting comprises skirmishes—that is, conflicts between small groups (sometimes just one or two warriors) or between a small group and a much larger force. We noted in Chapter 3 that there are three general types of battle descriptions in the *Heike:* one warrior fighting against another; one fighting against many; and many fighting against many (group combat). These three types, however, all come from accounts of battles or the clashes of armies. The first two types (one-against-one and one-against-many) are descriptions of particular parts of battles; they are not independent fights. *Gikeiki*, on the other hand, contains almost no battle accounts. Nearly all its fights are skirmishes between Yoshitsune, with his small band of followers, and the agents of Yoritomo who pursue him in the post-Gempei, fugitive phase of his life.

But *Gikeiki* differs perhaps most markedly from the regular war tales in its almost total lack of factuality. Apart from some information that can be historically corroborated, *Gikeiki* presents only legends *(densetsu)* about Yoshitsune. The brief phase of his life that is part of the historical record—his military career in the Gempei War—is summarized in a few sentences. In other words, *Gikeiki* jumps almost directly from the pre-Gempei to the post-Gempei legends.

Nearly three-quarters of *Gikeiki* is devoted to the post-Gempei legends of Yoshitsune. In this latter portion of the work, it is not Yoshitsune but others who hold center stage: figures like Satō no Tadanobu, Yoshitsune's mistress Shizuka, and, above all, the ever-faithful follower Musashibō Benkei. Like the other leading tragic heroes of the war tales—Yoshitomo and Yoshinaka—Yoshitsune becomes, in this final phase of his life, passive, uncertain, even bewildered by the events that envelop him. But Yoshitsune's "final phase," a product of *Gikeiki*, is far more elaborated than the final phases of Yoshitomo (in the *Heiji*) and Yoshinaka (in the *Heike*). And Yoshitsune's character in his final phase is much more significantly transformed than either of theirs. In the words of Helen McCullough, Yoshitsune becomes, in a reflection of the tastes of the Muromachi period, which produced *Gikeiki*, "a rather effeminate type of hero—[revealing] the same taste . . . responsible for the adulation of handsome temple pages *(chigo)* and the idealization of the fleeing Taira as elegant and bewildered aristocrats."[107]

The last scene of Yoshitsune's life as presented in *Gikeiki* shows him as the kind of hero McCullough describes. Fujiwara no Yasuhira, leading a force of twenty thousand warriors, attacks Yoshitsune and eight retainers, including Benkei and Ise no Yoshimori, at their Koromogawa residence. The retainers, with superhuman valor, hold off Yasuhira's horde while Yoshitsune, inside, recites a portion of the Lotus Sutra. One by one the retainers are killed or commit suicide; Benkei, after fighting like a man possessed, dies while still on his feet, and no one dares approach him until finally a gust of wind from a galloping horse blows him down. When Yoshitsune at last must take his own life, he is uncertain how best to do it. At the suggestion of one of his two remaining retainers, he disembowels himself (although he inserts his dagger in his chest rather than his stomach). He leaves to the retainer the unhappy task of killing his wife and two children. Thus the life of one of the greatest warrior heroes of the war tales ends, in the *Gikeiki* account, in a way more pitiful than heroic.

5
TAIHEIKI
CHRONICLE OF GREAT PEACE

Historical Background
Rise of the Hōjō

Minamoto no Yoritomo, who received the title of *sei-i tai-shōgun* in 1192,[1] died in 1199 and was succeeded as shogun by his sons Yoriie (r. 1199–1203) and Sanetomo (r. 1203–1219). Ineffectual as rulers, the sons were buffeted by factional fighting among the leading warrior families of the Kamakura Bakufu. One of these families was the Hōjō, who were related to the Minamoto by marriage: Hōjō Masako was Yoritomo's wife and the mother of Yoriie and Sanetomo.[2]

Gradually, during the first two decades of the thirteenth century, the Hōjō consolidated their control over the Bakufu. With the death of Sanetomo in 1219—he was assassinated by a nephew—the Hōjō under Yoshitoki, who was Masako's brother and Sanetomo's uncle, became the real rulers at Kamakura.[3] Of relatively obscure origins,[4] the Hōjō did not seek to take the office of shogun for themselves but instead brought, first, Fujiwara and, later, imperial princes to Kamakura to serve as titular heads of the Bakufu. Under these Kyoto shoguns, the Hōjō exercised real governing power as shogunal regents *(shikken)*.

During the long struggle for power at Kamakura that accompanied the rise of the Hōjō, there grew an anti-Bakufu faction at court led by the retired emperor Gotoba. Securing the support of an assortment of warriors from the central provinces and from among eastern warriors on guard duty in Kyoto,[5] Gotoba in 1221 issued an edict branding Yoshitoki a rebel and calling upon warriors throughout the country to rise and overthrow the Bakufu. Yoshitoki responded by dispatching a great Bakufu army to Kyoto that speedily destroyed Gotoba's defenses

159

and occupied the capital. Gotoba was sent into exile, and Kyoto and the court were brought under direct control of the Bakufu by the installation of two Kyoto magistrates *(tandai)*, known also as the Rokuhara magistrates because their offices were located in the Rokuhara section of southeastern Kyoto where the Ise Taira had formerly had their residences.

This brief clash of arms in 1221 is known, after the year era, as the Jōkyū (or Shōkyū) Conflict and is described in the war tale *Jōkyūki* (Chronicle of Jōkyū).[6] The Jōkyū Conflict was a critical event in the early medieval age because it enabled the Kamakura Bakufu to establish itself much more firmly as the de facto government of the country, both through its assertion of control over the key city of Kyoto and through the confiscation of vast holdings of estate lands from the losing Gotoba side. To these estate lands the Bakufu appointed vassals as stewards *(jitō)*, substantially augmenting the network of stewards that was first created by Yoritomo during the Gempei War. The estate-based stewards were, along with constables *(shugo)* appointed as policing officials to each of the provinces, the principal representatives of the Bakufu as a countrywide government.[7]

The Kamakura Bakufu under Hōjō rule is remembered in history perhaps best for its effectiveness in establishing laws for warriors and serving as a judicial body for handling the legal suits, dealing mostly with land, that were submitted to it from all sectors of society. The Jōei Code, compiled in 1232, served both as a starting point and as a model for the formulation of warrior law for centuries. Yet even as the Bakufu functioned impressively as a national government in the legal realm, it never exercised administrative control over the entire country: Many estates, especially in the central and western provinces, remained free of stewards and, hence, were essentially autonomous.

The Mongol Invasions

The Kamakura Bakufu was confronted with one of its greatest challenges in the Mongol invasions of 1274 and 1281. About the time when the Bakufu was being established in the late twelfth and early thirteenth centuries, North China came under the control of the Mongols, led by Chinggis Khan. In 1268, Chinggis' grandson, Khubilai Khan, sent the first of a series of letters to Japan calling upon it to become tributary to China—that is, to accept a relationship that the Japanese, alone among the peoples of East Asia, had for centuries avoided.[8] Assuming responsibility for dealing with this foreign threat in place of the Kyoto court, the Bakufu ignored Khubilai's demands, thus tacitly rejecting them.

In 1274 a Mongol armada, including among its troops both Chinese and Koreans, who were under Mongol domination, landed at Hakata Bay in northern Kyushu. This first Mongol invasion lasted only one day. The defending Kyushu warriors, accustomed to the kind of one-against-one combat on horseback that had for so long been the premier fighting style in Japan, were hard-pressed to resist the world-conquering Mongols, who used coordinated troop movements and weapons—including poisoned arrows, explosive shells launched by catapults, and crossbows—that were virtually unknown to the Japanese.[9] But suddenly a typhoon arose at night and forced the Mongols back onto their ships and out to the open sea, where many of the ships were sunk and the others sent straggling back to the continent.[10]

The Japanese were better prepared for the second Mongol invasion in 1281, a massive undertaking by a force of 140,000 invaders, and fought effectively during several weeks of warfare in northern Kyushu. But again the Mongols were driven away by a typhoon that decimated their armada as the earlier typhoon had shattered the armada of 1274. The Japanese believed these typhoons were *kamikaze*, "divine winds" sent by the Shinto gods to protect Japan during times of dire national peril.

The Imperial Succession Dispute

In 1272, two years before the first Mongol invasion, the senior retired emperor Gosaga died. Certainly no one at the time saw this as a significant event, inasmuch as the imperial family had been stripped of most of its remaining powers by the Bakufu after the Jōkyū Conflict of 1221. But the seeds of a very great problem indeed lay in Gosaga's failure to specify how he wished the imperial succession to be transmitted. One of his sons, Gofukakusa, was a retired emperor; another, younger son, Kameyama, was the reigning monarch. Each wanted his descendants to be the successors. Very likely Gosaga did not indicate his opinion about the matter in deference to the Bakufu, which had essentially dictated the succession's course since the Jōkyū Conflict.

The Bakufu could readily have settled the dispute between Gofukakusa and Kameyama at its inception by selecting the line of one or the other to be the successors; but it did not. It thereby allowed the dispute to fester, causing not only further polarization of the imperial family but also forcing virtually all the ministers at court to choose sides. Toward the end of the century, the Bakufu established a principle of alternate succession, which called for the emperorship to shift back and forth between the senior (Gofukakusa) and junior (Kameyama) lines. This arrangement brought peace, but not for long. For the

imperial family had by this time divided into two distinct and ultimately irreconcilable branches.[11]

The fight over imperial succession was not waged simply for the
honor of serving, with little political power, as emperor or senior
retired emperor. More important, the contending lines sought control
over the extensive blocks of estate lands still held by the imperial family. During the course of the succession dispute, these lands were per-
manently divided between the senior and junior branches, thus providing both lines with economic independence.

Decline and Fall of the Kamakura Bakufu

By the early fourteenth century, the Kamakura Bakufu was in
decline. The Mongol invasions had, in particular, greatly strained it as
a governing body. Whereas civil conflicts in the past had nearly always
provided warrior victors with the opportunity to seize spoils—mainly
lands—for distribution as rewards, the invasions produced no such
spoils. The Bakufu made what rewards it could from the lands available to it, but they were insufficient. Moreover, the Bakufu had to face
new demands for rewards from those warriors who maintained until
the end of the thirteenth century the defense of northern Kyushu
against a possible third Mongol invasion, which never occurred.

But the Mongol invasions were only one factor in the Bakufu's
decline. Known until this time for its fairness and justice, the Bakufu
was increasingly accused of injustice and corruption. These accusa-
tions came at a time when the Hōjō, who had earlier shared governing
power at Kamakura with other eastern warrior families, began alienat-
ing many of them by drawing dictatorial powers to themselves.

In 1318 Godaigo of the junior line became emperor. Unlike many
of his youthful predecessors, he was a mature man of thirty. He was
also, as became abundantly clear, a person of great determination
whose ambition did not stop at abolishing the alternate succession system and securing the emperorship solely for his line: He wished also to
assume genuine ruling powers at court. His hand was strengthened
when, in 1321, his father, Gouda, discontinued the office of senior
retired emperor *(in)*, thus making Godaigo, as emperor, the unchallenged leader of the court.

In 1324 an anti-Bakufu plot, involving both courtiers and warriors, was uncovered at court. Its leaders, forming a group called the
"Free and Easy Society" *(bureikō)*, secretly contrived their plot against
the "eastern barbarians" while meeting to eat, drink, and carouse with
young ladies.[12] Godaigo disclaimed knowledge of the plot, even
though he had probably encouraged it; and the Bakufu, showing sur-

prising leniency, did no more than exile the courtier, Hino Suketomo, who had organized the Free and Easy Society.

After this abortive plot, Godaigo became increasingly active in the anti-Bakufu movement at court, seeking support especially among warriors and Buddhist temples of the central provinces. His efforts were sabotaged, however, when in 1331:5 one of his closest advisers, the court minister Yoshida Sadafusa, revealed his plans to the Bakufu. The Bakufu did not act immediately against Godaigo, although it arrested several courtiers and priests who were his confidants and interrogated them, using torture. In 1331:8, Godaigo left Kyoto and, after visiting Nara, went to the Buddhist temple on Mount Kasagi, east of Nara.

The Rokuhara magistrates sent a military force to Kasagi, whose temple served as a fortress manned both by warriors and the temple's monks. After several unsuccessful assaults, the Bakufu force succeeded in burning the temple-fortress down. Godaigo escaped, but he was soon captured. Forced to abdicate in favor of Kōgon of the senior branch, he was exiled the following year to the Oki Islands in the Japan Sea.

Meanwhile, others rallied to Godaigo's loyalist cause. Chief among them was Kusunoki Masashige, a local chieftain of Kawachi province. Defending a fortress here, harassing a Bakufu position there, Masashige kept the fires of resistance burning, even against a great army sent by the Bakufu from the Kantō. Another loyalist stalwart at this time was Godaigo's son, Prince Moriyoshi (or Morinaga), who worked tirelessly to recruit support for his father.

In 1333:2 Godaigo escaped from the Oki Islands to mainland Honshu, where he was sheltered and defended by the loyalist warrior Nawa Nagatoshi. The following month the Bakufu, alarmed at the continuing inability of the Rokuhara magistrates to maintain order in the central provinces, dispatched another army from Kamakura, co-commanded by Ashikaga Takauji. But upon reaching the central provinces, Takauji turned against the Bakufu, attacking and destroying the offices of the Rokuhara magistrates in the capital. Almost simultaneously, Nitta Yoshisada, who, like Takauji, was the head of a leading Minamoto branch family and had also served the Bakufu, raised the loyalist flag in the east and attacked Kamakura. The Bakufu went down in flames, as the last Hōjō leader, Takatoki,[13] and hundreds of his kinsman and followers committed suicide. In 1333:6 Godaigo returned triumphantly to Kyoto, claiming that he had never willingly abdicated and announcing the commencement of an "imperial restoration," known in history as the Kemmu Restoration (1333–1336).

The Kemmu Restoration

The Kemmu Restoration occurred at a time of momentous change in Japanese history. Older institutions, such as the estate system of landholding, that had long provided order and stability in the country, had been severely weakened by developments during the Kamakura period. In the case of the estate system, it had been steadily fragmented by unrelenting attacks by land-hungry warriors, some of whom were Bakufu vassals. The decline of the estate system was accompanied by outbreaks of disorder, especially in the central and western provinces, that the Bakufu was increasingly unable to control.

As Godaigo began his restoration, the country was, in fact, lapsing into regionalism. Perhaps a truly remarkable ruler could have done something to stem the tide, although that seems doubtful. Historians have, in any case, long believed that Godaigo was not only ill-equipped by training and temperament to deal with the issues of the day—the most pressing of which was how to handle rewards for the warrior victors in the recent fighting—but had little sense of what was really happening to the country. Rather than look to the future, he turned to the past, seeking to restore something—direct imperial rule—that probably never existed.

Ruling without competition from a senior retired emperor (it will be recalled that his father discontinued that office in 1321) and refusing to appoint a Fujiwara regent or give the title of shogun (sei-i tai-shōgun) to a warrior leader,[14] Godaigo seemed intent upon turning the clock back five hundred years to the time of Emperor Daigo, who in the early tenth century supposedly ruled "directly" before the rise of the Fujiwara regents, the senior retired emperors, and the military. Godaigo revealed his fascination with the reign of Daigo by going against precedent to select as his own posthumous name "Daigo II."[15]

Seeing Godaigo as both reactionary and incompetent, historians have criticized in particular his handling—or mishandling—of the critical business of rewards for warriors who had fought to overthrow the Kamakura Bakufu. A passage from Taiheiki seems to support this criticism of the Kemmu regime's policy on rewards:

> After the reestablishment of peace there were unknown tens of thousands of fellows who had served loyally and wished rewards. But the only ones who have thus far received them are courtiers and their underlings. This is the reason why petitions have been abandoned and why suits are no longer submitted; others, resentful over their failure to receive rewards for loyal service and dissatisfied over unjust governing practices, have returned home to their provinces. . . .

Although the court should be seeking to dispel the resentment of the warriors, it has decided first to undertake repairs to the palace. For this purpose stewards of the various provinces are being levied one-twentieth of their incomes. How grievous it is that the burden should be placed on these men when they are still suffering from the ravages of war.[16]

Recently, however, some scholars have begun to reevaluate the role of Godaigo and the Kemmu Restoration in medieval history. Andrew Goble, for example, argues that earlier historians, knowing that the Kemmu regime was overthrown after only three years, sought retrospectively to explain the reasons for its "failure," placing most of the blame on Godaigo himself. Goble contends that Godaigo was a far-sighted statesman who even before the restoration had clear plans for establishing strong imperial rule over the country. Rejecting the characterization of Godaigo as a reactionary, Goble contends that he worked firmly and successfully to consolidate his regime, develop a coherent policy for handling land claims, assert authority over the courtiers and great religious institutions, and provide leadership for the provincial warrior class.[17]

However one may evaluate the success or failure of Godaigo and the Kemmu regime, they soon came to grief through military conflict over which they may have had little control. The chief threat to the regime was Ashikaga Takauji. Although a leading commander in the destruction of the Kamakura Bakufu and handsomely rewarded by Godaigo, Takauji remained largely detached from the activities of the restoration regime. But when in 1335 an uprising of former Hōjō supporters under Takatoki's son Tokiyuki erupted in the Kantō, Takauji went forth from Kyoto to suppress it. He requested from Godaigo the title of *sei-i tai-shōgun* to sanctify this military undertaking, but he was refused.

Upon reaching the Kantō, Takauji quickly and thoroughly defeated the insurgents. He then established an administrative base in Kamakura and, despite directives from the court, refused to return to Kyoto. Alarmed that Takauji now posed a threat to the court, Godaigo in 1335:11 commissioned Nitta Yoshisada to lead an expeditionary force to chastise him. Behind the dispatch of Yoshisada to the Kantō lay a smoldering rivalry between him and Takauji that was bound to burst into flames. As chieftains of the two leading branches of the Minamoto, both aspired to become the new leader *(tōryō)* of the country's warriors. Although Takauji was militarily the more powerful, Yoshisada ingratiated himself with Godaigo, thus securing the backing of the restoration court.[18]

The War Between the Courts

The dispatch of Nitta Yoshisada to the Kantō in 1335:11 to chastise Ashikaga Takauji marked the beginning of the long civil conflict that later became known as the war between the northern and southern courts (whose establishment we will consider shortly)—a conflict that was not concluded until 1392. Takauji defeated Yoshisada's expeditionary force in sharp combat in the Kantō and then pursued it back to the central provinces. In the first two months of 1336 the loyalists and the Ashikaga fought a series of battles in and around Kyoto. The loyalists got the better of this battling, mainly because they received timely support from the courtier-general Kitabatake Akiie, who brought a large army up from the northern Mutsu-Dewa region where he had been stationed from the beginning of the Kemmu Restoration.[19]

In 1336:2 Takauji withdrew from the central provinces and went by ship to Kyushu, where he remained for two months. After bringing most of Kyushu under his sway and adding greatly to the size of his force, Takauji departed Kyushu in 1336:4 for the return to the central provinces. Early in the fifth month, Takauji and his brother Tadayoshi, in a coordinated action by land and sea, engaged the loyalists under Nitta Yoshisada in a great battle at Minatogawa in Settsu province. The battle became a rout of the loyalists: Kusunoki Masashige, after a valiant stand, committed suicide; and Nitta Yoshisada escaped only with great difficulty.

Takauji triumphantly entered Kyoto, while Godaigo fled to sanctuary on Mount Hiei. When Godaigo returned to the capital at the end of the year, he was forced to relinquish the regalia to a new emperor, Kōmyō of the senior branch of the imperial family. Shortly thereafter, Godaigo escaped to Yoshino in the mountains of Kii province to the south of Kyoto. He claimed that, as he had given Kōmyō false regalia, he, Godaigo, was still the rightful sovereign. From this point there were two courts: the northern court in Kyoto, supported by the Ashikaga, and the southern court of Godaigo and his successors at Yoshino.

The half-century of war between the courts may be summarized briefly. The Ashikaga established a new Bakufu in Kyoto—the Ashikaga or Muromachi Bakufu—and completely dominated the northern court.[20] Since most of the courtiers remained in Kyoto, the southern court was always a limited establishment, although at times it was able to command substantial military support. Fighting spread throughout the country to regions as distant as the Kantō and Kyushu. Nitta Yoshisada tried to assert control over the Hokuriku region on the Japan Sea coast, but he died in battle in 1338. In the same year, Kitabatake Akiie brought his army up from Mutsu-Dewa to the central provinces for a second time, but he too died while fighting. All of the principal loyalist chieftains were by this time gone, and in 1339 Godaigo—long the focus of their loyalism—died at Yoshino.

Warriors changed allegiance frequently during the war between the courts, shifting from one side to the other. Loyalty meant little where personal advantage was involved. In some cases, warriors of the same family fought on opposite sides. From about midcentury, the southern court had little prospect of achieving final victory. But its hopes were temporarily buoyed when the Ashikaga Bakufu was raked with internal strife centering on the shogun Takauji and his brother Tadayoshi. During this time, the country was treated to the extraordinary spectacle of both Tadayoshi and Takauji, on separate occasions (1350, 1351), defecting to the southern court. Takauji managed to poison his brother in 1352, but the Bakufu continued to suffer from the repercussions of their fraternal rupture.

Takauji himself died in 1358. During the rule of his son and successor, Yoshiakira, the Bakufu steadily asserted its supremacy in the war between the courts. By the time Yoshiakira was succeeded by Yoshimitsu as the third Ashikaga shogun in 1368, the southern court had ceased to be a serious military threat, although it managed to survive as a government until 1392. In that year Yoshimitsu persuaded the southern emperor to return to Kyoto by promising to reinstitute the system of alternate succession to the emperorship. But Yoshimitsu never honored his promise, and all subsequent emperors—to this day —have been descendants of the senior, northern branch of the imperial family.

Taiheiki

Taiheiki is the longest of the major war tales, exceeding Heike Monogatari in length by about a third. It also covers by far the longest period of time. Whereas some war tales, such as Hōgen Monogatari and Heiji Monogatari, deal with the events of only a few days or weeks and others, like Mutsu Waki and the Heike, span a decade or more, Taiheiki tells the story of a half-century. It is, moreover, a half-century of turbulence and violence of a kind, scale, and duration not previously seen in Japan.

Taiheiki is usually thought to comprise three parts: Books 1–12, dealing with the period from the accession of Emperor Godaigo in 1318 until the overthrow of the Kamakura Bakufu and commencement of the Kemmu Restoration in 1333; Books 13–21, covering the years from the Kemmu Restoration until the death of Godaigo at Yoshino in 1339; and Books 22–40, a narrative of the shifting fortunes of the war between the northern and southern courts and the conflict within the Ashikaga Bakufu during the years until the death of the second Ashikaga shogun, Yoshiakira, in 1367.

Part One is the best-structured and best-composed portion of *Taiheiki*. Commencing with the introduction of its two leading characters, Emperor Godaigo and the Hōjō leader Takatoki, it describes in highly moralistic terms the disordered condition into which the country has fallen because of the virtueless rule of Takatoki and the Kamakura Bakufu and announces the great aim of the court and Godaigo to "destroy the eastern barbarians" and reassert imperial rule.[21] Throughout Part One, the ideal of an imperial restoration is held before the reader as a shining goal—a goal that he senses will be achieved no matter how the fighting shifts between the "imperial forces" *(kangun)* and the "enemies of the court" *(chōteki;* the Kamakura Bakufu). The final triumph of the imperial forces is the capstone of a mission made inevitable by its inherent rightness.

The shift in tone from Part One to Part Two is abrupt and harsh. We quickly learn that Godaigo, whatever his earlier worthy qualities, will not rule fairly or benevolently. Indeed, he will commit some of the classic sins of the Confucian "bad ruler," listening, for example, to the self-interested advice of ladies and other favorites at court, using public revenue for luxurious living, and failing to reward impartially those who have served him best (that is, the warriors who destroyed the Kamakura Bakufu). Many warriors, we are told, begin to wish for a return to military rule, and Ashikaga Takauji emerges to fulfill that wish. In the ensuing warfare of the early years of the war between the courts, as we have seen, all of the original loyalist heroes (the commanders of the imperial forces) perish—Nawa Nagatoshi, Kusunoki Masashige, Kitabatake Akiie, Nitta Yoshisada—and in 1339 Godaigo himself dies in virtual exile in Yoshino, his dream of imperial rule shattered (although there are those who will continue to pursue that dream).

Part Three of *Taiheiki* introduces us to a somber, even despairing world. Fighting is ceaseless, and those who clash one with another are seldom motivated by lofty goals. They contend for selfish ends, often ignoring the most fundamental standards of civilized behavior.

Literarily, Part Three lacks cohesion. One failing of *Taiheiki* as a work of literary history, compared especially to *Heike Monogatari*, is its surfeit of what are often repetitive-sounding battle accounts written in stereotyped language. Part Three confronts the reader with a seemingly endless sequence of such accounts. As Nagazumi Yasuaki observes, Part Three not only descends into the tedium of disjointed battle accounts but even loses its basic structure as a story.[22]

The name *Taiheiki*, literally meaning "Chronicle of Great Peace," has, so far as we know, always been attached to this war tale, and countless readers through the ages have wondered how a story of such great disorder could have been so named. One theory is that the original *Taiheiki* ended with what we now call Part One—that is, with the loyalist victory over the Kamakura Bakufu and inauguration of the Kemmu Restoration. Godaigo and his supporters are victorious, and a "great peace" is brought to the land. According to another theory, "great peace" is intended to have an ironic or cynical meaning, referring to the opposite of the disorder that prevails through most of the work. A third theory, widely held today, is that the name *Taiheiki* should be understood to mean "Chronicle of Great Pacification," for the work in fact ends at a time, in 1367, when the country is about to enter a period of order and reasonably effective central government under the third Ashikaga shogun, Yoshimitsu.[23]

There is more information in the records about the possible authorship and manner of composition of *Taiheiki* than about most, if not all, of the other war tales, although the questions of how and by whom the work was written have by no means been fully answered. Two things are clear: *Taiheiki* was composed over a long period of time —beginning by at least the 1340s, or within a decade or so of the start of its narrative—and it was written or compiled by several people, perhaps even teams of people, who gathered the great abundance of materials that make up its forty books.

The courtier Tōin Kinsada recorded in his diary, *Kinsada Kōki*, the following commentary for 1374:5:3: "I have heard that the priest Kojima died on the twenty-eighth or twenty-ninth [of the last month]. He was the author of *Taiheiki*, which is enjoying popularity in the country these days. Although of lowly social origins, he was regarded as a person of considerable talent. His passing is a pity."[24] Nothing else is known about the priest Kojima, although it is generally agreed that he was not the sole author of *Taiheiki*.

Information about *Taiheiki*'s possible authorship—and means of composition—is provided also in *Nan-Taiheiki*, written in 1402 by Imagawa Ryōshun (Sadayo), a commander of the Ashikaga forces in the war between the courts who played a major role in defeating the southern court's adherents in Kyushu. A noted poet and man of culture as well as a warrior chieftain, Ryōshun wrote *Nan-Taiheiki*, which can be translated as "The Difficulties with *Taiheiki*," to correct what he regarded as errors in *Taiheiki*, especially in its representation of the role played by himself and the Imagawa family during the war. Ryōshun claims that *Taiheiki* was written by a person or persons who deeply favored the "imperial" *(miyakata)* or anti-Ashikaga side in the war, egregiously altered facts, and even resorted to invention. Demonstrating that he is not the first member of the Ashikaga side to complain about these flaws in *Taiheiki*, he notes: "Long ago, the priest Echin of Hosshōji Temple brought the thirty books [or first thirty books] of this writing [*Taiheiki*] to Lord Nishikinokōji [Ashikaga Tadayoshi] at Tōjiji Temple. After looking at it himself, the lord had the priest Gen'e read it. Because [*Taiheiki*] had many distortions and mistakes, Tadayoshi ordered . . . that it be corrected and revised."[25]

Since the language of this quote from *Nan-Taiheiki* is ambiguous, we do not know whether the thirty books that Echin brought to Tadayoshi constituted the entirety of *Taiheiki* as it existed at that time—estimated to have been the 1340s—or whether they dealt with only its first part. A variant edition of *Nan-Taiheiki* identifies Echin as the author of this early version of *Taiheiki*.[26] Scholars think that both Echin and Gen'e were somehow involved in the composition of *Taiheiki*, although neither could have been responsible for compiling or editing all of the work as we have it today, since Gen'e died in 1350 and Echin in 1356, a decade or more before the terminal date of *Taiheiki*'s narrative, 1367. In any case, if Ryōshun's statement in *Nan-Taiheiki* is correct, some alterations to *Taiheiki* favorable to the Ashikaga side were apparently made in the 1340s, and possibly Ryōshun himself was able to effect additional pro-Ashikaga changes in the early fifteenth century.

The many versions of *Taiheiki* fall into two categories: the old text *(kotai-bon)* versions and the circulating text *(rufubon)* versions. The oldest extant old-text version is the Saigen'in text—estimated to have been written sometime during the period 1412–1421, or within a decade or two after Imagawa Ryōshun composed *Nan-Taiheiki*.[27] A distinctive feature of all old text versions of *Taiheiki* is the absence of Book 22. Although no one knows why this book, situated at the point of transition from Part Two to Part Three, is missing, it may have been deleted because of opposition to its contents by someone like Ryōshun.[28] The *rufubon* versions of *Taiheiki*, compiled during the Tokugawa period, all have Book 22; but *rufubon* Book 22 adds nothing to the overall narrative, since it was created by taking material from other books in Parts Two and Three.[29]

We have seen that the early medieval war tales, the *Hōgen*, *Heiji*, and *Heike*, all evolved during long periods of textual development from quasi-historical chronicles *(ki)* to tales *(monogatari)*. Under the influence primarily of tale singers, their original, chronologically arranged formats were altered by the insertion of stories and by other embellishments and were further obscured by the deletion of much of the dating of their passages and chapters. *Taiheiki* did not undergo such alteration, owing primarily to the fact that it was not used—and hence was not textually remolded—by tale singers. True to its title, "*Taihei* Chronicle," it has remained essentially a *ki*, the chronological progression of its passages and chapters clearly identified by the frequent use of dates. Although it contains more digressions—mostly excursions into Chinese history and literature—than any other war tale, the digressions, which were almost surely composed by its original authors, do not affect the fundamentally chronological structuring of the work.

Because *Taiheiki* was not remolded as the early medieval war tales were, its variant texts are very similar. I have, for example, compared entire chapters of the 1603 *rufubon* text used for this study with the corresponding chapters in the Saigen'in and Kanda old text versions and found them to be almost identical, differing only in the choice of certain words, phrases, and Chinese characters and in the use of some numbers (such as the numbers of troops in battles).[30]

Although *Taiheiki* was not adopted for use by tale singers, it was recited or read aloud in a practice called *Taiheiki-yomi* (*Taiheiki* reading). The oldest reference to *Taiheiki-yomi*, dated 1466, is in the diary *Onryōken Nichiroku* (or *Inryōken Nichiroku*) of the Kyoto Zen temple Shōkokuji.[31] But the practice became especiall·· popular as part of the *gunsho-yomi* (reading of military texts) of the *sengoku* and Tokugawa periods. *Taiheiki-yomi* entailed not only the straight reading of the work, but also the interpretation of various words and passages and the presentation of critiques of its political views and military tactics. The critiques were inspired by the polemical character of *Taiheiki*, which contains far more social and political criticism than any other war tale.

Scholars have shown that the authors of *Taiheiki* drew upon an extraordinarily large number of historical and literary works, both Chinese and Japanese. They were particularly inspired by *Heike Monogatari*, as we can deduce from the frequency of their direct references to the *Heike*, their use of *Heike*-like language in battle accounts, and even their occasional recreation, using *Taiheiki* characters, of famous scenes from the *Heike*. In this regard, it is interesting to note that *Taiheiki* was completed during the same period that the Kakuichi text of *Heike Monogatari* was being compiled. (The Kakuichi text was completed in 1371.)[32]

Taiheiki itself exerted a great influence on the writing of history during the Tokugawa period. It was used, for example, as a major primary source in the composition of both *Dai-Nihon Shi* by the Mito school and *Nihon Gaishi* by Rai San'yō. In modern times, *Taiheiki*'s historicity has been sharply attacked. Thus Kume Kunitake in 1891 published an article entitled "*Taiheiki* Is Worthless as a Historical Source."[33] But others have come to the work's defense, demonstrating that, beneath its hyperbole and obvious embellishments, it contains a considerable amount of historically reliable information.[34]

Warriors and Warfare

Taiheiki differs in many ways from the early medieval war tales in its descriptions of warriors and warfare. Some of the differences derive from the altered conditions of fighting in the fourteenth century. For example, the siege, unknown in the early medieval war tales (although found in such ancient tales as *Mutsu Waki* and *Ōshū Gosannen Ki*), becomes a major form of battle in *Taiheiki*; indeed, some of the most famous chapters in *Taiheiki* are accounts of sieges, especially those in which the defending force is commanded by Kusunoki Masashige. Other differences in *Taiheiki*'s descriptions of warriors and warfare are conceptual and stylistic; that is, they result from new or variant ways of seeing warriors and depicting them in battle. The following paragraphs consider some of the ways in which *Taiheiki*'s handling of warriors and warfare differs from the early medieval war tales.

DESCRIPTIONS OF BATTLE

Most of the battling in *Taiheiki* is presented as group combat. In part this is because of the frequency of sieges among the work's battles. By its nature, the siege is essentially a clash between two groups, attackers and defenders, and there is little opportunity for individual initiative or heroics. *Taiheiki*'s authors are obliged to describe sieges for what they are: almost exclusively group encounters. But even in their narration of "open field" battling, which, as in the past, featured the pairing off of mounted warriors in one-against-one fights, the authors give comparatively little attention to these fights and focus instead primarily on the larger conflicts. This is very different from *Heike Monogatari* in which such effective use is made of the battle description in terms of "overview" and "scenes," with the concentration—as, for example, in the Battle of Ichinotani—emphatically on the scenes. One may speculate that the infrequent use of scenes in *Taiheiki*'s battle accounts is mainly because, as noted, the work was not adopted and shaped by tale singers, who used the device of the scene to appeal to their audiences' tastes.

Taiheiki's limited use of the scene in its battle descriptions can be noted, for example, in the campaigns of Kusunoki Masashige, which include both sieges and nonsieges. In all of Masashige's fighting before and after the Kemmu Restoration, as recounted in *Taiheiki*, there is only one passage that might be called a scene: the account of the unsuccessful attempt by Masashige and his band at the Battle of Minatogawa (to be discussed later) to capture or kill Ashikaga Tadayoshi when his horse steps on an arrowhead and is disabled.[35] But even this is not a true scene in the *Heike* sense of an isolated encounter between two warriors or between one warrior and a small group; rather, it is a description of the pursuit of a single warrior within an overview presentation of a battle.

Although the *Heike* contains an abundance of exciting and dramatic scenes, its overviews tend to be skimpy. In this regard, *Taiheiki* is the richer work, since its long, detailed commentaries on battles give us a much better idea of tactics and the ebb and flow of combat. At the same time, as observed, the sheer number of battle commentaries in *Taiheiki* and the often excessive use of stock phrasing in them convey a strong sense of repetition that can deaden the reader's interest.

DRESSING AND NAME-ANNOUNCING

In addition to downplaying the scene in battle descriptions, *Taiheiki* makes only sparing use of two other devices that were highly favored by tale singers: dressing the hero and name-announcing. There are few hero dressings in *Taiheiki*. Name-announcings also appear much less frequently than in the early medieval war tales, although some of *Taiheiki*'s name-announcings are longer and more elaborate—and thus more informative—than many of those in the earlier tales.

WESTERN WARRIORS

From the standpoint of warriors and warfare, *Heike Monogatari* is a sustained paean to the battle skills of the Bandō warriors, those ferocious mounted fighters from the east. "Western" warriors (warriors from the central and western provinces) are generally feeble by contrast, despite their special capabilities in naval warfare. In *Taiheiki*, the Bandō warriors retain their superiority as fighting men in terms of sheer aggressiveness and power. But the western warriors have, by this time, developed their own ways of conducting battle on land. By carefully picking their terrains and setting their stages strategically, they are prepared to take on any foe.

The fighting methods of western warriors in *Taiheiki* appear to have evolved among local groups of *nobushi* warriors: literally, warriors who "hide in the fields."[36] These *nobushi* groups are presumably

the same as the armed bands identified in other records of the age as
akutō or "rowdy (literally, 'evil') bands"—that is, bands engaged in
essentially lawless activities, including the seizure of lands and crops
from others.[37] As fighters, the western warriors of *Taiheiki* are guerrillas.[38] They specialize particularly in erecting and defending fortresses
—that is, withstanding sieges. But they are also adept in hit-and-run
tactics of harassment. They recognize no rules in warfare and employ
unorthodox and wily stratagems. Many are organized as units of foot
soldiers and use spears *(yari)*, as well as bows and swords.

The two great models of western warrior leaders in *Taiheiki* are
Kusunoki Masashige and Akamatsu Norimura (Enshin).[39] Norimura, a
petty chieftain from Harima province, becomes, along with Masashige, a loyalist fighter for Godaigo and plays a major role in defeating
the Bakufu forces in the central provinces. But he is not well rewarded
during the Kemmu Restoration and later joins the Ashikaga against
Godaigo and the southern court.

The new methods of warfare of western warriors as found in
Taiheiki are discussed in detail in the section on Kusunoki Masashige.

WARRIOR TYPES

Taiheiki tends to present warriors more as types—often extreme
types—than the earlier war tales. Hence we find in its pages many one-
dimensional warriors who are readily identifiable as traitors, cowards,
or heroes. The traitors and cowards are often particularly despicable,
and the heroes are incredibly, even insanely, brave and devoted. There
is, for example, the case of the traitor Shimazu Shirō. In the battling
for Kamakura in 1333 that leads to the destruction of the Hōjō family,
Hōjō Takatoki selects Shirō for the vital task of guarding one of the
approaches to the city. Famed for his strength and martial demeanor,
Shirō is considered the "equal of a thousand" and one upon whom the
Hōjō can rely in a time of crisis. Takatoki toasts Shirō and bestows
upon him the "most famous horse *(meiba)* in the Kantō," equipped
with a silver-lined saddle. As Shirō rides off to defend against the
invaders of Kamakura, he is the envy of all who see him. But instead of
fighting magnificently when he encounters the enemy (the troops of
Nitta Yoshisada), he promptly dismounts, surrenders, and joins them.
Taiheiki informs us that "there were none, of either high or low station, who, upon seeing this, did not take back their words of praise and
detest [Shimazu Shirō]."[40]

Self-sacrificing heroes abound in *Taiheiki*. There is, for example,
the loyalist warrior who, at the battle of Yoshino in 1333:2, disembowels himself in view of the attacking enemy, claiming that he is

Prince Moriyoshi in order to enable the prince secretly to escape.[41] And in the last stages of the fighting for Kamakura, one warrior after another goes deliberately to his death in battle or commits suicide with the sole thought of repaying the Hōjō for favors received in the past.

The inclusion in *Taiheiki* of so many odious warrior villains on the one hand and peerless warrior heroes on the other can no doubt be attributed to facile stereotyping by the work's authors. At the same time, it also reflects, I believe, the times that produced *Taiheiki*. Good and bad or right and wrong—in terms of ethical rightness or sacred legitimacy—are major issues in *Taiheiki*, especially Part One, in a way not found, for example, in the *Heike*. Taira no Kiyomori certainly represents "bad" or "evil" in the *Heike's* first half. But Kiyomori dies at the beginning of the Gempei War, and in the work's second half, a narration of the war, there is little sense that the Minamoto represent the righteous side or the Taira the converse. To be sure, the Taira suffer bad karma because of Kiyomori's evil ways. But, as discussed in Chapter Three, they are also battered by the inscrutable forces of fate. Because the world, including the Taira, is so clearly seen to be in the grips of a destructive fate in the age of *mappō*, the question of which side is "right" and which is not is, at best, of secondary importance. What really matters in the war is military success: The Minamoto win because they are the best fighters, not because they represent a righteous cause.

Taiheiki also contains references to *mappō*, fate, and the world in decline. But again—especially in the early parts—these are of secondary importance. As scholars have observed, *Taiheiki* is much more a Confucian than a Buddhist work and is mainly concerned with questions of ethical rightness and legitimacy, leading its authors to draw many characters stereotypically as either obviously good or obviously bad.[42]

SUICIDE

The practice among warriors of suicide by disembowelment *(seppuku)* appears, as we have seen, in the early medieval war tales. But it does not appear often and is found only among eastern warriors. In *Taiheiki*, seppuku becomes one of the chief features of warrior behavior, and we read of warriors from all regions, in battle after battle, "cutting their bellies." Often the descriptions of these suicides are graphic—specifying, for example, not only how warriors bisect their stomachs or slice them in the form of a cross *(jūmonji)* but also, on occasion, pull out their entrails. Sometimes a warrior employs a companion as a second, who decapitates him after he has cut his stomach while in a seated position. In historical fact, the second became virtually essential in *seppuku*, since death by knife-inflicted wound to the stomach was likely to be slow and agonizing. Some of the warriors in *Taiheiki* commit *seppuku* to avoid capture in battle. In reality, this would have been unwise, unless a warrior was assured that some time—enough time to die—would elapse before the enemy reached him.

Seppuku is not the only method of suicide employed by warriors in *Taiheiki*. As in earlier war tales, some warriors fall on their swords.[43] Others engage in a form of double suicide by stabbing each other *(sashi-chigaete)* to death; a few perform the astounding feat of cutting off their own heads. The most famous of all suicides in *Taiheiki*, Kusunoki Masashige's, is part of a double suicide. When, at the Battle of Minatogawa in 1336, defeat is certain, Masashige and his brother Masasue die as they simultaneously stab each other and, in a common euphemism found in *Taiheiki* and later war tales, "lie down on the same pillow."[44] Nitta Yoshisada, on the other hand, is among those who decapitate themselves. He performs this act after being fatally wounded by an arrow that strikes him in the forehead in a battle in Echizen province in 1338.[45]

Taiheiki introduces us to an important new reason for the warrior to commit suicide: to follow his lord in death, usually called *junshi*. Isolated cases of warriors killing themselves after the deaths of their lords can be found in the earlier war tales and may be regarded as *junshi*, but it is not until *Taiheiki* that the practice begins to assume the form of something that is expected of the loyal warrior or is part of the warrior's unwritten code. At the fall of the Kamakura Bakufu in 1333, for example, a vast number of people—*Taiheiki* says more than six thousand—destroy themselves along with the Hōjō leader Takatoki in a mass *junshi*. It is a ghastly scene, with warriors and nonwarriors, women as well as men, committing *seppuku*, stabbing each other, cutting off their own heads, and running into blazing buildings.[46]

One may argue that this orgy of self-destruction is not truly *junshi*—the voluntary act of following one's lord in death—since most of the people who kill themselves probably assume they will be murdered by the enemy if captured. A clearer case of *junshi* in *Taiheiki* can be found, for example, in the suicide of three or more lieutenants after their commander, Nitta Yoshisada, decapitates himself, as noted above, in a battle in Echizen province in 1338. Yoshisada's head rolls into the deep mud of a rice paddy, and his body falls on top of it. An enemy runs up and, retrieving the head, fastens it to the tip of his spear and rushes back toward his fortress. Yoshisada's lieutenants, who could easily escape with the remnants of their army, instead go to Yoshisada's corpse and, kneeling before it, commit *seppuku*, their bodies "falling over one on top of another."[47]

SHIFTING WARRIORS

In *Heike Monogatari*, as we have seen, Yoshitsune's follower Ise no Yoshimori remarks: "These provincial warriors don't care whom they serve. They'll follow anyone who can quell the disturbances and restore order to the land." As observed in Chapter Four, this remark suggests that many of the warriors who fought in the Gempei War opportunistically shifted from one side to the other as conditions and their own selfish interests dictated. The *kari-musha* or temporarily assembled warriors, who appear in the armies of the Taira and scatter or decamp as soon as a battle starts to go badly, are extreme examples of unreliability among warriors recruited to fight the war, at least in the *Heike* account.

In *Taiheiki*, especially the early chapters, great emphasis is placed on the zeal and steadfast loyalty of the core supporters of the various armies or sides in battles. One thinks particularly of those who commit themselves wholeheartedly to Godaigo's loyalist cause, although the Hōjō before the Kemmu Restoration and the Ashikaga after it also have their shares of devoted warrior followers. But as we read through battle after battle in *Taiheiki*, especially the back-and-forth fighting between the loyalists and the Ashikaga after the restoration's failure that leads to the war between the courts, we realize that the two sides are frequently competing for the same shifting pools of warriors. In other words, they are repeatedly obliged to vie, one against another, for warriors of the regions where they fight in order to augment their bands of diehard followers.

This competition for warriors can be observed, for example, in the events of early 1336 that follow the great success of the loyalists' army, headed by Nitta Yoshisada and Kitabatake Akiie, in driving Ashikaga Takauji out of Kyoto and forcing him to flee by boat to Kyushu.[48] *Taiheiki* says that the warrior adherents of the Ashikaga in "Shikoku and the western provinces" are all dispirited, fleeing into the mountains and forests and trying to establish new alliances. If Yoshisada had without delay set out westward after the Ashikaga, "not a single one [of these former enemies] would have failed to join him."[49] But Yoshisada, like Yoshinaka in the *Heike* when he is attacked by the army of Yoshitsune and Noriyori, chooses instead to dally with a court lady— her name is Kōtō no Naishi—and misses what may have been a golden opportunity to amass an army sufficient in size to decisively defeat the

Ashikaga. As time passes and Yoshisada fails to march, the Ashikaga begin to regroup; and they attract so many warriors to their banner throughout the western regions that "even those who do not sympathize with the shogun's (Takauji's) cause are obliged to submit to him."[50]

But even as this great pool of western warriors swings again to the Ashikaga, a loyalist stalwart, Kojima Takanori of Bizen province, presents Yoshisada with an elaborate and ingenious strategy involving various fortresses and positions that he guarantees will, if followed, "cause all the forces of the western provinces, without exception, to join us."[51] In other words, it will cause the pool to flow back once more to the loyalists.

Kojima Takanori's strategy, in fact, works fairly well, and for a while the fortunes of the loyalists rise. But when the pool of fickle western warriors hears that the Ashikaga are returning from Kyushu with a "great army" (taigun), they begin absconding from the loyalists to join it. In a march to Hyōgo on the Inland Sea, where they plan to await the return of the Ashikaga from Kyushu, the loyalist army is reduced by desertion, according to Taiheiki, from one hundred thousand to twenty thousand.[52]

In Part Three of Taiheiki, dealing with the war between the courts after Godaigo's death in 1339, deceit and treachery become so common that even the most prominent warriors, including, as noted, Takauji and his brother Tadayoshi, are prepared to defect to the enemy when it suits their purposes. Loyalty among warriors sinks to the point where the work's authors somberly lament: "The heart of the warrior in these times is as difficult to rely upon as a rotted rope you might use to tether six horses."[53] And, near Taiheiki's end, we hear this anguished cry: "Whom can one, in these times, consider a true enemy or trust as an unswerving ally? The changeable heart has no more substance than a goose feather, while the steadfast spirit is as rare as the horn of a kirin."[54]

WARRIOR-COURTIERS

The Taira of Heike Monogatari, as observed, take on courtier ways during the decades of their ascendancy in Kyoto between the Heiji Conflict and the Gempei War, merging the bun and the bu and becoming courtier-warriors. In Taiheiki we encounter the reverse phenomenon of courtiers—and members of royalty—acquiring bu and becoming warrior-courtiers. (I will use the term warrior-courtiers to refer to both courtiers and royalty who behave like warriors.) The two best examples of warrior-courtiers are Prince Moriyoshi and Kitabatake Akiie, but there are many others who become directly involved in the warfare described in *Taiheiki*.[55] Thus whereas in the *Heike* courtiers and royalty are either helpless bystanders or are engaged, at most, in political intrigue during the Gempei War, in *Taiheiki* some are also active military participants in the fighting before and after the Kemmu Restoration.

An interesting example of courtier participation in the warfare in *Taiheiki* appears in the account of the Battle of Takenoshita in the Kantō in late 1335, fought between the Ashikaga and the loyalists under Nitta Yoshisada's brother Yoshisuke. One unit of the loyalists, under the command of an imperial prince, comprises some five hundred members of the guard companies that serve courtier families and retired emperors. Unfurling the imperial banner, members of the unit shout at the enemy, calling upon them to put down their helmets and surrender in order to avoid the "heavenly transgression" of drawing their bows and releasing arrows against the emperor's army. The warrior commanders on the Ashikaga side guess from the way these shouting loyalists handle their horses and from their banner that they are courtiers. Mockingly observing that, since they are forbidden to shoot arrows, they will use their swords instead, the Ashikaga warriors charge with drawn blades into the loyalists, who unceremoniously whip their horses as they desperately seek to escape. Most of them, however, are either killed or taken prisoner.[56]

The Failed Loyalist Hero

In the early medieval war tales we met the loser-hero and the tragic loser-hero. *Taiheiki* introduces us to another kind of loser-hero: the failed loyalist hero. The chief characteristic of the failed loyalist hero is unswerving devotion to Emperor Godaigo and the southern court, leading finally to death in battle in what, as we know in historical retrospect, was the southern court's losing cause. Chief among the failed loyalist heroes of *Taiheiki* are Kusunoki Masashige, Nitta Yoshisada, Nawa Nagatoshi, Kitabatake Akiie, and Kusunoki Masatsura.

In the failed loyalist hero we find the supreme personification in the war tales of Watsuji Tetsurō's idea of self-sacrificing *(kenshin)* loyalty. As we have seen, such loyalty appears from earliest times to have been one of the highest ideals among warriors—both in the war tales, which are only partly historical, and in actual history. But history and the war tales also provide so many examples of violations of the *kenshin* ideal—including blatant disloyalty (conspicuously observable, for example, in the shifting pool of western warriors discussed above)—that we must wonder how significant it was in shaping warrior relations through the ages.

Taiheiki's failed loyalist hero personifies self-sacrificing loyalty at its highest because the focus of his commitment is the emperor himself. There are ample references in the earlier war tales to warriors motivated by their devotion to emperors (and ex-emperors). But imperial loyalism does not emerge as a central belief governing warrior behavior in the war tales until *Taiheiki*. In *Hōgen Monogatari*, for example, although the contending sides are headed by an emperor and an ex-emperor and warrior chieftains make intermittent claims that the cause of one side or the other is just or legitimate, the reader gets little sense that there is really an issue of imperial justness or legitimacy involved in the Hōgen Conflict. Rather, the emperor and ex-emperor are figureheads for groups representing blatant factional (hence selfish) interests.

In *Heiji Monogatari*, Kiyomori and the Taira achieve a coup when they secretly transfer the emperor from Minamoto custody to Kiyomori's residence in the Rokuhara section of Kyoto. This makes the Taira the "emperor's army." But the *Heiji*, in describing the ensuing, decisive Battle of Taikenmon Gate, does not convey the impression that the Taira and Minamoto who clash attach much significance to this distinction.

And in *Heike Monogatari*, Emperor Antoku, who is indisputably the legitimate sovereign because he possesses the regalia, is with the Taira throughout the Gempei War. Yet the *Heike*'s author never accuses the Minamoto of violating the emperor or imperial sovereignty, even though they relentlessly pursue the Taira and Antoku and finally cause Antoku's death by drowning in the Battle of Dannoura. In fact, sovereignty seems to be represented more by the retired emperor Goshirakawa than by Antoku in the *Heike*, and Goshirakawa transfers his "sovereign" support back and forth from one warrior chief to another, depending on how the winds of fortune blow.[57]

In *Taiheiki*, imperial legitimacy is from the outset presented as the work's central issue. Godaigo, according to the first chapter, is a legitimate and virtuous emperor who has "rectified the three ways and five virtues and adheres to the way of the Duke of Chou and Confucius."[58] The Hōjō, after ruling for "nine generations," have brought disorder to the land and must be destroyed. Those who fight against the Hōjō and for Godaigo are, as observed, the "imperial army," a distinction that the loyalists retain in *Taiheiki* even after the collapse of the Kemmu Restoration and the beginning of the war between the courts.

When Godaigo fails to perform as a virtuous ruler in the Kemmu Restoration, his cause is clearly tarnished. And in the ensuing war between the courts the Ashikaga, drawing on the earlier practice of

Upon being summoned, Masashige goes immediately to Mount Kasagi. In response to the emperor's inquiry about how he might conquer the "eastern barbarians" (tōi) and bring peace to the land, he says:

> "The eastern barbarians, in their recent rebellion, have drawn the censure of heaven. If we take advantage of their weakness, resulting from the decline and disorder they have caused, what difficulty should we have in inflicting heaven's punishment upon them? But the goal of unifying the country must be carried out by means of both military tactics and carefully devised strategy. Even if we fight them force against force and although we recruit warriors throughout the more than sixty provinces of Japan to confront the men of the two provinces of Musashi and Sagami, we will be hard-pressed to win. But if we fight with clever scheming, the military force of the eastern barbarians will be capable of no more than breaking sharp swords and crushing hard helmets. It will be easy to deceive them, and there will be nothing to fear. Since the aim of warfare is ultimate victory, Your Majesty should pay no heed to whether we win or lose in any single battle. So long as you hear that Masashige alone is still alive, know that your imperial destiny will in the end be attained."[68]

Masashige makes the following points: The eastern barbarians have gone against heaven and must be punished (that is, destroyed); they cannot be destroyed by force alone, because they still possess great military might, but must be defeated also by clever scheming; Masashige himself will not only assume responsibility for devising and carrying out the schemes necessary to destroy the eastern barbarians, his life will become Godaigo's "imperial destiny" (seiun).

Masashige's comment about the forces of the Kamakura Bakufu —represented by "the two [Kantō] provinces of Musashi and Sagami" —confirms the belief, also noted earlier in the section on "Warriors and Warfare," that the eastern, Bandō warriors are still superior to all others in face-to-face—one-against-one—fighting. Even in its degenerate state, the Bakufu, according to Masashige, can mobilize a force of Bandō warriors who, in a clash of sheer military might, will defeat troops from the rest of the country. The Bandō warriors must be brought to their knees by a combination of force and stratagem.

Masashige and Yoshitsune

The reader of the war tales will inevitably compare Kusunoki Masashige with Minamoto no Yoshitsune, his chief competitor for the distinction of supreme fighting commander in the tales.[69] One difficulty in making such a comparison is that whereas Taiheiki's Masashige is a flawless character whose sterling qualities are never tarnished, but who also lacks the frailties that might make him more human, Yoshitsune of *Heike Monogatari* is a complex, unpredictable, and decidedly flawed—one might say fatally flawed—figure. Comparing the two is like holding a brilliant but erratic mortal up against a transcendent being.

Nevertheless, a comparison of Yoshitsune and Masashige as warrior leaders will help clarify the special qualities of both as they are presented in the *Heike* and *Taiheiki*. Yoshitsune, as we have seen, has a crafty, deceptive streak, but as a commander his principal motto might be "Ever Forward," and most of his great victories are marked by decisiveness, speed, and surprise, and even, at times, by death-defying recklessness. In his "reverse oars" dispute with Kajiwara no Kagetoki before the Battle of Yashima, Yoshitsune rejects as defeatist thinking Kagetoki's idea of equipping boats with special oars to enable them to retreat or advance according to the dictates of battle. Perhaps Yoshitsune opposes the reverse oars idea simply to challenge and embarrass Kagetoki. Still, the principle of not considering retreat is in keeping with his bravura style of dashing, inspirational leadership.

In Kusunoki Masashige, a model of the new kind of western warrior found in *Taiheiki*, we have a leader of a very different stamp. He will use any means or ruse to beguile, deceive, and entrap the enemy. Whereas Yoshitsune's career is highlighted by a series of great, decisive victories, Masashige avoids the decisive encounter, preferring instead to confound, frustrate, and wear his opponent down. We noted that Yoshitsune and his personal band may have had experience as guerrillas, and they often use guerrilla techniques in battle. In Masashige, we have the consummate guerrilla.

The guerrilla, in the true sense of the word, is a local fighter thoroughly familiar with the terrain—the home terrain—in which he operates. Yoshitsune conducted all his campaigns during the Gempei War on fields (and seas) far from what was presumably his home terrain, Mutsu. But Masashige fought for Godaigo's loyalist cause almost entirely in the three bordering provinces of Kawachi, Izumi, and Settsu, where, according to *Taiheiki*, he was already famous as a local fighter and where he undoubtedly had extensive connections and many supporters.

One of the most distinctive qualities of Yoshitsune in the *Heike*, as we have seen, is his close relationship with a small band of followers, including the Satō brothers, Ise no Yoshimori, and Musashibō Benkei. Indeed, Yoshitsune's character is to a large extent defined by how he treats and inspires these men. He frequently seeks their advice, he rallies them to perform great deeds, he succors them when they are dying. They, in turn, follow where he leads, without regard for safety or even their lives. So closely bound is Yoshitsune with this intimate band of followers that we cannot think of him without them: They are an integral part of the entity known as "Yoshitsune" in the *Heike*.

Masashige, too, is a warrior leader capable of inspiring his followers to perform superbly. But *Taiheiki* tells us almost nothing about who these followers are or what personal relationships they may have with Masashige. Only two of the followers are, in fact, mentioned by name. One is Wada Masatō, identified only as a subcommander at the Battle of Akasaka;[70] the other is Masashige's brother Masasue, who remains merely a name until the Battle of Minatogawa, when he and Masashige commit suicide by stabbing each other.[71]

Siege Warfare and the Battle of Akasaka

Shortly after Godaigo's meeting with Masashige in *Taiheiki*, Bakufu forces attack the fortress on Mount Kasagi and, after several unsuccessful attempts to break down its defenses by conventional daytime assaults, finally destroy it with fire in a night attack, confirming again the excellence of the night attack and arson as means for achieving victory in battle. Godaigo flees Kasagi, but he is captured and, the following year, sent into exile on the Oki Islands. Against his will, he is replaced as emperor by Kōgon of the senior line. Meanwhile, Kusunoki Masashige, openly raising the banner of the loyalist cause and defying the Bakufu, takes up a position with some five hundred warriors on Mount Akasaka in Kawachi, near his home.

Taiheiki uses various terms for the defensive fortifications or fortresses established at places like Kasagi and Akasaka during the wars of the restoration and the northern and southern courts—terms such as *shiro* and *jōkaku*, which can be variously translated as stronghold, fortress, castle, or citadel. Although very little remains from either the written records or the physical sites to inform us of the exact character of these fortifications, we know that they became focal points of the new kind of siege warfare that appeared at this time, especially in the central and western provinces. The loyalist (later, southern court) forces particularly favored the use of such fortifications, probably because they were often greatly outnumbered by their opponents. Kusunoki Masashige may have been a major figure in the development of fortifications and siege warfare during the early fourteenth century.[72]

Mutsu Waki and *Ōshū Gosannen Ki* tell of the use of defensive fortifications called *saku* or stockades in the fighting in the northern, Mutsu-Dewa region in the late eleventh century; and Minamoto no

Yoshiie in particular is obliged to sustain long, grueling sieges in order to defeat the Kiyowara in the Ōshū account of the Later Three Years War. Otherwise, the ancient and early medieval war tales say little about sieges. In the one-against-one type of fighting between mounted warriors that prevailed throughout this period, the preferred setting for battle remained the open field, where mobility and maneuverability were keys to success.

The principal fortification in *Heike Monogatari* is the Taira fortress at Ichinotani. But it is clear from the *Heike* description of the Battle of Ichinotani in its various phases that the Taira have only erected simple barricades—such as the wooden spikes called *sakamogi*—around the fortress and have no intention of trying to hold it defensively against attackers. Even as the battle begins, the Taira open the fortress gates and rush forward to meet the advancing Minamoto.

The development of defensive fortresses in the warfare of the fourteenth century saw the movement of fortification sites from level ground to mountaintops.[73] But fortresses built on such elevated, difficult-to-approach locations were not intended to be enduring strongholds. Rather, they were constructed for specific strategic purposes or campaigns. Often, as in the case of Kasagi, Buddhist temples on mountaintops were temporarily converted into fortresses. The mountaintop temple not only provided buildings but might also afford additional manpower and resources if the monks joined the warriors as defenders.[74] *Taiheiki* informs us that the monks of Kasagi Temple did not immediately commit themselves as fighters to Godaigo, but rallied to him when they heard that loyalists had defeated Bakufu troops in fighting near Kyoto.[75]

Here is *Taiheiki*'s description of Kasagi Fortress:

> The mountain upon which Kasagi Fortress (*shiro*) stood soared into the sky, its peak partially buried in white clouds. Valleys, whose paths were blocked by moss-covered rocks, yawned far below, and the twisting road to the mountain's peak was a mile and a half in length. Boulders had been excavated to create a moat, and rocks were piled high to form walls. Even if there were no defenders, it would be no easy matter to ascend Kasagi's heights to attack the fortress.[76]

The descriptions in *Taiheiki* of such fortresses seldom lack hyperbole and obviously cannot be accepted as entirely accurate. But they are valuable in conveying a general sense of the fourteenth-century fortress. Among the principal features of these fortresses were moats (*hori*), wooden walls (*hei*), watchtowers (*yagura*), and outer gates (*kido*)—gates that were structurally installed on the outer sides of the fortress walls.[77] From the few drawings of them that remain, and from otherwise fancifully elaborated descriptions of them in *Taiheiki*, these fortresses appear to have been none too sturdy. In many cases moats were just ditches, wooden walls were weakly constructed and often plastered with mud to reduce the threat of incineration by flaming arrows, and watchtowers were rickety structures erected mainly to provide elevated positions for archers.

Kasagi Fortress was destroyed by forces dispatched by the Roku-hara magistrates of Kyoto, even as an army sent by the Bakufu from Kamakura approached the capital region to give assistance. *Taiheiki* pictures the warriors of this eastern army, frustrated in having missed out on the Kasagi campaign, hurrying with great eagerness to assault Kusunoki Masashige's position on Mount Akasaka.[78] But to the distress of these warriors, all aflame to perform meritoriously and obtain rewards, the Akasaka Fortress, as they approach it, presents a sorry sight: It is a hastily erected structure with a half-dug moat or ditch, only one mud-covered wall instead of the usual two or more, and a mere twenty to thirty watchtowers (evidently regarded as insufficient because each could accommodate only a few archers). Hoping that, by some miracle, the position will hold out for at least a day to enable them to distinguish themselves in battle, the warriors of the Bakufu's army—*Taiheiki*, noted for its lavish use of numbers, says there are three hundred thousand of them—rush forward "Me first!" to storm Akasaka Fortress.[79]

Drawing upon a famous concept in Chinese military history, *Taiheiki* says: "Masashige was by nature the kind of commander who, alone inside his headquarters, could devise a plan for victory thousands of miles away."[80] Waiting until the attackers reach the base of the fortress, Masashige signals his archers, positioned on the watchtowers and at every opening in the walls, to unleash a hail of arrows that in a moment slays a thousand. And when the amazed enemy withdraw to rest and regroup, three hundred of Masashige's horsemen, previously concealed in the surrounding hills, charge into their midst, killing many and scattering the others in all directions. Next the fortress gates open and another two hundred horsemen pour forth to complete the rout of the vast Bakufu army.[81]

When the Bakufu warriors, still convinced that Akasaka Fortress is too flimsy to withstand a powerful assault, again approach it and seek to scale its wall, the defenders cut the ropes that hold the wall, actually a sham facade, and it crashes down, crushing many of the attackers. The defenders slaughter still more attackers by throwing down huge logs and boulders. And when, in yet another attack on the fortress, the Bakufu warriors try to pull down its real wall with bear-claw *(kumade)* rakes, the defenders, using ten- to twenty-foot-long ladles, pour boiling water on them. Seeping through the openings in helmets and armor, the scalding water, although it does not kill the attackers, causes such horrible burns that many of them are left utterly incapacitated.[82]

Scholars have pointed out that many of the methods used by Masashige at Akasaka and in other battles—throwing logs and rocks, for example, and pouring boiling water down on attackers—were the fighting methods of commoners and rowdies, tactics apparently adopted by the western warriors who formed *akutō*. Okabe Shūzō suggests that Masashige was also a student of the art of the *ninja*. Citing various references to *ninja* practices in *Taiheiki*, Okabe contends that the *ninja* art was widespread, at least in the central provinces, at this time.[83]

One of the most interesting of *Taiheiki's ninja* practices, as identified by Okabe, is the *rakugaki*, or anonymous satirical verse.[84] Posted at prominent locations in Kyoto and elsewhere, *rakugaki* were used to mock the failures of warrior leaders, thus serving as weapons in what today would be called psychological warfare. Just before the Battle of Kasagi Fortress, for example, a chieftain named Takahashi Matashirō attempts, with three hundred followers, to be first in battle by attacking the fortress before the arrival of the Bakufu's main contingent. When he is ambushed and routed by the defenders and forced to flee ignominiously, someone posts this verse at Byōdōin Temple in Uji:

> Because the waves flow swiftly
> Over the rocky shoals of Kizu River,
> The tall bridge collapsed
> As soon as it was erected.[85]

Punning on the name Takahashi, "tall bridge," the verse's author cleverly satirizes how Takahashi Matashirō encountered military disaster when he and his men arrived at Kizu River at the base of Mount Kasagi and were put to flight by a force of loyalist defenders lying in wait.

After three disastrous attempts to take Akasaka Fortress by storm, the Bakufu army, while lamenting that it cannot achieve an impressive victory at arms, decides to starve the defenders into submission. In fact, Masashige was not able to stock the fortress with enough food to withstand a long siege. Ever flexible in his thinking and planning, he explains to his men the need always to look to the final victory and not be concerned about winning every battle. He decides that, with all save one of the men, he will secretly escape from Aka-

saka Fortress on a dark night. The one left behind will set fire to the
fortress, and the charred bodies of companions killed earlier in the
fortress's defense will convince the Bakufu army that Masashige and
all the defenders chose to die rather than surrender.

Masashige's secret escape from Akasaka Fortress, as recounted in
Taiheiki, is accompanied by new signs of sacred or heavenly approval
of him. Heaven, we are told, displays its favor by quickly presenting
Masashige with a dark, rainy night to facilitate the escape; and when
an archer shoots point-blank at him as he attempts to pass through the
enemy's camp, the arrow strikes an amulet inscribed with the Kannon
Sutra that he has carried for years and his life is saved.[86]

The Battle of Chihaya

Akasaka Fortress was abandoned and burned in 1331:10, and
early the following year, 1332, Godaigo was sent into exile. During the
remainder of 1332, the loyalist cause was kept alive largely by
Masashige and Prince Moriyoshi fighting in the central provinces.
Showing himself to be as fine a commander in mobile warfare as in
holding a fortress, the usually outnumbered Masashige kept the
Bakufu forces constantly at bay.

In the *Taiheiki* account we read how Masashige retakes Akasaka
Fortress (which has presumably been rebuilt) with a Trojan Horse ploy
—sending in his followers disguised as the bearers of supplies, but carrying bags that actually contain weapons.[87] And on another occasion
we find him allowing the enemy to occupy a position, Tennōji Temple,
then causing them to abandon it by lighting signal fires throughout the
countryside and making them believe they are encircled by a huge
army.[88]

By 1333:3, Akasaka Fortress, which Masashige had left to others
to defend, had surrendered to Bakufu attackers and Prince Moriyoshi
was forced to abandon a position he had held at Yoshino in Yamato
province. In the *Taiheiki* account of this third battle of Akasaka Fortress, there is a competition to be first in battle between two warriors
named Hitomi and Homma. Scholars have pointed to this competition
as a prime example of imitation of *Heike Monogatari* by the authors of
Taiheiki, since it is so reminiscent of the famous rivalry between
Kumagae no Naozane and Hirayama no Sueshige to be first at the Battle of Ichinotani in the *Heike*'s version of the Gempei War;[89] indeed,
reference is made in this *Taiheiki* story of Hitomi and Homma to
Naozane and Sueshige. But whereas Naozane and Sueshige—and most
of the other warriors who contend to be first in battle in the *Heike*—do
so for rewards, Hitomi and Homma deliberately sacrifice their lives

out of a sense of obligation to the Hōjō. They are not concerned about waiting for others to witness their daring and bravery. Both set out alone for the fortress before dawn on the day it is to be attacked and, meeting on the road, ride together to the fortress and fight at its gate until they are killed.[90]

When Homma's son learns of his father's death, he resolves to die the same way. A priest attempts to dissuade him, arguing disingenuously that the father had, in fact, forfeited his life for reward for his family. But the son, imbued with the same self-sacrificing spirit as his father, sets out for the fortress anyway. At the fortress gate he announces his name, informing the defenders of his determination to fulfill his filial duty and die as his father died. After fighting furiously, he places his sword in his mouth and perishes by falling on his face.[91]

We find here a theme that recurs in *Taiheiki:* the warrior son who follows his father in death. This theme appears again, for example, in the very next chapter, "The Battle of Yoshino Fortress." As the fortress, commanded by Prince Moriyoshi, is about to be overrun by Bakufu attackers, Murakami Yoshiteru implores the prince to escape, saying that he himself will die in the prince's place. Reluctantly, Moriyoshi leaves the fortress. Yoshiteru, climbing one of the towers, disembowels himself in front of the enemy, proclaiming himself to be the prince. Although Yoshiteru persuades his son Yoshitaka not to die with him in the fortress, the son, accompanying Prince Moriyoshi from the fortress, relinquishes his life shortly thereafter as he fights alone to enable Moriyoshi to escape.[92]

When the defenders of Akasaka Fortress surrender to the Bakufu besiegers, they do so in the belief that they will be spared because the Bakufu commanders will wish to use an act of leniency to persuade other loyalists, defending other fortresses, also to surrender. In negotiations, the Bakufu commanders not only promise to spare the defenders if they surrender but even say they will bestow rewards upon some. But when the defenders open the fortress gates and lay down their arms, they are seized, bound, and carried off to Kyoto, where all are beheaded as blood sacrifices to the gods of war.[93]

Masashige, meanwhile, has taken up a position at Chihaya Fortress, a short distance south of Akasaka. In 1333:3 Bakufu forces attack Chihaya. The disparity in numbers between attackers and defenders, as given in *Taiheiki*, is mind-boggling: more than one million versus barely one thousand.[94] As at the first siege of Akasaka Fortress in 1331, the Bakufu attackers, scorning what they regard as a puny fortress, greatly underestimate Masashige's power of resistance. Rushing wildly "Me first!" to the base of the fortress, they are soon dispersed by an assortment of rocks and expertly aimed arrows. The attackers suffer so many casualties, we are told, that "in recording the dead and wounded, twelve scribes did not put their brushes down for three days and nights."[95]

One of the ploys Masashige uses in the siege of Chihaya to befuddle and outwit the enemy is, along with the false wall trick at Akasaka Fortress, probably the most famous of the many brilliant military maneuvers ascribed to him in *Taiheiki*. Placing some twenty to thirty life-size dolls, outfitted with armor and helmets, at the base of the fortress during nighttime darkness, Masashige at dawn has a group of his warriors hiding behind the dolls shout their battle cries, deceiving the Bakufu force into believing that all the defenders are coming out of the fortress at once to engage in open battle. As the attackers, enticed by the prospect of slaughtering Masashige's meager contingent, rush pell-mell "Me first!" once again toward the fortress, Masashige pulls the group behind the dolls back into the fortress. And when the attackers reach the fortress's base, he rains down thirty to forty boulders, squashing more than three hundred of the duped attackers and leaving another five hundred "half-dead and half-alive."[96]

In still another attempt to take Chihaya Fortress, the attackers bring some five hundred carpenters from Kyoto to construct a huge bridge. Lowering the bridge by ropes to span the ravine that separates a neighboring peak from Chihaya, the attackers start across it. But Masashige, prepared for this kind of assault, has his men light torches and throw them onto the bridge. They then pour oil on the torches with pumps. The attackers in front, seeing the impending disaster, try to move backward, but those behind, who know nothing of what is happening, continue to press forward. When the bridge finally collapses, thousands of the attackers plunge to their deaths in the valley far below.[97]

Between its futile attacks on Chihaya Fortress, the Bakufu army resorts to the time-honored siege tactic of trying to force the defenders into submission by waiting until their supplies, including water and food, are exhausted. Masashige, however, has stocked the fortress much more fully than he was able to stock Akasaka Fortress, thus reducing the effectiveness of this tactic. But the principal reason why the waiting game is of dubious value to the Chihaya besiegers is that they must destroy Masashige's fortress as quickly as possible. For the fortress's value is not strategic but symbolic. So long as it holds out, the Bakufu has not put down the loyalist insurgency in the central provinces, and warriors will continue to be drawn to the loyalist cause.

But even before the Chihaya besiegers are able to mount another assault upon the fortress their strength is greatly reduced when Prince Moriyoshi mobilizes local fighters or "field warriors" (nobushi), including at least some peasants who have acquired armor and helmets from fallen warriors, to cut off the approaches—and thus the supply lines—to Chihaya. As increasingly larger groups of warriors desert the besieging army, it is reduced in size from eight hundred thousand (we were told at the chapter's beginning that the army numbered more than a million) to only a hundred thousand. In their frantic eagerness to get away, the deserters behave in a manner that Taiheiki calls unprecedented shamelessness, abandoning their horses and discarding their armor (including priceless family heirlooms) and even their underclothes. Oblivious to humiliation, they run from Chihaya, attempting to cover their nakedness at least partially with reeds and grasses.[98]

Meanwhile, as the Chiyaha siege drags on, Godaigo escapes from the Oki Islands. And the loyalist efforts in the central provinces are greatly bolstered when Akamatsu Norimura—who, as noted earlier, is along with Masashige the archetype of the "western warrior," the guerrilla leader in Taiheiki—joins the cause against the Bakufu. Finally, in 1333:5, the Bakufu is overthrown by the joint attacks of Ashikaga Takauji and Nitta Yoshisada upon its offices in Kyoto and Kamakura.

The Battle of Minatogawa

The Kemmu Restoration failed and the country lapsed into what became the war between the courts when, as noted, Godaigo in late 1335 disptached an army under Nitta Yoshisada to the Kantō to chastise Ashikaga Takauji. Defeated in several key battles, Yoshisada retreated to the central provinces with the enemy at his heels.

In the Taiheiki account of the fighting that ensues between the loyalists and the Ashikaga in the central provinces at the end of 1335 and the first half of 1336, Kusunoki Masashige reappears as a battle commander. The supreme leader of the loyalists is Yoshisada, although he shares his leadership in the beginning with Kitabatake Akiie, head of the army brought up from Mutsu-Dewa. When Masashige is described in combat during this period, he is almost always said to be in charge of a group of "five hundred warriors." In view of the unrealistically enormous troop figures that are routinely given in Taiheiki—eighty thousand, one hundred thousand, even a million—we may interpret "five hundred warriors" to be the authors' conventionalized way of reaffirming that Masashige, who is repeatedly identified as possessing unmatched valor (yūki) and incomparable resourcefulness *(chibō)*,[99] is able to win victories with minuscule forces.

On one occasion, we are told, Masashige and his five hundred defeat more than fifty thousand of the enemy by fastening together shields to form a defensive line like the "wall of a fortress" *(kai-date)*.[100] After the enemy, having suffered defeat in this and other clashes, withdraws from the field of battle, Masashige offers advice to Yoshisada. It is interesting that he, the leader of only five hundred, should be allowed to advise a chieftain of Yoshisada's stature. But in the *Taiheiki* version of this period of battling, Masashige is regularly included in strategy deliberations among Yoshisada and the other high-ranking loyalist chieftains. And, as we will see, he and Yoshisada spend the night before the Battle of Minatogawa, in which Masashige dies, discussing plans and reminiscing.

In his advice to Yoshisada after the victory over the Ashikaga, Masashige remarks that, although the enemy have been defeated, they have not suffered many casualties. He recommends that the loyalists, after a day's rest, resume their attack; otherwise, their men will "become interested in treasures" (engage in looting?) and will not only fail to respond to the call to muster but may flock again to the enemy.[101] Here the shrewd Masashige draws Yoshisada's attention to what we have observed as the unreliability of the warriors and "field warriors" recruited by both the loyalist and Ashikaga armies in battling during this period.

As the loyalists, upon Masashige's advice, prepare to go on the offensive again, Masashige dupes the enemy, who have retreated to Kyoto, with an elaborate hoax. He sends twenty or thirty priests to look in the environs of the capital for the corpses of himself, Yoshisada, Akiie, and other loyalist leaders, instructing the priests to tell anyone who asks that these leaders have been killed in the recent fighting. The enemy are thus fooled into believing that all the loyalist leaders are dead and they can achieve an easy victory by riding out of Kyoto and smashing the opposing army, which has no one to command it. The Ashikaga contribute to their own deception by "identifying" and displaying heads taken from corpses that they are convinced are those of Yoshisada and Masashige.[102]

Rushing forth from Kyoto, the over confident and tactically ill-prepared Ashikaga are defeated again, providing the loyalists with the opportunity, which they promptly seize, to reoccupy Kyoto. In a revealing passage in *Taiheiki*, Takauji claims that his recent battlefield losses are not the result of military failure, but because he is an "enemy of the court" *(chōteki)*. He instructs a priest with connections at court to obtain from retired emperor Kōgon of the senior branch of the imperial family an edict authorizing him to quell the loyalists.[103] From this point, both the loyalists and the Ashikaga claim imperial legitimacy for their actions.

Takauji's retreat by boat to Kyushu in the first month of 1336 is not so much an admission of defeat as a strategic maneuver to regroup. In preparation for his return, Takauji stations lieutenants in various provinces of central and western Honshu.[104] Meanwhile, according to *Taiheiki*, Nitta Yoshisada wastes valuable time consorting with a mistress (see the section "Warriors and Warfare"). And when Takauji starts back from Kyushu in 1336:4, the bulk of that great pool of shifting warriors of Honshu's central and western provinces deserts the loyalists for him.[105] Their ranks now severely reduced, the loyalists establish themselves at Minatogawa on the coast of Hyōgo province to await the impending great battle with the Ashikaga.

The description of the Battle of Minatogawa is the dramatic high point of *Taiheiki*. As Yoshisada and the loyalists take up their position in Hyōgo, Godaigo summons Masashige and orders him to join them forthwith. Masashige opines that the reduced loyalist force will surely lose in a head-on clash with the rejuvenated Ashikaga. Reiterating his credo that only the final victory matters, he suggests that the loyalists temporarily relinquish Kyoto and that Yoshisada accompany the emperor to sanctuary on Mount Hiei. Meanwhile he, Masashige, will return to his base in Kawachi and work to sever the supply lines to the capital. Once the lines have been cut, the "shifting warriors" will gradually become tired and hungry and again desert, this time back to the loyalists. Yoshisada and he will then be able to defeat the remaining Ashikaga force in a coordinated pincer movement from Mount Hiei and Kawachi.[106]

Godaigo, however, rejects Masashige's plan. His reasons are: It would be demeaning for him, as emperor, to be driven from Kyoto a second time in one year (he had been forced to flee the capital when the Ashikaga occupied it in 1336:1); the loyalists have won victories before while outnumbered and can do so again; loyalist victories derive, in any case, not from superior military planning but from the blessings bestowed by heaven on Godaigo's imperial fortune *(seiun)*.[107]

Without further demurral, Masashige departs with his usual five hundred for Minatogawa. Or at least so the *rufubon* version of *Taiheiki* tells us. We observed in the section on the textual development of *Taiheiki* that much if not most of the work's old text versions are substantively almost identical to the *rufubon* versions. This is certainly true of nearly the entire chapter relating Masashige's meeting with Godaigo, the rejection of his advice, and his departure for Minatogawa. But the Saigen'in old text version, the oldest of all the *Taiheiki* texts, contains the following additional—and quite extraordinary—remarks about Masashige's reaction to the insistence that a stand be made at Minatogawa: "The scheme to achieve victory by deceiving a numerically superior enemy apparently does not suit His Majesty. Instead, he issues a decree calling upon peerless warriors to throw themselves against this great foe, which is the same as ordering them to go to their deaths."[108]

We may imagine that these remarks, severely critical of Godaigo, were deleted, perhaps during the Tokugawa period, because they detract from the image of Masashige as the pristine loyalist who stoically and without complaint goes to his death when ordered by his sovereign. In still another deletion from the *rufubon* texts, Masashige asserts: "To cherish honor *(gi)* and ignore death—that is the way of the loyal subject, the brave warrior *(chūshin yūshi)*."[109]

In his advice to Godaigo before Minatogawa, Masashige proposes that Yoshisada play a major role in the strategy of luring the Ashikaga back to Kyoto, cutting off their supplies, and then defeating them in a pincer movement. But *Baishōron*, a historical record compiled about 1349 that presents the events of this period primarily from the Ashikaga perspective, claims that Masashige has something very different in mind for Yoshisada: Instead of using the Nitta chieftain as his commander-in-chief, Godaigo should destroy Yoshisada and arrange for peace with Ashikaga Takauji. According to *Baishōron*, Godaigo and his court advisers simply laugh at this advice, as though it were a joke.[110]

We cannot know whether the historical Masashige was, in fact, pro- or anti-Yoshisada. *Taiheiki* consistently portrays him as cooperative with and sympathetic toward the Nitta leader. But in view of Yoshisada's many military failures, it would not be surprising if Masashige, who is lavishly praised for his valor and martial acuity in various writings of the age (for example, in *Baishōron*[111] and *Masukagami*,[112] as well as *Taiheiki*), had a low opinion of his fellow commander.

As Masashige, in the *Taiheiki* account, makes his way to Minatogawa, he stops at Sakurai Station near Osaka to direct his eleven-year-old son Masatsura, who has accompanied him to this point, to return home to Kawachi. To readers and audiences of *Taiheiki* over the centuries, this scene of the parting at Sakurai Station has probably been the most moving as well as the most inspiring passage of the entire work. Masashige's words to his young son Masatsura are:

"The coming battle will decide the fate of the country. I fear this is
the last time I will see your face in this life. If you hear that
Masashige has died in battle, you will know that the country has
fallen into the hands of the shogun [Takauji]. But you must never
surrender, thus forsaking the long-standing loyalty of our family to
the emperor, merely to preserve your transient life. So long as even
one of the young men of our family survives, he must establish a
position near Mount Kongō [in Kawachi]; and when the enemy
attacks, he must be prepared to expose himself to the arrows of Yang
Yu [a famous archer] and fight with a devotion comparable to the loyalty of Chi Hsin. This will be your most important filial duty
to me."[113]

Thus Masashige bequeaths to Masatsura and his other offspring
the ideal of unqualified, self-sacrificing loyalty to Emperor Godaigo
and the loyalist cause. At his first meeting with Godaigo at Kasagi in
1333, Masashige told the emperor that, so long as he, Masashige, still
lived, the loyalist cause would prevail in the end. Godaigo has now
rejected Masashige's advice and sent him to what we know will be his
death in a battle the loyalists cannot win. But Masashige's spirit, a gift
from the gods, will be perpetuated by others, at least for a while.

Arriving in Minatogawa, Masashige, as noted, spends the night
before the great battle with Nitta Yoshisada. Yoshisada agrees that,
given the disparity in numbers, the coming battle can only end in
defeat for the loyalists. He nevertheless feels compelled to fight the
battle at all costs in order to redeem himself in the eyes of those who
have mocked him for his various failures and retreats since undertaking the expedition to the Kantō in late 1335. Masashige seeks to com-
fort his companion by saying: "You should pay no heed to the criticism
of those who know nothing of the way of the warrior. The fine commander is one who, when sensing victory, advances; when realizing
the time is not right, withdraws."[114] Yoshisada is much pleased with
these words, and he and Masashige remain together through the night
talking and drinking sake.

In the opening "exchange of arrows" phase of the Battle of Minatogawa as described in *Taiheiki* there is a scene—no doubt inspired by
the opening scene in the *Heike Monogatari* account of the Battle of
Dannoura—of competition between archers from the two sides to
shoot "long arrows." After a loyalist archer launches a powerful shot
that travels a great distance and then taunts the enemy to match it,
Takauji inquires who among his men is the best candidate to shoot the
arrow back. His lieutenant, Kō no Moronao, informs him there is no
one among the Kantō warriors in their army who is sufficiently capa-

ble, but a man from Kyushu—the "strongest archer of the western provinces"—can match the shot. Before this western archer can dispatch his arrow, however, another warrior from the Ashikaga side decides to take his own shot at the loyalists. Whether this brash fellow is merely weak or his bowstring catches on his armor, his arrow travels only a short distance and plops into the water. This elicits great laughter from the loyalists and brings to a premature end the exchange of long arrows.[115]

Yoshisada has positioned Masashige to meet that half of the Ashikaga army (commanded by Ashikaga Tadayoshi) coming by land from the west, while he defends against the half (commanded by Takauji) approaching by sea. But the seaborne half decides to land farther east than Yoshisada had anticipated, and in shifting along the coast of Settsu province to the enemy's actual landing point, Yoshisada leaves Masashige exposed and isolated.

Attacked from both the front and rear, Masashige, along with his brother Masasue and seven hundred followers (rather than the usual five hundred), fights furiously for six hours. Even when his force is reduced to a mere seventy-three, Masashige still has the chance to break through the enemy encirclement and escape. But he has decided that this will be his last battle. Refusing to retreat "even one step," he and his men continue to struggle until totally exhausted. They then withdraw to a peasant's house north of Minatogawa, where they prepare to commit suicide.[116]

The Death of Masashige

Upon removing his armor, Masashige finds that he has been wounded in eleven places. None of the other men has fewer than three wounds. While Masashige and Masasue watch, some of the followers who have accompanied them—thirteen other Kusunoki kinsmen and fifty vassals—align themselves in two rows in the reception hall of the house and, after reciting the *nembutsu* (a prayer to Amida Buddha) ten times, together commit *seppuku*.[117] Interestingly, the Saigen'in old text version of *Taiheiki* says simply that the kinsmen and vassals "recited the *nembutsu* and, as one, cut their bellies."[118] Apparently the *rufubon* version was embellished to have the kinsmen and vassals line up formally in two rows and recite the *nembutsu* ten times to provide greater solemnity to an event that sets the stage for *Taiheiki*'s dramatic and symbolic high point: the suicide of Masashige.[119]

After this mass suicide, Masashige turns to Masasue and remarks: "It is said that one's last thought in this life determines the goodness or evil of one's next incarnation. Into which of the nine lev-

els of existence would you like to be reborn?" Laughing loudly, Masasue replies: "It is my wish to be reborn again and again for seven lives
into this same existence in order to destroy the enemies of the court!"
Greatly pleased, Masashige says that, although his brother's wish is
deeply sinful, it matches exactly what he has in mind. Pledging that
they will fulfill their shared wish through reincarnation, they stab
each other and fall dead "on the same pillow."[120]

Komatsu Shigetō speaks of *Heike Monogatari* as a "literature of
death,"[121] and indeed dying and death are the central images of the
Buddhist doctrine of impermanence that pervades that work. With one
notable exception—Taira no Kiyomori—those warriors whose deaths
are described in the *Heike* do not struggle against their fates once they
have determined to die or cannot avoid dying. Most of the Taira who
perish in battle or are executed, for example, die reciting the *nembutsu*, seeking to banish all thoughts of their lives and to prepare
themselves for rebirth in Amida's Pure Land paradise after death.
Many warriors in *Taiheiki*, such as those kinsmen and vassals who join
Masashige and Masasue in suicide at the Battle of Minatogawa, similarly die with the *nembutsu* on their lips. But there are also a number
of prominent characters, including Masashige and Masasue, who in
their final moments are, like the *Heike*'s Kiyomori, consumed only
with thoughts of vengeance. They are men whose principal agony is
not that they must die but that they must leave the world while their
enemies still live and are ascendant.

Thus, whereas revenge is a relatively minor theme in the *Heike*,
in *Taiheiki* it assumes major importance. In the case of Masashige,
revenge is essential to the idea that his spirit—his unswerving devotion to the loyalist cause—transcends mortality and will live even after
his death.[122] But in this and other cases, the desire for revenge may
also be fostered by the particular nature of the conflict that *Taiheiki*
describes: a protracted, seemingly endless sequence of fighting in
which deceit, treachery, and other base acts are commonplace and ani-
mosities become so intense that they can only be satisfied by revenge.

After noting the suicides, following those of Masashige and Masasue, of more Kusunoki kin and vassals, *Taiheiki*'s authors present the
following eulogy to Masashige:

> From the Genkō era [1331–1333], tens of millions of people gra-
> ciously came forth in response to His Majesty's [Godaigo's] call,
> served loyally, and distinguished themselves in battle. But since this
> rebellion [of Ashikaga Takauji] erupted, people ignorant of the way of
> benevolence have flouted the imperial favor and joined the enemy.
> Feckless individuals, hoping to escape death, have surrendered and,

contrary to their expectations, have been executed. Other ignorant people, not comprehending the trend of the times, have gone against the way. In the midst of this, [Kusunoki] Masashige, a man combining the three virtues of wisdom, benevolence, and courage, whose fidelity is unequaled by anyone from ancient times to the present, has chosen death as the proper way. His and his brother's deaths by suicide are omens that a sagely sovereign has again lost the country and traitorous subjects are running amok.[123]

The praise heaped upon Masashige does not surprise us, since *Taiheiki*'s authors have already made abundantly clear that, for his service to the loyalist cause, he deserves nothing less. The striking part of the eulogy is the reference to Godaigo as a "sagely sovereign" *(seishu)*, a reference that raises the issue of the conflicting portrayals of Godaigo found in *Taiheiki*: On the one hand, he is extolled as one of the most enlightened and splendid—sagely—emperors in Japanese history; on the other hand, he is shown to possess flaws and shortcomings as a ruler that contribute not only to the failure of the Kemmu Restoration but, as in the case of Minatogawa, to loyalist defeats in battle.

Nitta Yoshisada

Kusunoki Masashige, as portrayed in *Taiheiki*, is a nearly godlike figure who betrays no human weaknesses. His spirit invests the loyalist cause of Godaigo with a shining quality that has moved and inspired countless generations of Japanese readers and audiences. In the early twentieth century, the Japanese government decided that, in textbooks for primary-school children, Godaigo's southern court, rather than the northern court of the senior branch of the imperial family, should be presented as the legitimate court during the period 1336–1392.[124] The government did this in large part because Masashige had espoused Godaigo's cause: It was unthinkable that Masashige—the supreme model for children of selfless loyalty to the emperor—could have fought and died for an "illegitimate" cause.

The Masashige of *Taiheiki*, however, is largely a creation of the work's authors, a *deus ex machina* introduced to enhance Godaigo and the loyalist cause. If Masashige were removed from *Taiheiki*, both Godaigo and the cause would lose much of their luster. I do not wish to inquire further into the possible failures of Godaigo as a ruler during the Kemmu Restoration. As described in *Taiheiki*, his inadequacies as a leader become even clearer after the restoration in his relations with his warrior supporters, including Masashige and especially Nitta Yoshisada.

All of the failed loyalist heroes in *Taiheiki* are, by definition, unalterably faithful to the loyalist cause. Even in the face of egregiously bad decisions, stubborn-mindedness, and, as we will see, virtual betrayal by Godaigo and his courtier advisers, they remain steadfast. Masashige's going to his death at Minatogawa after his advice is summarily rejected by Godaigo is a prime example of such steadfastness. But nowhere are the results of constancy to Godaigo and the loyalist cause more tragically revealed than in the case of Nitta Yoshisada. Although Yoshisada does not fit the precise definition of tragic loserhero (as I used that term to analyze a particular hero type found in the early medieval war tales), he is certainly a tragic figure—not only because, like all the failed loyalist heroes of *Taiheiki*, he goes to his death in the ill-fated loyalist cause, but also because his personal failings and military ineptitude contribute greatly to the cause's ultimate demise.

We have noted that during the night he spends with Masashige before the Battle of Minatogawa, Yoshisada expresses his determination to take a stand against the Ashikaga at Minatogawa. For if he does not fight there, he may be forced to endure more of the mockery people heaped upon him after the routs he suffered when driven back from the Kantō to the central provinces by Takauji in the previous year, 1335. Minatogawa, of course, ends in disastrous defeat for Yoshisada and the loyalists. In the agony of this and subsequent losses incurred as he desperately struggles to prevent the Ashikaga from reoccupying Kyoto, Yoshisada—always gallant and brave,[125] if not wise—seeks, in a highly unusual passage in *Taiheiki*, to take the entire burden of the loyalist cause onto his own shoulders:

"The disorder in the land is ceaseless, and for all too long the people, who are blameless, have known no peace. This is called a struggle between two lines of the imperial family, but in fact it is a confrontation between two men: Yoshisada and Lord Takauji. Rather than cause the suffering of many to achieve great merit for myself alone, I propose to settle the fight by myself, and hence come to this gate of my fortress [to challenge Lord Takauji to single combat]."[126]

Inflamed by this challenge, Takauji proclaims his willingness to meet Yoshisada alone in combat, but he is dissuaded by one of his lieutenants who observes that Yoshisada is merely suggesting a desperate means to extricate himself from a desperate situation.

Shortly after this, Kyoto falls again to the Ashikaga. Anxious to settle the dynastic dispute within the imperial family, Takauji persuades Godaigo, who has once more taken haven at Enryakuji Temple on Mount Hiei, to return to Kyoto with the promise that the "government of the country will be given back to the courtiers."[127] Godaigo impetuously agrees to return without consulting any of his court advisers and without a word to Yoshisada, commander of the loyalist forces. This prompts Takauji, who has no intention of fulfilling his promise, to observe "how easy it is to deceive [His Majesty]."[128]

Upon learning of Godaigo's intent to return to Kyoto, one of Yoshisada's followers, Horiguchi Sadamitsu, goes to Enryakuji Temple and confronts Godaigo as he and his entourage are about to descend the mountain for the capital. In an astonishing indictment of the emperor, Sadamitsu speaks of the great sacrifices that Yoshisada and the Nitta family have made for the loyalist cause, asserting that one hundred and thirty-two family members and some eight thousand followers have given their lives since Yoshisada first undertook to destroy the Hōjō regime. Now the emperor has betrayed Yoshisada's selfless loyalty and accumulated merit of years and has bestowed his favor instead on the great traitor Takauji. Recently the loyalist forces have suffered a number of defeats in and around Kyoto. These defeats are in no sense the result of military deficiencies, but are entirely because of failures of "imperial virtue" (teitoku). If the emperor now plans to return to Kyoto to embrace Takauji, he should summon Yoshisada and his family and behead them as criminals.[129]

The emperor, we are told, is filled with shame, lamenting the "mistake" he has made, and both he and his attendants bow their heads in recognition of the truth of Sadamitsu's words. Summoning Yoshisada to Mount Hiei, Godaigo acknowledges his error in not informing the Nitta chieftain about his return to Kyoto, saying that he has agreed to a temporary truce with Takauji merely to gain time until the loyalist forces can revitalize themselves and destroy the enemies of the court. He then instructs Yoshisada to proceed to Echizen province in the Hokuriku region to rally loyalist support there. To make clear the legitimacy of Yoshisada's mission, he orders the crown prince, Prince Tsuneyoshi, and Prince Takayoshi to accompany him.[130]

The Death of Yoshisada

Entering Echizen in 1336:10, Yoshisada and his army encounter unusually severe winter weather. Many of the men die of the cold, and others are incapacitated.[131] Yoshisada establishes his principal position at Kanegasaki Fortress on Tsuruga Bay. But when Ashikaga partisans, led by the Shiba family, lay siege to the fortress, the defenders find themselves dangerously short of supplies. Yoshisada and his brother Yoshisuke secretly escape to a nearby fortress, but the other defenders are reduced to eating their horses and, finally, to cannibalizing the bodies of their dead comrades.[132]

As Kanegasaki Fortress is about to fall, thirty-two of the loyalist defenders commit *seppuku*. Yoshisada's oldest son, Nitta Yoshiaki, pleads with Prince Takayoshi to save himself by surrendering. But the resolute prince, observing that he is the titular head of the defenders, insists upon joining the others in death and asks Yoshiaki to show him how to perform *seppuku*. Yoshiaki thereupon cuts his stomach and, before falling over dead, places the bloody dagger in front of the prince. Wrapping the weapon with his sleeve, Takayoshi inserts it into his stomach, the skin of which is "white as snow," and topples over upon the body of Yoshiaki. More than three hundred other defenders also commit *seppuku* or stab each other to death.[133]

Cannibalism and the *seppuku* of a prince are grim signs of the harshness of the conflict in the Hokuriku. For Yoshisada, the Hokuriku fighting differs from his earlier struggle with the Ashikaga because he is now in a secondary theater of the war and no longer confronting Takauji or Tadayoshi directly.[134]

The tide of the Hokuriku fighting shifts back and forth between the loyalists and their foes. After several victories, Yoshisada becomes stubbornly determined to destroy an enemy fortress at Kuromaru in Echizen and, according to *Taiheiki*, fails to seize the opportunity to return to the central provinces, where the warrior-monks of Enryakuji have shown a desire to join him in an assault on Kyoto.[135] Finally, Emperor Godaigo, who has established the southern court at Yoshino, sends a personal letter to Yoshisada urging him to return to the central provinces to save a loyalist army under siege in Yawata Fortress.[136] Yoshisada dispatches part of his army, now swollen in size by reinforcements from Echigo province, to Yawata under his brother Yoshisuke.[137] But on the way, Yoshisuke learns of the fall of Yawata Fortress —burned to the ground by Kō no Moronao—and returns to Echizen.[138] Once again, the Nitta brothers devote their full attention to the fighting in the Hokuriku.

Of warrior death scenes in the war tales, none is finer as literature or more moving than that of Minamoto no Yoshinaka in *Heike Monogatari*. In *Taiheiki*, Kusunoki Masashige's death by suicide at Minatogawa is the most dramatic death scene. But the mortal wounding, and consequent suicide, of Yoshisada in a forlorn setting in Echizen province in 1338 is the saddest and most affecting of the work's portrayals of death.

Yoshisada's death occurs as his fortunes are on the rise. His army, with the Echigo troops, has increased to three hundred thousand and, in a solemn and resplendent ceremony before its assembled ranks as they prepare for battle, everyone is impressed with the thought that "surely it is Lord Yoshisada who will wrest the country from Lord

Takauji."[139] But even at this exhilarating moment there are ominous portents. When Yoshisada mounts his horse and heads through the gate of his encampment, the beast suddenly bucks, trampling two grooms and leaving them "half dead and half alive."[140] And as Yoshisada crosses a river, the horse of his standard-bearer collapses and throws its rider into the water. Members of the army wonder whether these are signs that they should avoid the field of battle that day. But they continue on, outwardly maintaining their calm even as they are filled with foreboding.[141]

Yoshisada divides his army into seven units, directing each to attack an enemy fortress after first constructing a "facing fortress" (mukaijō). But the men of the unit assigned to attack Fujishima Fortress, manned by warrior-monks of Heisenji Temple, believe their target is ready to be toppled and, ignoring the order to build a facing fortress, rush to the assault. The Heisenji monks, as the attackers soon discover, are surprisingly determined fighters, and the battling drags on through the day. When Yoshisada learns that the attackers at Fujishima Fortress may be repulsed, he leaps astride a mount and, with only fifty accompanying horsemen, starts winding his way through the rice paddies to the fortress. Before long, he runs directly into a force of three hundred enemy horsemen, whose supporting foot soldiers set up their shields in the paddies and unleash a withering barrage of arrows. Yoshisada has no foot soldiers and no shields. The horsemen in front try to form a line to protect him, but they are struck down one after another.[142]

An aide implores Yoshisada to retreat to safety, but the Nitta chieftain asserts: "It is not my intention, when my men are losing their lives, to save myself from death,"[143] and whips his horse forward. But the horse, a magnificent animal capable, under ordinary circumstances, of leaping easily across moats, has been greatly weakened by five arrow wounds. Stumbling into a small ditch, it "collapses like a folding screen,"[144] pinning Yoshisada's left leg under its body. At that moment, an arrow smashes through Yoshisada's helmet and into his forehead. Still conscious and aware that the end has come, Yoshisada draws his sword and decapitates himself, his head dropping into the deep mud of a rice paddy and his body toppling over onto it. An enemy warrior rushes forward and, retrieving the head and affixing it to the tip of his spear, hurries away, taking with him Yoshisada's armor and weapons. Several of Yoshisada's commanders perform junshi—suicide to follow their lord in death—before his body.[145] Summing up the disastrous results of this chance encounter with a superior enemy force, Taiheiki somberly observes that Yoshisada and the others who perish with him have "died like dogs" *(inujini)* without killing a single enemy.[146]

Many elements combine to heighten the sense of sadness, horror, and tragedy in Yoshisada's death scene in *Taiheiki:* the great chieftain fighting on a distant field, confronted with dark portents even as his fortunes appear to rise; the chieftain's rash decision to ride to his wavering troops with only a small band of companions; the sudden meeting with an enemy force; the chieftain's brave refusal to desert his men and his reckless charge forward; the collapse of the chieftain's horse and "the pity of his fortune coming to an end as his life is taken by the arrow of a common bowman."[147] Satō Kazuhiko observes that Yoshisada was the last of a breed: the cavalry commander who persistently formed his armies around units of horsemen, failing to appreciate the value of foot soldiers armed with bows and arrows.[148]

Once Yoshisada's head and body are identified by the enemy, the corpse is buried in a nearby temple and the head is sent, in a vermillion-lacquered Chinese box, back to Kyoto, where it is publicly displayed on the gate of a jail.[149] *Taiheiki* at this point recounts the love affair of Yoshisada and the young court beauty Kōtō no Naishi. This lady, who had distracted Yoshisada when he should have been campaigning westward after Ashikaga Takauji withdrew to Kyushu in early 1336, was on her way to Echizen when she received word of Yoshisada's death. Like so many women of warriors in *Heike Monogatari* and other war tales, she becomes a Buddhist nun to pray for her dead lover's soul.[150]

When Yoshisuke learns of his brother's death, he vows to lead the Nitta army forth to "die in the place where the commander *(taishō)* died."[151] But the prospect that they may be led on a suicide mission greatly alarms the army, and during the night many of its members either abscond, take Buddhist vows, or surrender to the enemy.[152] By morning, a grand army of three hundred thousand has been reduced to less than two thousand. The Nitta campaign in the Hokuriku region has ended in failure.

Although *Taiheiki* gives a special place to Kusunoki Masashige as the spirit of Godaigo's loyalist cause, Nitta Yoshisada was really its heart and soul. Godaigo himself acknowledges this on his deathbed at Yoshino the following year, 1339. When reminded by a priest—as Masasue was reminded by Masashige—that one's last thought before dying determines the realm into which he will be reborn, Godaigo, joining those in *Taiheiki* who face death with their minds fixed on vengeance, says that his only wish is for the ultimate destruction of the enemies of the court.[153] He notes that the hopes of his cause have heretofore been sustained by the loyal subjects Nitta Yoshisada and Yoshisuke; henceforth the burden of the cause must be borne by their descendants among the Nitta family.[154]

Kusunoki Masatsura

No discussion of the loyalist movement and failed loyalist heroes in *Taiheiki* would be complete without comment on the career of Kusunoki Masashige's oldest son, Masatsura. The stories about Masatsura's relationship with his father and his emergence as a leading loyalist general in the late 1340s are among the best known in *Taiheiki*. In the course of them, Masatsura becomes the chief reviver of Masashige's spirit of unqualified devotion to the loyalist cause. Masatsura's period at center stage in the war between the courts is brief: He commits suicide in battle in the first month of 1348, less than a year after his first campaign against the forces of the Ashikaga. Yet during this brief period he displays qualities that, as delineated in *Taiheiki*, place him just behind his father among the failed loyalist heroes most admired by the Japanese of later centuries.

Masatsura enters *Taiheiki* in the days before the Battle of Minatogawa when, as a child of ten, he is sent home from Sakurai Station by Masashige who, as observed, passionately enjoins him to fulfill his filial duty by awaiting the time when he and other young Kusunoki kinsmen reach adulthood and can give themselves wholly as fighters to the loyalist cause. The Masatsura of *Taiheiki* is one of the supreme exemplars in Japanese literature not only of imperial loyalty but also filial piety. But this piety, in terms of fidelity to the last request of his father, is sorely tested in the days following Masashige's death at Minatogawa.

After Minatogawa, Masashige's head is sent to Kyoto, where it is displayed on the gate of a jail. Having been fooled by what they thought was Masashige's head earlier in the year, the people of Kyoto are dubious about this one.[155] But Ashikaga Takauji recognizes it as genuine and, in a gesture of compassion unusual for this age of bitter and vengeful strife, returns it to Masashige's family in Kawachi. Viewing the head, Masashige's widow and his son Masatsura are overcome with grief; and when Masatsura withdraws to a nearby chapel, the suspicious mother follows him, arriving just as he is about to disembowel himself with the sword bearing his father's "floating chrysanthemum" *(kikusui)* crest that Masashige gave him as a keepsake before Minatogawa.[156] Berating her son for this rash, unthinking behavior—she says it can only sully his father's name and cancel Masatsura's own future responsibilities to the emperor—the mother prevents the *seppuku* by

seizing the sword.[157] From this time, we are told, Masatsura thinks
only of performing his filial duty by carrying out his father's final
wishes. Even in games with other children, he burns with a passion to
undertake this duty. As he attacks and topples his young comrades in
mock warfare, for example, he shouts that he is "taking the heads of
enemies of the court"; and as he rides astride a bamboo horse, he proclaims that he is "pursuing the shogun (Takauji)."[158]

One of the most memorable events in Masatsura's short career as
a southern court commander, as recounted in *Taiheiki*, occurs at the
Battle of Abeno in Kawachi province in the ninth month of 1347. In
the course of this battle, a bridge over a river collapses and five hundred of the enemy are pitched into the water. The time is dawn and the
water is frigid. Although all five hundred are fished alive from the
river, they are not likely to survive without aid. The aid is promptly
rendered by Masatsura who, *Taiheiki* informs us, is a person of compassion *(nasake)*. He has the men change into dry, warm clothing; he
gives them medicine and cares for their wounds. After allowing the
men to rest for four or five days, Masatsura provides horses, armor, and
helmets to those who need them. Although enemies, the men are so
moved that they ask to become Masatsura's followers. Intent only
upon repaying the obligation to him, all five hundred die with Masatsura at the Battle of Shijō-Nawate the following year.[159]

This inspiring passage harks back to earlier tales—to stories of
the personal compassion or parental-like love displayed by commanders of the ancient and early medieval ages for their men, commanders
such as Minamoto no Yoriyoshi in *Mutsu Waki*, Minamoto no Yoshiie
in *Ōshū Gosannen Ki*, and Minamoto no Yoshitsune in *Heike Monogatari*. The love of these commanders for their men is an idealized form
of behavior much admired in the ancient and early medieval war tales,
but somewhat out of place in *Taiheiki*. Although *Taiheiki* speaks frequently of loyalty—and disloyalty—among warriors, it gives scant
attention to the intimately personal bonds among lords and vassals
that we find so memorably described in the earlier war tales.

The rise of Masatsura and the victories he achieves in the central
provinces in the last months of 1347 give renewed hope to the southern court and cause alarm among the Ashikaga and the northern court
in Kyoto. Appointing the Kō brothers, Moronao and Moroyasu, as co-
commanders, Takauji assembles an army to oppose Masatsura.[160] In
the first month of 1348, Masatsura and the Kō clash in the Battle at
Shijō-Nawate in Kawachi province.

Before this battle, Masatsura and his younger brother Masatoki
go to Yoshino for an audience with Emperor Gomurakami, Godaigo's

son and successor. In audiences of this sort, an emperor customarily spoke through an intermediary. But Masatsura, recounting the great sacrifices of his father and others of the Kusunoki family for the loyalist cause over the years and expressing his determination to take the heads of the Kō brothers in the coming battle or die in the effort, makes the unusual request that Gomurakami appear before them personally and allow them to gaze upon his imperial countenance once in this lifetime. Raising the curtains that conceal him, Gomurakami summons Masatsura and Masatoki to his side and, while speaking of various strategies in the coming battle against the enemy, declares that Masatsura and the Kusunoki are the "hands and feet" necessary to achieve final victory.[161]

Shijō-Nawate is a ferocious battle that rages from morning until night on 1348:1:5. *Taiheiki* describes the division of forces on both sides into subunits—comprising both cavalry and foot soldiers—that charge and clash, charge and clash, in a series of encounters over a broad battlefield. Although the Kō army is superior in numbers, Masatsura and his force, having selected the site for the battle, are able to take good advantage of the terrain. The outstanding feature of the *Taiheiki* description of the battle is Masatsura's single-minded determination to fulfill his pledge to take the heads of Kō no Moronao and Moroyasu—or, specifically, Moronao, since Moroyasu remains mostly on the periphery of the battle and thus out of reach.

After hours of relentless fighting, Masatsura and his men are reduced to less than two hundred. They have abandoned their horses— each wounded by no less than three or four arrows—and face the enemy on foot. They seek Moronao, but he is elusive. Masatsura engages an enemy, takes his head, and believes it is Moronao's. In fact, the head belongs to Ueyama Rokurōzaemon, who has donned Moronao's armor and sacrificed himself to protect the commander.[162] Finally, Masatsura advances to within a hundred yards of Moronao. He is exhausted from more than thirty encounters with the enemy, his small band of remaining men have all been wounded, and Moronao is shielded by seventy or eighty mounted guards. Nevertheless, Masatsura and his band run wildly forward, each "striving to be first."[163]

The desperate attack might have succeeded. But one of the enemy—a warrior from Kyushu named Susuki Shirō, known for his power and quickness with a bow *(tsuyoyumi no yatsugibaya)*— launches a hail of arrows at the attacking band.[164] After hours of fighting, the lacings in the armor of the attackers have loosened and Shirō's arrows find their way between the lames, sinking deeply into the attackers' bodies. Before long all the attackers are bristling with shafts.

Realizing the end has come and determined to avoid capture, Masa-tsura and his brother Masatoki stab each other to death (just as their father and uncle had done at Minatogawa); the others cut their bellies, falling one on top of another.[165]

The defeat at Shijō-Nawate is a devastating blow to the southern court loyalists. According to *Taiheiki*, there were none at the time who did not believe that the imperial fortune had ended and that the power of the military (the Ashikaga) would henceforth long endure.[166]

Taiheiki, *Part Three*

Although the story of Masatsura as hero appears in it, Part Three of *Taiheiki*, as noted earlier in this chapter, lacks the structural cohesion of the rest of the work. Often interrupted by digressions, it meanders through a seemingly endless series of battle accounts. Moreover, of the estimated two thousand or more characters who appear in *Taiheiki*'s pages,[167] a goodly number make their entries and exits in Part Three. So difficult is it for the reader to follow the twists and turns of Part Three's narrative and to keep track of its revolving door of characters, that some Japanese graduate students have facetiously suggested that, in this part, *Taiheiki*'s title should be changed from "Chronicle of Great Peace" to "Chronicle of Great Horror" *(Tai-henki)*.[168] ("Great horror" can also, of course, refer to the agony and terror of the fighting recorded in Part Three.)

A number of Part Three's digressions tell stories of supernatural characters, including ghosts, goblins *(tengu)*, and demons *(oni)*. In one of these stories, Kusunoki Masashige returns as a warrior ghost *(shura)* in an attempt to obtain a magical sword from Ōmori Hikoshichi, an Ashikaga adherent who fought against him at the Battle of Minato-gawa. Only with this sword, Masashige contends, can he vanquish once and for all the great traitor Ashikaga Takauji. Remarking to Hikoshichi that he has become a ghost because of the grave sin of thinking only of vengeance at the time of his death, Masashige says that among the other ghosts who have accompanied him from heaven are Emperor Godaigo, Prince Moriyoshi, Nitta Yoshisada, and—from an earlier age—Taira no Tadamasa, Minamoto no Yoshitsune, and Taira no Noritsune![169] Hikoshichi, however, is an intrepid warrior and, despite many threats, earth-shakings, and outright attacks by Masa-shige and the others, refuses to relinquish the sword. Finally, Hikoshi-chi pacifies the ghosts through readings of the Prajñā Pāramitā Sutra.[170]

Another Part Three digression concerning supernatural creatures that also reflects the urge to revenge on the part of dead loyalist heroes relates the story of a visit to earth by a group of goblins who are the ghosts of three clerics, one of whom is related to Emperor Godaigo, and Prince Moriyoshi. The purpose of the visit is to devise a scheme to throw the world into further disorder. One goblin suggests that they enter the mind of a well-known priest and cause him to preach heretical doctrines; another proposes that they arrange to have leaders of the Bakufu fight among themselves.[171] But the scheme that is adopted is the diabolically perverse proposal that the spirit of Prince Moriyoshi enter the womb of Ashikaga Tadayoshi's wife and be reborn into the world as her child. Confounding the doctors, who cannot believe that a woman over forty can be fertile, Tadayoshi's wife becomes pregnant and in due course gives birth to a boy. There is great rejoicing among the Ashikaga and their supporters, both warriors and courtiers: None fails to look upon the boy as a child of great good fortune.[172]

Let me explain briefly why Prince Moriyoshi, as his story is told in *Taiheiki*, might have taken particular pleasure in wreaking his vengeance upon Ashikaga Tadayoshi. We noted in the section "Warriors and Warfare" that Prince Moriyoshi is one of the prime examples of a warrior-courtier in *Taiheiki*. Practiced in the military arts, he plays a leading role, along with Kusunoki Masashige, in keeping alive—after the exiling of Godaigo in 1332—the loyalist insurgency in the central provinces that leads to the overthrow of the Kamakura Bakufu in 1333. Like Masashige, Moriyoshi is essentially a guerrilla. Despite his royal background, he knows the fighting ways of the *akutō*.[173]

After Godaigo returns to Kyoto and commences his Kemmu Restoration, Moriyoshi remains in the provinces, refusing orders from his father the emperor to disband his military force. Moriyoshi insists that Ashikaga Takauji is planning rebellion and demands that he be appointed *sei-i tai-shōgun* to chastise him. Godaigo reluctantly gives Moriyoshi the *shōgun* title but forbids him to move against Takauji. Still determined to destroy the Ashikaga chieftain, Moriyoshi returns to Kyoto with his troops, who, according to *Taiheiki*, behave like thugs, attacking people on the streets and even murdering some. The prince himself is vainglorious and self-indulgent, making no effort to control his men.[174]

In exasperation and probably also in fear that Moriyoshi might threaten the Restoration government itself, Godaigo arranges to have him arrested and turned over to Takauji's brother Tadayoshi, who is in Kamakura. Tadayoshi incarcerates Moriyoshi in a small cave-like jail that is so low in height he cannot stand. The jail, moreover, admits almost no light and is constantly damp from water seeping into it.[175] Kept for more than half a year in this inhuman state of captivity,

Moriyoshi is finally murdered by one of Tadayoshi's henchmen, a warrior named Fuchibe, when Tadayoshi is forced to leave Kamakura in 1335 because of the uprising of Hōjō Takatoki's son Tokiyuki (discussed in the section "Historical Background").

The description of Prince Moriyoshi's murder is one of the most gruesome accounts in *Taiheiki*. When Fuchibe opens Moriyoshi's jail door, the prince, surmising that he is about to be killed, rushes out and attempts to seize Fuchibe's sword. But his legs have been severely weakened by his long incarceration in the jail, where he was unable to stand, and Fuchibe easily knocks him over. When Fuchibe attempts to behead him, however, Moriyoshi constricts his head and neck and the sword becomes stuck in the neck. Fuchibe is able to withdraw the sword but discards it because its tip has snapped off. He finally succeeds in stabbing Moriyoshi to death with his dirk, and takes his head with the intent of showing it to Tadayoshi. But, when he examines the head, he not only finds the eyes open and staring as though they still possessed life but discovers the tip of his sword in Moriyoshi's mouth. Interpreting the staring eyes and sword tip as bad omens, Fuchibe throws the head away.[176]

If we disregard supernatural stories, such as those described above, one of the most shocking incidents in *Taiheiki*—indeed, in all the war tales—appears in Part Three, and involves the Ashikaga commander Toki Yoritō. Returning with another warrior chief, Nikaidō Yukiharu, and their followers to Kyoto one evening in the ninth month of 1342 after a day of martial games and picnicking, Yoritō encounters the entourage of the retired emperor Kōgon in the streets of the capital. When Kōgon's attendants peremptorily demand that the warriors dismount and perform obeisance to the retired emperor in the customary manner, Yukiharu promptly complies. But Yoritō, probably inebriated, loudly demands to know what kind of fool *(bakamono)* has the temerity to order him to dismount. He then charges into the attendants, scattering them. When one of the attendants shouts that the order is from the *in* (retired emperor), Yoritō retorts: "Did you say *in*? Or did you say *inu* (dog)? If it's a dog, perhaps I should shoot it down!" He thereupon fires arrows into Kōgon's cart. Although Kōgon is not injured, his cart is tipped over and its wheels and axles broken. Only with great difficulty is the vehicle dragged unceremoniously back to Kōgon's palace.[177]

Even to people of this age, hardened by countless instances of rude and harsh treatment of royalty and courtiers, Toki Yoritō's assault upon retired emperor Kōgon is an appalling commission of lese majesty. Ashikaga Tadayoshi, acting as chief aide to his brother, the shogun Takauji, declares Yoritō's behavior an outrage unmatched in the histories of either China or Japan, and he claims that even the most severe of punishments—such as using carriages to tear Yoritō's body apart and then pickling it in brine—would not be retribution enough. Although Tadayoshi does not, in fact, impose such a grisly punishment, he insists that Yoritō be executed (by the usual method of decapitation), even ignoring a plea for mercy from Musō Soseki, the leading Zen priest of the day. People are impressed with Tadayoshi's handling of the affair, interpreting it as an indication that at least some semblance of order and justice remains in the world.[178]

I will conclude this chapter with a brief discussion of another Ashikaga commander, who, in Taiheiki, not only matches Toki Yoritō in his disrespect for the imperial family but also undergoes the first stage of transformation into one of the most hateful of villains in Japanese history and legend. The commander is Kō no Moronao, scion of a family whose men had for generations served as vassals to the Ashikaga. Moronao first appears in Taiheiki as an aide to Ashikaga Takauji when Takauji, having come down from Kamakura in 1333 as co-commander of a Bakufu army to put down the loyalist insurgency in the central provinces, turns coat and attacks the offices of the Rokuhara magistrates in Kyoto.

When the country lapses into the war between the courts after the Kemmu Restoration, Moronao and his brother Moroyasu become two of Takauji's closest advisers. Moronao is appointed shitsuji, or personal lieutenant, to Takauji as Ashikaga family head, and Moroyasu is named chief of the Board of Retainers (samurai-dokoro) of the newly established Ashikaga Bakufu. Both win important military victories for the Ashikaga, including, as we have seen, the Battle of Shijō-Nawate in 1348 that resulted in the death of Kusunoki Masatsura.

Moronao displays his personal bravery as well as his authority as a battle commander at Shijō-Nawate when he rallies the Ashikaga troops, who are starting to retreat, by shouting: "This is disgraceful! Come back! The enemy has only a small force and I, Moronao, am here. If you desert me and flee back to Kyoto, how do you expect to hold your heads up and face the shogun? Our fate lies with heaven. Forget your personal concerns!"[179]

Victory at Shijō-Nawate enables Moronao to launch a direct attack on Yoshino, seat of the southern court. The southern court emperor, Gomurakami, is warned in advance and flees; and when Moronao arrives at Yoshino, nobody is there. With Yoshino at his mercy, Moronao orders that all the buildings, including those of Buddhist temples and Shinto shrines, be burned to the ground. Taiheiki

describes this as a wanton act of arson, and predicts that heaven will
punish Moronao.[180] This is the first indication we are given that Moronao, as warrior commander, is headed for a fall.

In addition to accounts of the Kō brothers' military campaigns,
Part Three of the *Taiheiki* periodically describes their behavior as
members of the new warrior elite resident in Kyoto. Taking full advantage of their status as senior members of the Ashikaga Bakufu, the
brothers lead lives of extravagant luxury, even confiscating the man-
sions of courtiers and others for their own uses. They also gobble up
landholdings, sometimes through outright confiscation and sometimes through the issuance of illegal decrees. When their vassals and
others complain that they have not been sufficiently rewarded, the
brothers do not hesitate to confiscate land for them as well. So greedy
for land does Moronao become that he even expresses resentment that
the spaces in Kyoto taken up by the palaces of the emperor and retired
emperor are not available to him. In exasperation, he suggests that
their majesties be banished. If there must be an emperor and retired
emperor, he reasons, "why not make them out of wood or cast them in
metal?"[181]

The Kō brothers—especially Moronao—are thus described in Part
Three in most unflattering terms. But there are many villains in
Taiheiki. If Moronao's "bad" behavior had been limited to that just
described, he might have escaped the extraordinary notoriety that
awaited him in later centuries. His greatest sin was his lechery.
Taiheiki informs us that he was insatiable in seducing court ladies,
even reaching for his victims into the personal quarters of the imperial
palace. But Moronao's most scandalous affair—one that was not actually consummated—was with the wife of a provincial warrior sup-
porter of the Ashikaga, Enya Hangan Takasada.

Told that the wife, a court lady just slightly beyond her prime, is a
great beauty, Moronao becomes determined to have her, even recruiting Yoshida Kenkō, author of *Tsurezuregusa*, to write a love letter for
him. But when the lady rebuffs all his overtures, Moronao slanders her
husband, Enya Hangan, telling Takauji and Tadayoshi that Hangan is
planning rebellion. When Hangan tries to escape to his home province
with his family and retainers, he is pursued by Bakufu forces. The wife
is killed and Hangan commits suicide. Echoing the words of Kusunoki
Masasue at the time of his and Masashige's suicides at the Battle of
Minatogawa, Hangan prays that he will be reborn seven times to
become again and again the enemy of Kō no Moronao.[182]

As is well known to all students of Japanese theater, the name of
Kō no Moronao was used some three and a half centuries later by play-

wrights in place of the real name of the villain in the story of the Forty-Seven Rōnin (Masterless Samurai). This story, greatly embellished by the playwrights, is based on events of the opening years of the eighteenth century, when a *daimyō* was forced to commit *seppuku* because he drew his sword in the shogun's palace and wounded one of the palace ministers, Kira Yoshinaka, for having humiliated him. The Forty-Seven (actually forty-six) Rōnin were vassals of the *daimyō* who, two years later, avenged their lord's death by attacking Kira's mansion and killing him. The Rōnin were subsequently sentenced to commit *seppuku* by the Tokugawa Bakufu for having broken its laws.

In the play *Chūshingura* (Treasury of Loyal Retainers), the *Taiheiki* tale of Kō no Moronao and Enya Hangan is superimposed on the story of the Forty-Seven Rōnin.[183] Thus, whereas the issue between the *daimyō* and Kira seems to have arisen from the *daimyō's* failure to bribe Kira to assist him in preparing for the official responsibility of receiving imperial envoys from Kyoto at the shogun's palace, in *Chūshingura* the lubricious Kō no Moronao (Kira) attempts to seduce Hangan's (the *daimyō's*) wife. His name thereby indelibly imprinted upon what became without question the most beloved of Japanese plays, the historical Kō no Moronao himself was consigned to the front ranks of insidious villains in the popular imagination.

Kō no Moronao and his brother Moroyasu were killed in 1351 by allies of Ashikaga Tadayoshi. They were victims of a complex internal struggle in the Bakufu centering on Tadayoshi and his brother, the shogun Takauji. In this struggle, which, as noted in the section "Historical Background," caused both Tadayoshi and Takauji on separate occasions (in 1350 and 1351) to defect to the southern court and finally led to Tadayoshi's poisoning by Takauji in 1352, the Kō stood staunchly with the shogun. Perhaps *Taiheiki's* authors, themselves bewildered by the events of this struggle, sought to set the stage for the killings of the Kō brothers and Tadayoshi—that is, sought to explain why they were fated to die—by either contriving or embellishing the stories of supernatural beings, wanton destruction, lese majesty, uncontrolled extravagance, and lechery described in this section.[184]

Conclusion

THE IMPERIAL-BUREAUCRATIC state created under Chinese influence during the Taika Reform period of the late seventh century conscripted peasants as foot soldiers to serve in provincial military units *(gundan)* and as frontier guards in Kyushu and court guards in the capital. Armies that were assembled to deal with rebellions and other emergencies comprised foot soldiers and mounted officers, the latter recruited from local (district) elite families. But from the late eighth century, the court largely abandoned the conscription of peasant foot soldiers, who proved inadequate in combat, and sought instead the best ways to employ mounted warriors to meet the military needs of the state.

During the ninth and tenth centuries, a warrior class emerged in the provinces from among the horse-riding fighters of the local elite families, especially those of the Kantō (or Bandō), a frontier region noted from antiquity for the high quality of its warriors—and also (along with Mutsu province to the north) for its horses. As great value was placed on warfare with bow and arrow on horseback, the way of the warrior at this time and for many centuries to come was known as the "way of the bow and horse." In battle, warriors typically paired off to fight one-against-one.

The genre of writings called war tales appeared almost simultaneously with the emergence of a provincial warrior class. In the first tale, *Shōmonki*, a record of the Taira no Masakado Revolt in the Kantō in the 930s, we read of the evolving ethos of warrior society, including the warrior's devotion to the military arts, his great concern about "name" (implying honor, face, and fame as well as pride in family), and his sense of shame or fear that he might be dishonored. Armies described in *Shōmonki* are highly unstable, usually forming before battles and dissolving after them. Although these armies generally include foot soldiers, the foot soldiers are often reliable only so long as the tide of battle goes well. The principal fighters in *Shōmonki*, as in all of the war tales discussed in this study, are mounted warriors.

The Former Nine Years War and Later Three Years War fought by Minamoto armies in Mutsu-Dewa in the middle and late eleventh century were crucibles of combat for the evolving warrior class. Much of what we know about these conflicts derives from two war tales, *Mutsu Waki* and *Ōshū Gosannen Ki*. From the standpoint of this study, *Mutsu* and *Ōshū* are probably most valuable in informing us about the development of the lord/vassal relationship in warrior society. In its idealized form, as found in these and other war tales, the relationship joins, on the one hand, a lord who not only provides for the material needs of his vassal but also gives him the love *(nasake)* a parent might give to a child and, on the other hand, a vassal who serves his lord in a spirit of absolute self-sacrifice *(kenshin)* and is ready to die for him at a moment's notice.

The golden period of the war tales was the early and mid-medieval age, spanning the late twelfth through fourteenth centuries. A trio of tales—*Hōgen Monogatari, Heiji Monogatari,* and *Heike Monogatari* —describe the political competition and armed struggle between the Ise Taira and various branches of the Minamoto that ushered in the medieval age (1185–1573). A fourth tale, *Taiheiki,* narrates the protracted warfare that accompanied the overthrow of the Kamakura Bakufu in 1333, Emperor Godaigo's ill-fated Kemmu Restoration (1333–1336), and the founding and first decades of the Ashikaga or Muromachi Bakufu (1336–1573). The principal setting of all these tales is Kyoto, and all inform us not only about the fighting among warrior armies during the tumultuous periods of history with which they deal, but also about relations between warriors and courtiers during these disordered times. In *Taiheiki,* some courtiers actually participate in the fighting on the side of the loyalists against the Ashikaga armies.

The war tales of the golden period provide far more information about the ethos and behavior of warriors than any of their Heian period precursors. *Heike Monogatari* is particularly rich in delineating the way of the warrior; and *Taiheiki* is notable for its detailed battle accounts.

I have devoted considerable attention to analyzing certain types of heroes identifiable in the early and mid-medieval war tales: the loser-hero and his variant, the tragic loser-hero, who appear in the *Hōgen, Heiji,* and *Heike,* and the failed loyalist hero of *Taiheiki.* All

these heroes meet sad and untimely, if not tragic, ends. Their prominence reflects the taste of the tales' anonymous authors as well as their
medieval audiences. They are tastes that bequeathed to future generations perceptions of the medieval warrior as gallant and courageous but
often fated for an early death, perhaps because of some personal flaw,
such as impolitic behavior, or because of steadfast (although not necessarily wise) commitment to a losing cause.

NOTES

INTRODUCTION

1. This was the Hokke or northern branch.

2. *Sesshō* was the regent for a minor emperor and *kampaku* for an adult emperor.

3. William Wayne Farris, *Heavenly Warriors* (Cambridge: Harvard University Press, 1992), p. 53.

4. The crossbow was a continental weapon imported from China. But we do not know the precise kind of crossbow used in Japan, since none have been found in archaeological sites and no drawings of crossbows remain. Karl Friday, suggesting that the Japanese crossbow may have been a multiple-arrow launcher of a rather unwieldy size, refers to it as an artillery piece. See Friday, *Hired Swords* (Stanford: Stanford University Press, 1992), pp. 41–43.

5. Quoted in Endō Motoo and Ōmori Shirō, eds., *Nihon Shi Handobukku* (Tokyo: Asakura Shoten, 1963), p. 82.

6. Ibid.

7. Kobata Atsushi and Wakamori Tarō, *Nihon Shi Kenkyū* (Tokyo: Zokubundō, 1956), p. 89.

8. For other thoughts about the move from Nara see Ronald P. Toby, "Why Leave Nara?", *Monumenta Nipponica* 40 (3) (Autumn 1985): 331–347.

9. The principal occasions were the Jinshin Conflict of 672 that made Temmu emperor, the Fujiwara no Hirotsugu Revolt in Kyushu in 740, and the Fujiwara no Nakamaro Revolt of 764. See Farris, *Heavenly Warriors*, pp. 44, 64, and 73–75.

10. Friday, *Hired Swords*, pp. 124–125.

11. See the discussion in Naoki Kōjirō, *Kodai Kokka no Seiritsu* (Tokyo: Chūō Kōron Sha, 1965), pp. 247–251.

12. In this study I will use Bandō, which means "East of the [Ashigara] Barrier," interchangeably with Kantō. But originally Bandō meant the Kantō plus Mutsu province and sometimes Dewa province.

13. *Mutsu Waki* in Hanawa Hokiichi, ed., *Gunsho Ruijū*, vol. 20 (Tokyo: Zoku Gunsho Ruijū Kansei Kai, 1959), p. 32.

14. See Takahashi Takashi, *Sakanoue no Tamuramaro* (Tokyo: Yoshi-kawa Kōbunkan, 1959), pp. 131–135.

15. Ibid., pp. 137–138.

16. Farris, *Heavenly Warriors*, p. 101.

17. See Farris' remarks about the crossbow and the Japanese abandon-ment of it at this time; ibid., pp. 113–116.

18. Hayakawa Shōhachi, *Ritsuryō Kokka* (Tokyo: Shōgakukan, 1974), p. 428.

19. Karl Friday points out that these former officials of the provincial governments also usually maintained residences in Kyoto and continued to keep abreast of political affairs in the capital; *Hired Swords*, pp. 79–81.

20. Quoted in Kitayama Shigeo, *Heian-kyō* (Tokyo: Chūō Kōron Sha, 1965), p. 320.

21. Ibid., pp. 312–313.

22. Ibid., p. 319.

23. Ibid., pp. 322–326.

24. Yomiuri Shimbun Sha, ed., *Nihon no Rekishi*, vol. 3 (Tokyo: Yomiuri Shimbun Sha, 1959), pp. 211–212.

25. Sakamoto Shōzō, *Sekkan Jidai* (Tokyo: Shōgakukan, 1974), pp. 165–166.

CHAPTER 1

1. Genealogies state that Takamochi had either eight or ten sons. See Judith N. Rabinovitch, trans., *Shōmonki: The Story of Masakado's Rebellion* (Tokyo: Monumenta Nipponica, 1986), p. 11.

2. A chart showing Masakado's place in the line of the Kammu Taira can be found in Rabinovitch, trans., *Shōmonki*, p. 142. The opening lines of *Shōmonki* also provide genealogical information about Masakado.

3. Koten Isan no Kai, ed., *Shōmonki, Kenkyū to Shiryō* (Tokyo: Shin-doku Shosha, 1963), p. 209. *Shōmonki* says nothing about why Masakado decided to support such a sinister character, except that he approved of Haruaki's wish to attack the Hitachi vice-governor, Fujiwara no Korechika.

4. For a discussion of the position of *ōryōshi*, see Friday, *Hired Swords*, pp. 141–148.

5. Yomiuri Shimbun Sha, ed., *Nihon no Rekishi*, vol. 3 (Tokyo: Yomiuri Shimbun Sha, 1959), p. 216.

6. Koten Isan no Kai, ed., *Shōmonki*, p. 276.

7. Yomiuri Shimbun Sha, ed., *Nihon no Rekishi*, vol. 3, p. 217.

8. See the comments about this and other manifestations of Masakado worship in Rabinovitch, trans., *Shōmonki*, pp. 3–5.

9. Koten Isan no Kai, ed., *Shōmonki*, p. 278. The oldest extant *Shōmonki* texts are the *Shinpukuji-bon* (dated 1099) and the *Yō Shukei Kyūzō-bon* (from the tenth or eleventh centuries). The *Shinpukuji-bon*, used in this study of *Shōmonki*, is a much longer, more complete work. The *Yō Shukei Kyūzō-*

bon, which contains only *Shōmonki's* middle portion, is useful primarily to check variant phraseology and the like. See Rabinovitch, trans., *Shōmonki*, pp. 33–39.

10. See Judith Rabinovitch's discussion of this subject in *Shōmonki*, pp. 44–45.

11. Aoki Kazuo, *Kodai Gōzoku*, in *Nihon no Rekishi*, vol. 5 (Tokyo: Shōgakukan, 1974), pp. 309–310.

12. Rabinovitch, trans., *Shōmonki*, p. 53.

13. Sasaki Hachirō describes the language as Chinese *(kambun)* with a "Japanese scent"; *Chūsei Senki Bungaku* (Tokyo: Tsuru Shobō, 1943), p. 20.

14. Takeuchi Rizō, *Bushi no Tōjō*, in *Nihon no Rekishi*, vol. 6 (Tokyo: Chūō Kōron Sha, 1965), p. 82.

15. Koten Isan no Kai, ed., *Shōmonki*, p. 262.

16. Fukuda Toyohiko, *Taira no Masakado no Ran* (Tokyo: Iwanami Shoten, 1981), pp. 92–93. The mounted warriors—the commander's close followers—are usually identified in *Shōmonki* as *jūrui*.

17. Koten Isan no Kai, ed., *Shōmonki*, p. 233.

18. Ibid., p. 267.

19. Ibid., p. 205.

20. Frances Gies, *The Knight in History* (New York: Harper & Row, 1984).

21. Koten Isan no Kai, ed., *Shōmonki*, p. 150.

22. Ibid., p. 255.

23. William Wayne Farris observes that the straight sword was imported from China in early times and was of two kinds: the *tachi*, sharpened on one edge, and the double-edged *tsurugi*. The *tsurugi* was apparently used largely for ceremonial purposes.See Farris, *Heavenly Warriors*, pp. 19, 101–102.

24. Ishii Susumu, *Kamakura Bakufu*, in *Nihon no Rekishi*, vol. 7 (Tokyo: Chūō Kōron Sha, 1965), p. 120. A type of curved sword may have been introduced to the Japanese by the Emishi during the fighting in Mutsu-Dewa in the late eighth century. See Farris, *Heavenly Warriors*, pp. 102–103.

25. Koten Isan no Kai, ed., *Shōmonki*, p. 158.

26. Ibid., p. 172.

27. Ibid., p. 174.

28. Ibid., p. 163.

29. Ibid., p. 263.

30. Warriors sometimes had cape hoods known as *horo* that billowed as they rode and were also intended to deflect arrows.

31. Kajiwara Masaaki, *Heike Monogatari* (Tokyo: Kōdansha, 1967), pp. 155–156. Henceforth this work will be identified as *Heike Monogatari* (Kōdansha) to distinguish it from another work with the same title by the same author published by Shōgakukan.

32. Ishii, *Kamakura Bakufu*, p. 116.

33. Nagazumi Yasuaki and Shimada Isao, eds., *Hōgen Monogatari, Heiji Monogatari*, in *Nihon Koten Bungaku Taikei*, vol. 31 (Tokyo: Iwanami Shoten, 1961), p. 106. *Hōgen Monogatari* has been translated into English by William

R. Wilson in *Hōgen Monogatari: Tale of the Disorder in Hōgen* (Tokyo: Sophia University, 1971). An abridged translation of the *Hōgen* can be found in Edward R. Kellogg, "*Hōgen Monogatari*," *Transactions of the Asiatic Society of Japan* 45 (pt. 1) (1917): 25–117.

34. Japanese horses were smaller than European horses, but were strong and fast.

35. Koten Isan no Kai, ed., *Shōmonki*, p. 220.

36. See Kajiwara Masaaki's discussion of *arauma-nori* (riding untamed horses) in *Heike Monogatari* (Kōdansha), pp. 153–154.

37. This is known as *uma-ate* (being hit by horses); ibid., p. 152. Kajiwara remarks that using horses to trample on people was a major technique of warfare.

38. Lynn White, Jr., *Medieval Technology and Social Change* (London: Oxford University Press, 1962), pp. 15–16.

39. Koten Isan no Kai, ed., *Shōmonki*, p. 185.

40. Ibid., p. 150.

41. Ibid., p. 263.

42. Ibid., p. 162.

43. Ibid., p. 174.

44. Ibid., p. 266.

45. Ibid., p. 163.

46. Ibid., p. 158.

47. Ibid., p. 171.

48. Ruth Benedict, *The Chrysanthemum and the Sword* (Tokyo: Tuttle, 1954), p. 223.

49. The best discussion of Japanese feudalism in English is John W. Hall, "Feudalism in Japan—A Reassessment," in John W. Hall and Marius B. Jansen, eds., *Studies in the Institutional History of Early Modern Japan* (Princeton: Princeton University Press, 1968).

50. See William Wayne Farris' summary remarks about Japanese feudalism in *Heavenly Warriors*, pp. 371–379.

51. Fukuda, noting how readily warriors shifted from one commander to another as they sought to take advantage of the flow of power, states that there was no true lord/vassal relationship in the age of *Shōmonki*. See "Ōchō Gunji Kikō to Nairan," in Iwanami Shoten, ed., *Iwanami Kōza Nihon Rekishi* (Tokyo: Iwanami Shoten, 1976), vol. 4, p. 88.

52. Fukuda Toyohiko observes that marriage ties were frequently stronger than blood ties in bringing warriors together; ibid., p. 87.

53. Quoted in Hall, "Feudalism in Japan—A Reassessment," p. 30.

54. See Karl Friday's remarks about the kinds of rewards warrior chiefs of the Heian period gave their followers; *Hired Swords*, pp. 116–117.

55. Aoki, *Kodai Gōzoku*, p. 305.

56. That is, *fudai* or hereditary vassals.

57. Owada Tetsuo, *Sengoku Bushō* (Tokyo: Chūō Kōron Sha, 1981), p. 91.

58. Katsumata Shizuo, "The Development of Sengoku Law," in John W.

Hall et al., eds., *Japan before Tokugawa* (Princeton: Princeton University Press, 1981), p. 105.

59. Koten Isan no Kai, ed., *Shōmonki*, pp. 151–152.

60. Fukuda, *Taira no Masakado no Ran*, pp. 99–100. Fukuda Toyohiko points out that *jūrui* houses were usually situated near the commander's, whereas those of the *banrui*, the peasants recruited into armies, were scattered across the countryside.

61. Aoki, *Kodai Gōzoku*, p. 318.

62. Takeuchi, *Bushi no Tōjō*, p. 76.

63. Watanabe Tamotsu, *Genji to Heishi* (Tokyo: Shibundō, 1955), p. 31.

64. Quoted in George Sansom, *A History of Japan to 1334* (Stanford: Stanford University Press, 1958), p. 248. Takeuchi Rizō suggests two possible reasons for Tadatsune's surrender: First, Tadatsune had so devastated the farming in the Bōsō Peninsula during his revolt that he lacked the supplies to continue fighting; second, he may have hoped to become Yorinobu's vassal. See *Bushi no Tōjō*, p. 38.

65. Korehira was appointed governor of Ise in 1006.

66. Marian Ury, *Tales of Times Now Past* (Berkeley: University of California Press, 1979), p. 2.

67. This style is known as *wakan konkō bun*, "mixed Japanese and Chinese."

68. Yamada Yoshio et al., eds., *Konjaku Monogatari Shū*, vol. 4 in *Nihon Koten Bungaku Taikei*, vol. 25 (Tokyo: Iwanami Shoten, 1962), p. 368. The Book 25 warrior stories in *Konjaku* have been translated into English by William Ritchie Wilson in "The Way of the Bow and Arrow: The Japanese Warrior in *Konjaku Monogatari*," *Monumenta Nipponica* 28 (2) (1973): 177–234.

69. Yamada et al., eds., *Konjaku Monogatari Shū*, vol. 4, pp. 368–370.

70. Ishii, *Kamakura Bakufu*, pp. 117–122.

71. Ibid., p. 117. This occurred before the battle of Fujigawa in 1180.

72. One of the references is in this story about Mitsuru and Yoshifumi. An arrow shot by Yoshifumi strikes Mitsuru's sword scabbard. See Yamada et al., eds., *Konjaku Monogatari Shū*, vol. 4, p. 369.

73. Ishii, *Kamakura Bakufu*, pp. 117–122.

74. Ibid., pp. 120–121.

75. Ibid.

76. Ibid., p. 125.

77. Nagazumi and Shimada, eds., *Hōgen Monogatari*, p. 99.

78. Nagazumi Yasuaki and Shimada Isao, eds., *Hōgen Monogatari, Heiji Monogatari*, in *Nihon Koten Bungaku Taikei*, vol. 31 (Tokyo: Iwanami Shoten, 1961), p. 234. About a third of *Heiji Monogatari* has been translated into English by Edwin Reischauer in Edwin Reischauer and Joseph K. Yamagiwa, eds. and trans., *Translations from Early Japanese Literature* (Cambridge: Harvard University Press, 1951). Marisa Chalitpatanangune has translated the first two of the three books of the oldest extant version of the work in "*Heiji Monogatari*: A Study and Annotated Translation of the Oldest Text" (unpublished dissertation, University of California, Berkeley, 1987).

79. Nagazumi and Shimada, eds., *Heiji Monogatari*, pp. 253–254.

80. Yamada et al., eds., *Konjaku Monogatari Shū*, vol. 4, pp. 374–375.

81. Ibid., pp. 375–376.

82. Ibid., pp. 377–378.

83. Ibid., p. 378.

84. Ibid., pp. 379–381.

85. Ibid., p. 381.

86. See, for example, the description of Masakado himself as such a warrior in Koten Isan no Kai, eds., *Shōmonki*, p. 188.

87. In later war tales, especially *Heike Monogatari*, the two terms *ienoko* (kin vassals) and *rōdō* (non-kin vassals) appear frequently together to indicate the followers of a chieftain.

88. Both of these phrases can be found, for example, in Yamada et al., eds., *Konjaku Monogatari Shū*, vol. 4, p. 399.

89. I have translated this from the original *Mutsu Waki* rather than the version contained in *Konjaku Monogatari Shū*. See Hanawa Hokiichi, ed., *Mutsu Waki*, in *Gunsho Ruijū*, vol. 20 (Tokyo: Zoku Gunsho Ruijū Kansei Kai, 1959), p. 25. *Mutsu Waki* has been translated into English by Helen Craig McCullough in "A Tale of Mutsu," *Harvard Journal of Asiatic Studies* 25 (1964–1965): 178–211.

90. *Mutsu Waki*, p. 25.

91. See Karl Friday's comments in *Hired Swords*, pp. 93–95, about the inadvisability of using the Japanese historians' term *bushidan* in discussing warrior bands.

92. Karl Friday suggests that the forerunners of the Heian period warrior bands may have been provincial groups of armed robbers (discussed in the Introduction) dating back to the late eighth century; *Hired Swords*, pp. 96–97.

93. *Mutsu Waki*, p. 28.

94. Watsuji Tetsurō, *Nihon Rinri Shisō Shi*, vol. 1 (Tokyo: Iwanami Shoten, 1952), pp. 290–318. Uwayokote Masataka points out that Watsuji, writing in the pre–World War II period, was influenced in his interpretation of what he called the *kenshin* ethic of premodern warriors by equating it with the spirit of absolute loyalty and self-sacrifice to the emperor that was expected of all Japanese subjects in the propaganda of that time. Put another way, Watsuji believed that the *kenshin* spirit of warriors in the war tales should serve as a model for the modern Japanese. See Uwayokote, "Chūsei-teki Rinri to Hō," in Nihon Kenkyū Kai, ed., *Kōza Nihon Bunka Shi*, vol. 3 (Tokyo: Sanjū-ichi Shobō, 1962), p. 156.

95. Yamada et al., eds., *Konjaku Monogatari Shū*, vol. 4, p. 373.

96. James Legge, trans., *Li-chi*, in *The Sacred Books of the East* (Oxford, 1885), vol. 27, p. 92.

97. See H. Paul Varley, *The Samurai* (London: Weidenfeld & Nicolson, 1970), p. 31. See also Norman F. Cantor, *Medieval History* (New York: Macmillan, 1963), pp. 127–129.

98. There are two translations of *Soga Monogatari* into English: Thomas J. Cogan, trans., *The Tale of the Soga Brothers* (Tokyo: University of Tokyo

Press, 1987); and Hiroshi Kitagawa, *The Tale of the Soga Brothers* (Shiga: Faculty of Letters, Shiga University, 1988).

99. Examples of the desire for vengeance in forms other than *katakiuchi* will be found in the medieval war tales, especially *Taiheiki*.

100. Yamada et al., eds., *Konjaku Monogatari Shū*, vol. 4, p. 391.

101. Takagi Ichinosuke et al., eds., *Heike Monogatari*, vol. 1, in *Nihon Koten Bungaku Taikei*, vol. 32 (Tokyo: Iwanami Shoten, 1959), p. 373. *Heike Monogatari* has been translated into English by A. L. Sadler, "The *Heike Monogatari*," *Transactions of the Asiatic Society of Japan* 46 (pt. 2) (1918); by Hiroshi Kitagawa and Bruce T. Tsuchida, *The Tale of the Heike*, 2 vols. (Tokyo: University of Tokyo Press, 1975); and by Helen Craig McCullough, *The Tale of the Heike* (Stanford: Stanford University Press, 1988).

102. Gotō Tanji and Kamada Kisaburō, eds., *Taiheiki*, vol. 1, in *Nihon Koten Bungaku Taikei*, vol. 34 (Tokyo: Iwanami Shoten, 1960), p. 210. The first third of *Taiheiki* has been translated into English by Helen Craig McCullough in *The Taiheiki: A Chronicle of Medieval Japan* (New York: Columbia University Press, 1959).

103. The origins of the Abe are obscure, although they may have been one of a number of families in Mutsu and Dewa that took the Abe surname from the seventh-century general Abe no Hirafu. They are referred to simply as Emishi. The six districts controlled by the Abe covered the area of what is today Iwate prefecture.

104. The source for this information is the war tale *Mutsu Waki* (p. 22). See Takeuchi, *Bushi no Tōjō*, p. 51, for comments on the reliability of *Mutsu Waki* as history.

105. The designation Former Nine Years War seems to have come from a reference in *Heike Monogatari* to nine years of fighting. Originally the conflict was called the "twelve years war"—from 1051, when Minamoto no Yoriyoshi went to Mutsu, until 1062, when the Abe were finally defeated. See Watanabe, *Genji to Heishi*, p. 62.

106. Hanawa, ed., *Mutsu Waki*, p. 26.

107. Ibid., p. 32.

108. McCullough, "A Tale of Mutsu," p. 181.

109. See note 104.

110. Hanawa, ed., *Mutsu Waki*, p. 23.

111. Ibid., p. 29.

112. Ibid., p. 25.

113. Ibid.

114. Watanabe, *Genji to Heishi*, p. 75.

115. Yasuda Motohisa, *Minamoto no Yoshiie* (Tokyo: Yoshikawa Kōbunkan, 1966), p. 25.

116. Hanawa, ed., *Mutsu Waki*, p. 31.

117. Ibid.

118. The court called Yoshiie's war a "private fight." See Takeuchi, *Bushi no Tōjō*, p. 73.

119. William Wayne Farris argues that the court, far from abandoning

responsibility for military control of the provinces during the Heian period, continued to supply, through the provincial governments, substantial military support to warrior commanders. The court gave such support to Yoriyoshi in the Former Nine Years War but denied it to Yoshiie in the Later Three Years War. See *Heavenly Warriors*, p. 239.

120. *Ōshū Gosannen Ki*, in Hanawa Hokiichi, ed., *Gunsho Ruijū*, vol. 20 (Tokyo: Zoku Gunsho Ruijū Kansei Kai, 1959), p. 48.

121. See the discussion of *Ōshū Gosannen Ki* in Yasuda, *Minamoto no Yoshiie*, pp. 84–86.

122. Hanawa, ed., *Ōshū Gosannen Ki*, p. 33.

123. Ibid., p. 40.

124. Ibid., pp. 39–40. I have not been able to identify the Masafusa book. But the lore about birds being disturbed by soldiers in hiding comes from Sun Tzu: "Birds rising in flight is [sic] a sign that the enemy is lying in ambush; when the wild animals are startled and flee he is trying to take you unaware." See Sun Tzu, *The Art of War*, trans. Samuel B. Griffith (Oxford: Clarendon Press, 1963), p. 119.

125. Ibid., pp. 38–39.

126. Nagazumi and Shimada, eds., *Hōgen Monogatari*, pp. 110–111.

127. Takagi et al., eds., *Heike Monogatari*, vol. 2, p. 208. Still another reference to Kagemasa and his feat in the Later Three Years War can be found in *Taiheiki*; Gotō and Kamada, eds., *Taiheiki*, vol. 2, p. 138.

128. Yasuda, *Insei to Heishi*, p. 104.

129. Nakamikado no Munetada, *Chūyūki*, 1106:7:16, in Zōho Shiryō Taisei Kankō Kaihen, ed., *Zōho Shiryō Taisei* (Tokyo: Rinsui Shoten, 1965), vol. 11, p. 129.

130. Yamada et al., eds., *Konjaku Monogatari Shū*, vol. 4, p. 68.

131. Nakamikado no Munetada, *Chūyūki*, 1108:1:24, p. 322.

132. Ibid., 1108:1:29, p. 325.

CHAPTER 2

1. Yasuda Motohisa, *Taira no Kiyomori* (Tokyo: Kiyomizu Shoten, 1971), p. 47.

2. Ibid., p. 59.

3. One of Toba's grievances toward his grandfather Shirakawa concerned Toba's son, the future Emperor Sutoku. Sutoku's mother, Taikenmon'in, had been provided as a wife to Toba by Shirakawa. But it was widely believed that Shirakawa was Sutoku's real father and that Sutoku was therefore Toba's *ojiko*, "uncle child." See Takeuchi, *Bushi no Tōjō*, pp. 318–319.

4. Takagi et al., eds., *Heike Monogatari*, vol. 1, pp. 84–88. The phrase of the song given in the *Heike* can be taken to have several meanings: "The Ise Heishi (or Heike; Tadamori) is squint-eyed," for example, or "The bottle from Ise is a roughly made article (or 'is a vinegar bottle')."

5. Okami Masao and Akamatsu Toshihide, eds., *Gukanshō*, in *Nihon Koten Bungaku Taikei*, vol. 85 (Tokyo: Iwanami Shoten, 1967), p. 206. *Gukanshō* has been translated into English in Delmer Brown and Ichirō Ishida, *The Future and the Past: A Translation and Study of the Gukanshō* (Berkeley: Uni-

versity of California Press, 1979). *Gukanshō* has also been partially translated by Johannes Rhader: "Miscellany of Personal Views of an Ignorant Fool," *Acta Orientalia* 15 (3) (1936): 173–230.

6. Yasuda, *Insei to Heishi*, p. 242.

7. Nagazumi and Shimada, eds., *Hōgen Monogatari*, p. 75.

8. Ibid., p. 76.

9. Yasuda, *Insei to Heishi*, p. 244.

10. Iida Yukiko, *Hōgen, Heiji no Ran* (Tokyo: Kyōikusha, 1979), p. 109.

11. *Futsū Shōdō Shū.* See the comments in Nagazumi Yasuaki, *Hōgen Monogatari, Heiji Monogatari* (Tokyo: Kadokawa Shoten, 1976), p. 16.

12. Ibid., p. 18.

13. In *Hōgen Monogatari: Tale of the Disorder in Hōgen,* William Wilson has translated a composite version of the *Hōgen* edited from a number of *rufubon* texts by Yoshimura Shigenori in *Hōgen Monogatari Shinsaku* (Tokyo: Daidōkan, 1927).

14. Nagazumi, *Hōgen Monogatari, Heiji Monogatari*, p. 19.

15. Nagazumi and Shimada, eds., *Hōgen Monogatari*, p. 84.

16. Ibid., pp. 84–85.

17. Hanawa, ed., *Mutsu Waki*, p. 27.

18. Nagazumi and Shimada, eds., *Hōgen Monogatari*, p. 92.

19. Ibid., pp. 117–118.

20. Hanawa, ed., *Mutsu Waki*, p. 30.

21. Koten Isan no Kai, ed., *Shōmonki*, p. 151.

22. Nagazumi and Shimada, eds., *Hōgen Monogatari*, p. 123.

23. Takagi et al., eds., *Heike Monogatari*, vol. 1, p. 100.

24. This is a central theme in Ivan Morris, *The Nobility of Failure: Tragic Heroes in the History of Japan* (New York: Holt, Rinehart & Winston, 1975).

25. Nagazumi, *Hōgen Monogatari, Heiji Monogatari*, p. 82.

26. Nagazumi and Shimada, eds., *Hōgen Monogatari*, p. 81. The Nakaraibon and *rufubon* versions of the *Hōgen* contain similar descriptions of Tametomo. But the Nakaraibon *Hōgen* adds that Tametomo's bow requires three men to string it *(sannin-bari)*; Nakaraibon *Hōgen Monogatari* in Koten Kenkyū Kai, ed., *Hōgen Monogatari*, vol. 1 (Tokyo: Namifuru Shoten, 1972), p. 138. And *rufubon Hōgen* states that it takes five men to string the bow *(gonin-bari)*: *rufubon* (identified as *kokatsujibon* or "old-type text") *Hōgen Monogatari* in Nagazumi and Shimada, eds., *Hōgen Monogatari, Heiji Monogatari*, p. 356. Most bows could be strung by one or two men. *Sannin-bari* is a conventional term used in the war tales to identify a powerful warrior who needs a powerful bow. *Gonin-bari* suggests a warrior of extraordinary strength. In *Heike Monogatari,* as we will see, the best Bandō warriors are said to use *gonin-bari.*

27. Ibid., pp. 99–100. The story of the brothers is cited also in Chapter 1 in the section "The Taking of Heads," which describes one brother, Itō Go, taking the head of his brother (Itō Roku), who has been slain by Minamoto no Tametomo, to prevent the head from falling into enemy hands.

28. Ibid., p. 99.

29. Neither Nakaraibon *Hōgen* nor *rufubon Hōgen* refers to Kiyomori's wish to attack a gate other than the one guarded by Tametomo. Since *rufubon Hōgen* is closer in content to the Nakaraibon or old text version than to Kotohirabon *Hōgen* (see Wilson, trans., *Hōgen Monogatari: Tale of the Disorder in Hōgen*, p. vi), it appears that this passage, picturing Kiyomori as cowardly, was the work of the tale singers who developed Kotohirabon.

30. Ibid., pp. 137–138. Nakaraibon *Hōgen* contains essentially the same account of Tametomo's plan, but *rufubon Hōgen* (p. 376) does not include the idea of establishing a capital in the Kantō like Masakado's.

31. Ibid., p. 175.

32. Ibid.

33. See, for example, the *rufubon* version (pp. 396–399).

34. Nagazumi and Shimada, eds., *Hōgen Monogatari*, p. 106. In Nakaraibon *Hōgen* (p. 191) and *rufubon Hōgen* (p. 363), Masakiyo does not hold Yoshitomo back; rather, Yoshitomo orders Masakiyo to go forward and test Tametomo.

35. Ibid., pp. 106–107.

36. Takeuchi, *Bushi no Tōjō*, pp. 84–85.

37. Nagazumi and Shimada, eds., *Hōgen Monogatari*, p. 75.

38. Ibid., p. 94.

39. Kenneth Dean Butler, "The *Heike Monogatari* and the Japanese Warrior Ethic," *Harvard Journal of Asiatic Studies* 29 (1969): 104.

40. Nagazumi and Shimada, eds., *Hōgen Monogatari*, p. 69.

41. Ibid., p. 99. See the comments about this incident in note 29. In Nakaraibon *Hōgen* (p. 174) and *rufubon Hōgen* (p. 361), it is not Kiyomori but one of his vassals, Itō Kagetsuna, who performs the name-announcing and challenges Tametomo.

42. Ibid., p. 114.

43. Ibid., p. 115. Neither this statement nor the statement in the next sentence appears in either Nakaraibon *Hōgen* or *rufubon Hōgen*.

44. Ibid.

45. Ibid., p. 99.

46. See the section on "Tametomo and the Loser as Hero." This is, once again, the story of Itō Go and Itō Roku.

47. See the section on "The Ever-Faithful Follower."

48. Takagi et al., eds., *Heike Monogatari*, vol. 2, p. 79. The warrior is Saitō no Sanemori, whose story will be told in the next chapter. His special reason is that he wishes to disguise his age. He is over seventy but does not want to be treated as other than a worthy opponent in battle.

49. Ibid., p. 220.

50. Ibid., p. 204.

51. Mizuhara Hajime, ed., *Gempei Seisui Ki* (Tokyo: Shin-Jimbutsu Ōrai Sha, 1988), vol. 5, pp. 55–56.

52. For example, Taira no Koremochi is "dressed" in some detail as he prepares to lead his vassals in pursuit of Fujiwara no Morotō the morning after Morotō's night attack on Koremochi's residence. See Yamada et al., eds., *Konjaku Monogatari Shū*, vol. 4, pp. 378–379.

53. See the discussion in Ishimoda Shō, *Heike Monogatari* (Tokyo: Iwanami Shoten, 1957), pp. 168–169.

54. Nagazumi and Shimada, eds., *Hōgen Monogatari*, p. 101. The hood *(horo)* was attached to the back of a warrior's armor. When not in use, it billowed behind the warrior as he rode on his horse.

55. Iida Yukiko suggests that Shinzei persuaded Kiyomori to pursue this strategy; *Hōgen, Heiji no Ran*, p. 116.

56. Nagazumi and Shimada, eds., *Hōgen Monogatari*, p. 147. *Rufubon Hōgen* does not contain Tameyoshi's statement to Masakiyo and the other executioners about attaining no glory. Instead, it has a lengthy moralistic passage (p. 380) about Yoshitomo having violated righteousness *(gi)* itself in carrying out the execution of his father. This passage reflects the Confucian didacticism of *rufubon Hōgen* as opposed to the Kotohirabon version.

57. Ibid., p. 156. In *rufubon Hōgen* (p. 382), Otowaka predicts that Yoshitomo and the Minamoto house will be destroyed by Kiyomori within two or three years.

58. Nagazumi and Shimada, eds., *Hōgen Monogatari*, p. 70. This statement does not appear in either Nakaraibon or *rufubon Hōgen*.

59. Ibid., p. 72. *Rufubon Hōgen* states (p. 351) that Chikaharu was not able to commit suicide *(jigai)*, but it does not mention cutting the belly.

60. See, for example, *rufubon Hōgen*, p. 399.

61. Chiba Tokuji, *Seppuku no Hanashi* (Tokyo: Kōdansha, 1972), p. 73.

62. Ibid., p. 81.

63. For example, the *Hōgen* states that four wet nurses (and two warrior guards) cut their stomachs after the execution of Yoshitomo's four infant brothers. See Nagazumi and Shimada, eds., *Hōgen Monogatari*, pp. 156–157.

64. Chiba, *Seppuku no Hanashi*, p. 94.

65. See the discussion in Iida Yukiko, *Hōgen, Heiji no Ran*, p. 162.

66. Chalitpatanangune, trans., "*Heiji Monogatari*," p. 22.

67. Nagazumi, *Hōgen Monogatari, Heiji Monogatari*, pp. 190–191. Marisa Chalitpatanangune has translated the first two of the three books of the Yōmei-Gakushūin version of the *Heiji* in "*Heiji Monogatari*."

68. Nagazumi, *Hōgen Monogatari, Heiji Monogatari*, p. 191.

69. Chalitpatanangune, trans., "*Heiji Monogatari*," p. 22.

70. Nagazumi and Shimada, eds., *Heiji Monogatari*, p. 189.

71. Ibid., p. 197. In Yōmei-Gakushūin *Heiji*, Kiyomori and his party on the pilgrimage to Kumano receive a report, which proves untrue, that Yoshihira is waiting to attack them at Abeno in Settsu province (Chalitpatanangune, "*Heiji Monogatari*," p. 72). The text, however, does not relate any discussion between Yoshihira and Nobuyori about whether to move south against Kiyomori or await his return to the capital.

72. There are many similarities between the *Hōgen* Tametomo and the *Heiji* Yoshihira. But whereas Tametomo dominates the warfare, accepting directions from no one, Yoshihira is simply one of several Minamoto commanders who follow Yoshitomo's orders. Yoshihira is very much a team player, sacrificing his personal will (Komatsu Shigetō speaks of Yoshihira's spirit of *kenshin*) for the good of the group, his warrior band. See Komatsu Shi-

getō, "*Hōgen Monogatari, Heiji Monogatari* no Jimbutsu Zō," in *Chūsei Gunki-mono no Kenkyū* (Tokyo: Ōfūsha, 1962), p. 11.

73. The battle is described in Nagazumi and Shimada, eds., *Heiji Monogatari*, pp. 222–233.

74. Ibid., p. 253. In Yōmei-Gakushūin *Heiji* (p. 137), Yoshihira is directed to go to Kai and Shinano provinces.

75. Ibid., p. 270. This exchange between Kiyomori and Yoshihira does not appear in either Yōmei-Gakushūin *Heiji* or *rufubon Heiji* (such as the *rufubon* version identified as *kokatsujibon* or "old-type text" *Heiji Monogatari* in Nagazumi and Shimada, eds., *Hōgen Monogatari, Heiji Monogatari*).

76. See note 8.

77. Nagazumi and Shimada, eds., *Hōgen Monogatari*, p. 106. This statement by Yoshitomo is not in either Nakaraibon *Hōgen* or *rufubon Hōgen*.

78. Iida, *Hōgen, Heiji no Ran*, p. 170.

79. Nagazumi and Shimada, eds., *Heiji Monogatari*, p. 224.

80. Ibid., p. 241.

81. Ibid., pp. 248–249. In Yōmei-Gakushūin *Heiji* (p. 120), the followers request permission to leave Yoshitomo's party.

82. Nagazumi and Shimada, eds., *Heiji Monogatari*, p. 251.

83. Ibid., pp. 253–254. In Yōmei-Gakushūin *Heiji* (p. 138) and *rufubon Heiji* (p. 442), Tomonaga asks his father to kill him. There is reference in "The Taking of Heads" section of Chapter 1 to Yoshitomo's killing Tomonaga and taking his head to prevent it from later coming into the possession of the enemy.

84. Nagazumi and Shimada, eds., *Heiji Monogatari*, p. 263.

85. For example, the Heiji Scrolls.

86. I. Bottomley and A. P. Hopson, *Arms and Armor of the Samurai* (New York: Crown Publishers, 1988), p. 24. Karl Friday informs me that the *naginata* resembled the Western glaive.

87. Ishii, *Kamakura Bakufu*, p. 134.

88. Nagazumi and Shimada, eds., *Heiji Monogatari*, p. 230. *Rufubon Heiji* (p. 428) tells how Nukemaru became famous in the possession of Yorimori's and Kiyomori's father, Tadamori.

89. Attendants are, in fact, sometimes also found in the Heiji Scrolls wearing full ō-yoroi armor.

90. Ishii, *Kamakura Bakufu*, p. 141.

91. Ibid.

92. A warrior in the war tales also often designates one of his vassals as a standard-bearer (*hatasashi*) to make himself readily identifiable in battle.

93. Nagazumi and Shimada, eds., *Hōgen Monogatari*, p. 93.

94. Nagazumi and Shimada, eds., *Heiji Monogatari*, p. 219.

95. See note 82.

96. Nagazumi and Shimada, eds., *Heiji Monogatari*, p. 227.

97. Takagi et al., eds., *Heike Monogatari*, vol. 1, p. 367. The expedition terminated in the ill-fated (for the Taira) Battle of Fuji River, which will be described in Chapter 3.

98. Ishii, *Kamakura Bakufu*, pp. 119–120. Karl Friday contends that the armor of this age should not be described as "light," since it weighed some 30 kilograms and was rigidly constructed.

99. Takagi et al., eds., *Heike Monogatari*, vol. 2, p. 203.

100. Nagazumi and Shimada, eds., *Heiji Monogatari*, p. 292.

101. Takagi et al., eds., *Heike Monogatari*, vol. 1, p. 409.

CHAPTER 3

1. Takagi et al., eds., *Heike Monogatari*, vol. 1, p. 92.

2. Uwayokote Masataka, *Heike Monogatari no Kyokō to Shinjitsu* (Tokyo: Hanawa Shobō, 1985), vol. 1, p. 36.

3. See Jeffrey P. Mass, "The Emergence of the Kamakura Bakufu," in John W. Hall and Jeffrey P. Mass, eds., *Medieval Japan: Essays in Institutional History* (New Haven: Yale University Press, 1974). See also Uwayokote, *Heike Monogatari no Kyokō to Shinjitsu*, vol. 1, p. 59.

4. Farris argues that the Taira did, in fact, develop an "independent, national military system"; *Heavenly Warriors*, p. 275. See chap. 7 of *Heavenly Warriors* for a detailed discussion of this revisionist view.

5. Kuroita Katsumi, ed., *Azuma Kagami*, in *Kokushi Taikei*, vol. 32 (Tokyo: Kokushi Taikei Kankō Kai, 1932), pp. 28–29. The first part of *Azuma Kagami*, covering the period 1180–1185, has been translated into English by Minoru Shinoda in *The Founding of the Kamakura Shogunate* (New York: Columbia University Press, 1960).

6. For an excellent survey of the Gempei War, see Jeffrey P. Mass, "The Kamakura Bakufu," in Kozo Yamamura, ed., *The Cambridge History of Japan* (Cambridge: Cambridge University Press, 1990), vol. 3, pp. 52–58.

7. *Azuma Kagami*, 1180:10:20. Ishii Susumu suggests that there were far more substantial reasons for the sudden withdrawal of the Taira army than the fluttering of birds: The army was not well provisioned and its morale was not high; most important, it was probably very much smaller in size than usually thought, perhaps numbering only four thousand. See Ishii, *Kamakura Bakuku*, pp. 69–72. Farris contends that most battles during the Gempei War involved only a few hundred horsemen, at most several thousand. He believes that in both numbers and military technology armies of the late twelfth century differed little from those of the tenth century. See *Heavenly Warriors*, p. 302.

8. Ishii, *Kamakura Bakufu*, p. 53.

9. Takagi et al., eds., *Heike Monogatari*, vol. 1, p. 409.

10. *Heike Monogatari* mistakenly states that Yoritomo was appointed *sei-i shōgun* (that is, *sei-i tai-shōgun*) by Goshirakawa during the time when Yoshinaka occupied Kyoto in 1183. See Sugimoto Keisaburō, ed., *Heike Monogatari*, vol. 8 (Tokyo: Kōdansha, 1987), p. 116. Yoritomo became *sei-i tai-shōgun* in 1192, seven years after the Gempei War and after the death of Goshirakawa.

11. See the discussion of the debate over this edict in Jeffrey P. Mass, *Warrior Government in Early Medieval Japan* (New Haven: Yale University Press, 1974), pp. 74–76.

12. See the discussion in Kajiwara Masaaki, *Heike Monogatari* (Tokyo: Shōgakukan, 1982), pp. 16–17. Henceforth this work will be identified as *Heike Monogatari* (Shōgakukan) to distinguish it from another work with the same title by the same author published by Kōdansha.

13. Ibid., p. 16.

14. See ibid., p. 18, for a chart of the names of these people.

15. Donald Keene, trans., *Essays in Idleness: The Tsurezuregusa of Kenkō* (New York: Columbia University Press, 1967), p. 186. *The Dance of the Seven Virtues* is a poem by Po Chü-i. See Kenneth Butler's interpretation of this *Tsurezuregusa* passage in "The Textual Evolution of the *Heike Monogatari,*" *Harvard Journal of Asiatic Studies* 26 (1965–1966): 16–23.

16. Ibid., p. 18.

17. Ibid., p. 6.

18. Takagi et al., eds., *Heike Monogatari*, vol. 1, p. 83.

19. The third Noble Truth is that there is a way to achieve salvation or release from suffering; the fourth Noble Truth identifies that way as the Eightfold Noble Path (right views, right intention, right speech, right action, right livelihood, right effort, right mindfulness, and right concentration).

20. During the age of the flourishing of the Law *(shōbō)* there is teaching *(kyō)*, practice *(gyō)*, and result *(shō)*; in the age of decline of the Law *(zōhō)*, result is lost; during *mappō*, there is only teaching and, eventually, the Law itself is extinguished.

21. Okami and Akamatsu, eds., *Gukanshō*, pp. 265–266.

22. See Ishida Ichirō, "Structure and Formation of *Gukanshō* Thought," in Brown and Ishida, *The Future and the Past*, pp. 420–450.

23. *Matsudai* (final generation) and *matsuyo* (final world) are often used in the *Heike* with essentially the same meaning as *mappō*.

24. See Ishimoda, *Heike Monogatari*, p. 9.

25. In 1183, when the Minamoto under Yoshinaka are driving toward Kyoto, both the Minamoto and the Taira solicit the support of Enryakuji Temple. The temple's monks, in the *Heike* account, reason: "Why should this temple alone support the Heike (Taira), whose karma *(shukuun)* is coming to an end, and go against the Genji (Minamoto), whose good fortune *(unmei)* is beginning?" See Takagi et al., eds., *Heike Monogatari*, vol. 2, p. 88. In this case the reference is to the Taira karma, or retribution for sins; however, there are frequent references elsewhere in the *Heike* to their fate or fortune *(unmei)* running out.

26. The *rufubon* of the *Hōgen* and *Heiji*, which were compiled in the Tokugawa period, are more imbued with Confucian didacticism than earlier versions of the works. Komatsu Shigetō observes that the *Heike* takes the idea of *unmei* found in the *Hōgen* and *Heiji* and transforms it into a worldview. See "Gunki-mono ni Okeru Unmei (Ichi)," in *Chūsei Gunki-mono no Kenkyū*, pp. 36–37.

27. It might be argued that the future portends well for the Minamoto. But the two most prominent Minamoto field commanders in the *Heike* (and, along with Taira no Kiyomori, its leading characters), Yoshinaka and Yoshi-

tsune, become tragic loser-heroes; and Yoritomo, the supreme Minamoto commander, plays a curiously insignificant role in the *Heike*. In other words, even the Minamoto, as portrayed in the *Heike*, give support to the proposition that the past is better than the present and the future will bring further decline.

· 28. Yasuda Motohisa, *Heike no Gunzō* (Tokyo: Hanawa Shinsho), pp. 17–18.

29. Nagazumi and Shimada, eds., *Heiji Monogatari*, p. 233.

30. Chalitpatanangune, trans., "*Heiji Monogatari*," p. 117.

31. Okami and Akamatsu, eds., *Gukanshō*, p. 235.

32. Takagi et al., eds., *Heike Monogatari*, vol. 1, p. 83.

33. Ibid.

34. Komatsu Shigetō, "*Heike Monogatari* ni Okeru Mujō," in *Chūsei Gunki-mono no Kenkyū*, p. 56.

35. See, for example, Tomikura Tokujirō, *Heike Monogatari* (Tokyo: NHK, 1972), p. 56.

36. There is one passage in the *Heike* in which Shigemori performs a military function. In Book 1 he assumes responsibility for the defense of several gates of the imperial palace when warrior-monks of Enryakuji Temple enter Kyoto to demand the punishment of two men accused of destroying the buildings of a provincial temple associated with Enryakuji. See Takagi et al., eds., *Heike Monogatari*, vol. 1, p. 135.

37. Ibid., pp. 171–172.

38. Ibid. The four obligations are to heaven and earth, to one's sovereign, to one's parents, and to mankind.

39. Ibid.

40. Ibid., p. 173.

41. Sovereignty, of course, rested with the emperor. Moreover, historically the *in* of late Heian times did not even resemble the remote, largely nonacting emperors of the period but rather were very active political figures who readily invited challenges to their efforts to be the real rulers in Kyoto. See Uwayokote, *Heike Monogatari no Kyokō to Shinjitsu*, vol. 1, p. 80.

42. Although in this interpretation I have drawn a fairly sharp distinction between karma and fate, the line separating the two is not always clear in the *Heike*. Thus Komatsu Shigetō characterizes *unmei* as an irresistible governing force that may also contain an element of retribution; "Gunki-mono ni Okeru Unmei (Ichi)," p. 23. At the start of his admonition to Kiyomori following the Shishigatani affair, Shigemori himself speaks of a possible connection between karma and fate: "When a person's fortune *(unmei)* is falling, he invariably conceives of evil acts [that will bring karmic retribution]"; Takagi et al., eds., *Heike Monogatari*, vol. 1. p. 172.

43. The idea of evil acts and karmic retribution in the same lifetime is called *jungengō*. See Kajiwara, *Heike Monogatari* (Shōgakukan), p. 46.

44. Komatsu, "*Heike Monogatari* ni Okeru Mujō," p. 56.

45. Kajiwara, *Heike Monogatari* (Shōgakukan), p. 47.

46. Takagi et al., eds., *Heike Monogatari*, vol. 2, p. 116. This passage appears after the Taira have left Kyoto and have spent a night at Fukuhara on

the shore of the Inland Sea. And, in a slightly earlier passage, we read: "Yesterday they were miraculous dragons dispensing rain from above the clouds; today they are like dried fish out of water on display in a shop." Ibid., p. 101.

47. Ibid., p. 176.

48. Ibid., vol. 1, pp. 241–244. The *Heike's* Shigemori is invested with the power to see into the future; Ishimoda, *Heike Monogatari*, p. 21.

49. Takagi et al., eds., *Heike Monogatari*, vol. 1, p. 409.

50. Komatsu, "*Heike Monogatari* ni Okeru Shi," in *Chūsei Gunki-mono no Kenkyū*, p. 75.

51. Koremori deserts the Taira camp at Yashima and goes to Mount Kōya, the seat of Shingon Buddhism, where he takes Buddhist vows. After a pilgrimage to the Kumano Shrines, he commits suicide by leaping into the waters of the Inland Sea, chanting the name of Amida Buddha and concentrating on rebirth in the Pure Land. Among warriors in the *Heike*, only the Taira—not the Minamoto—pray to Amida as they face death. Yet even this is anachronistic, since Pure Land Buddhism was just being popularized and established as an independent sect by Hōnen around the time of the Gempei War. The widespread enthusiasm (apart from the eastern Minamoto) for Pure Land Buddhism in the *Heike* reflects more accurately the sentiments of Japanese of the late thirteenth or fourteenth centuries—that is, the time of the later textual development of the *Heike*—than the late twelfth century. In any case, the chapters in Book 10 of the *Heike* devoted to Koremori's desertion, religious conversion, and suicide are among the most poignant in the entire work.

52. Takagi et al., eds., *Heike Monogatari*, vol. 1, pp. 372–373. The reference to penetrating two or three suits of armor with an arrow is reminiscent of Minamoto no Yoshiie's performing just such a feat, according to *Mutsu Waki*, after the Former Nine Years War. See the section "Minamoto no Yoshiie" in Chapter 1. The statement that "a strong bow requires five or six stout men to string" seems a considerable exaggeration, even for a war tale. The *Enkei-bon Heike* (p. 440) refers to only "two men" and *Gempei Seisui Ki* (vol. 3, p. 155) says "three to five men." In the *Gempei Seisui Ki's* account (ibid.) of Sanemori's remarks, Sanemori says that eastern warriors select their horses carefully, ride them from morning to evening hunting deer and foxes, and "make the mountains and forests their homes."

53. Nagazumi and Shimada, eds., *Heiji Monogatari*, p. 244.

54. Takagi et al., eds., *Heike Monogatari*, vol. 1, p. 371.

55. Ibid., vol. 2, p. 77.

56. This is an example of a common phenomenon in this age: a vassal changing lords. See Kajiwara, *Heike Monogatari* (Shōgakukan), p. 208.

57. Takagi et al., eds., *Heike Monogatari*, vol. 2, p. 81.

58. Ibid., pp. 79–80. Kenneth Butler, in his article "The *Heike Monogatari* and the Japanese Warrior Ethic," uses the story of Sanemori's end to illustrate how some *Heike* heroes were created entirely during the textual evolution of the work. He points out (pp. 101–102) that in *Shibu Kassenjō*, the oldest surviving version of the *Heike*, Sanemori flees from the Battle of Shinohara like all the other warriors of the Taira army. It is because he is old that he is overtaken and killed by a young Minamoto warrior.

59. Takagi et al., eds., *Heike Monogatari*, vol. 2, pp. 80–81.

60. Nagazumi and Shimada, eds., *Hōgen Monogatari*, pp. 98–99. Tametomo says that on the battlefield seniority among brothers based on age does not matter. The only criterion is ability. In Nakaraibon *Hōgen* (pp. 169–170) and *rufubon Hōgen* (p. 361), Tametomo and his older brother Yorikata engage in a personal dispute over who will lead the defense against the enemy. As the dispute becomes heated, Tametomo, concerned about family harmony, defers to Yorikata.

61. Nagazumi and Shimada, eds., *Heiji Monogatari*, p. 229.

62. *Gempei Seisui Ki* (vol. 4, p. 271) says that Ikezuki was, in keeping with his name, prepared to bite both man and beast, whichever came near him.

63. Takagi et al., eds., *Heike Monogatari*, vol. 2, p. 170. In a written report of the Battle of the Uji River sent to Yoritomo in Kamakura, Takatsuna and Kagesue are officially listed as the first and second to cross the river; ibid., p. 172.

64. *Gempei Seisui Ki*, vol. 4, p. 271.

65. Ibid., pp. 269–270.

66. *Heike Monogatari*, pp. 170–171. In *Enkei-bon Heike* (pp. 718–719) the young warrior's given name is Suetsugu and he is not identified as Shigetada's godson (*eboshigo*, literally "a child upon whom one has placed the hat in his coming-of-age [*gempuku*] ceremony"). Suetsugu grasps the top of Shigetada's helmet in midstream and, without Shigetada's knowing, gets a free ride to the river's opposite shore.

67. The main Minamoto assault force *(ōte)* at Ichinotani, under Noriyori, attacked from the east at Ikuta-no-mori. The rear assault force *(karamete)* was under the command of Yoshitsune and assigned to attack from the west. But Yoshitsune turned over the command to Doi no Sanehira and himself led a group of riders in a surprise assault down Hiyodorigoe Cliff from the north.

68. Professor Imai Masaharu has pointed out to me that warriors took fierce pride in their home provinces and displayed it by announcing themselves as the residents of such-and-such provinces.

69. Takagi et al., eds., *Heike Monogatari*, vol. 2, pp. 205–206.

70. *Daimyō* derives from *daimyōden*, "large (holdings of) name-fields." Agricultural lands were called "name-fields" because their holders often took the geographical names of these lands as surnames.

71. See the section "Sanemori and the Bandō Warrior."

72. From *shōmyōden*, "small (holdings of) name-fields."

73. *Azuma Kagami*, 1180:11:7.

74. Ibid., 1182:6:5.

75. Uwayokote Masataka observes that those leading an attack did not actually start fighting until others from their army arrived to serve as witnesses; *Heike Monogatari no Kyokō to Shinjitsu*, vol. 2, p. 42. More will be said of witnesses to battlefield exploits later in this chapter.

76. Takagi et al., eds., *Heike Monogatari*, vol. 2, p. 207.

77. Ibid., p. 208.

78. Ibid., pp. 199–201.

79. The *Gempei Seisui Ki* account of Naozane's name-announcing and the Taira "response" is quite different. See the section "Finding a 'Worthy Foe' " in Chapter 2.

80. The other warrior is Narida no Gorō. Having cautioned Sueshige that he should not rush ahead until he is certain that there are fellow warriors to witness what he does, Narida himself tries to gallop past Sueshige. But Sueshige has the faster horse and soon overtakes and outdistances Narida. See Takagi et al., eds., *Heike Monogatari*, vol. 2, pp. 201–202.

81. Ibid., p. 202.

82. Ibid., pp. 204–205.

83. Komatsu Shigetō, "Gunki-mono ni Okeru Kassen Byōsha," in *Chūsei Gunki-mono no Kenkyū, Zoku* (Tokyo: Ōfūsha, 1971), pp. 66–67.

84. See the "Order of Battle" section of Chapter 1 for a description of a more elaborate (and probably seldom followed) classical order of battle.

85. Komatsu, "Gunki-mono ni Okeru Kassen Byōsha," pp. 67–68.

86. Takagi et al., eds., *Heike Monogatari*, vol. 2, p. 204.

87. Nagazumi and Shimada, eds., *Hōgen Monogatari*, pp. 101–102.

88. Ibid., p. 102.

89. Ibid.

90. Ibid., p. 105. In *rufubon Hōgen* (p. 363) the groom does not try to fight the enemy, but instead retrieves his master's body and carries it back to the Taira camp.

91. Takagi et al., eds., *Heike Monogatari*, vol. 2, pp. 201–202. In *Gempei Seisui Ki* (vol. 5, pp. 56–59), Naozane ponders the problem of attacking without witnesses while he, Naoie, and the standard bearer wait alone before the Taira position. When Sueshige arrives, he and Naozane discuss the importance of witnesses.

92. Takagi et al., eds., *Heike Monogatari*, vol. 2, pp. 206–207. The Kawara brothers are members of Noriyori's main assault force at the eastern, Ikuta-no-mori approach to Ichinotani. They attack the fortress together on foot. Nagano Jōichi observes that the brothers abandon their horses and fight on foot because the obstacles the Taira have placed before their fortress make it difficult to maneuver on horseback. See *Heike Monogatari no Kanshō to Hihyō* (Tokyo: Meiji Shoin, 1975), pp. 306–307.

93. Ibid., p. 207. Neither the *Enkei-bon Heike* nor *Gempei Seisui Ki* contains this substitute name-announcing in its account of the deaths of the Kawara brothers.

94. Sugimoto Keisaburō remarks that the account of the deaths of the Kawara brothers is a classic example in the war tales of warriors sacrificing their lives to gain rewards for their surviving families; Sugimoto, ed., *Heike Monogatari*, vol. 9, p. 206.

95. *Katō Kiyomasa no Shichikajō*, in Suchi Masakazu, ed., *Nihon no Kakun* (Tokyo: Nihon Bungei Sha, n.d.), p. 160.

96. Saiki Kazuma et al., eds., *Mikawa Monogatari, Hagakure*, in *Nihon Shisō Taikei*, vol. 26 (Tokyo: Iwanami Shoten, 1974), p. 220.

97. Yoshinaka was sometimes called Kiso instead of Minamoto because he was raised in the Kiso region of Shinano province.

98. Takagi et al., eds., *Heike Monogatari*, vol. 2, p. 123.

99. Farris cites "the Great Famine of 1180–1182" as a principal reason for the failure of the Taira in the Gempei War; *Heavenly Warriors*, p. 309.

100. Takagi et al., eds., *Heike Monogatari*, vol. 2, pp. 139–141.

101. Ibid., p. 160. Even as he thinks about assuming one of these exalted offices, Yoshinaka displays gross ignorance in remarking that as emperor he would have to style himself like a boy (when only a minor emperor would be so styled) and as retired emperor he would be obliged to become a Buddhist monk (when taking the tonsure, or Buddhist vows, was optional for a retired emperor).

102. Nagazumi Yasuaki observes that the *Heike*'s account of Yoshinaka's behavior in Kyoto is in the same negative category as the behavior of Kiyomori and the other "rebels" of China and Japan listed at the *Heike*'s beginning. See *Heike Monogatari o Yomu* (Tokyo: Iwanami Shoten, 1980), pp. 128–129.

103. Takagi et al., eds., *Heike Monogatari*, vol. 2, pp. 172–173.

104. Ibid., p. 176.

105. Ichiko Teiji, ed., *Heike Monogatari* (Tokyo: Shōgakukan, 1985), vol. 3, pp. 164–165.

106. Takagi et al., eds., *Heike Monogatari*, vol. 2, p. 176.

107. *Gempei Seisui Ki*, vol. 4, p. 308.

108. Yamada Shōzen, *Heike Monogatari no Hitobito* (Tokyo: Shin Jimbutsu Ōrai Sha, 1972), p. 130.

109. Takagi et al., eds., *Heike Monogatari*, vol. 2, p. 176. The *Enkei-bon Heike* (p. 724) introduces Tomoe not as a *binjo* but as a *bijo* or "beautiful woman." This characterization has prompted commentators to speculate that she was one of Yoshinaka's mistresses. There is also reference in the opening sentence of "The Death of Kiso" to a woman named Yamabuki, but we are told nothing about her except that she became sick and remained in Kyoto.

110. Takagi et al., eds., *Heike Monogatari*, vol. 2, pp. 178–179.

111. Ibid., p. 179.

112. Yamada, *Heike Monogatari no Hitobito*, pp. 130–132. In *Gempei Seisui Ki* (vol. 4, pp. 310–311) Yoshinaka, in dismissing Tomoe, expressly directs her to take the story of his final battle back to his home province of Shinano. *Gempei Seisui Ki* also says that, after the Gempei War, Tomoe is summoned to Kamakura by Yoritomo and marries one of Yoritomo's chief administrators, Wada no Yoshimori, by whom she has a son. After this son is killed in 1213, when the Wada family is destroyed by the Hōjō, Tomoe becomes a nun and lives until age ninety-one (vol. 4, pp. 311–312).

113. Takagi et al., eds., *Heike Monogatari*, vol. 2, p. 175.

114. Ibid., p. 177. Yoshinaka seems to judge Ichijō no Jirō a worthy foe solely because he leads some six thousand warriors and not because of any knowledge of his family status.

115. Kajiwara Masaaki points out that the theme of the defeated warrior whose armor feels heavier than usual can be found also in *Hōgen Monogatari* and other war tales. See *Heike Monogatari* (Kōdansha), pp. 174–175.

116. Takagi et al., eds., *Heike Monogatari*, vol. 2, p. 180.

117. Ibid., p. 181.

118. Ibid.

119. Nagazumi, *Heike Monogatari o Yomu*, p. 145.

120. Takagi et al., eds., *Heike Monogatari*, vol. 2, pp. 280–284. See also note 51.

121. Kajiwara, *Heike Monogatari* (Shōgakukan), p. 230.

122. Takagi et al., eds., *Heike Monogatari*, vol. 2, p. 103.

123. Ibid., pp. 215–216. Neither *Enkei-bon Heike* (p. 762) nor *Gempei Seisui Ki* (vol. 5, p. 87) mentions these *kari-musha*. They describe Tadanori as riding away from Ichinotani alone.

124. Takagi et al., eds., *Heike Monogatari*, vol. 2, p. 216. There is no reference to prayers to Amida in *Enkei-bon Heike*.

125. Takagi et al., eds., *Heike Monogatari*, vol. 2, pp. 79–80.

126. Ibid., p. 217.

127. Ibid., pp. 211–212.

128. Ibid., pp. 219–220.

129. See Kenneth Butler's comments on this theme in "The *Heike Monogatari* and the Japanese Warrior Ethic," pp. 106–107.

130. Takagi et al., eds., *Heike Monogatari*, vol. 2, p. 78. The story of Nagatsuna and Yukishige does not appear in *Enkei-bon Heike*.

131. Takagi et al., eds. *Heike Monogatari*, vol. 2, p. 78.

132. Ibid., p. 221.

133. In *Gempei Seisui Ki* (vol. 5, p. 106), *Enkei-bon Heike* (p. 771), and several other medieval literary works Naozane, after the Gempei War, takes the tonsure and is ordained a priest by Hōnen, founder of the Pure Land sect of Buddhism. In historical fact, Naozane did take the tonsure, probably in 1192, seven years after the Gempei War. The most likely reason for his decision to become a priest at that time was frustration caused by a long-standing dispute over a landholding. See Uwayokote, *Heike Monogatari no Kyokō to Shinjitsu*, vol. 2, pp. 48–49. As Uwayokote points out, there is no documentary proof that Naozane actually killed Atsumori. Concerning Naozane's taking of the tonsure, see also Miyazaki Fumiko, "Religious Life of the Kamakura Bushi, Kumagai Naozane and His Descendants," *Monumenta Nipponica* 47 (4) (Winter 1992): 435–467.

134. A translation into English of *Atsumori* can be found in Arthur Waley, trans., *The Nō Plays of Japan* (New York: Grove Press, 1957).

135. Takagi et al., eds., *Heike Monogatari*, vol. 2, p. 220.

136. Ibid., p. 221.

137. *Gempei Seisui Ki* (vol. 5, p. 95), however, suggests that Atsumori puts up a fairly good fight against Naozane. Naozane prevails because he is the older (and presumably more experienced) warrior, but only after the two wrestle "first one on top and then the other."

138. Uwayokote, *Heike Monogatari no Kyokō to Shinjutsu*, vol. 2, p. 65.

139. Takagi et al., eds., *Heike Monogatari*, vol. 1, p. 385.

140. Ibid., p. 381.

141. Ibid., pp. 381–382.

142. In *Enkei-bon Heike* (pp. 457–458) Shigehira does not call for a fire;

and his follower does not burn peasant houses but attacks the Nara temples directly, setting them ablaze on his own initiative.

143. Takagi et al., eds., *Heike Monogatari*, vol. 2, p. 194.

144. See, for example, Ishimoda, *Heike Monogatari*, p. 164. Ishimoda notes that the horror and brutality not in the *Heike* can be found in *Gempei Seisui Ki*.

145. Takagi et al., eds., *Heike Monogatari*, vol. 1, p. 383.

146. Neither *Enkei-bon Heike* (see note 142) nor *Gempei Seisui Ki* (vol. 3, pp. 186-187) records that Shigehira ordered a fire to be set.

147. Takagi et al., eds., *Heike Monogatari*, vol. 2, pp. 217-219.

148. Ibid., p. 247. It is not stated in either *Enkei-bon Heike* (see p. 801) or *Gempei Seisui Ki* (see vol. 5, p. 138) that the lady becomes a nun to pray for Shigehira's enlightenment.

149. Takagi et al., eds., *Heike Monogatari*, vol. 2, p. 249.

150. Ibid., pp. 250-251.

151. The one exception is Minamoto no Yorimasa who, in Book 4, invokes Amida's name as he prepares to commit disembowelment following the failure of Prince Mochihito's revolt in 1180:5; ibid., vol. 1, p. 316. But Yorimasa, whose refusal to support Minamoto no Yoshitomo in the Heiji Conflict caused Yoshitomo's defeat (see Chapter 2), was the only ranking Minamoto to remain in Kyoto during the years after the Heiji Conflict when the Ise Taira of Kiyomori prospered. He is portrayed in the *Heike* as becoming, like the Taira, a courtier-warrior. Hence we are not surprised that he shares the Taira belief in Pure Land Buddhism.

152. Ibid., vol. 2, pp. 260-261.

153. Ibid., p. 266.

154. Ibid.

155. Ibid., p. 378.

CHAPTER 4

1. *Azuma Kagami*, 1180:10:21.

2. See, for example, Uwayokote, *Heike Monogatari no Kyokō to Shinjitsu*, vol. 2, p. 83. Watanabe Tamotsu observes that virtually all the "tales" *(monogatari)* about Yoshitsune's early life (when he was known by the childhood name of Ushiwaka) take this *Azuma Kagami* account as their starting point. See *Minamoto no Yoshitsune* (Tokyo: Yoshikawa Kōbunkan, 1966), p. 14. A survey of the legends about Yoshitsune's life before the meeting with Yoritomo at Kisegawa, most of which were contrived during the Muromachi period (1336-1573), can be found in Helen Craig McCullough, trans., *Yoshitsune* (Stanford: Stanford University Press, 1966), pp. 37-53.

3. Watanabe, *Minamoto no Yoshitsune*, p. 8.

4. Uwayokote, *Heike Monogatari no Kyokō to Shinjitsu*, vol. 2, p. 88.

5. Watanabe, *Minamoto no Yoshitsune*, p. 24.

6. Ibid., pp. 47, 61.

7. Quoted in ibid., p. 40.

8. Taira no Kiyomori, seeking to establish a capital away from his ene-

mies in Kyoto, moved the court to Fukuhara in 1180:6. But the move proved unsuccessful, and Kiyomori returned with the court to Kyoto five months later.

9. *Azuma Kagami*, 1184:8:8.

10. Ibid., 1185:3:9.

11. Ibid., 1184:6:20.

12. Ibid., 1184:6:21.

13. The appointments were made on 8:6. *Azuma Kagami*, 1184:8:17. *Azuma Kagami* says that it was because of these court appointments bestowed upon Yoshitsune without his approval that Yoritomo decided not to give Yoshitsune a new commission against the Taira at this time.

14. Uwayokote, *Heike Monogatari no Kyokō to Shinjitsu*, vol. 2, p. 83. Professor Uwayokote remarks that, although *hōgan biiki* is a Tokugawa period term, the expression of sympathy for Yoshitsune that it conveys arose during Yoshitsune's lifetime.

15. *Azuma Kagami*, 1184:8:17.

16. For speculations about how Yoshitsune assembled his victorious Dannoura naval force see Nagano Jōichi, *Heike Monogatari no Kanshō to Hihyō*, pp. 420–423.

17. *Azuma Kagami*, 1185:3:24.

18. Takagi et al., eds., *Heike Monogatari*, vol. 2, p. 169. *Gempei Seisui Ki* (vol. 4, pp. 283–296) presents a far more detailed account of the crossing of the Uji River. In this account, Yoshitsune plays a major role in directing and inspiring his army as it undertakes the difficult crossing with enemy archers firing arrows from the opposite bank. The *Enkei-bon Heike* version of the crossing is similar to *Gempei Seisui Ki*'s.

19. Takagi et al., eds., *Heike Monogatari*, vol. 2, pp. 193–194.

20. *Azuma Kagami*, 1184:2:7.

21. Takagi et al., eds., *Heike Monogatari*, vol. 2, p. 198.

22. Ibid., pp. 198–199. The story about following an old horse does not appear in *Gempei Seisui Ki*. And Musashibō Benkei does not simply bring the hunter to Yoshitsune; rather, Yoshitsune directs Benkei to seek out someone to guide them (vol. 5, pp. 44–47). This is interesting because, as we will see, Benkei's name appears only infrequently and fleetingly in the *Heike*. In *Gempei Seisui Ki*, on the other hand, he is presented as an important aide to Yoshitsune, and we are given substantial information about his background, appearance, and character. *Enkei-bon Heike* contains neither the story about the old horse nor the account of the acquisition of Washinoo no Yoshihisa as guide.

23. See the remarks on this point in Ishimoda, *Heike Monogatari*, pp. 99–102. See also the quotation in the section "First in Battle" in Chapter 3 citing the warrior who says "a chieftain *(daimyō)* gains fame through the exploits of his vassals. But we vassals have to earn our reputations ourselves."

24. See note 22.

25. Takagi et al., eds., *Heike Monogatari*, vol. 2, p. 313. There is no reference to this war of words in *Enkei-bon Heike*.

26. Ibid., p. 365. The Koshigoe Letter appears in *Azuma Kagami*, 1185:5:24.

27. Ishii Susumu believes it unlikely that Yoshitsune assembled his personal band of followers during his early life (that is, before meeting Yoritomo in 1180). He hypothesizes that the band comprised men of the central provinces whom Yoshitsune acquired as followers from the late fall of 1183, when he became an active military commander in that region. See *Kamakura Bakufu*, p. 156.

28. See, for example, Uwayokote, *Heike Monogatari no Kyokō to Shinjitsu*, vol. 2, p. 90.

29. Takagi et al., eds., *Heike Monogatari*, vol. 2, pp. 209–210.

30. Ibid., p. 211.

31. Ibid.

32. Ishii Susumu reproduces the battle cry as *"Ei-ei! Ō-ō!"* See *Kamakura Bakufu*, p. 118.

33. See the section entitled "The Taira as Courtier-Warriors: Atsumori" in Chapter 3 for a description of the chaos at the boats as the Taira attempt to escape in them.

34. Kajiwara, *Heike Monogatari* (Kōdansha), pp. 152–154.

35. Takagi et al., eds., *Heike Monogatari*, vol. 2, p. 292.

36. Ibid., pp. 302–304.

37. Ibid., pp. 304–305. In *Gempei Seisui Ki* (vol. 5, p. 237) Yoshitsune, responding to the insult of being called a "wild boar warrior," orders men to seize Kagetoki, and several high-ranking chieftains, including Miura no Yoshizumi, Hatakeyama no Shigetada, and Toi no Sanehira, must physically restrain Yoshitsune, Kagetoki, and their retinues. The *Enkei-bon Heike* (pp. 853–855) account is similar to that of *Gempei Seisui Ki*.

38. Takagi et al., eds., *Heike Monogatari*, vol. 2, pp. 207–209. See the section "First in Battle" in Chapter 3.

39. Ibid., p. 329.

40. Uwayokote Masataka observes that *Azuma Kagami*, rather than the *Heike*, portrays Kagetoki's "evil" side, or, stated more accurately, portrays Kagetoki as a slanderer. But much of this portrayal appears in passages dealing with the period of Yoritomo's successor as shogun, Yoriie, when Kagetoki, in historical fact, was expelled from Bakufu service because of his slandering. See *Heike Monogatari no Kyokō to Shinjitsu*, vol. 2, p. 124.

41. *Gempei Seisui Ki* (vol. 5, p. 240) claims that only five boats left for Shikoku because there were not enough crewmen to man the other boats.

42. Takagi et al., eds., *Heike Monogatari*, vol. 2. p. 312.

43. Ibid., p. 314. Neither *Enkei-bon Heike* nor *Gempei Seisui Ki* speaks of this band of warriors protecting Yoshitsune.

44. Takagi et al., eds., *Heike Monogatari*, vol. 2, p. 315.

45. Ibid., p. 316.

46. See Chapter 1.

47. In both *Enkei-bon Heike* (p. 863) and *Gempei Seisui Ki* (vol. 5,

p. 268), Yoshitsune at Yashima uses this same stereotyped phrase, tearfully reminding Tsuginobu that they had pledged to "die in the same place."

48. Takagi et al., eds., *Heike Monogatari*, vol. 2, pp. 316–317.

49. Ibid., p. 317. In *Gempei Seisui Ki* (vol. 5, pp. 257–258), Yoichi's older brother, Jūrō, is first selected to shoot at the Taira fan. But Jūrō claims his bow arm was injured at the Battle of Ichinotani and recommends that Yoichi take the shot instead. Yoichi agrees to replace his brother without demurral.

50. *Gempei Seisui Ki*, vol. 5, p. 256.

51. Takagi et al., eds., *Heike Monogatari*, vol. 2, pp. 318–319.

52. Ibid., p. 332.

53. Ibid., p. 333.

54. Ibid., pp. 319–320. Neither *Enkei-bon Heike* (p. 867) nor *Gempei Seisui Ki* (vol. 5, p. 261) attributes this shooting to an order from Yoshitsune. The Minamoto as a group debate whether or not the dancer should be shot, and a large majority favors shooting him.

55. Takagi et al., eds., *Heike Monogatari*, vol. 2, p. 322. See note 26 in Chapter 2 for comments on the stringing of bows.

56. Ibid., p. 330.

57. Ibid., pp. 322–323.

58. Ibid., pp. 324–325.

59. Ibid., p. 325.

60. Watanabe, *Minamoto no Yoshitsune*, p. 60.

61. Nagano, *Heike Monogatari no Kanshō to Hihyō*, p. 406.

62. Of course, Yoshitsune had left nearly two hundred boats at Watanabe in Settsu when he chose to cross the Inland Sea with his small band in only five boats during a gale. The larger group of boats, under the command of Kajiwara no Kagetoki, arrived at Yashima after the Battles of Yashima and Shido. Presumably the total of two hundred boats formed at least part of the nucleus for the Dannoura navy.

63. Takagi et al., eds., *Heike Monogatari*, vol. 2, pp. 327–328.

64. *Azuma Kagami*, 1185:4:4.

65. Nagano, *Heike Monogatari no Kanshō to Hihyō*, p. 420.

66. Takagi et al., eds., *Heike Monogatari*, vol. 2, pp. 327–328.

67. Ibid., pp. 328–329. This second clash between Yoshitsune and Kagetoki does not appear in either *Enkei-bon Heike* or *Gempei Seisui Ki*.

68. Takagi et al., eds., *Heike Monogatari*, vol. 2, p. 330.

69. Ibid., pp. 334–335. The Taira had placed the emperor, his entourage, and high-ranking warriors on the fighting boats; the warriors who were to do the actual fighting were put on the Chinese-style ships that were normally used for noncombatant dignitaries.

70. Ibid., pp. 330–331.

71. Ibid., pp. 336–337. *Azuma Kagami*, as noted earlier in this chapter, states that a Taira woman, Lady Azechi, leapt into the sea with Antoku and that Kiyomori's widow (the child's grandmother), Taira no Tokiko, jumped in by herself.

72. Takagi et al., eds., *Heike Monogatari*, vol. 2, p. 342.

73. Ibid., p. 340.
74. Ibid.
75. Ibid.
76. Ibid., p. 341.
77. Ibid., pp. 338–340.
78. Ibid., pp. 362–363, 367–368.
79. Ibid., pp. 370–371.
80. *Azuma Kagami*, 1185:4:21.
81. Ibid., 1185:4:29.
82. Ibid., 1185:5:7.
83. Ibid., 1185:5:24.
84. Ibid., 1185:6:13.
85. Watanabe, *Minamoto no Yoshitsune*, p. 140.
86. Ibid., p. 143.
87. Ibid., p. 152.
88. Ishii, *Kamakura Bakufu*, p. 164.
89. Yukiie was captured and killed in Izumi province in 1186:5; ibid., p. 188.
90. Watanabe, *Minamoto no Yoshitsune*, p. 172.
91. Ishii, *Kamakura Bakufu*, p. 189.
92. Ibid., p. 188.
93. Ibid., p. 192.
94. Takagi et al., eds., *Heike Monogatari*, vol. 2, p. 357.
95. Ibid., p. 363. Kagetoki's slander as recorded in *Azuma Kagami* is much more damaging to Yoshitsune.
96. *Gempei Seisui Ki* (vol. 5, pp. 212–213) says that Yoshitsune secretly went to Kamakura in 1184:6 to refute charges of slander by Kajiwara no Kagetoki. We can presume that he saw Yoritomo at that time. As note 98 indicates, he also saw Yoritomo when he took the Taira prisoners Munemori and his son to Kamakura at the end of the Gempei War.
97. The Ox King amulets were talismans given to pilgrims who visited the Kumano Shrines and other shrines during the medieval age.
98. Takagi et al., eds., *Heike Monogatari*, vol. 2, pp. 364–366. In both *Enkei-bon Heike* (pp. 907, 912) and *Gempei Seisui Ki* (vol. 6, pp. 83, 90) Yoshitsune takes Munemori and son to Kamakura, enters the city, and even has an audience with Yoritomo during which both men are restrained and say little. Thus the entire story about Koshigoe and the Koshigoe Letter is absent from these works.
99. Takagi et al., eds., *Heike Monogatari*, vol. 2, p. 297.
100. Yoritomo's mother was the daughter of an official of the Atsuta Shrine. Tokiwa served the Kujō family. See Uwayokote, *Heike Monogatari no Kyokō to Shinjitsu*, vol. 2, p. 89.
101. Takagi et al., eds., *Heike Monogatari*, vol. 2, p. 138. "He [Yoritomo] had a large face and was small of stature; he was elegant and comely and spoke without an accent [that is, there was no provincial distortion to his speech]."

102. Ibid., pp. 388–389.
103. Ibid., p. 391.
104. *Azuma Kagami*, 1185:11:3.
105. *Gempei Seisui Ki* (vol. 6, pp. 145–150) provides a summary of Yoshitsune's entire life.
106. Helen McCullough provides an excellent survey of the development of the Yoshitsune legends in *Yoshitsune*, her translation of *Gikeiki*.
107. McCullough, *Yoshitsune*, p. 54.

CHAPTER 5

1. Yoritomo received the title from Emperor Gotoba after the death of the senior retired emperor Goshirakawa. He voluntarily resigned the title in 1194.

2. From about this time in history the possessive *"no"* is dropped from most Japanese names. Hence we speak of Hōjō Masako instead of Hōjō no Masako (Masako of the Hōjō).

3. Sanetomo was assassinated by Kugyō, the son of his brother Yoriie. Scholars have long speculated that Kugyō was in league with Yoshitoki, Sanetomo's uncle (and Kugyō's great-uncle). See H. Paul Varley, "The Hōjō Family and Succession to Power," in Jeffrey P. Mass, ed., *Court and Bakufu in Japan* (New Haven: Yale University Press, 1982), pp. 157–158.

4. The Hōjō, a Kantō family, claimed to be of Taira descent. But little is known about the family before Hōjō Tokimasa, who served as Yoritomo's warden when he was exiled to the east after the Heiji Conflict and whose daughter, Masako, married the future Minamoto leader.

5. See Ishii, *Kamakura Bakufu*, pp. 366–367.

6. The various versions of *Jōkyūki* appear to differ more radically than those of any other war tale, with the possible exception of *Heike Monogatari*, if we regard *Gempei Seisui Ki* as a variant of the *Heike*. William McCullough has translated into English the Jikōji text of *Jōkyūki*, thought to be the oldest of its versions, in *"Shōkyūki:* An Account of the Shōkyū War of 1221," *Monumenta Nipponica* 19 (1964): 163–215; 186–221. See the introduction to this translation for more information about the textual development of *Jōkyūki*. A well-edited version of the *Jōkyūki rufubon* can be found in Matsubayashi Yasuaki, *Jōkyūki* (Tokyo: Gendai Shichō Sha, 1974).

7. For a discussion of the various functions of the stewards and constables, see Jeffrey P. Mass, "The Kamakura Bakufu," in Yamamura, ed., *The Cambridge History of Japan*, vol. 3, pp. 80–87.

8. Throughout premodern times China conducted its foreign affairs by means of a tributary system. Other countries were expected to send periodic missions to China, missions which, by engaging in various rituals and following certain symbolic procedures, acknowledged the supremacy of China in a hierarchical "world order." Japan had refused to enter into a tributary relationship with China since at least the seventh century.

9. Ishii Susumu, "The Decline of the Kamakura Bakufu," in Yamamura, ed., *The Cambridge History of Japan*, vol. 3, p. 139. See also Bottomley and Hopson, *Arms and Armor of the Samurai*, p. 48.

10. One source of the time says that the Mongols lost more than 13,500 men in this invasion, most of whom drowned in the storm at sea. The loss was about one-third of the entire Mongol force. See Ishii, "The Decline of the Kamakura Bakufu," p. 140.

11. For a discussion of the succession dispute, see H. Paul Varley, *Imperial Restoration in Medieval Japan* (New York: Columbia University Press, 1971), pp. 50–59. See also Andrew Goble, "Go-Daigo and the Kemmu Restoration" (unpublished dissertation, Stanford University, 1987), chap. 1.

12. Information about the Free and Easy Society comes primarily from *Taiheiki*. See Gotō and Kamada, eds., *Taiheiki*, vol. 1, pp. 44–47.

13. Takatoki was the Hōjō family head, but from 1326 he transferred the office of shogunal regent to vassals.

14. Godaigo appointed his son Prince Moriyoshi *sei-i tai-shōgun* in 1333:6.

15. The names I have been using for emperors—that is, the names that are customarily used for them—are actually posthumously selected names. Godaigo's personal name during his lifetime was Takaharu.

16. Gotō and Kamada, eds., *Taiheiki*, vol. 2, p. 16.

17. Goble, "Go-Daigo and the Kemmu Restoration," p. 451.

18. Goble discusses the weakness of Yoshisada's position in the Kantō even after he destroyed the Hōjō regime at Kamakura. Under Ashikaga pressure, he was forced to shift to the central provinces, "a general without an army and . . . an implacable foe of the Ashikaga"; "Go-Daigo and the Kemmu Restoration," p. 225. Yoshisada had no alternative but to try to counter Ashikaga power by aligning himself with Godaigo.

19. Kitabatake Akiie was the son of Kitabatake Chikafusa, author of *Jinnō Shōtōki* (Chronicle of the Direct Descent of Gods and Sovereigns), a history of Japan that argues the legitimacy of the Godaigo line (from 1336, the southern court) in the succession dispute. *Jinnō Shōtōki* has been translated into English in H. Paul Varley, *A Chronicle of Gods and Sovereigns* (New York: Columbia University Press, 1980).

20. The offices of the Bakufu were established in the Muromachi section of northeastern Kyoto in the late fourteenth century.

21. *Taiheiki* portrays Takatoki as what is known in the Chinese Confucian tradition of historiography as a "bad last ruler"—the evil ruler of a dynasty that is about to come to an end. See Gotō and Kamada, eds., *Taiheiki*, vol. 1, pp. 36–37. We will observe in the next paragraph that Godaigo too, according to *Taiheiki*, behaves like a "bad ruler" (albeit not a "bad *last* ruler") once he comes to power in the Kemmu Restoration.

22. Nagazumi Yasuaki, *Taiheiki* (Tokyo: Iwanami Shoten, 1984), pp. 45–46.

23. Aoki Akira, "Kaidai," in Yamazaki Masakazu, trans., *Taiheiki* (Tokyo: Kawade Shobō, 1990), p. 327.

24. *Tōin Kinsada Nikki*, in Tōkyō Teikoku Daigaku, *Bunka Daigaku Shishi Sōsho* (Tokyo, 1897–1908), vol. 48, p. 27.

25. Imagawa Ryōshun, *Nan-Taiheiki*, in Hanawa Hokiichi, ed., *Gunsho Ruijū* (Tokyo: Zoku Gunsho Ruijū Kansei Kai, 1931), vol. 21, pp. 612–613.

26. Mori, *Taiheiki no Gunzō*, p. 288

27. Washio Junkei, ed., *Saigen'in-bon Taiheiki* (Tokyo: Toe Shoin, 1936), p. 5.

28. Nagazumi, *Taiheiki*, p. 271.

29. Washio, ed., *Saigen'in-bon Taiheiki*, p. 5.

30. The Kanda old-text version of *Taiheiki* can be found in Takahashi Teiichi, ed., *Taiheiki* (Kyoto: Shibunkaku, 1976).

31. Washio, ed., *Saigen'in-bon Taiheiki*, p. 7. There are also references to *Taiheiki-yomi* in Fushimi-no-miya Sadafusa's diary *Kanmon Gyoki*, which covers the period 1416–1448.

32. See the discussion in Nagazumi Yasuaki, *Gunki Monogatari no Sekai* (Tokyo: Asahi Shimbun Sha, 1978), pp. 97–106.

33. Kume Kunitake, "*Taiheiki* wa Shigaku ni Eki Nashi," *Shigaku Zasshi* 2 (1891):230–240.

34. See the comments in Varley, *Imperial Restoration in Medieval Japan*, pp. 127–128. See also Nagazumi, *Taiheiki*, p. 134, for the observation that, upon close examination, one discovers a "surprisingly large" number of entries in *Taiheiki* based on fact.

35. Gotō and Kamada, eds., *Taiheiki*, vol. 2, p. 158.

36. Nagazumi, *Taiheiki*, p. 41.

37. A discussion of *akutō* can be found in Lorraine F. Harrington, "Social Control and the Significance of *Akutō*," in Mass, ed., *Court and Bakufu in Japan*. Harrington observes that *akutō* were "part of a rising tide of lawlessness in the late Kamakura period" (p. 226) and "that all Kamakura *akutō* incidents occurred after the Jōkyū War and that most took place in the central and western provinces" (p. 227).

38. Kuroda Toshio notes that the warriors of Kyushu who defended against the Mongol invasions of 1274 and 1281 fought in the traditional one-against-one method of the Japanese and were sorely tested, if not outdone, by the Mongol invaders fighting in disciplined groups. Kuroda judges that the new way of "western" fighting found in *Taiheiki* evolved among *akutō* in the half-century after the invasions. See Kuroda, *Mōko Shūrai* (Tokyo: Chūō Kōron Sha, 1965), p. 482.

39. See ibid., pp. 487–488, for a discussion of Norimura's fighting methods.

40. Gotō and Kamada, eds., *Taiheiki*, vol. 1, pp. 337–338.

41. Ibid., pp. 213–215.

42. Mori Shigeaki, citing Watsuji Tetsurō, points out that although *Taiheiki* appears, especially in its early parts, to be strongly Confucian, it contains many beliefs and sentiments that derive from other systems of thought and religion, including Buddhism and Shinto; *Taiheiki no Gunzō* (Tokyo: Kadokawa Shoten, 1991), p. 309. A good survey of the "thought" *(shisō)* in *Taiheiki* can be found in Nagazumi, *Taiheiki*, pp. 198–216.

43. An acrobatic way of doing this was to place the tip of the sword in one's mouth and leap backwards off one's horse. This is how, as we saw in Chapter 3, Minamoto no Yoshinaka's ever-faithful follower, Imai no Kanehira,

commits suicide in the *Heike*. Some warriors in *Taiheiki* too kill themselves in this or a similar manner. See, for example, the section on "The Battle of Chihaya," which describes the suicide of a warrior who places his sword in his mouth and falls on his face.

44. Gotō and Kamada, eds., *Taiheiki*, vol. 2, p. 159.

45. Ibid., p. 320.

46. Ibid., vol. 1, pp. 358–360.

47. Ibid., vol. 2, p. 320.

48. I have chosen to focus on this period. But many examples of warrior unreliability can also be found in the mass desertions of loyalists in the *Taiheiki* account of the fighting in late 1335, when Nitta Yoshisada is defeated in the Kantō and driven back to the central provinces by Ashikaga Takauji. Loyalist desertions reach their high point at the beginning of the new year when word reaches Kyoto that Takauji is about to attack the city with a huge army of eight hundred thousand. So many of the warriors gathered to defend Kyoto flee "to the four directions" that the loyalist force is reduced to less than ten thousand, and they are so dispirited that they ignore the orders of their superiors. To bolster these warriors, the court promises immediate, "same-day" rewards to those who distinguish themselves in the pending battle with the Ashikaga; ibid., p. 72.

49. Ibid., pp. 132–133.

50. Ibid., p. 133. *Taiheiki* cites this as a "good example of how a woman can bring down a country." But Mori Shigeaki points out that the story of Yoshisada's affair with Kōtō no Naishi cannot be verified in any other source; *Taiheiki no Gunzō*, p. 196.

51. Gotō and Kamada, eds., *Taiheiki*, vol. 2, pp. 136–137.

52. Ibid., p. 149.

53. Ibid., vol. 3, p. 365. My attention was drawn to this and the following quotation by Nagazumi Yasuaki in *Gunki Monogatari no Sekai*, pp. 115–116.

54. Gotō and Kamada, eds., *Taiheiki*, vol. 3, p. 430. A *kirin* is a fabulous animal, part deer and part horse.

55. Such as the warrior-courtier Chigusa Tadaaki, who played an important role in the destruction of the Rokuhara magistrates in 1333 and was killed in fighting against the Ashikaga in 1336.

56. Gotō and Kamada, eds., *Taiheiki*, vol. 2, pp. 60–61.

57. One might suppose that imperial loyalism would be a primary concern in *Jōkyūki*, since it deals with a conflict (in 1221) between a senior retired emperor, Gotoba, and the Kamakura Bakufu, headed by Hōjō Yoshitoki, whom Gotoba brands a rebel. But *Jōkyūki* portrays Gotoba as a headstrong man who listens to the wrong ministers, makes a very bad decision in challenging the Bakufu militarily, and gets what he deserves (exile). A century later Kitabatake Chikafusa, writing in *Jinnō Shōtōki*, says of Gotoba and his cause: "How then could the Kyoto court expect so readily to overthrow the Bakufu if it did not have an administration of equal merit to that of Kamakura? . . . The Jōkyū incident cannot be likened to a conflict in which enemies of the throne rise in

rebellion and are victorious. Since the time for opposing the Kamakura regime had not yet arrived, heaven clearly would not permit Gotoba's action to succeed." See Varley, trans., *A Chronicle of Gods and Sovereigns*, p. 225.

58. Gotō and Kamada, eds., *Taiheiki*, vol. 1, p. 37.

59. A survey of the history of the debate over the fourteenth-century legitimacy issue can be found in Murata Masashi, *Namboku-chō Shi Ron* (Tokyo, 1949).

60. Ivan Morris states: "Among historical figures the man most revered by kamikaze pilots was the loyalist warrior, Kusunoki Masashige." *The Nobility of Failure*, p. 314.

61. Nagazumi, *Taiheiki*, p. 97.

62. Gotō and Kamada, eds., *Taiheiki*, vol. 1, pp. 96–97.

63. Ibid., p. 97.

64. Okabe Shūzō, *Namboku-chō no Kyozō to Jitsuzō* (Tokyo: Yūzankaku, 1975), p. 242. Uemura Seiji summarizes the research that has been done to determine whether or not Masashige was descended from the Tachibana. See *Kusunoki Masashige* (Tokyo: Shibundō, 1962), pp. 26–30.

65. Okabe, *Namboku-chō no Kyozō to Jitsuzō*, p. 242. Uemura Seiji remarks that this office, which was part of the imperial guard unit *hyōefu*, could be bestowed directly by the court or at the request of a temple or the Bakufu; *Kusunoki Masashige*, pp. 34–35.

66. Among the theories about Masashige are: He was a former vassal of the Kamakura Bakufu and turned against it; he had received land from the court and was committed to supporting it even before Godaigo summoned him to Mount Kasagi. One of the most intriguing theories about Masashige contends that his nephew became the famous *nō* actor and playwright Kan'ami. See Ino Akira, "Kusunoki Masashige no Gunryaku," in Satō Kazuhiko, ed., *Kusunoki Masashige no Subete* (Tokyo: Shin-Jimbutsu Ōrai Sha, 1989), pp. 52–53.

67. Ibid. See also Hayashiya Tatsusaburō, *Namboku-chō* (Tokyo: Sōgensha, 1957), pp. 48–53.

68. Gotō and Kamada, eds., *Taiheiki*, vol. 1, p. 98.

69. Hayashiya Tatsusaburō says that if he were asked to name the most popular figures in Japanese history, he would without hesitation cite Yoshitsune, the late-sixteenth-century unifier Toyotomi Hideyoshi, and Kusunoki Masashige. All three are great warrior heroes in the war tales, but, unlike the other two, Hideyoshi is remembered as a commander of armies, not as a leader in combat. See *Namboku-chō*, p. 57.

70. Gotō and Kamada, eds., *Taiheiki*, vol. 1, p. 115. The editors remark in a note that nothing is known about Wada Masatō apart from this and a second reference to him (at the Battle of Minatogawa) in *Taiheiki*.

71. The names of several other followers of Masashige appear immediately after the account of the double suicide of Masashige and Masasue. They too destroy themselves at Minatogawa; ibid., vol. 2, p. 159.

72. Owada Tetsuo, *Shiro to Jōkamachi* (Tokyo: Kyōiku-sha, 1979), p. 49.

73. Ibid., p. 48.

74. Owada Tetsuo cites as the two most distinctive features of fortresses during this age their location on mountains or steep heights and their use of Buddhist temples for buildings, manpower, and supplies; ibid., p. 50.

75. Gotō and Kamada, eds., *Taiheiki*, vol. 1, p. 96.

76. Ibid., pp. 100–101.

77. Owada, *Shiro to Jōkamachi*, p. 51. Imai Masaharu points out that fortifications with stone walls did not appear in Japan until the *sengoku* period. See "Kusunoki Masashige" in *Chūsei o Ikita Nihon-jin* (Tokyo: Gakusei Sha, 1992), p. 253.

78. Owada Tetsuo notes that Akasaka Fortress was just one in a network of fortresses Masashige constructed in his home region of Kawachi; *Shiro to Jōkamachi*, p. 49.

79. Gotō and Kamada, eds., *Taiheiki*, vol. 1, p. 114.

80. Ibid., pp. 114–115.

81. Ibid., pp. 115–116.

82. Ibid., pp. 116–118.

83. Okabe, *Namboku-chō no Kyozō to Jitsuzō*, p. 247.

84. Ibid., p. 249.

85. Gotō and Kamada, eds., *Taiheiki*, vol. 1, p. 99.

86. Ibid., pp. 119–120.

87. Ibid., pp. 185–186. Okabe Shūzō identifies this Trojan Horse ploy as another example of a *ninja* trick; *Namboku-chō no Kyozō to Jitsuzō*, p. 247.

88. Gotō and Kamada, eds., *Taiheiki*, vol. 1, pp. 189–193.

89. Nagazumi, *Gunki Monogatari no Sekai*, pp. 103–104.

90. Gotō and Kamada, eds., *Taiheiki*, vol. 1, pp. 199–201.

91. Ibid., pp. 201–203.

92. Ibid., pp. 214–215.

93. Ibid., p. 207.

94. Ibid., p. 216. George Sansom observes that the opposing armies at Austerlitz numbered only eighty thousand; *A History of Japan, 1334–1615* (Stanford: Stanford University Press, 1961), p. 14.

95. Gotō and Kamada, eds., *Taiheiki*, vol. 1, p. 217.

96. Ibid., p. 221.

97. Ibid., pp. 222–223.

98. Ibid., pp. 223–224.

99. He is so identified, for example, in the chapter on the Battle of Chihaya; ibid., p. 218.

100. Ibid., vol. 2, p. 109.

101. Ibid., p. 110.

102. Ibid., pp. 111–112.

103. Ibid., p. 113.

104. See Nagahara Keiji, *Nairan to Minshū no Seiki* (Tokyo: Shōgakukan, 1988), pp. 46–47.

105. Yoshisada also devoted (wasted?) much time in laying siege to a fortress held by Akamatsu Enchin rather than preparing for Takauji's return. Enchin had been a major participant in the destruction of the Rokuhara magis-

trates in 1333, but turned against Godaigo and the loyalists because of dissatisfaction over his rewards during the Kemmu Restoration. See Higuchi Kunio, "Minatogawa Kassen," in Satō, ed., *Kusonoki Masashige no Subete*, p. 119.

106. Gotō and Kamada, eds., *Taiheiki*, vol. 2, pp. 149–150.

107. Ibid., pp. 150–151. Masashige's plan is rejected and the reasons for rejection are enumerated by the courtier Fujiwara Kiyotada; but we can assume that he was acting and speaking on behalf of Godaigo.

108. Washio, ed., *Saigen'in-bon Taiheiki*, p. 444.

109. Ibid.

110. Yashiro Kazuo and Kami Hiroshi, eds., *Baishōron* (Tokyo: Gendai Shichō Sha, 1975), p. 124. A study of *Baishōron* can be found in Shuzo Uyenaka, "A Study of *Baishōron*: A Source for the Study of the Ideology of Imperial Loyalism in Medieval Japan" (unpublished dissertation, University of Toronto, 1979).

111. Yashiro and Kami, eds., *Baishōron*, p. 125.

112. Kawamata Keiichi, ed., *Ima Kagami, Masukagami* (Tokyo: Nihon Bungaku Sōsho Kankō Kai, 1926), pp. 308, 312.

113. Gotō and Kamada, eds., *Taiheiki*, vol. 2, p. 151. In *The Nobility of Failure* (pp. 131–132), Ivan Morris cites "a patriotic song which was popular in Japanese schools before the war" about the parting of Masashige and Masatsura at Sakurai Station. Two of the verses are:

> "Not for *my* sake do I send you hence," the father says.
> "Soon, when I no longer live,
> This land will be in Takauji's hands.
> You, my son, grow quickly and become a man
> So that you may serve our Emperor and his realm!
>
> "Here is the precious sword
> That His Majesty bestowed upon me many years ago.
> Now I am giving it to you
> In memory of this, our last farewell.
> Go, Masatsura, back to our village,
> Where your aging mother waits!"

114. Gotō and Kamada, eds., *Taiheiki*, vol. 2, p. 152.

115. Ibid., pp. 154–157.

116. Ibid., pp. 158–159.

117. Ibid., p. 159.

118. Washio, ed., *Saigen'in-bon Taiheiki*, p. 452.

119. Nagazumi, *Gunki Monogatari no Sekai*, p. 134.

120. Gotō and Kamada, eds., *Taiheiki*, vol. 2, p. 159. Inspired by this scene in *Taiheiki*, several *kamikaze* units during World War II used the slogan "Reborn seven times to serve the nation" (*shichishō hōkoku*). See Morris, *The Nobility of Failure*, p. 453.

121. Komatsu, "*Taiheiki* ni Okeru Shi," in *Chūsei Gunki Monogatari no Kenkyū*, p. 88.

122. Ibid., p. 93.
123. Gotō and Kamada, eds., *Taiheiki*, vol. 2, p. 160.
124. See Varley, *Imperial Restoration in Medieval Japan*, pp. 156–183. See also Shuzo Uyenaka, "The Textbook Controversy of 1911: National Needs and Historical Truth," in John S. Brownlee, ed., *History in the Service of the Japanese Nation* (Toronto: University of Toronto-York, 1983).
125. See Nagazumi, *Taiheiki*, p. 147, for an assessment of Yoshisada's qualities, both good (his loyalty, bravery) and bad (his weaknesses as a strategist and politician).
126. Gotō and Kamada, eds., *Taiheiki*, vol. 2, p. 201.
127. Ibid., p. 206.
128. Ibid., p. 207.
129. Ibid., p. 208.
130. Ibid., pp. 209–210.
131. Yashiro and Kami, eds., *Baishōron*, p. 135; Satō Kazuhiko, *Namboku-chō Nairan* (Tokyo: Shōgakukan, 1974), p. 77.
132. Gotō and Kamada, eds., *Taiheiki*, vol. 2, p. 244.
133. Ibid., pp. 244–245.
134. Nakanishi Tatsuharu, *Taiheiki Ron Josetsu* (Tokyo: Ōfūsha, 1985), p. 119.
135. Gotō and Kamada, eds., *Taiheiki*, vol. 2, p. 302.
136. Ibid., p. 305.
137. Ibid., p. 309.
138. Ibid., pp. 311–312. It is customary to use the *"no"* in the name Kō no Moronao, even though the practice, as noted at the beginning of this chapter, was largely discontinued at approximately the beginning of the medieval age.
139. Ibid., p. 318.
140. Ibid.
141. Ibid.
142. Ibid., p. 319.
143. Ibid.
144. Ibid., p. 320.
145. Ibid. Yoshisada's suicide and the *junshi* of his commanders are also described in the passage on "Suicide" earlier in this chapter.
146. Ibid.
147. Ibid., p. 321.
148. Satō, *Namboku-chō Nairan*, pp. 80–81.
149. Gotō and Kamada, eds., *Taiheiki*, vol. 2., pp. 321–323.
150. Ibid., pp. 333–334.
151. Ibid., p. 322.
152. Ibid.
153. Ibid., p. 342.
154. Ibid.
155. See "The Battle of Minatogawa" in this chapter.

156. Ivan Morris observes that the Meiji period statesman and soldier Saigō Takamori used *kikusui* as a password and that *kikusui* was the most popular emblem selected by *kamikaze* pilots. See *The Nobility of Failure*, pp. 303, 380.

157. Gotō and Kamada, eds., *Taiheiki*, vol. 2, pp. 170–171.

158. Ibid., p. 171.

159. Ibid., vol. 3, p. 14.

160. Ibid.

161. Ibid., pp. 15–16.

162. Ibid., pp. 23–25.

163. Ibid., p. 26.

164. We have noted in earlier war tales archers who are famous for accuracy, strength, and distance (see the discussion in "The Battle of Yashima" in Chapter 4). Shooting arrows rapid-fire was another skill admired among archers in the war tales, and the phrase *yatsugibaya* (shooting arrows rapidly, one after another) has become a modern word for "quickly."

165. Ibid., pp. 26–27.

166. Ibid., p. 28.

167. Satō Kazuhiko, *Taiheiki o Yomu* (Tokyo: Gakusei Sha, 1991), p. 10.

168. Ibid., p. 11.

169. Gotō and Kamada, eds., *Taiheiki*, vol. 2, pp. 392–395. Masashige is in the form of a thousand-headed demon riding a seven-headed ox. In addition to the six men mentioned, he is accompanied by all the Minamoto and Taira killed in the Hōgen and Heiji conflicts, the Gempei War, and the fighting that led to the Kemmu Restoration.

170. Ibid., pp. 399–400.

171. Ibid., pp. 447–449. The suggestion to magically cause leaders of the Bakufu—including Ashikaga Takauji and Tadayoshi and the Kō brothers, Moronao and Moroyasu—to fight among themselves in fact prefigures the internal strife that shook the Bakufu in the late 1340s and early 1350s (mentioned in the section "Historical Background" and also at the end of this section). Carmen Blacker describes a *tengu* as "half-man and half-hawk, with a large beak, long wings and glittering eyes, but a man's body, arms and legs." *The Catalpa Bow* (London: George Allen & Unwin, 1975), p. 182.

172. Ibid., pp. 449–450.

173. Nagazumi, *Taiheiki*, p. 87.

174. Gotō and Kamada, eds., *Taiheiki*, vol. 1, pp. 424–425.

175. Ibid., p. 428. *Taiheiki*'s author, frequently critical of Godaigo, denounces him here for turning Prince Moriyoshi over to the "enemy," and sees in the emperor's action a sign that the court's fortunes will again decline and the military (the Ashikaga) will flourish (p. 431).

176. Ibid., vol. 2, pp. 31–32.

177. Ibid., pp. 403–404.

178. Ibid., pp. 404–406.

179. Ibid., vol. 3, p. 22.

180. Ibid., p. 32.

181. Ibid., p. 49.

182. Ibid., vol. 2, p. 364.

183. See Donald Keene, trans., *Chūshingura* (New York: Columbia University Press, 1971).

184. This thought was suggested to me by Satō Kazuhiko. See *Taiheiki o Yomu*, p. 137.

GLOSSARY

akusho 悪所	rough terrain
akusho-otoshi 悪所落	riding over rough terrain
akusō 悪僧	rowdy monk
akutō 悪党	rowdy band
aramusha 荒武者	rough warrior
arauma 荒馬	wild, untamed horse
arauma-nori 荒馬乗	riding wild horses
asahi shōgun 朝日将軍	Morning-Sun General
awanu kataki 合わぬ敵	unworthy foe
aware 哀	sadness
baishin 陪臣	rear vassal
banrui 伴類	peasant foot soldier
binjo 便女	attendant, servant
biwa 琵琶	lute
biwa hōshi 琵琶法師	tale singer
bu 武	military
bubi no ie 武備の家	military house
bugei 武芸	military arts
bun 文	civil/cultural
bunbu nidō 文武二道	two ways of the civil/cultural and military
bureikō 無礼講	Free and Easy Society
bushi 武士	warrior
bushidan 武士団	warrior band

bushidō 武士道	warrior way
buyū no michi 武勇の道	way of the military
chibō 智謀	resourcefulness
chinjufu shōgun 鎮守府将軍	general for pacification
chōnin 重任	extension of term
chōteki 朝敵	enemy of the court
chūshin yūshi 中臣勇士	loyal subject, brave warrior
daijō daijin 太政大臣	chancellor
daimyō 大名	chieftain
denjōbito 殿上人	courtier with right of attendance on emperor
densetsu 伝説	legend
dōmaru 胴丸	corselet (armor)
edo 穢土	world of filth
furubon 古本	old text
fushū 俘囚	relocated Emishi
gempuku 元服	initiation to manhood
ge'nin 下人	groom
geyu 解由	document of release
gi 義	honor, righteousness
gōza 剛座	bravery seat
gun 郡	district
gundan 軍団	military unit
gunji 郡司	district magistrate
gunsho-yomi 軍書読	reading of military texts
haji 恥	shame
hara o kiru 腹を切る	cut the belly
haramaki 腹巻	corselet (armor)
hatasashi 旗指	standard bearer
hei 塀	wooden wall
hentai kambun 変体漢文	variant Chinese (language)
hōgan 判官	lieutenant
hōgan biiki 判官贔屓	sympathy for the lieutenant (Yoshitsune)
hoko 矛	straight-bladed spear
hori 堀	moat

hoshi kabuto 星兜	star helmet
ichinin tōsen no tsuwamono 一人当千の兵	warrior worth a thousand
ie 家	family
ienoko 家の子	kin vassal
ikki-uchi 一騎打	single mounted warrior
ikusa 軍	army, battle, warrior band
in 院	senior retired emperor
inga 因果	karma as retribution
ippō no taishō 一方の大将	leading commander
jigai 自害	commit suicide
jiriki 自力	self-power
jitō 地頭	steward
jōba no rōdō 乗馬の郎等	mounted retainer
jōgō 成功	purchase of office
jōkaku 城郭	fortress, castle
jūmonji 十文字	cross-shaped (cutting of stomach)
junshi 殉死	following one's lord in death
jūrui 従類	warrior follower
kabura-ya 鏑矢	arrow with turnip-shaped head
kabuto 兜	helmet
kachihashiri 徒走	foot soldier
kachi-nanori 勝名乗	victory name-announcing
kageyushi 勘解由使	release commissioner
kaidate 垣楯	shield barrier
kamikaze 神風	divine wind
kampaku 関白	regent for an adult emperor
kangun 官軍	imperial army
karamete 搦手	rear force
kari-musha 駆武者	temporarily assembled warriors
kasa-jirushi 笠標	hat marker
katakiuchi 敵討	vendetta
kataribon 語り本	recitative text
katarite 語り手	teller of tales
Kebiishichō 検非違使庁	Bureau of Metropolitan Police
ke'nin 家人	vassal

kenshin 献身	absolute self-sacrifice
kenzoku 眷族	vassal
ki 記	chronicle
kido 木戸	outer gate (of castle)
kikusui 菊水	floating chrysanthemum (crest)
kiroku 記録	chronicle
kokugaryō 国衙領	holdings attached to office of provincial governor
kokuō no on 国王の恩	obligation to sovereign
kokushi 国司	provincial governor
kubi-jikken 首実検	inspection of heads
kugyō 公卿	senior noble/courtier
kumade 熊手	bear-claw rake
kusazuri 草摺	protective skirt (armor)
kuwagata 鍬形	horn-shaped decoration for helmet
kyūba no michi 弓馬の道	way of the bow and horse
mappō 末法	end of the Buddhist Law
meiba 名馬	famous horse
menboku 面目	face, fame
mokudai 目代	surrogate
monogatari 物語	tale
mujō 無常	impermanence
mukaijō 向城	facing fortress
musha 武者	warrior
musha no narai 武者の習	warrior way
na 名	name
naginata 長刀	curve-bladed polearm
nanbokuchō jidai 南北朝時代	period of the northern and southern courts
nanori 名乗	name-announcing
narabinaki tsuwamono 並び無き兵	warrior without peer
nasake 情	love, compassion
ninja 忍者	person of secret methods
nobushi 野伏	warrior who hides in the fields
odoshi 縅	armor lacing

ōhō 王法	Imperial Law
okuza 臆座	cowardice seat
on 恩	obligation
oni 鬼	demon
ōryōshi 押領使	sheriff
ō-sode 大袖	great sleeves
ōte 大手	main force
ō-yoroi 大鎧	Great Armor
ōyumi 弩	crossbow
rakugaki 落書	satirical verse
rōdō 郎等	non-kin vassal
rōnin 浪人	wave person (absconding peasant, masterless samurai)
rufubon 流布本	circulating text
ruiban 類伴	vassal
sakamogi 逆茂木	spikes
sakigake 先駆	first in battle
sakimori 防人	border guard
saku 柵	stockade
samurai 侍	one who serves, warrior
samurai-dokoro 侍所	Samurai Unit, Board of Retainers
sannin-bari 三人張	bow requiring three men to string
sanzoku 山賊	mountain bandit
sashi-chigaete 刺し韋へて	stabbing each other to death
sei-i tai-shōgun 征夷大将軍	barbarian-subduing great general
seishu 聖主	sagely sovereign
seiun 聖運	imperial destiny
sengoku jidai 戦国時代	age of provincial wars
senjin 先陣	first in battle
seppuku 切腹	disembowelment
sesshō 摂政	regent for a minor emperor
setsuwa bungaku 説話文学	literature of stories
shikken 執権	shogunal regent
shikoro 錏	neck guard (armor)
shinkō 新皇	new emperor
shinkoku 神国	divine land

shiro 城	fortress, castle
shitsuji 執事	assistant to shogun
shōen 荘園	private estate
shōgun 将軍	general
shojū 所従	groom
shōnin 證人	witness
shūba no tō 僦馬の党	band of packhorse handlers
shugo 守護	constable
shujū 主従	lord/vassal, patron/client
shukuun 宿運	karma
shura 修羅	warrior ghost
sōga 爪牙	claws and teeth
suiko 出挙	loan
suke 介	vice-governor
taigun 大軍	army
Taiheiki-yomi 太平記読	reading of *Taiheiki*
tai-shōgun 大将軍	great general
tandai 探題	magistrate
tariki 他力	other power
teitoku 帝徳	imperial virtue
tendō 天道	way of heaven
tengu 天狗	goblin
tennō 天皇	emperor/empress
tō 党	gang
tōi 東夷	eastern barbarians
toki 鬨	battle cry
toneri 舎人	groom
tō no ya 当の矢	answering arrow
tōryō 棟梁	overlord
tsuitōshi 追討使	subjugator
tsuwamono 兵	warrior
tsuwamono no michi 兵の道	warrior way
tsuyoyumi 強弓	powerful with bow and arrow
uchikomi no ikusa 打ち込みの軍	mass attack
ukina 憂名	sully one's name
uma-ate 馬当	hitting with hooves

un 運	fate
un ga tsuku 運が尽く	luck/fate runs out
unmei 運命	fate
wakan konkō bun 和漢混淆文	mixed Chinese and Japanese
warawa 童	page
ware saki ni 我先に	Me first!
ya-awase 矢合せ	exchange of arrows
yagura 矢倉	watchtower
yamabushi 山伏	mountain priest
yamadachi 山立	mountain bandit
yari 槍	spear
yoki kataki 良き敵	worthy foe
yomibon 読本	text to be read
yōnin 遙任	absentee appointment
youchi 夜討	night attack
yūki 勇気	valor
yunzei 弓勢	powerful with bow and arrow
zainin 罪人	criminal
zoku 賊	rebel
zuihyō 随兵	warrior follower
zuryō 受領	provincial governor

BIBLIOGRAPHY

Akagi Munenori. *Taira no Masakado*. Tokyo: Kadokawa Shoten, 1970.

Amino Yoshihiko. *Mōko Shūrai*. Tokyo: Shōgakukan, 1974.

Anbe Motoo. *Gunki-mono no Genzō to Sono Tenkai*. Tokyo: Ōfūsha, 1976.

Aoki Kazuo. *Kodai Gōzoku*. Tokyo: Shōgakukan, 1974.

Benedict, Ruth. *The Chrysanthemum and the Sword*. Tokyo: Tuttle, 1954.

Blacker, Carmen. *The Catalpa Bow*. London: George Allen & Unwin, 1975.

Bottomley, I., and A. P. Hopson. *Arms and Armor of the Samurai*. New York: Crown Publishers, 1988.

Brown, Delmer, and Ichirō Ishida, trans. *The Future and the Past: A Translation and Study of the Gukanshō*. Berkeley: University of California Press, 1979.

Butler, Kenneth Dean. "The *Heike Monogatari* and the Japanese Warrior Ethic." *Harvard Journal of Asiatic Studies* 29 (1969): 93–108.

———. "The Textual Evolution of the *Heike Monogatari*." *Harvard Journal of Asiatic Studies* 26 (1965–1966): 5–51.

Cantor, Norman F. *Medieval History*. New York: Macmillan, 1963.

Chalitpatanangune, Marisa, trans. "*Heiji Monogatari*: A Study and Annotated Translation of the Oldest Text." Unpublished dissertation, University of California at Berkeley, 1987.

Chiba Tokuji. *Seppuku no Hanashi*. Tokyo: Kōdansha, 1972.

Cogan, Thomas J., trans. *The Tale of the Soga Brothers*. Tokyo: University of Tokyo Press, 1987.

Endō Motoo and Ōmori Shirō, eds. *Nihon Shi Handobukku*. Tokyo: Asakura Shoten, 1963.

Farris, William Wayne. *Heavenly Warriors: The Evolution of Japan's Military, 500–1300*. Cambridge: Harvard University Press, 1992.

Friday, Karl. *Hired Swords: The Rise of Private Warrior Power in Early Japan*. Stanford: Stanford University Press, 1992.

———. "Teeth and Claws: Provincial Warriors and the Heian Court." *Monumenta Nipponica* 43 (2) (Summer 1988): 153–185.

Fukuda Toyohiko. "Ōchō Gunji Kikō to Nairan." In Iwanami Shoten, eds., *Iwanami Kōza Nihon Rekishi*, vol. 4. Tokyo: Iwanami Shoten, 1976.

———. *Taira no Masakado no Ran*. Tokyo: Iwanami Shoten, 1981.

Gies, Frances. *The Knight in History*. New York: Harper & Row, 1984.

Goble, Andrew. "Go-Daigo and the Kemmu Restoration." Unpublished dissertation, Stanford University, 1987.

Gotō Tanji and Kamada Kisaburō, eds. *Taiheiki*. In *Nihon Koten Bungaku Taikei*, vols. 34–36. Tokyo: Iwanami Shoten, 1960.

Hall, John W. *Government and Local Power in Japan, 500 to 1700*. Princeton: Princeton University Press, 1966.

Hall, John W., et al., eds. *Japan before Tokugawa*. Princeton: Princeton University Press, 1981.

Hall, John W., and Marius B. Jansen, eds. *Studies in the Institutional History of Early Modern Japan*. Princeton: Princeton University Press, 1968.

Hall, John W., and Jeffrey P. Mass, eds. *Medieval Japan: Essays in Institutional History*. New Haven: Yale University Press, 1974.

Hall, John W., and Toyoda Takeshi, eds. *Japan in the Muromachi Age*. Berkeley: University of California Press, 1977.

Hanawa Hokiichi, ed. *Mutsu Waki*. In *Gunsho Ruijū*, vol. 20. Tokyo: Zoku Gunsho Ruijū Kansei Kai, 1959.

———. *Ōshū Gosannen Ki*. In *Gunsho Ruijū*, vol. 20. Tokyo: Zoku Gunsho Ruijū Kansei Kai, 1959.

Hayakawa Shōhachi. *Ritsuryō Kokka*. Tokyo: Shōgakukan, 1974.

Hayashiya Tatsusaburō. *Namboku-chō*. Tokyo: Sōgensha, 1957.

Hesselink, Reinier H. "The Introduction of the Art of Mounted Archery into Japan." *Transactions of the Asiatic Society of Japan*, 4th series, vol. 6 (1991): 27–47.

Hurst, G. Cameron. *Insei: Abdicated Sovereigns in the Politics of Late Heian Japan, 1086–1185*. New York: Columbia University Press, 1976.

Igarashi Chikara. *Gunki-monogatari Kenkyū*. Tokyo: Waseda Daigaku, 1931.

———. *Senki Bungaku*. Tokyo: Kawade Shobō, 1935.

Iida Yukiko. *Hōgen, Heiji no Ran*. Tokyo: Kyōikusha, 1979.

Imagawa Ryōshun. *Nan-Taiheiki*. In Hanawa Hokiichi, ed., *Gunsho Ruijū*, vol. 21. Tokyo: Zoku Gunsho Ruijū Kansei Kai, 1931.

Imai Masaharu. *Chūsei o Ikita Nihon-jin*. Tokyo: Gakusei Sha, 1992.

Ishii Susumu. *Kamakura Bakufu*. Tokyo: Chūō Kōron Sha, 1965.

Ishimoda Shō. *Heike Monogatari*. Tokyo: Iwanami Shoten, 1957.

Kadokawa Genyoshi and Takada Minoru. *Minamoto no Yoshitsune*. Tokyo: Kadokawa Shoten, 1966.

Kajiwara Masaaki, ed. *Gikeiki*. In *Nihon Koten Bungaku Zenshū*, vol. 31. Tokyo: Shōgakukan, 1971.

———. *Heike Monogatari*. Tokyo: Kōdansha, 1967.

———. *Heike Monogatari*. Tokyo: Shōgakukan, 1982.

———. *Shōmonki*. 2 vols. Tokyo: Heibonsha, 1975.

Kawamata Keiichi, ed. *Ima Kagami, Masukagami*. Tokyo: Nihon Bungaku Sōsho Kankō Kai, 1926.

Kazue Kyōichi. *Minamoto no Yoshitsune no Higeki*. Tokyo: Futami Shoin, 1966.

Keene, Donald, trans. *Chūshingura*. New York: Columbia University Press, 1971.

———. *Essays in Idleness: The Tsurezuregusa of Kenkō*. New York: Columbia University Press, 1967.

Kellogg, Edward R., trans. "*Hōgen Monogatari*." *Transactions of the Asiatic Society of Japan* 45 (pt. 1) (1917): 25–117.

Kitagawa, Hiroshi. *The Tale of the Soga Brothers*. 2 vols. Shiga: Faculty of Economics, Shiga University, 1981.

Kitagawa, Hiroshi, and Bruce T. Tsuchida, trans. *The Tale of the Heike*. 2 vols. Tokyo: University of Tokyo Press, 1975.

Kitayama Shigeo. *Heian Kyō*. Tokyo: Chūō Kōron Sha, 1965.

Kobata Atsushi and Wakamori Tarō. *Nihon Shi Kenkyū*. Tokyo: Zokubundō, 1956.

Komatsu Shigetō. *Chūsei Gunki-mono no Kenkyū*. Tokyo: Ōfūsha, 1962.

———. *Chūsei Gunki-mono no Kenkyū, Zoku*. Tokyo: Ōfūsha, 1971.

Koten Isan no Kai, ed. *Shōmonki, Kenkyū to Shiryō*. Tokyo: Shindoku Shosha, 1963.

Koten Kenkyū Kai, ed. *Hōgen Monogatari*. 2 vols. Tokyo: Namifuru Shoten, 1972.

Kume Kunitake. "*Taiheiki* wa Shigaku ni Eki Nashi." *Shigaku Zasshi* 2 (1891): 230–240.

Kuroda Toshio. *Mōko Shūrai*. Tokyo: Chūō Kōron Sha, 1965.

Kuroita Katsumi, ed. *Azuma Kagami*. In *Kokushi Taikei*, vol. 32. Tokyo: Kokushi Taikei Kankō Kai, 1932.

Legge, James, trans. *Li-chi*. In *The Sacred Books of the East*, vol. 27. Oxford, 1885.

Mabuchi Kazuo et al., eds. *Konjaku Monogatari Shū*. In *Nihon Koten Bungaku Zenshū*, vol. 23. Tokyo: Shōgakukan, 1974.

McCullough, Helen C., trans. "A Tale of Mutsu." *Harvard Journal of Asiatic Studies* 25 (1964–1965): 178–211.

———. *The Taiheiki: A Chronicle of Medieval Japan*. New York: Columbia University Press, 1959.

———. *The Tale of the Heike*. Stanford: Stanford University Press, 1988.

———. *Yoshitsune: A Fifteenth-Century Japanese Chronicle*. Stanford: Stanford University Press, 1966.

McCullough, William, trans. "*Azuma Kagami* Account of the Shōkyū War." *Monumenta Nipponica* 23 (1–2) (1968): 102–155.

———. "*Shōkyūki*: An Account of the Shōkyū War of 1221." *Monumenta Nipponica* 19 (1964): 163–215; 186–221.

Mass, Jeffrey P. *Warrior Government in Early Medieval Japan*. New Haven: Yale University Press, 1974.

———, ed. *Court and Bakufu in Japan*. New Haven: Yale University Press, 1982.

Matsubayashi Yasuaki. *Jōkyūki*. Tokyo: Gendai Shichō Sha, 1974.

Miyazaki Fumiko. "Religious Life of the Kamakura Bushi, Kumagai Naozane and His Descendants." *Monumenta Nipponica* 47 (4) (Winter 1992): 435–467.

Mizuhara Hajime, ed. *Gempei Seisui Ki.* Tokyo: Shin-Jimbutsu Ōrai Sha, 1988.

Mori Shigeaki. *Taiheiki no Gunzō.* Tokyo: Kadokawa Shoten, 1991.

O Morris, Ivan. *The Nobility of Failure: Tragic Heroes in the History of Japan.* New York: Holt, Rinehart & Winston, 1975.

Murata Masashi. *Namboku-chō Shi Ron.* Tokyo, 1949.

Nagahara Keiji. *Nairan to Minshū no Seiki.* Tokyo: Shōgakukan, 1988.

Nagano Jōichi. *Heike Monogatari no Kanshō to Hihyō.* Tokyo: Meiji Shoin, 1975.

Nagazumi Yasuaki. *Gunki Monogatari no Sekai.* Tokyo: Asahi Shimbun Sha, 1978.

———. " 'Gunki-mono' no Kōzō to Sono Tenkai." *Kokugo to Kokubungaku* (April 1960): 1–15.

———. *Heike Monogatari no Kōsō.* Tokyo: Iwanami Shoten, 1989.

———. *Heike Monogatari o Yomu.* Tokyo: Iwanami Shoten, 1980.

———. *Hōgen Monogatari, Heiji Monogatari.* Tokyo: Kadokawa Shoten, 1976.

———. *Taiheiki.* Tokyo: Iwanami Shoten, 1984.

Nagazumi Yasuaki and Shimada Isao, eds. *Hōgen Monogatari, Heiji Monogatari.* In *Nihon Koten Bungaku Taikei,* vol. 31. Tokyo: Iwanami Shoten, 1961.

Nakamikado no Munetada. *Chūyūki.* In Zōho Shiryō Taisei Kankō Kaihen, ed., *Zōho Shiryō Taisei,* vol. 11. Tokyo: Rinsui Shoten, 1965.

Nakanishi Tatsuharu. *Taiheiki Ron Josetsu.* Tokyo: Ōfūsha, 1985.

Naoki Kōjirō. *Kodai Kokka no Seiritsu.* Tokyo: Chūō Kōron Sha, 1965.

Okabe Shūzō. *Namboku-chō no Kyozō to Jitsuzō.* Tokyo: Yūzankaku, 1975.

Okami Masao, ed. *Gikeiki.* In *Nihon Koten Bungaku Taikei,* vol. 37. Tokyo: Iwanami Shoten, 1959.

Okami Masao and Akamatsu Toshihide, eds. *Gukanshō.* In *Nihon Koten Bungaku Taikei,* vol. 85. Tokyo: Iwanami Shoten, 1967.

Ōmori Kitayoshi. *Taiheiki no Kōzō to Hōhō.* Tokyo: Meiji Shoin, 1988.

Owada Tetsuo. *Sengoku Bushō.* Tokyo: Chūō Kōron Sha, 1981.

———. *Shiro to Jōkamachi.* Tokyo: Kyōiku-sha, 1979.

O Rabinovitch, Judith N., trans. *Shōmonki: The Story of Masakado's Rebellion.* Tokyo: Monumenta Nipponica, 1986.

O Reischauer, Edwin, trans. "*Heiji Monogatari.*" In Edwin Reischauer and Joseph K. Yamagiwa, eds. and trans., *Translations from Early Japanese Literature.* Cambridge: Harvard University Press, 1951.

Rhader, Johannes. "Miscellany of Personal Views of an Ignorant Fool." *Acta Orientalia* 15 (3) (1936): 173–230.

Sadler, A. L., trans. "The *Heike Monogatari.*" *Transactions of the Asiatic Society of Japan* 46 (pt. 2) (1918): 10–278 and 49 (pt. 1) (1921): 1–354.

Saeki Arikiyo et al. *Masakado no Ran.* Tokyo: Yoshikawa Kōbunkan, 1976.

Saiki Kazuma et al., eds. *Mikawa Monogatari, Hagakure.* In *Nihon Shisō Taikei,* vol. 26. Tokyo: Iwanami Shoten, 1974.

Sakamoto Shōzō. *Sekkan Jidai.* Tokyo: Shōgakukan, 1974.

Sansom, George. *A History of Japan to 1334.* Stanford: Stanford University Press, 1958.

———. *A History of Japan, 1334–1615.* Stanford: Stanford University Press, 1961.

Sasaki Hachirō. *Chūsei Senki Bungaku.* Tokyo: Tsuru Shobō, 1943.

Satō Kazuhiko, ed. *Kusunoki Masashige no Subete.* Tokyo: Shin-Jimbutsu Ōrai Sha, 1989.

———. *Namboku-chō Nairan.* Tokyo: Shōgakukan, 1974.

———. *Taiheiki o Yomu.* Tokyo: Gakusei Sha, 1991.

Satō Shin'ichi. *Namboku-chō no Dōran.* Tokyo: Chūō Kōron Sha, 1965.

Shimizu, Yoshiaki, ed. *Japan: The Shaping of Daimyō Culture, 1185–1868.* Washington: National Gallery of Art, 1988.

Shinoda, Minoru. *The Founding of the Kamakura Shogunate, 1180–1185.* New York: Columbia University Press, 1960.

Stramigioli, Giuliana. "Preliminary Notes on the *Masakadoki* and the Taira no Masakado Story." *Monumenta Nipponica* 28 (3) (1973): 261–293.

Suchi Masakazu, ed. *Nihon no Kakun.* Tokyo: Nihon Bungei Sha, n.d.

Sugimoto Keisaburō. *Gunki Monogatari no Sekai.* Tokyo: Meichō Kankō Kai, 1985.

———, ed. *Heike Monogatari.* Tokyo: Kōdansha, 1987.

Sun Tzu. *The Art of War.* Trans. by Samuel B. Griffith. Oxford: Clarendon Press, 1963.

Takagi Ichinosuke et al., eds. *Heike Monogatari.* In *Nihon Koten Bungaku Taikei,* vols. 32–33. Tokyo: Iwanami Shoten, 1959–1960.

Takahashi Takashi. *Sakanoue no Tamuramaro.* Tokyo: Yoshikawa Kōbunkan, 1959.

Takahashi Teiichi, ed. *Heiji Monogatari.* Tokyo: Kōdansha, 1952.

———. *Taiheiki.* 2 vols. Kyoto: Shibunkaku, 1976.

Takeuchi Rizō. *Bushi no Tōjō.* Tokyo: Chūō Kōron Sha, 1965.

Tanigaki Itao. *Taiheiki no Setsuwa Bungaku-teki Kenkyū.* Osaka: Izumi Shoin, 1989.

Toby, Ronald. "Why Leave Nara?" *Monumenta Nipponica* 40 (3) (Autumn 1985): 331–347.

Tōin Kinsada. *Tōin Kinsada Nikki.* In Tōkyō Teikoku Daigaku, *Bunka Daigaku Shishi Sōsho,* vol. 48. Tokyo, 1897–1908.

Tomikura Tokujirō. *Heike Monogatari.* Tokyo: NHK, 1972.

Tsuda Sōkichi. *Bungaku ni Arawaretaru Waga Kokumin Shisō no Kenkyū.* Tokyo: Rakuyōdō, 1917.

Tsukamoto Tessan, ed. *Gempei Seisui Ki.* 2 vols. Tokyo: Yubōdō, 1929.

Uemura Seiji. *Kusunoki Masashige.* Tokyo: Shibundō, 1962.

Ury, Marian. *Tales of Times Now Past.* Berkeley: University of California Press, 1979.

Uwayokote Masataka. "Chūsei-teki Rinri to Hō." In Nihon Kenkyū Kai, ed., *Kōza Nihon Bunka Shi,* vol. 3. Tokyo: Sanjū-ichi Shobō, 1962.

———. *Heike Monogatari no Kyokō to Shinjitsu.* 2 vols. Tokyo: Hanawa Shobō, 1985.

Uyenaka, Shuzo. "A Study of *Baishōron:* A Source for the Study of the Ideology of Imperial Loyalism in Medieval Japan." Unpublished dissertation, University of Toronto, 1979.

———. "The Textbook Controversy of 1911: National Needs and Historical Truth." In John S. Brownlee, ed., *History in the Service of the Japanese Nation*. Toronto: University of Toronto–York, 1983.

Varley, H. Paul, trans. *A Chronicle of Gods and Sovereigns*. New York: Columbia University Press, 1980.

———. *Imperial Restoration in Medieval Japan*. New York: Columbia University Press, 1971.

———. *The Samurai*. London: Weidenfeld & Nicolson, 1970.

Waley, Arthur, trans. *The Nō Plays of Japan*. New York: Grove Press, 1957.

Washio Junkei, ed. *Saigen'in-bon Taiheiki*. Tokyo: Toe Shoin, 1936.

Watanabe Sadamaro. *Heike Monogatari no Shisō*. Tokyo: Hōzō Kan, 1991.

Watanabe Tamotsu. *Genji to Heishi*. Tokyo: Shibundō, 1955.

———. *Minamoto no Yoshitsune*. Tokyo: Yoshikawa Kōbunkan, 1966.

Watsuji Tetsurō. *Nihon Rinri Shisō Shi*. 2 vols. Tokyo: Iwanami Shoten, 1952.

White, Lynn, Jr. *Medieval Technology and Social Change*. London: Oxford University Press, 1962.

Wilson, William R., trans. *Hōgen Monogatari: Tale of the Disorder in Hōgen*. Tokyo: Sophia University, 1971.

———. "The Way of the Bow and Arrow: The Japanese Warrior in *Konjaku Monogatari*." *Monumenta Nipponica* 28 (2) (1973): 177–234.

Yamada Shōzen. *Heike Monogatari no Hitobito*. Tokyo: Shin-Jimbutsu Ōrai Sha, 1972.

Yamada Yoshio et al., eds. *Konjaku Monogatari Shū*. In *Nihon Koten Bungaku Taikei*, vol. 25. Tokyo: Iwanami Shoten, 1962.

Yamamura, Kozo, ed. *The Cambridge History of Japan*. Vol. 3: *Medieval Japan*. Cambridge: Cambridge University Press, 1990.

Yamashita Hiroaki. *Gunki-monogatari no Hōhō*. Tokyo: Yūseidō, 1983.

Yamazaki Ken. *Taira no Masakado*. Tokyo: Sanseidō, 1971.

Yamazaki, Masakazu, trans. *Taiheiki*. Tokyo: Kawade Shobō, 1990.

Yashiro Kazuo and Kami Hiroshi, eds. *Baishōron*. Tokyo: Gendai Shichō Sha, 1975.

Yasuda Motohisa. *Heike no Gunzo*. Tokyo: Hanawa Shinsho, 1967.

———. *Minamoto no Yoshiie*. Tokyo: Yoshikawa Kōbunkan, 1966.

———. *Taira no Kiyomori*. Tokyo: Kiyomizu Shoten, 1971.

Yasui Hisayoshi. *Namboku-chō Gunki to Sono Shūhen*. Tokyo: Kasama Shoin, 1985.

Yomiuri Shimbun Sha, ed. *Nihon no Rekishi*, vol. 3. Tokyo: Yomiuri Shimbun Sha, 1959.

Yoshimura Shigenori. *Hōgen Monogatari Shinsaku*. Tokyo: Daidōkan, 1927.

INDEX

About the Author

PAUL VARLEY is professor of Japanese history in the Department of East Asian Languages and Cultures at Columbia University, where he received both his M.A. and Ph.D. degrees. From 1991 to 1993 he held the Sen Sōshitsu XV Professorship in Japanese Cultural History at the University of Hawaii. His publications include *The Ōnin War, Imperial Restoration in Medieval Japan, The Samurai, Japanese Culture,* and *A Chronicle of Gods and Sovereigns.* He is coeditor, with Kumakura Isao, of *Tea in Japan.*